Emotional Intelligence:
Key Readings on the Mayer and Salovey Model

Edited by:

Peter Salovey, Ph. D., Yale University
Marc A. Brackett, Ph. D., Yale University
John D. Mayer, Ph.D., University of New Hampshire

DUDE
PUBLISHING

DUDE PUBLISHING
A Division of
National Professional Resources, Inc.
Port Chester, New York

Cover/Book Design & Production by Andrea Cerone,
National Professional Resources, Inc., Port Chester, NY

© 2004

Dude Publishing
A Division of National Professional Resources, Inc.
25 South Regent Street
Port Chester, New York 10573
Toll free: (800) 453-7461
Phone: (914) 937-8879

Visit our web site: www.NPRinc.com

Printed in the United States of America

ISBN 1-887943-72-2

Acknowledgements

The authors wish to express appreciation to all the co-authors who contributed to the included works, as well as to Elyse Schneiderman and Shinzong Lee, undergraduate research assistants at Yale University. They also are appreciative of the support provided by the staff of their publisher, National Professional Resources, Inc./Dude Publications, particularly Andrea Cerone, Becky Abel, Lisa Hanson, Nancy Cassone, and Dorothy Romanello.

Contact Information of Editors

Peter Salovey
Dean of the Graduate School of Arts and Sciences
& Chris Argyris Professor of Psychology
Yale University
P O Box 208205
New Haven, CT 06520
Email: peter.salovey@yale.edu

Marc A. Brackett
Associate Director, Health, Emotions, & Behavior Laboratory
Department of Psychology
Yale University
P O Box 208205
New Haven, CT 06520
Email: marc.brackett@yale.edu

John (Jack) D. Mayer
Professor of Psychology
Department of Psychology
University of New Hampshire
10 Library Way
Durham, NH 03824
Email: jack.mayer@unh.edu

TABLE OF CONTENTS

Part III
Application of EI: Everyday Behavior, Education, and the Workplace

Introduction

The term *Emotional Intelligence (EI)* refers to the processes involved in the recognition, use, understanding, and management of one's own and others' emotional states to solve emotion-laden problems and to regulate behavior (Mayer & Salovey, 1997; Salovey & Mayer, 1990). It is a member of an emerging group of cognitive abilities alongside social (Cantor and Kihlstrom, 1987), practical (Sternberg, 1995), and personal (Gardner, 1983) intelligences. Unlike general intelligence (e.g., verbal-propositional), which relies on cold cognitive processes, EI operates on "hot" cognitive-emotional processes that are of importance to the individual and the surrounding environment (Abelson, 1963).

Work on EI is as an outgrowth of two areas of psychological research that emerged toward the end of last century. In the 1980's psychologists began to examine how emotions interact with thought and vice versa (e.g., Bower, 1981; Isen, Shalker, Clark & Karp, 1978; Zajonc, 1980). For instance, researchers studied how mood states can assist cognition and influence thought processes and personal judgments (Mayer & Bremer, 1985; Palfai & Salovey, 1993-1994; Salovey & Birnbaum, 1989). At the same time, there was a gradual loosening of the concept of intelligence to include a broad array of mental abilities rather than a monolithic "g" (e.g., Cantor & Kihlstrom, 1987; Gardner, 1983; Sternberg, 1995). Gardner, for instance, advised educators and scientists to place a greater emphasis on the search for multiple intelligences. He was primarily interested in helping educators appreciate students with diverse learning styles and potentials.

The term Emotional Intelligence, however, was not formally defined until two articles were published in 1990. The first article defined EI as "the ability to monitor one's own and others' feelings and emotions, to discriminate among them and to use this information to guide one's thinking and actions" (Salovey & Mayer, 1990, p. 189). The second article presented an empirical demonstration of how EI could be tested as a mental ability (Mayer, DiPaolo, & Salovey, 1990). Findings from the empirical study demonstrated that emotion and cognition could be combined to perform sophisticated information processing. For example, some people were better than others at identifying the emotional content in designs and colors.

The public and academia were mostly unaware of EI until 1995, when Daniel Goleman popularized the construct in his trade book, *Emotional Intelligence: Why it can Matter more than IQ*. Emotional intelligence quickly captured the interest of the media, general public, and researchers. Goleman (1995) made extraordinary and difficult-to-substantiate claims about the importance of EI, and wrote that it was "as powerful and at times more powerful than IQ" in predicting success in life (p. 34). Goleman's definition of EI was not confined to the abilities described by Salovey and Mayer (1990); it encompassed a broad array of personal attributes, including political awareness, self-confidence, conscientiousness, and achievement motive, among other desirable personality attributes (Goleman, 1995, pp. 26-28; Goleman, 1998). Moreover, some of the claims he made about EI went far beyond the evidence available (Davies, Stankov, & Roberts, 1998; Epstein, 1998; Hedlund & Sternberg, 2000; Matthews, Zeidner, & Roberts, 2002; Mayer & Cobb, 2000; Mayer, Salovey, & Caruso, 2000).

In the years that followed, educators, psychologists, human resource professionals began to consult and write about EI, using the term to represent traits and skills related to character and achieving "success" in life. On the other hand, we—the editors of this book and authors/coauthors of its articles— have focused our definition of EI on a set of abilities (Mayer & Salovey, 1997; see also Mayer et al., 2000) pertaining to (a) accurately perceiving and expressing emotion, (b) using emotion to facilitate cognitive activities, (c) understanding emotions, and (d) managing emotions for both emotional and personal growth (Mayer & Salovey, 1997).

Today, the field is filled with journal articles, as well as both popular and scholarly books on EI. There are also a number of published tests to measure the construct. These include: the performance-based test, the *Mayer-Salovey-Caruso Emotional Intelligence Test* (MSCEIT; Mayer, Salovey, & Caruso, 2002), which operationalizes the four-branch model of EI (Mayer & Salovey, 1997); Self-report inventories such as the *Emotional Quotient Inventory* (EQ-i; Bar-On, 1997), which measures EI as set of self-reported attributes pertaining to intra-and inter-personal skills, stress management, and adapatability; and 360-degree assessments such as the *Emotional Competence Inventory* (ECI; Boyatzis, Goleman, & Rhee, 2000), which measures an individual's initiative and organizational awareness, among other variables, using composite ratings by all the people in a particular individual's social environment.

As a result of the various definitions, claims, books, and tests of EI, the field has become extremely diverse: some have worried that "EI appears to be more myth than science" (Mathews, Zeidner, & Roberts, 2002, p. 547). We have made efforts to clarify the field by distinguishing (both theoretically and empirically) our four-branch ability model of EI from others' "mixed" conceptions of the construct (Mayer et al., 2000; Brackett & Mayer, 2003). In our view EI is an intelligence that is defined and measured as a set of mental abilities (Mayer, Caruso, & Salovey, 1999; Mayer, Salovey, Caruso, & Sitarenios, 2002, 2003). Mixed conceptions are labeled as such because they combine an ability conception of EI with numerous self-reported personality attributes including optimism, self-awareness, initiative, and self-actualization (e.g., Bar-On, 1997; Boyatzis et al., 2000; Goleman, 1995,1998). We believe the traits and competencies covered by mixed-models are predictive of real-life criteria, but that they are better addressed directly and as distinct from ability EI. In our view, keeping EI restricted to an ability model that strictly focuses on emotion-related processing makes it possible to analyze the degree to which EI specifically contributes to a person's behavior over and above traditional personality attributes.

The purpose of this book of readings is to introduce the theory, measurement, and applications of our ability model of EI. We carefully selected the most up-to-date book chapters and peer-reviewed articles to accomplish this goal. There are thirteen readings that are divided into three parts: I. Conceptualization and Development of EI Theory, II. Measurement of EI with the MSCEIT, and III. Application of EI: Everyday Behavior, Education and the Workplace. Because we only represent key readings, we encourage readers who become seriously interested in EI to use the reference sections that follow each article to guide their further exploration.

Research on EI is still in its beginning stages. After all, it was introduced to a broader psychological audience just 13 years ago, and reliable and valid measures of the construct have only been used in scientific investigations for about 5 years. The most widely used scales of analytic intelligence (IQ), the Wechsler Intelligence scales, are the product of almost 100 years of clinical assessment and research. Therefore, there is much to be learned about EI and the fate of EI is, in part, in the hands of educators, theorists, and investigators who will explore the topic in greater detail. For example, there are no carefully designed studies assessing explicitly how EI is developed (Denham, 1998, and Saarni, 1999). We are also only now learning what EI predicts about a person's everyday behavior, as well as academic and work performance. Recall, our performance-based test of EI, the MSCEIT, measures EI by having individuals solve tasks pertaining to the perception, use, understanding, and management of emotion. We are certain that future research will bring about new tasks to assess the construct and additional ways to objectively assess the four abilities we have identified as part of EI.

We hope this snapshot of the theory, measurement, and application of EI helps the reader gain insight into this exciting new area of psychological inquiry. We also hope these readings stimulate students, teachers, and researchers into thinking more critically about the great breadth of human functioning and abilities, and the value of investigations to understand EI and its implications for people's lives and society as a whole.

References

Abelson, R. P. (1963). Computer simulation of "hot cognition." In S. S. Tomkins & S. Mesick (Eds.), *Computer simulations of personality*. New York: Wiley.

Bar-On, R. (1997). *Bar-On Emotional Quotient Inventory: Technical manual.* Toronto, Canada: Multi-Health Systems.

Bower, G. H. (1981). Mood and memory. *American Psychologist, 36*, 129-148.

Boyatzsis, R. E., Goleman, D., & Rhee, K. S. (2000). Clustering Competence in Emotional Intelligence. In R. Bar-On, & J. D. A. Parker (Eds.). *The handbook of emotional intelligence.* (pp. 33-362). San Francisco: Jossey-Bass.

Brackett, M., & Mayer, J. D. (2003). Convergent, discriminant, and incremental validity of competing measures of emotional intelligence. *Personality and Social Psychology Bulletin, 29*.

Cantor, N., & Kihlstrom, J.F. (1987). *Personality and social intelligence.* Englewood Cliffs, NJ: Prentice Hall.

Davies, M., Stankov, L., & Roberts, R. D. (1998). Emotional intelligence: In search of an elusive construct. *Journal of Personality and Social Psychology, 75,* 989-1015.

Denham, S. A. (1998). *Emotional development in young children.* New York: Guilford

Epstein, S. (1998). *Constructive thinking: The key to emotional intelligence.* New York: Praeger Publishers.

Gardner, H. (1983). *Frames of mind: The theory of multiple intelligences.* New York: Basic Books.

Goleman, D. (1995). *Emotional intelligence.* New York: Bantam Books.

Goleman, D. (1998). *Working with emotional intelligence.* New York: Bantam.

Hedlund, J., & Sternberg, R. J. (2000). Too many intelligences? Integrating social, emotional, and practical intelligence. In R. Bar-On & J. D. A. Parker (Eds.), *Handbook of emotional intelligence* (pp. 136-167). New York: Jossey-Bass.

Isen, A. M., Shalker, T. E., Clark, M., & Karp, L. (1978). Affect, accessibility of material in memory, and behavior: A cognitive loop? *Journal of Personality and Social Psychology, 36,* 1-12.

Mathews, G., Zeidner, M., & Roberts, R. D. (2002). *Emotional intelligence: Science and myth.* Cambridge, MA: MIT Press

Mayer, J. D., & Cobb, C. D. (2000). Educational policy on emotional intelligence: Does it make sense? *Educational Psychology Review, 12,* 163-183.

Mayer, J. D., & Salovey, P. (1997). What is emotional intelligence? In P. Salovey & D. Sluyter (Eds.), *Emotional development and emotional intelligence: Educational implications* (pp. 3-31). New York: Basic Books.

Mayer, J. D., Caruso, D. R., & Salovey, P. (1999). Emotional intelligence meets traditional standards for an intelligence. *Intelligence, 27,* 267-298.

Mayer, J. D., DiPaolo, M. T., & Salovey, P. (1990). Perceiving affective content in ambiguous visual stimuli: A component of emotional intelligence. *Journal of Personality Assessment, 54,* 772-781.

Mayer, J. D., Salovey, P., & Caruso, D. R. (2000). Models of emotional intelligence. In R. J. Sternberg (Ed.), *Handbook of intelligence* (pp. 396-420). Cambridge, England: Cambridge University Press.

Mayer, J. D., Salovey, P., & Caruso, D. R. (2002). *Mayer-Salovey-Caruso Emotional Intelligence Test (MSCEIT) User's Manual.* Toronto, Canada: MHS Publishers.

Mayer, J. D., Salovey, P., Caruso, D. R., & Sitarenios, G. (2001). Emotional intelligence as a standard intelligence. *Emotion, 1,* 232-242.

Mayer, J. D., Salovey, P., Caruso, D. R., & Sitarenios, G. (2003). Measuring emotional intelligence with the MSCEIT V2.0. *Emotion, 3,* 97-105.

Mayer, J.D., & Bremer, D. (1985). Assessing mood with affect-sensitive tasks. *Journal of Personality Assessment, 49,* 95-99.

Palfai, T. P., & Salovey, P. (1993-1994). The influence of depressed and elated mood on deductive and inductive reasoning. *Imagination, Cognition & Personality, 13,* 57-71.

Saarni, C. (1999). *The Development of emotional competence.* New York: Guilford.

Salovey, P., & Birnbaum, D. (1989). Influence of mood on health-relevant cognitions. *Journal of Personality and Social Psychology, 57,* 539-551.

Salovey, P., & Mayer, J. D. (1990). Emotional intelligence. *Imagination, Cognition, and Personality, 9,* 185-211.

Sternberg, R. J., Wagner, R. K., Williams, W. M., & Horvath, J. A. (1995). Testing common sense. *American Psychologist, 50,* 912-927.

Zajonc, R. B. (1980). Feeling and thinking: Preferences need no inferences. *American Psychologist, 35,* 151-175.

Part I

Conceptualization and Development of EI Theory

This first section is comprised of four articles pertaining to the conceptualization and development of EI theory. The initial article, *Emotional intelligence,* was the first published manuscript on EI by Salovey and Mayer (1990). The authors offered a formal definition of EI as a set of skills pertaining to the accurate appraisal and expression of emotion in oneself and others, the use of emotions, and the effective regulation of emotion in self and others. The article also briefly reviewed various components of EI and discussed the possible links between EI and psychological health.

The second reading is titled, *What is emotional intelligence?* In this book chapter, Mayer and Salovey (1997) presented a revised definition of EI, which formally introduced their four-branch theoretical model of EI: (a) perception of emotion, (b) use of emotion to facilitate thought, (c) understanding of emotion, and (d) management emotions to promote personal growth.

The third reading is a book chapter, *The positive psychology of emotional intelligence* by Salovey, Mayer, and Caruso (2002). Here, the authors updated the 1997 chapter, and provided a brief history of the EI concept and a review of recent studies that have examined the predictive validity of EI.

The final article in this section is *Models of emotional intelligence* by Mayer, Salovey, and Caruso (2000). This book chapter goes into great detail distinguishing the ability model of EI from mixed models of EI. The focus is on theoretical distinctions between EI conceived as a mental ability and measured with performance-based tests and EI conceived as a set of personality traits and skills that is measured with self-report instruments.

Emotional Intelligence

Peter Salovey, Yale University
John D. Mayer, State University of New York

Acknowledgements

We gratefully acknowledge the helpful feedback on earlier drafts of this manuscript provided by Mahzarin R. Banaji, Seymour Epstein, Stephanie Fishkin, Paula M. Niedenthal, Ann M. O'Leary, Jerome L. Singer, and Robert J. Sternberg. Bob Sternberg also provided valuable assistance in guiding us to the modern literature on social intelligence. John D. Mayer especially thanks his mother, Edna Mayer, who drew attention to many of the issues that later contributed to the concept of emotional intelligence. We would both like to thank Chloe Drake for her painstaking assistance in preparing this manuscript.

The preparation of this manuscript was supported in part by NIH Biomedical Research Support Grant S07 RR07015, NIH Grant CA42101, NCHS Contract 200-88-7001, and by a grant from the Yale Social Science Faculty Research Fund to Peter Salovey as well as a New York State/Union of University Professionals New Faculty Development Award and a SUNY-Purchase President's Award to John D. Mayer.

Abstract

This article presents a framework for *emotional intelligence*, a set of skills hypothesized to contribute to the accurate appraisal and expression of emotion in one's self and in others, the effective regulation of emotion in self and others, and the use of feelings to motivate, plan, and achieve in one's life. We start by reviewing the debate about the adaptive versus maladaptive qualities of emotion. We then examine the literature on intelligence, and especially social intelligence, to examine the place of emotion in traditional intelligence conceptions. This examination leads to a framework for integrating the research on emotion-related skills. Next, we review the components of emotional intelligence. To conclude the review, the role of emotional intelligence in mental health is discussed and avenues for further investigation are suggested.

Emotional Intelligence

Is "emotional intelligence" a contradiction in terms? One tradition in Western thought has viewed emotions as disorganized interruptions of mental activity, so potentially disruptive that they must be controlled. Writing in the first century B.C., Publilius Syrus stated, "Rule your feelings, lest your feelings rule you" (Publilius Syrus, c. 100 BC/1961). More recently, in psychology, Young (1943) defined emotions as "acute disturbance[s] of the individual as a whole" (p. 263), and modern introductory texts described emotion as "a disorganized response, largely visceral, resulting from the lack of an effective adjustment" (Schaffer, Gilmer, & Schoen, 1940, p. 505). In this view, pure emotion is seen as causing a "complete loss of cerebral control" and containing no "trace of conscious purpose" (Young, 1936, p. 457-458). In this vein, Woodworth (1940) suggested that a scale to measure IQ should contain tests demonstrating not being afraid, angry, grieved, or inquisitive over things that arouse the emotions of younger children.

A second tradition (Leeper, 1948) views emotion as an organizing response because it adaptively focuses cognitive activities and subsequent action (Easterbrook, 1959). Rather than characterizing emotion as chaotic, haphazard, and something to outgrow, Leeper suggested that emotions are primarily motivating forces; they are "processes which arouse, sustain, and direct activity" (Leeper, 1948, p. 17). Modern theories of emotion also see it as directing cognitive activities adaptively (Mandler, 1975; Simon, 1982). Artificial intelligence researchers have recently considered the value of adding emotions to computers so as to prioritize and direct their processing (Mayer, 1986; Sloman & Croucher, 1981). The full expression of emotions seems to be a primary human motive (Izard & Buechler, 1980; Plutchik, 1980; Tomkins, 1962), and it may therefore be worthwhile to consider it from a functionalist perspective.

A Definition of Emotions

We view emotions as organized responses, crossing the boundaries of many psychological subsystems, including the physiological, cognitive, motivational, and experiential systems. Emotions typically arise in response to an event, either internal or external, that has a positively or negatively valenced meaning for the individual. Emotions can be distinguished from the closely related concept of mood in that emotions are shorter and generally more intense. In the present paper, we view the organized response of emotions as adaptive and as something that can potentially lead to a transformation of personal and social interaction into enriching experience.

Emotional Intelligence and Its Relationship to Other Intelligences

At the paper's outset, we asked whether emotional intelligence was a contradiction in terms. Far from emotion being contradictory to intelligence, constructs such as emotional intelligence have played a part within the traditions of the intelligence field. Intelligence researchers have often examined specific intelligence about such subareas as social behavior, and occasionally, emotions (Gardner, 1983).

Intelligence Defined

Intelligence has been defined differently in different epochs. Definitions have ranged from Diogenes's (c. 300 A.D./1925, Vol. II, p. 347) description of Pythagoras's none-too-helpful description of intelligence as "winds" to Descartes's definition that intelligence is the ability to judge true from false. The most often cited definition is Wechsler's statement that "intelligence is the aggregate or global capacity of the individual to act purposefully, to think rationally, and to deal effectively with his environment" (Wechsler, 1958). Such a definition has the advantage of broadly encompassing what people think of as intelligence, as opposed to more restrictive definitions, such as those proposed by Terman and others (e.g., the ability to carry on abstract thinking). It includes the broad areas historically designated as involving intelligence, such as the distinction among Abstract (Verbal), Mechanical (Visual/Spatial), and Social (E.L. Thorndike, 1920) intelligences, as well as those distinctions proposed by more contemporary theorists such as Gardner (1983) and Sternberg et al. (1981).

Intelligence versus models of intelligence — In the present paper, it is critical to distinguish between intelligence per se and models of intelligence. Intelligence, according to the view described above, is a broad set of abilities. Models of intelligence, however, are (generally) more restrictive organizations of the field that serve to describe interrelations or causes of mental abilities. For example, we would consider Spearman's unifactorial, "g" view of intelligence as a model of intelligence. This model holds that all mental abilities are intercorrelated. It is not contradictory to say that emotional intelligence can be an intelligence, and yet may not necessarily conform to the "g" model. That is, emotional intelligence may or may not correlate with other types of intelligence, and this should not reflect on its classification as a type of intelligence, although it might reflect on the "g" model. What is more critical is that it fits within the boundaries of conceptual definitions of intelligence, such as those provided, for example, by Wechsler.

Social Intelligence

The notion that there are different types of intelligence has been a part of the intelligence field almost since its inception. One type was social intelligence, defined initially as "the ability to understand and manage people" (R.L. Thorndike & Stein (1937, p. 275). These social/intellectual skills might also be directed inward and so social intelligence might include, by extension, the ability to understand and manage oneself. The concept of social intelligence has a long history among intelligence researchers (Walker & Foley, 1973). E.L. Thorndike (1920) originally distinguished social intelligence from other forms of intelligence, and defined it as "the ability to understand men and women, boys and girls — to act wisely in human relations." In essence, Thorndike defined social intelligence as the ability to perceive one's own and others' internal states, motives, and behaviors, and to act toward them optimally on the basis of that information. Social intelligence, however, was often defined in a more manipulative fashion. Weinstein (1969) noted that social intelligence "boils down to the ability to manipulate the responses of others..." (p. 755). Or, as the Bureau of Public Personnel Administration (1930) more crassly put it, "The essential thing is that the person...is able to get others consistently and voluntarily to do the things he wants them to do and even like doing so..." (p. 73). Traditional views of social intelligence may take on manipulative connotations because they omit consideration of one's own and others' emotions that may guide conduct in a more prosocial fashion (Dienstbier, 1984; Hoffman, 1984).

The independence of social intelligence from other types of intelligence such as abstract and mechanical was not so readily demonstrable. One problem was that social intelligence was defined so broadly so as to blend imperceptibly into verbal and visual/spatial intelligence. For instance, the intelligence test item that asks what you would do if you found a letter on the sidewalk that was addressed and had a stamp on it is considered a measure of verbal intelligence, and yet to answer the question requires social knowledge and even morality (Wechsler, 1958).

By 1960, Cronbach had reached his well known conclusion that despite "50 years of intermittent investigation...social intelligence remains undefined and unmeasured" (1960, p. 319). Most researchers accepted Cronbach's conclusions that "enough attempts were made...to indicate that this line of approach is fruitless" (1960, p. 319; see, for example, Chlopan, McCain, Carbonell, & Hagen, 1985). Few had considered on what basis these conclusions were drawn. The sole basis for his statements and those of others (e.g., Ford & Tisak, 1983; Walker & Foley, 1973) was an article of R.L. Thorndike and Stein (1937). Yet, a careful reading of that article leaves one optimistic that social intelligence might be a viable construct. Thorndike and Stein concluded that "whether there is any unitary trait corresponding to social intelligence remains to be demonstrated" (1937, p. 284), but not that this demonstration would be impossible. In fact, they suggested that with further investigation (relying on scales with less verbal content than their own and taking a multidimensional view of social intelligence), the construct might ultimately be measurable.

There is at present a resurgence of interest in social intelligence and its measurement. Sternberg, Conway, Ketron, and Bernstein (1981) asked lay people to describe an intelligent person. Many of the characteristics elicited were such socially relevant attributes as: accepts others for what they are, admits mistakes, and displays interest in the world at large. Sternberg and Smith (1985) have attempted to operationalize social intelligence. For example, in one study they asked subjects to view photographs of couples and to judge whether they were strangers posing together or actually involved in a dating or marital relationship. Similarly, Ford (1982) developed the Social Competence Nomination Form which measures attitudinal, goal directedness, and social goal variables. Factorial results indicated that a social intelligence component could be distinguished from general academic abilities.

Recently, Cantor and Kihlstrom (1985, 1987) have proposed social intelligence as a unifying construct for understanding personality. Social problem solving, according to their view, is a central personality process that underpins social behavior. It places the locus of individual differences in varied social and personal schemata stored in memory. For instance, Cantor and her colleagues have focused on fitting individual personality styles into social situations by exploring how high school students adapt to the transition to college (Cantor, Norem, Niedenthal, Langston, & Brower, 1987). In a similar vein, Epstein and Meier have argued that constructive thinking, defined as dealing creatively with the environment, is a core component of personality. They believe that people who lead their lives successfully have, for example, learned the advantages of flexible thinking (Epstein & Feist, 1988). We find these conceptualizations of social intelligence exciting and useful.

Emotional Intelligence

We define emotional intelligence as the subset of social intelligence that involves the *ability to monitor one's own and others' feelings and emotions, to discriminate among them and to use this information to guide one's thinking and actions*. We posit that life tasks such as those described by Cantor and her colleagues and constructive thinking defined by Epstein (1984) are laden with affective information, that this affective information must be processed (perhaps differently than the cognitive information), and that individuals may differ in the skill with which they do so. Emotional intelligence is also a part of Gardner's (1983) view of social intelligence, which he refers to as the personal intelligences. Like social intelligence, the personal intelligences (divided into inter- and intrapersonal intelligence) include knowledge about the self and about others. One aspect of the personal intelligences relates to feelings and is quite close to what we call emotional intelligence:

> The core capacity at work here is access to one's own feeling life —
> one's range of affects or emotions: the capacity instantly to effect
> discriminations among these feelings and, eventually, to label them, to
> enmesh them in symbolic codes, to draw upon them as a means of
> understanding and guiding one's behavior. In its most primitive form, the
> intrapersonal intelligence amounts to little more than the capacity to
> distinguish a feeling of pleasure from one of pain...At its most advanced
> level, intrapersonal knowledge allows one to detect and to symbolize
> complex and highly differentiated sets of feelings...to attain a deep
> knowledge of...feeling life (p. 239).

Interpersonal intelligence involves, among other things, the ability to monitor others' moods and temperaments and to enlist such knowledge into the service of predicting their future behavior. As was the case with social intelligence, emotional intelligence is a subset of Gardner's personal intelligences. Emotional intelligence does not include the general sense of self and appraisal of others. It focuses, rather, on the processes described specifically above, that is, the recognition and use of one's own and others' emotional states to solve problems and regulate behavior.

Emotional Intelligence: Conceptualization and Scope

There is an exciting body of research that, for lack of a theoretical concept, is dismembered and scattered over a diversity of journals, books, and subfields of psychology. This collection of studies has in common the examination of how people appraise and communicate emotion, and how they use that emotion in solving problems. It is different from research on the interaction of cognition and affect, traditionally conceived (e.g., Blaney, 1986; Clark & Fiske, 1982; Izard, Kagan, & Zajonc, 1984; Mayer & Salovey, 1988; Singer & Salovey, 1988), because it concentrates not on memory or judgment per se, but on more general contributions of emotionality to personality. As long as this research remains scattered without a guiding framework, its contribution to psychology will be minimal. But by integrating this research conceptually, its contribution to psychology will be readily grasped.

Much of the research to be studied is descriptive in nature. And the descriptive qualities of the work have been developed through the agency of scale development and measurement. For this reason, some sections of the current review will integrate a number of instances of scale development, such as those concerning alexithymia, emotional expression, and empathy. Although we are not interested in the scales per se, we are interested in the constructs that underlie them and the means by which they operationalize portions of what we will call emotional intelligence.

We hope to reveal the implications of this scattered set of findings that have not yet been appreciated: that there is a set of conceptually related mental processes involving emotional information. The mental processes include (a) appraising and expressing emotions in the self and others, (b) regulating emotion in the self and others, and (c) using emotions in adaptive ways. An outline of these components is provided in Figure 1. Although these processes are common to everyone, the present model also addresses individual differences in processing styles and abilities. Such individual differences are important for two reasons. First, there has been a century-long tradition among clinicians recognizing that people differ in the capacity to understand and express emotions. Second, such differences may be rooted in underlying skills that can be learned and thereby contribute to peoples' mental health.

In the next portion of the paper, each of these processes are discussed in turn, operationalizations are described, and pertinent experimental results are presented.

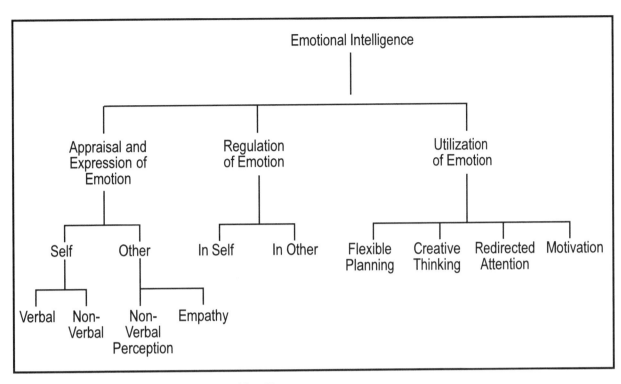

Figure 1. Conceptualization of emotional intelligence.

Appraisal and Expression of Emotion

Emotion in the Self

The processes underlying emotional intelligence are initiated when affect-laden information first enters the perceptual system. Emotional intelligence allows for the accurate appraisal and expression of feelings, and stable laws may govern them (e.g., Arnold, 1960; Frijda, 1988; Lazarus, 1966; Roseman, 1984; Smith & Ellsworth, 1985; Weiner, 1985). These emotional appraisals, in turn, in part determine various expressions of emotion.

Verbal — One medium through which emotions are appraised and expressed is language. Learning about emotions depends in part upon speaking clearly about them. This social learning interacts with the ability to introspect and form coherent propositions on the basis of that introspection. Recent psychological examinations of expression have concentrated upon the dimensions underlying expressions of the content of emotion (e.g., Pleasant-Unpleasant and Arousal-Calm; Mayer & Gaschke, 1988; Watson & Tellegen, 1985). There is a considerably smaller psychological literature on individual differences in the styles or ability to appraise and express emotions, and much of the following research is reported in the psychiatric literature.

The term *alexithymia* (Sifneos, 1972) was introduced to refer to psychiatric patients who are unable to appraise and then verbally express their emotions. Certain physiological explanations for alexithymia have been proposed, among them that it may be due to blocking of impulses from the right to left hemisphere at the corpus callosum (TenHouten, Hoppe, Bogen, & Walter, 1985, 1986) or to a disconnection between limbic system and higher cortical activities (MacLean, 1949). Although such theorizing has been interesting, associated operationalizations do not yet bear on such physiological theories. Operationalizations have, however, been provided for emotional expressiveness itself.

The first scale to measure emotional expressiveness was the Beth Israel Hospital Psychosomatic Questionnaire (Sifneos, 1973), which presented brief scenarios to patients who were asked to respond in an open ended fashion. For example, patients were asked to react to situations described verbally such as a truck advancing toward them at 90 miles per hour, and their verbal responses were recorded. This protocol is then scored for emotion-communication. A normative response to the above item might be "I'd feel terror". But an alexithymic might reply, "like I want to get out of the way." For several years, the Beth Israel Hospital Psychosomatic Questionnaire served as the instrument of choice for researchers in this area (e.g., Krystal, Giller, & Cicchetti, 1986). Its subjective scoring procedure, however, resulted in low reliability (Taylor, 1984), and so the Schalling-Sifneos Personality Scale was introduced as an alternative to the Beth Israel (Apfel & Sifneos, 1979), albeit with little improvement in reliability. A number of projective measures of alexithymia appeared as well but were limited by the projective procedure itself (Cohen, Auld, Demers, & Catchlove, 1985; Defourny, Hubin, & Luminet, 1976/77; Vogt, Burckstummer, & Ernst, 1977). Finally, a method of scoring alexithymic tendencies in natural language samples using the Gottschalk-Gleser (1969) system was developed by TenHouten et al. (1985, 1986).

A group administrable and objectively scored scale in this area was clearly indicated (Thayler-Singer, 1977; Wolff, 1977), and an alexithymia scale based on the Minnesota Multiphasic Personality Inventory was developed by Kleiger and Kinsman (1980). The construction of this measure was flawed, however, due to the use of small non-representative samples, capitalization on chance during item selection, and arbitrary criteria for excluding otherwise adequate items. These procedures can be assumed to have yielded a non-optimal test.

Three new scales that address emotional expression have been developed to measure more specific attitudes about emotions. These are the State and Trait Meta-Mood Scale (SMMS; Mayer & Gaschke, 1988; TMMS; Salovey & Mayer, 1988) and the Toronto Alexithymia Scale (Bagby, Taylor & Ryan, 1986; Taylor, Ryan, & Bagby, 1985). Such attitudes are important in themselves, but in so far as they indirectly predict actual emotional reactions, they are probably not best classed with a scale such as the Beth Israel.

Another problem with most discussions of alexithymia is that they concentrate on negative emotions and ignore positive feelings, mixed emotions, or neutral states. Thus, it is unclear whether alexithymia pertains to ego-threatening feelings, or to feelings of all kinds. Additionally, might not some individuals exhibit hyper-emotionality in neutral situations? Some of these problems were addressed in a study by Mayer, Gomberg-Kaufman, and Salovey (1988). Participants reacted to 32 emotional and non-emotional situations by checking three of twelve pre-classified alternatives that represented their response to each situation. Patterns of responses fell along three broad dimensions of feeling/thought, defensive/openness, and coping/troubled. The thinking pole of the first dimension and the defensive pole of the second dimension both appear close to psychiatric conceptions of alexithymia. The fact that two dimensions might describe alexithymia suggests that the "alexithymic" classification may need to be reconceptualized.

Nonverbal — One reason the appraisal and expression of emotion have been overlooked as mental abilities may be that they often take place on a nonverbal level, and such nonverbal communication did not fit the format of early measures of mental abilities. Many investigators, however, have explored nonverbal appraisals and expressions of emotion (e.g., Ekman & Friesen, 1975) since Darwin's now classic study of facial expression (Darwin, 1872/1965). Much emotional communication occurs through nonverbal channels. And, individual differences in the clarity of the perception of these signals is illustrated in its expression, sometimes termed "nonverbal sending accuracy" (Buck, 1984).

Two scales, the Affect Expression Rating Scale (Buck, 1975, 1977) and the Affective Communication Test (Freedman, Prince, Riggio, & DiMatteo, 1980), have been developed for this purpose. The first of these is used to assess the emotional expressiveness of children, as rated by, for example, their teachers; but a self-report adult version of the scale has also been developed (Buck, 1979). The Affective Communication Test involves self-report items, such as, "I show that I like someone by hugging or touching them."

Together, these and similar scales have been used to relate emotional expressiveness to several dispositional variables. Consistent associations have been found between emotional communication, empathy (Notarius & Levenson, 1979), and depression (which yields a reverse relationship; Gerson & Pearlman, 1979; Prkachin, Craig, Papageorgis, & Reith, 1977). Such expressive ability is less clearly related to non-affective domains. Mixed or contradictory results have been obtained when predicting from emotional communication to intelligence (Harper, Wiens, & Matarazzo, 1979), extraversion (Buck, Miller, & Caul, 1974; Buck, Savin, Miller, & Caul, 1972; but see Harper et al., 1979; Notarius & Levenson, 1979), and field dependence (Sabatelli, Dreyer, & Buck, 1979, 1983; Shennum, 1976).

Summary — We have suggested that appraising and expressing emotions accurately is a part of emotional intelligence. This is the case because those who are more accurate can more quickly perceive and respond to their own emotions and better express those emotions to others. Such emotionally intelligent individuals can also respond more appropriately to their own feelings because of the accuracy with which they perceive them. These skills are emotionally intelligent because they require the processing of emotional information from within the organism, and because it is clear that some level of minimal competence at these skills is necessary for adequate social functioning.

Emotion in Others

Nonverbal perception of emotion — From an evolutionary standpoint it was important that people be able to perceive emotions not only in themselves, but also in those around them. Such perceptual abilities insure smoother interpersonal cooperation by, for example, permitting the monitoring of displeasure. There are several indications that individual differences exist in the interpretation of emotions through facial expressions.

Various measures of individual differences in non-verbal receiving of other's emotion have been developed (cf. Buck, 1984). The Affect Sensitivity Test (Campbell, Kagan, & Krathwohl, 1971; Kagan, 1978) presents videotaped interactions between pairs of individuals; subjects respond by indicating the emotions and thoughts that targets are expressing. The Communication of Affect Receiving Ability Test (CARAT) consists of a videotape of people watching scenic, unpleasant, unusual, and sexual slides (Buck, 1976). Subjects must guess what slide the target is observing by studying the target's facial expressions. The Affect Sensitivity Test has moderate internal consistency and a good test-retest reliability, although different versions of the test have had surprisingly low intercorrelations (Kagan, 1978). The Profile of Nonverbal Sensitivity (PONS; Rosenthal, Hall, DiMatteo, Rogers, & Archer, 1979) has one of the best item samples of emotional expression, including face, body, and face and body combined. Another scale oriented to a more general class of stimuli combines faces, colors, and designs, and finds they define a unifactorial construct of emotional receiving (Mayer, DiPaulo, & Salovey, 1988). Several other scales or procedures exist (Archer & Akert, 1977; Ekman & Friesen, 1974) including, for example, measures of the recognition of tachistoscopically presented facial expressions.

Differences in nonverbal perceptions of emotion have been associated with various criteria. CARAT scores are higher among artists than scientists, and they correlate with Rotter's (1966) interpersonal trust scale. More accurate perceptions may relate to effective mental-health counseling (Campbell, et al., 1971). A number of researchers (Boucher & Carlson, 1980; Ekman, 1982; Hall, 1978; Kirouac, & Doré, 1983, 1985; Wagner, MacDonald, & Manstead, 1986) have found that women are generally better in recognizing emotions in facial expressions than are men, with the exception of anger perception (Wagner, MacDonald, & Manstead, 1986). The unifactorial faces, colors, and designs scale correlates moderately with empathy (Mayer, DiPaulo, & Salovey, 1988). On the whole, scales examining intercorrelations among nonverbal perception measures are diverse, and unsurprisingly for that reason, have yielded diverse results. The different operationalizations suggest they are measuring different underlying skills (Fields & O'Sullivan, 1976; Klaiman, 1979). Buck (1984) concluded that either these instruments were, "sensitive to different aspects of nonverbal receiving ability, or, non-verbal receiving ability is not a unidimensional construct..." (p. 263).

Empathy — A particularly exciting communality among emotional appraisal and expression is that they appear related to empathy, the ability to comprehend another's feelings and to re-experience them oneself. Rogers believed an active striving to understand another person and to empathize with them is a priceless gift as well as a prerequisite for helping another grow (Rogers, 1951). Empathy may be a central characteristic of emotionally intelligent behavior. As social support researchers have made clear in recent years, a person's relatives, friends, and neighbors are critical contributors to his or her well being (Kessler, Price, & Wortman, 1985; Thoits, 1986). When people relate positively to one another, they experience greater life satisfaction, and lower stress. For example, the empathy of an advice giver is an important determinant of whether the advice is perceived as good (Mayer, Gottlieb, Hernandez, Smith, & Gordis, 1988). Empathy is also a motivator for altruistic behavior (Batson, 1987). People who behave in an emotionally intelligent fashion should have sufficient social competence to weave a warm fabric of interpersonal relations. Clearly, the greater number of emotionally intelligent friends, relatives, and coworkers, the more empathic and supportive a social structure will surround a person.

Empathy researchers, in turn, have noted its dependence on subsidiary abilities similar to appraising and expressing emotion (cf. Batson, Fultz, Schoenrade, 1987; Wispé, 1986): to understand another person's point of view (Dymond, 1949; Hogan, 1969), to identify accurately another's emotions (Buck, 1984), to experience the same or other appropriate emotion in response to them (Batson & Coke, 1981, 1983; Mehrabian & Epstein, 1972), and finally, to communicate and/or act on this internal experience (Batson, O'Quin, Fultz, Vanderplas, & Isen, 1983; Krebs, 1975).

Much of the work on empathy has treated it as a dispositional variable (Chlopan, McCain, Carbonell, & Hagen, 1985). Two scales examining empathy are Hogan's (1969) and Mehrabian and Epstein's (1972). Hogan's scale was constructed according to judges' ratings of California Q-sort items that were intended to reflect empathic and unempathic individuals. The complexity of the scale development techniques reported in Hogan (1969) make it clear that broad attributes other than empathy were considered as part of the criterion including humor, imaginative play, and insight into motives. Although we are sympathetic to this approach, which is similar to emotional intelligence in its generality, the scale may for this reason lack discriminant validity for empathy, as more narrowly considered here. A scale developed by Meharabian and Epstein (1972) more specifically measures emotional responsiveness to others and includes such subscales as emotional contagion, appreciation of distant others' feelings, and being moved by others' positive and negative emotional experiences (e.g., "It makes me sad to see a lonely stranger in a group;" "I like to watch people open presents"). Other empathy scales have been reported, but are less widely used (e.g., Dymond, 1949; Kerr & Speroff, 1954).

Developmental perspectives on empathy suggest that appraisal of one's own feelings and those of others are highly related, and that, in fact, one may not exist without the other. For example, according to Hoffman's (1984) perspective, contributors to empathy include (a) *primary circular reactions* in which an infant cries in response to other infants crying and (b) *classical empathic conditioning* in which one views another's emotional reaction (through facial expressions or body posture) to the same situation one is in oneself, thereby learning situational determinants of an affect. It is clear that while these may provide information about others' feelings, they also enable the child to learn about what one's feelings in response to a situation should be. Thus, empathy scales may measure not only one's ability to feel toward others, but general access to one's own feelings as well.

Summary — We have included the skillful recognizance of other's emotional reactions and empathic responses to them as a component of emotional intelligence. These skills enable individuals to gauge accurately the affective responses in others and to choose socially adaptive behaviors in response. Such individuals should be perceived as genuine and warm by others while individuals lacking these skills should appear oblivious and boorish.

Regulation of Emotion

People experience mood on both a direct and a reflective level. In their reflective experience, individuals have access to knowledge regarding their own and others' moods. This experience, in part, represents a willingness and ability to monitor, evaluate, and regulate emotions. Previously, we discussed the skills needed to appraise and express emotions. We now turn to processes that undergird differences in the ability to regulate one's own emotions. Later, we will discuss how similar processes might apply to attempts to regulate, even manipulate, the affective reactions of other people. Much of the research in this domain concerns mood rather than emotions. Moods, although less intense and generally longer lasting than emotions, should be just as effectively regulated and managed by individuals with emotionally intelligent skills.

Regulation of Emotion in the Self

There are a variety of experiences that one has about one's mood; these *meta-experiences of mood* can be conceptualized as the result of a regulatory system that monitors, evaluates, and sometimes acts to change mood (Mayer & Gaschke, 1988). Although many aspects of mood regulation occur automatically (it is, for instance, unnecessary to make a conscious decision to become sad in the presence of tragedy), some meta-experiences of mood are conscious and open to inquiry. For example, two scales designed expressly to measure mood regulation are the State and Trait Meta-Mood Scales (SMMS, Mayer & Gaschke, 1988; TMMS, Salovey & Mayer, 1988). As the names suggest, one scale measures momentary regulation, the other, longer-term regulatory style.

The co-occurrence of mood with meta-experiences of mood (e.g., which moods are typical, which are not; which moods are understandable, which are not) over many situations provides data for individuals to build theories about the situations that bring about moods. For instance, if one experiences a pleasant, acceptable mood when dancing, then the cause of the mood (dancing) could be sought after in the future so as to bring about the mood again. In this way, it would serve as a foundation upon which rules could be constructed that would themselves direct behavior to bring about moods.

Additionally, one can regulate mood by choosing one's associates. Associating with other people whose successes are not threatening to us generally results in positive affects like pride (Tesser, Millar & Moore, 1988), although associating with people whose successes are in areas considered important to one's sense of self can lead to negative affective states like envy (Salovey & Rodin, 1984). Individuals try to maintain positive and avoid negative moods by seeking information that helps them maintain a positive view of themselves. Tesser (1986, Tesser & Campbell, 1983) has termed this motive "self-evaluation maintenance." Further, individuals may act helpfully to others as a way of terminating negative moods, the so-called "negative state relief" view of altruistic behavior (Cialdini & Kenrick, 1976; Salovey & Rosenhan, in press). And, it makes greater evolutionary sense that the individuals of a species, rather than becoming happy by directly deciding to do so, do so instead by regulating behavior, as for example by engaging in altruistic acts (Mayer & Gaschke, 1988; Mayer & Salovey, 1988; Minsky, 1985).

Another quite different way that meta-mood experience may affect mood-change is by positively augmenting a person's overall internal experience. A negative mood that is evaluated as unacceptable and long-lasting is devastating; but were the evaluations reversed so as to view the mood as under control and soon-to-change, the overall feelings would be far less destructive of one's equanimity. Such countervailing evaluations may assist individuals to persevere in times of negative moods, and thereby enter new situations that have the potential to improve their future moods (Mayer & Gaschke, 1988).

Mood may be modified directly, as well. The earliest evidence for the self-regulation of mood stemmed from observations that the impact of mood on memory encoding and recall was generally stronger for positive than negative mood states. To explain this asymmetry, Isen (1984) has suggested that individuals are generally motivated to maintain, even prolong, pleasant moods but attempt to attenuate the experience of unpleasant ones. These processes have been labeled "mood maintenance" and "mood repair" (Isen, 1985). This motivational view assumes that individuals attempt to maximize pleasurable experiences and terminate aversive ones. They seem to use conscious (controlled) mechanisms to counteract automatic associations produced by negative moods (Clark & Isen, 1982; Fiske & Taylor, 1984), and to "take charge of their minds' propensity to jump from gloomy thought to gloomy thought. . .[by] counting your blessings, looking for the silver lining and trying to remember your favorite things" (Fiske & Taylor, 1984, p. 328). The assumption thus far, and, in fact, a long-standing tradition within psychology has been that individuals seek to maximize time spent in pleasant affective states and to terminate negative emotions. Researchers working from a variety of psychological perspectives predict that pleasant experiences are more likely to be sought (and then retained in memory) as compared with unpleasant ones (Rapaport, 1942; Singer & Salovey, 1988). Individuals' interactions with others and their private imagery are often oriented to a pleasure seeking goal.

However, people's actions are more complex than this. Individuals may be motivated to seek emotional experiences of any kind and to try to prolong these emotional experiences (Tomkins, 1962, 1963). We attend plays, read fiction, listen to symphonies even when these experiences lead to sorrow. Sorrow, though, may not be unpleasant; tragedy is considered by some the highest form of art (Aristotle, c. 355 BC/ 1970). Aesthetic appreciation may involve special qualities of emotional perception and awareness (Barten, 1983) possibly related to the internal experience of emotional intelligence. These aesthetic experiences allow us to practice feeling negative affect (with little consequence), perhaps so as to become more motivated to seek pleasant experiences and to avoid negative ones that do matter. We must empathize with the down-trodden in order to feel positively about our own advantages, and the experience of profound sadness, at times, can be uplifting. Perhaps the positive affect that accompanies aesthetically generated sorrow is rooted in contrast: one must experience, sorrow, at least temporarily, in order to feel joy (cf. Solomon, 1980).

Regulation of Emotion in Others

Emotional intelligence includes the ability to regulate and alter the affective reactions of others. For example, an emotionally intelligent orator can elicit strong reactions in an audience. Similarly, an emotionally intelligent job candidate understands the contribution of behaviors such as promptness and dress in creating a favorable impression (cf. Jones, 1964).

Goffman (1959) eloquently described the ways in which individuals present themselves and their activities to others in order to guide and control the impressions formed of them. His influential chapter on "The Arts of Impression Management" described the important consequences of deliberately "creating a scene," or having the "presence of mind" to suppress emotional responses to private problems. In addition, the skilled impression manager knows when not to attend to the behaviors of others (cf. Geller & Laor, 1988). Such management techniques have recently been expanded by Hochschild (1983), who has investigated the commercialization of emotional impression management by large corporations and other institutions.

Since Goffman, the actual processes underlying such interpersonal mood-regulation have been examined in greater detail. Jones (1964) studied emotional regulation through ingratiation. Rosen, Johnson, Johnson, and Tesser (1973) investigated the MUM effect, in which people suppress negative communications to others so as to enhance their interpersonal relations. Similarly, Mayer and Gordis (1988) demonstrated how advice givers sometimes compromise honesty to provide more interpersonal support when the two conflict. Wasielewski (1985) has developed a theory of charisma, in which it is viewed as an emotional regulation of followers by leaders.

Summary — We have included the regulation of emotion in the construct of emotional intelligence because it may lead to more adaptive and reinforcing mood states. Most people regulate emotion in themselves and others (Mayer & Gaschke, 1988). Emotionally intelligent individuals, however, should be especially adept at this process and do so to meet particular goals. On the positive side, they may enhance their own and others' moods and even manage emotions so as to charismatically motivate others toward a worthwhile end. On the negative side, those whose skills are channelled antisocially may create manipulative scenes or sociopathically lead others to nefarious ends.

Utilizing Emotional Intelligence

Individuals also differ in their ability to harness their own emotions in order to solve problems. Moods and emotions subtly but systematically influence some of the components and strategies involved in problem solving (see Isen, 1987, and Mayer, 1986, for reviews). First, emotion swings may facilitate the generation of multiple future plans. Second, positive emotion may alter memory organization so that cognitive material is better integrated and diverse ideas are seen as more related (Isen, 1987). Third, emotion provides interrupts for complex systems, "popping" them out of a given level of processing and focusing them on more pressing needs. Moods such as anxiety and depression, for example, may focus attention on the self (Pyszczynski & Greenberg, 1987; Salovey & Rodin, 1985; Wood, Saltzberg, & Goldsamt, 1988). Finally, emotions and moods may be used to motivate and assist performance at complex intellectual tasks (Alpert & Haber, 1960; Cantor, Norem, Niedenthal, Langston, & Brower, 1987; Showers, 1988).

Flexible Planning

One central aspect of personality is the mood swing wherein individuals differ in the frequency and amplitude of their shifts in predominant affect (Eysenck, 1982; Larsen, Diener, & Emmons, 1986). Those with the strongest mood swings will experience concomitant changes in their estimates of the likelihood of future events depending upon the valence of those events. People in good moods perceive positive events as more likely and negative events as less likely to occur and that the reverse holds true for people in unpleasant moods (Bower, 1981; Johnson & Tversky, 1983; Mayer & Bremer, 1985; Mayer & Volanth, 1985; Mayer, Mamberg, & Volanth, 1988; Salovey & Birnbaum, 1988). Mood swings may assist such people in breaking set when thinking about the future and consider a wider variety of possible outcomes. As a consequence, they may be more likely to generate a larger number of future plans for themselves and thereby be better prepared to take advantage of future opportunities (Mayer, 1986).

Creative Thinking

Mood may also assist problem solving by virtue of its impact on the organization and use of information in memory. For example, individuals may find it easier to categorize features of problems as being related or unrelated while they experience positive mood (Isen & Daubman, 1984). This clarity in categorizing information may have positive impact on creative problem solving (Isen, Daubman, & Nowicki, 1987).

Standard creativity tasks such as the remote associates task and cognitive categorization tests have commonly been used as the dependent variables in this research. For example, Isen et al. (1987) demonstrated that positive mood can facilitate more creative responses to Duncker's candle task. It seems that subjects experiencing positive mood are more likely to give especially unusual or creative first associates to neutral cues (Isen, Johnson, Mertz, & Robinson, 1985). Moreover, happy individuals may be more likely to discover category organizing principles and use them to integrate and remember information (Isen, Daubman, & Gorgoglione, 1987).

Mood Redirected Attention

The third principle states that attention is directed to new problems when powerful emotions occur. Thus, when people attend to their feelings, they may be directed away from an ongoing problem into a new one of greater immediate importance. The salesperson who is undergoing a divorce may be directed away from trivial work-related problems and toward understanding of her own interpersonal relations through the pain that emerges from her marital situation (Easterbrook, 1959; Mandler, 1975; Simon, 1982). In this fashion, individuals learn to capitalize on the capacity of emotional processes to refocus attention on the most important stimuli in their environment. Rather than merely disrupting ongoing cognitive activities, affect can help individuals to reprioritize the internal and external demands on their attention, and allocate attentional resources accordingly.

Motivating Emotions

Finally, moods may be used to motivate persistence at challenging tasks. For example, some individuals can channel the anxiety created by evaluative situations (such as tests and impending performances) to motivate them to prepare more thoroughly and attain more exacting standards (Alpert & Haber, 1960). Others may imagine negative outcomes as a method of motivating performance (Cantor, Norem, Niedenthal, Langston, & Brower, 1987; Showers, 1988). People may use good moods to increase their confidence in their capabilities and thus persist in the face of obstacles and aversive experiences (Bandura, 1986; Kavanagh & Bower, 1985; Salovey, 1986; Salovey & Birnbaum, 1988). Finally, individuals with positive attitudes toward life construct interpersonal experiences that lead to better outcomes and greater rewards for themselves and others (Epstein & Feist, 1988).

Summary

When people approach life tasks with emotional intelligence, they should be at an advantage for solving problems adaptively. And it is for this reason that such skills are included within the construct of emotional intelligence. The sorts of problems people identify and the way they frame them will probably be more related to internal emotional experience than will be the problems addressed by others. For example, such individuals are more likely to ask not how much they will earn in a career, but rather whether they will be happy in such a career. Having framed a problem, individuals with such skills may be more creative and flexible in arriving at possible alternatives to problems. They are also more apt to integrate emotional considerations when choosing among alternatives. Such an approach will lead to behavior considerate and respectful of the internal experience of themselves and others.

Conclusions and Implications

People who have developed skills related to emotional intelligence understand and express their own emotions, recognize emotions in others, regulate affect, and use moods and emotions to motivate adaptive behaviors. Is this just another definition of a healthy, self-actualized individual? These and other considerations relating emotional intelligence to the individual will be considered as we conclude.

The Utility of a Concept of Emotional Intelligence

Throughout this paper, we have presupposed that the construct of emotional intelligence is of heuristic value in drawing together literatures that are often left unintegrated. But do the abilities represented by these literatures reflect a coherent construct? For the emotional intelligence framework to be useful, the component skills need not intercorrelate. For example, in models of cognition, it would not be considered any less useful were individual differences in the component parts (e.g., attention, memory, metacognition) not intercorrelated. Such models have a useful status whether underlying components form a single factor or are a set of independent but conceptually related processes. Of course, it may be that these skills are intercorrelated, but such a conclusion awaits the findings of well designed experiments and correlational studies. What is important is that the skills share the fact that they (a) involve emotional processing and (b) are necessary for a minimum level of competence and adequate, intelligent functioning. We believe that each of our topic areas satisfies these criteria.

Emotional Intelligence and Adjustment

Emotional intelligence and health — The person with emotional intelligence can be thought of as having attained at least a limited form of positive mental health. These individuals are aware of their own feelings and those of others. They are open to positive and negative aspects of internal experience, are able to label them, and when appropriate, communicate them. Such awareness will often lead to the effective regulation of affect within themselves and others, and so contribute to well being. Thus, the emotionally intelligent person is often a pleasure to be around and leaves others feeling better. The emotionally intelligent person, however, does not mindlessly seek pleasure, but rather attends to emotion in the path toward growth. Emotional intelligence involves self-regulation appreciative of the fact that temporarily hurt feelings or emotional restraint is often necessary in the service of a greater objective. Helping others, which may make one feel better in the long run, may require sacrifice and emotional toughness (Dienstbier, 1988). Thus, emotionally intelligent individuals accurately perceive their emotions and use integrated, sophisticated approaches to regulate them as they proceed toward important goals.

Deficits in emotional intelligence — In contrast, many problems in adjustment may arise from deficits in emotional intelligence. People who don't learn to regulate their own emotions may become slaves to them. Individuals who can't recognize emotions in others, or who make others feel badly, may be perceived as cloddish or oafish and ultimately be ostracized. Other peculiarities of emotional deficits exist as well. Sociopaths, who are impoverished in their experience of emotion, seem to over-regulate mood in others for their own purposes (Rosenhan & Seligman, 1984). A far more common ailment may involve people who cannot recognize emotion in themselves and are therefore unable to plan lives that fulfill them emotionally. Such planning deficits may lead to lives of unrewarded experience lived by individuals who become depressed, even suicidal. A society of such individuals could create a culture in which people are insufficiently rewarded and so regulate their emotions in alienating ways (Skinner, 1986).

Future Research in Emotional Intelligence

Just as emotional intelligence may provide a framework for organizing personality, it may also suggest an outline for personality researchers who study emotion. Investigators may wish to examine emotions in the self, the appraisal of others' emotions, the ways in which emotion is regulated, or the adaptive uses of emotion. But, in addition, others may choose a research strategy that involves the identification of emotionally intelligent individuals through the use of laboratory tasks or conventional scales. They might also examine the acquisition of emotionally intelligent skills and interventions to promote them. We would hope as well that researchers in this area might examine the role played by emotional intelligence in understanding other complex social processes such as the development of friendships and other close relationships. In the end, by recognizing the contribution of emotional intelligence to a healthy personality, and how to foster it, we may come to recognize advantageous qualities or needed changes in social institutions and cultural practices.

References

Alpert, R., & Haber, R. (1960). Anxiety in academic achievement situations. Journal of Abnormal Psychology, 61, 207-215.

Apfel, R.J., & Sifneos, P.E. (1979). Alexithymia: Concept and measurement. Psychotherapy and Psychosomatics, 32, 180-190.

Archer, D. & Akert, R. M. (1977). Words and everything else: Verbal and nonverbal cues in social interpretation. Journal of Personality and Social Psychology, 35, 443-449.

Aristotle (c. 355 BC/1970). The poetics. G. F. Else (Trans.) Ann Arbor, MI: The University of Michigan Press.

Arnold, M. (1960). Emotion and personality. New York: Columbia University Press.

Bandura, A. (1986). Social foundations of thought and action. Englewood Cliffs, NJ: Prentice-Hall.

Barten, S.S. (1983). The aesthetic mode of consciousness. In S. Wapner & B. Kaplan (Eds.), Toward a holistic developmental psychology. Hillsdale, NJ: Lawrence Erlbaum Associates.

Batson, C.D. (1987). Prosocial motivation: Is it ever truly altruistic? In L. Berkowitz (Ed.), Advances in experimental social psychology (Vol. 20, pp. 65-123). New York: Academic Press.

Batson, C.D., & Coke, J.S. (1981). Empathy: A source of altruistic motivation for helping? In J. P. Rushton, & R. M. Sorrentino (Eds.). Altruism and helping behavior (pp. 167-187). Hillsdale, NJ: Erlbaum.

Batson, C.D., & Coke, J.S. (1983). Empathic motivations of helping behavior. In J.T. Cacciopo & R.E. Petty (Eds.). Social psychop-hys-iology: A sourcebook (pp. 417-433). New York: Guilford.

Batson, C.D., Fultz, J., & Schoenrade, P.A. (1987). Distress and empathy: Two qualitatively distinct vicarious emotions with different motivational consequences. Journal of Personality, 55, 19-39.

Batson, C.D., O'Quin, K., Fultz, J., Vanderplas, M., & Isen, A. (1983). Self-reported distress and empathy and egoistic versus altruistic motivation for helping. Journal of Personality and Social Psychology, 45, 706-718.

Blaney, P. (1986). Affect and memory: A review. Psychological Bulletin, 99, 229-246.

Boucher, J.D., & Carlson, G.E. (1980). Recognition of facial expression in three cultures. Journal of Cross-Cultural Psychology, 11, 263-280.

Bower, G.H. (1981). Mood and memory. American Psychologist, 36, 129-148.

Buck, R. (1975). Nonverbal communication of affect in children. Journal of Personality and Social Psychology, 31, 644-653.

Buck, R. (1976). A test of nonverbal receiving ability: Preliminary studies. Human Communication Research, 2, 162-171.

Buck, R. (1977). Nonverbal communication accuracy in preschool children: Relationships with personality and skin conductance. Journal of Personality and Social Psychology, 33, 225-236.

Buck, R. (1979). Individual differences in nonverbal sending accuracy and electrodermal responding: The externalizing-internalizing dimension. In R. Rosenthal (Ed), Skill in nonverbal communication: Individual differences. Cambridge, MA: Oelgeshlager, Gunn, & Hain.

Buck, R. (1984). The communication of emotion. New York: The Guilford Press.

Buck, R., Miller, R.E., & Caul, W.F. (1974). Sex, personality, and physiological variables in the communication of emotion via facial expression. Journal of Personality and Social Psychology, 30, 587-596.

Buck, R., Savin, V.J., Miller, R.E., & Caul, W.F. (1972). Nonverbal communication of affect in humans. Journal of Personality and Social Psychology, 23, 362-371.

Bureau of Personnel Administration (1930). Partially standardized tests of social intelligence. Public Personnel Studies, 8, 73-79.

Campbell, R.J., Kagan, N.I., and Krathwohl, D.R. (1971). The development and validation of a scale to measure affective sensitivity (empathy). Journal of Counseling Psychology, 18, 407-412.

Cantor, N., & Kihlstrom, J.F. (1985). Social intelligence: The cognitive basis of personality. In P. Shaver (Ed.). Review of Personality and Social Psychology, 6, 15-33.

Cantor, N., & Kihlstrom, J.F. (1987). Personality and social intelligence. Englewood Cliffs, NJ: Prentice Hall.

Cantor, N., Norem, J.K., Niedenthal, P.M., Langston, C.A., Brower, A.M. (1987). Life tasks, self-concept ideals, and cognitive strategies in a life transition. Journal of Personality and Social Psychology, 53, 1178-1191.Chlopan, B. E., McCain, M. L.,

Carbonell, J. L., & Hagen, R. L. (1985). Empathy: Review of Available Measures. Journal of Personality and Social Psychology, 48, 635-653.

Cialdini, R.B., & Kenrick, D.T. (1976). Altruism as hedonism: A social development perspective on the relationship of negative mood state and helping. Journal of Personality and Social Psychology, 34, 907-914.

Clark, M.S., & Fiske, S.T. (1982). Affect and cognition. Hillsdale, NJ: Erlbaum.

Clark, M.S., & Isen, A.M. (1982). Toward understanding the relationship between feeling states and social behavior. In A.H. Hastorf, & A.M. Isen (Eds.) Cognitive social psychology. (pp. 73-108). New York: Elsevier North-Holland.

Cohen, M. A., Auld, F., Demers, L., & Catchlove, R. (1985). Alexithymia: The development of a valid and reliable projective measure (the Objectively Scored Archetypal$_9$ Test). Journal of Nervous and Mental Disease, 173, 621-627.

Cronbach, L. J. (1960). Essentials of psychological testing (2nd ed.) New York: Harper & Row.

Darwin, C. (1872/1955). Expression of the emotions in man and animals. New York: Philosophical Library.

Defourny, M., Hubin, P. & Luminet, D. (1976/1977). Alexithymia: "Pensée opératoire" and predisposition to coronopathy." Psychotherapy and Psychosomatics, 27, 106-114.

Dienstbier, R.A. (1984). The role of emotion in moral socialization. In C.E. Izard, J. Kagan, & R.B. Zajonc (Eds.), Emotions, cognition, and behavior. (pp. 484-514). | New York: Cambridge Press.

Dienstbier, R.A. (June, 1988). Toughening. Paper presented at the 6th International Conference on Affect and Motivation. Nags Head, NC.

Diogenes Laertius (1925). Lives of eminent philosphers (R.D. Hicks, trans.). Cambridge, MA: Harvard University Press.

Dymond, R. F. (1949). A scale for the measurement of empathic ability. Journal of Consulting Psychology, 13, 228-233.

Easterbrook, J.A. (1959). The effects of emotion on cue utilization and the organization of behavior. Psychological Review, 66, 183-200.

Ekman, P. (1982). Emotion in the human face. New York: Cambridge University Press.

Ekman, P., & Friesen, W.V. (1974). Nonverbal behavior and psychopathology. In R.J. Friedman & H.M. Katz (Eds.), The psychology of depression: Contemporary theory and research. New York: Wiley.

Ekman, P., & Friesen, W.V. (1975). Unmasking the face: A guide to recognizing the emotions from facial clues. Englewood Cliffs, NJ: Prentice-Hall.

Epstein, S. (1984). Controversial issues in emotion theory. In P. Shaver (Ed.), Review of personality and social psychology: Emotions, relationships, and health. (pp. 64-88). Beverly Hills, CA: Sage Publications.

Epstein, S. (1986). The development of an inventory of constructive thinking. Unpublished manuscript.

Epstein, S., & Feist, G.J. (1988). Relation between self- and other-acceptance and its moderation by identification. Journal of Personality and Social Psychology, 54, 309-315.

Eysenck, H.J. (1982). Personality, genetics, and behavior. New York: Praeger Publishers.

Fields, B., & O'Sullivan, M. (April, 1976). Convergent validation of five person-perception measures. Paper presented at the annual meeting of Western Psychological Association.

Fiske, S.T., & Taylor, S.E. (1984). Social cognition. Reading, MA: Addison-Wesley.

Ford, M.E. (1982). Social cognition and social competence in adolescence. Developmen-tal Psychology, 18, 323-340.

Ford, M.E., & Tisak, M. (1983). A further search for social intelligence. Journal of Educational Psychology, 75, 196-206.

Freedman, H.S., Prince, L.M., Riggio, R.E., & DiMatteo, M.R. (1980). Understanding and assessing nonverbal expressiveness: The Affective Communication Test. Journal of Personality and Social Psychology, 39, 333-351.

Frijda, N.H. (1988). The laws of emotion. American Psychologist, 43, 349-358.

Gardner, H. (1983). Frames of mind. New York: Basic Books.

Geller, J., & Laor, N. (1988). Nose picking and the automobile: A psychosomatic parapraxis. Unpublished manuscript.

Goffman, E. (1959). The presentation of self in everyday life. Garden City, NY: Doubleday & Co.

Gottschalk, L.A., & Gleser, G. (1969). The measurement of psychological states through the content analysis of verbal behavior. Berkeley, CA: University of California Press.

Hall, J.A. (1978). Gender effects in encoding nonverbal cues. Psychological Bulletin, 85, 845-857.

Harper, R.G., Wiens, A.N., & Matarazzo, J.B. (1979). The relationship between encoding-decoding of visual nonverbal emotional cues. Semiotica, 28, 171-192.

Hochschild, A.R. (1983). The managed heart: Commercialization of human feeling. Berkeley, CA: University of California Press.

Hoffman, M.L. (1984). Interaction of affect and cognition in empathy. In C.E. Izard, J. Kagan, & R.B. Zajonc (Eds.), Emotions, cognition, and behavior (pp. 103-131). Cambridge: Cambridge University Press.

Hogan, R. (1969). Development of an empathy scale. Journal of Consulting and Clinical Psychology, 33, 307-316.

Isen, A.M. (1984). Toward understanding the role of affect in cognition. In R. Wyer & T. Srull (Eds.), Handbook of social cognition (Vol 3., pp. 179-236). Hillsdale, NJ: Erlbaum.

Isen, A.M. (1985). The asymmetry of happiness and sadness in effects on memory in normal college students. Journal of Experimental Psychology: General, 114, 388-391.

Isen, A.M. (1987). Positive affect, cognitive processes, and social behavior. In L. Berkowitz (Ed.), Advances in experimental social psychology (Vol. 20, pp. 203-253). New York: Academic Press.

Isen, A.M., & Daubman, K.A. (1984). The influence of affect on categorization. Journal of Personality and Social Psychology, 47, 1206-1217.

Isen, A.M., Daubman, K.A., & Gorgoglione, J.M. (1987). The influence of positive affect on cognitive organization: Implications for education. In R. Snow & M. Farr (Eds.), Aptitude, learning, and instruction: Affective and conative factors. Hillsdale, NJ: Erlbaum.

Isen, A.M., Daubman, K.A., & Nowicki, G.P. (1987). Positive affect facilitates creative problem solving. Journal of Personality and Social Psychology, 52, 1122-1131.

Isen, A.M., Johnson, M.M.S., Mertz, E., & Robinson, G. (1985). The influence of positive affect on the unusualness of word associations. Journal of Personality and Social Psychology, 48, 1413-1426.

Izard, C.E., & Buechler, S. (1980). Aspects of consciousness and personality in terms of differential emotions theory. In R. Plutchik & H. Kellerman (Eds.), Emotion: Theory, research, and experience (Vol. 1, pp. 165-187). New York: Academic Press.

Izard, C.E., Kagan, J., & Zajonc, R.B. (1984). Emotions, cognition, and behavior. Cambridge: Cambridge University Press.

Johnson, E.J., & Tversky, A. (1983). Affect, generalization, and the perception of risk. Journal of Personality and Social Psychology, 15, 294-301.

Jones, E.E. (1964). Ingratiation: A social psychological analysis. New York: Appleton-Century-Crofts.

Kagan, N. (September, 1978). Affective sensitivity test: Validity and reliability. Paper presented at the meeting of the American Psychological Association, San Francisco.

Kavanagh, D.J., & Bower, G.H. (1985). Mood and self-efficacy: Impact of joy and sadness on perceived capabilities. Cognitive Therapy and Research, 9, 507-525.

Kerr, W.A., & Speroff, B. J. (1954). Validation and evaluation of the empathy test. The Journal of General Psychology, 50, 269-276.

Kessler, R.C., Price, R.H., & Wortman, C.B. (1985). Social factors in psychopathology: Stress, social support, and coping processes. Annual Review of Psychology, 36, 531-572.

Kirouac, G., & Doré, F. (1983). Accuracy and latency of judgment of facial expression of emotion. Perceptual and Motor Skills, 57, 683-686.

Kirouac, G., & Doré, F. (1985). Accuracy of the judgment of facial expression of emotions as a function of sex and level of education. Journal of Nonverbal Behavior, 9, 3-7.

Klaiman, S. (1979). Selected perceptual, cognitive, personality, and socialization variables as predictors of nonverbal sensitivity. Doctoral dissertation, University of Ottawa.

Kleiger, J.H. & Kinsman, R.A. (1980). The development of an MMPI alexithymia scale. Psychotherapy and Psychosomatics, 34, 17-24.

Krebs, D.L. (1975). Empathy and altruism. Journal of Personality and Social Psychology, 32, 1134-1146.

Krystal, J.H., Giller, E.L., Cicchetti, D.V. (1986). Assessment of alexithymia in post-traumatic stress disorder and somatic illness: Introduction of a reliable measure. Psychosomatic Medicine, 48, 84-94.

Larsen, R.J., Diener, E., & Emmons, R.A. (1986). Affect intensity and reactions to daily life events. Journal of Personality and Social Psychology, 51, 803-814.

Lazarus, R.S. (1966). Psychological stress and the coping process. New York: McGraw-Hill.

Leeper, R. W. (1948). A motivational theory of emotions to replace "emotions as disorganized response." Psychol-ogi-cal Review, 55, 5-21.

Mandler, G. (1975). Mind and emotion. New York: Wiley.

Mayer, J.D. (1986). How mood influences cognition. In N.E. Sharkey (Ed.), Advances in cognitive science (Vol. 1, pp. 290-314). Chichester: Ellis Horwood.

Mayer, J.D., & Bremer, D. (1985). Assessing mood with affect-sensitive tasks. Journal of Personality Assessment, 49, 95-99.

Mayer, J.D., DiPaulo, M., & Salovey, P. (1988). Perceiving affective content in ambiguous visual stimuli. Manuscript submitted for publication.

Mayer, J.D., & Gaschke, Y.N. (1988). The experience and meta-experience of mood. Journal of Personality and Social Psychology, 55, 102-111.

Mayer, J.D., Gomberg-Kaufman, S., & Salovey, P. (1988). Style of emotional reaction. Manuscript submitted for publication.

Mayer, J.D., & Gordis, F. (1988). Honest and not-so-honest advice. Unpublished manuscript.

Mayer, J.D., Gottlieb, A.N., Hernandez, M., Smith, J., & Gordis, F. (1988). Sought advice and self-regulation. Unpublished manuscript.

Mayer, J.D. & Salovey, P. (1988). Personality moderates the effects of affect on cognition. In J. Forgas & K. Fiedler (Eds.), Affect, Cognition, and Social Behavior. (pp. 87-99). Toronto: Hogrefe.

Mayer, J.D., Mamberg, M., & Volanth, A.J. (1988). Cognitive domains of the mood system. Journal of Personality, 56, 453-486.

Mayer, J.D., & Volanth, A.J. (1985). Cognitive involvement in the emotional response system. Motivation and Emotion, 9, 261-275.

Mehrabian, A., & Epstein, N. (1972). A measure of emotional empathy. Journal of Personality, 40, 525-543.

Minsky, M. (1985). The society of mind. New York: Simon & Schuster.

Notarius, C. I., & Levenson, R. W. (1979). Expressive tendencies and physiological response to stress. Journal of Personality and Social Psychology, 37, 1204-1201.

Plutchik, R. (1980). A general psychoevolutionary theory of emotion. In R. Plutchik & H. Kellerman (Eds.), Emotion: Theory, reseach, and Experience (Vol. 1, pp.3-33). New York: Academic Press.

Prkachin, K.N., Craig, K.B., Papageorgis, D., & Reith, G. (1977). Nonverbal communication deficits and response to performance feedback in depression. Journal of Abnormal Psychology, 86, 224-234.

Publilius Syrus (c. 100 BC/1961). Sententiae. In J.W. Duff & A.M. Duff (Eds.), Minor latin poets. Cambridge, MA: Harvard University Press.

Pyszczynski, T., & Greenberg, J. (1987). Self-regulatory perseveration and the depressive self-focusing style: A self-awareness theory of reactive depression. Psychological Bulletin, 102, 122-138.

Rapaport, D. (1942). Emotions and memory. Baltimore: Williams & Wilkins.

Rogers, C.R. (1951). Client-centered therapy: Its current practice, implications and theory. Boston: Houghton Mifflin.

Roseman, I.J. (1984). Cognitive determinants of emotion: A structural theory. Review of Personality and Social Psychology, 5, 11-36.

Rosen, S., Johnson, R.D., Johnson, M.J., & Tesser, A. (1973). Interactive effects of news valence and attraction on communicator behavior. Journal of Personality and Social Psychology, 28, 298-300.

Rosenhan, D.L., & Seligman, M.E.P. (1984). Abnormal psychology. New York: Norton.

Rosenthal, R., Hall, J.A., DiMatteo, M.R., Rogers, P.L., & Archer, D. (1979). Sensitivity to nonverbal communication: The PONS test. Baltimore: Johns Hopkins University Press.

Rotter, J.B. (1966). Generalized expectancies for internal versus external control of reinforcement. Psychological Monographs, 80, (1, Whole No. 609).

Sabatelli, R., Dreyer, A., & Buck, R. (1979). Cognitive style and the sending and receiving of facial cues. Perceptual and Motor Skills, 49, 203-212.

Sabatelli, R., Dreyer, A., & Buck, R. (1983). Cognitive style and marital complaints. Journal of Personality, 51, 192-201.

Salovey, P. (1986). The Effects of Mood and Focus of Attention on Self-Relevant Thoughts and Helping Intention. Unpublished doctoral dissertation, Yale University.

Salovey, P., & Birnbaum, D. (1988). The influence of mood on health-relevant cognitions. Unpublished manuscript, Yale University.

Salovey, P., & Mayer, J.D. (1988). The trait meta-mood scale. Unpublished manuscript.

Salovey, P. & Rodin, J. (1984). Some antecedents and consequences of social-comparison jealousy. Journal of Personality and Social Psychology, 47, 780-792.

Salovey, P. & Rodin, J. (1985). Cognitions about the self: Connecting feeling states to social behavior. In P. Shaver (Ed.), Self, Situations, and Social Behavior: Review of Personality and Social Psychology. (Volume 6). (pp. 143-166). Beverly Hills, CA: Sage.

Salovey, P. & Rosenhan, D.L. (in press). Mood states and prosocial behavior. In H. Wagner & A. Manstead (Eds.), Handbook of psychophysiology: Emotion and social behavior. New York: Wiley and Sons.

Schaffer, L.F., Gilmer, B, & Schoen, M. (1940). Psychology. New York: Harper & Brothers (Pp. xii, 521).

Shennum, W.A. (1976). Field-dependence and facial expression. Perceptual and Motor Skills, 43, 179-184.

Shower, C. (1988). Motivational consequences of considering negative possibilities for upcoming events. Submitted for publication.

Sifneos, P.E. (1972). Short-term psychotherapy and emotional crisis. Cambridge, MA: Harvard University Press.

Sifneos, P.E. (1973). The prevalence of "alexithymic" characteristics in psychosomatic patients. Psychotherapy and Psychosomatics, 22, 225-262.

Simon, H.A. (1982). Comments. In M.S. Clark & S.T. Fiske (Eds.), Affect and cognition. (pp. 333-342). Hillsdale, NJ: Erlbaum.

Singer, J.A., & Salovey, P. (1988). Mood and memory: Evaluating the network theory of affect. Clinical Psychology Review, 8, 211-251

Skinner, B. F. (1986). What is wrong with daily life in the Western World? American Psychologist, 41, 568-574.

Sloman, A., & Crocher, M. (1981). Why robots will have emotions. In A. Drinan (Ed.), Proceedings of the seventh International Joint Conference on Artificial Intelligence, (Vol 1.). Vancouver, BC.

Smith, C.A., & Ellsworth, P.C. (1985). Patterns of cognitive appraisal of emotion. Journal of Personality and Social Psychology, 48, 813-838.

Solomon, R.L. (1980). The opponent process theory of acquired motivation: The costs of pleasure and the benefits of pain. American Psychologist, 35, 691-712.

Sternberg, R. J., Conway, B. E., Ketron, J. L., & Bernstein, M. (1981). People's conceptions of intelligence. Journal of Personality and Social Psychology, 41, 37-55.

Sternberg, R.J., & Smith, C. (1985). Social intelligence and decoding skills in nonverbal communication. Social Cognition, 3, 168-192.

Taylor, G.J. (1984). Alexithymia: Concept, measurement, and implications for treatment. The American Journal of Psychiatry, 141, 725-732.

Taylor, G.J., Ryan, D. & Bagby, R.M. (1985). Toward the development of a new self-report alexithymia scale. Psychotherapy and Psychosomatics, 44, 191-199.

TenHouten, W.D., Hoppe, K.D., Bogen, J.E., & Walter, D.O. (1985). Alexithymia and the split brain: IV. Gottschalk-Gleser content analysis, an overview. Psychotherapy and Psychosomatics, 44, 113-121.

TenHouten, W.D., Hoppe, K.D., Bogen, J.E., & Walter, D.O. (1986). Alexithymia: An experimental study of cerebral commissurotomy patients and normal control subjects. American Journal of Psychiatry, 143, 312-316.

Tesser, A. (1986). Some effects of self-evaluation maintenance on cognition and action. In R.M. Sorrentino, & E.T. Higgins (Eds.) The Handbook of Motivation and Cognition (Pp. 435-464). New York: Guilford.

Tesser, A. & Campbell, J. (1983). Self-definition and self-evaluation maintenance. In J. Suls, & A. Greenwald (Eds.). Social psychological perspectives on the self. (Vol. 2; Pp. 1-31). Hillsdale, NJ: Erlbaum.

Tesser, A., Millar, M., Moore, J. (1988). Some affective consequences of social comparison and reflection processes: The pain and pleasure of being close. Journal of Personality and Social Psychology, 54, 49-61.

Thayler-Singer, M. (1977). Psychological dimensions in psychosomatic patients. Psychotherapy and Psychosomatics, 28, 13-27.

Thoits, P. (1986). Social support as coping assistance. Journal of Consulting and Clinical Psychology, 54, 416-423.

Thorndike, E.L. (1920). Intelligence and its uses. Harper's Magazine, 140, 227-235.

Thorndike, R.L., & Stein, S. (1937). An evaluation of the attempts to measure social intel-ligence. Psychological Bulletin, 34, 275-284.

Tomkins, S.S. (1962). Affect, imagery, and consciousness, Vol 1: The positive affects. New York: Springer.

Tomkins, S.S. (1963). Affect, imagery, and consciousness, Vol 2: The negative affects. New York: Springer.

Vogt, R., Burckstummer, G., & Ernst, L. (1977). Differences in fantasy life of psychosomatic and psychoneurotic patients. Psychotherapy and Psychosomatics, 28, 13-23.

Wagner, H.L., MacDonald, C.J., & Manstead, A.S.R. (1986). Communication of individual emotions by spon-taneous facial expres-sion. Journal of Personality and Social Psychology, 50, 737-743.

Walker R. E. & Foley, J. M. (1973). Social Intelligence: Its history and measurement. Psychological Reports, 33, 839-864.

Wasielewski, P.L. (1985). The emotional basis of charisma. Symbolic Interaction, 8, 207-222.

Watson, D., & Tellegen, A. (1985). Toward a consensual structure of mood. Psychological Bulletin, 98, 219-235.

Wechsler, D. (1958). The measurement and appraisal of adult intelligence. Baltimore, MD: Williams & Wilkins.

Weiner, B. (1985). An attributional theory of achievement motivation and emotion. Psychological Review, 92, 549-573.

Weinstein, E. A. (1969). The development of interpersonal competence. In D. A. Goslin (Ed.) Handbook of socialization theory and research. Chicago: Rand McNally.

Wispé, L.G. (1986). The distinction between sympathy and empathy: To call forth a concept, a word is needed. Journal of Personality and Social Psychology, 50, 314-321.

Wolff, H. (1977). The contribution of the interview situation to the restriction of fantasy life and emotion experience in psychosomatic patients. Psychotherapy and Psychosomatics, 28, 58-67.

Wood, J.V., Saltzberg, J.A., & Goldsamt, L.A., (1988). Does affect induce self-focused attention? Unpublished manuscript.

Woodworth, R. S. (1940). Psychology, 4th Edition. New York: Henry Holt.

Young, P. T. (1936). Motivation of behavior. New York: John Wiley & Sons.

Young, P. T. (1943). Emotion in man and animal: its nature and relation to attitude and motive. New York: John Wiley & Sons.

What is Emotional Intelligence?

John D. Mayer, University of New Hampshire
Peter Salovey, Yale University

The authors gratefully acknowledge the support of the Fetzer Institute, which sponsored several conferences on emotional literacy which we attended. Many of the conferees, including the other authors and commentators of this volume, made valuable suggestions that improved this chapter. Other educators, psychologists, and like-minded individuals contributed their comments as well. We are especially indebted to David Caruso, Kevin M. Carlsmith, Deborah Davis, Karol DeFalco, Deborah Hirsch, Dan Smith, and Chip Wood. Kevin M. Carlsmith also helped design and construct Figure 1.

Introduction

A fourth grade boy was shivering on a school playground when a teacher asked him if he owned a warmer coat. He replied that he did not (and his friend agreed). That afternoon, the teacher and the school nurse called the boy's home and offered to buy him a new coat. The boy's mother was delighted, and so the next morning, they outfitted the boy. Two boys noticed the child's new coat at recess, and accused him of stealing it. When the boy denied it, the accusers launched such a venomous attack that none of the other children dared to defend the boy. Teachers and staff arrived and began to break up the confrontation. One of the accusers yelled "suck eggs," at the school nurse. "You suck eggs!" she replied. The teacher who had bought the coat was disturbed that her gift had caused such pain. The school nurse wondered how she could have said, "suck eggs," to a child. The teacher whose class contained the trouble-makers wondered how her boys could have acted that way. The staff-members discussed what had happened and tried to determine what to do next.[1]

Reasoning about this situation requires sophisticated problem solving: What social rules have been followed or broken? What perceptions were logical or illogical? Does community support exist for disciplining the children? How can such problems be avoided in the future? Implicit in each of these questions is also information about feelings. Why were the accusers so angry? What can be done about the nurse's guilt? A feeling-blind response to the situation is possible: An administrator could declare that henceforth teachers should not give gifts to students. Such a response radically de-emphasizes feelings, however, in that it punishes those who care, and would embarrass the boy who received the coat. Alternative courses of action deal better with the feelings intrinsic to this situation. Reasoning that takes emotions into account is part of what we have referred to as *emotional intelligence.*

The concept of emotional intelligence has received considerable attention in various books, magazines, and journals.[2] Each new discussion of the concept, however, seems to employ a different definition or make a different claim for its importance. This interest has prompted us to further clarify the concept of emotional intelligence. In the remainder of this chapter we discuss the general scope and origin of emotional intelligence; the development of the concept of emotional intelligence; a revised definition and conceptualization of emotional intelligence; the assessment of emotional intelligence; and applications of emotional intelligence in the schools and beyond.

The General Scope and Origin of Emotional Intelligence

Understanding the concept of emotional intelligence requires exploring its two component terms, *intelligence* and *emotion.* Since the eighteenth century, psychologists have recognized an influential three-part division of the mind into cognition (or thought), affect (including emotion), and motivation (or conation).[3] The cognitive sphere includes such functions as human memory, reasoning, judgment, and abstract thought. Intelligence is typically used by psychologists (and those who came before) to characterize how well the cognitive sphere functions. That is, intelligence pertains to abilities such as the "power to combine and separate" concepts, to judge and to reason, and to engage in abstract thought.[4,5]

Emotions belong to the second, so-called affective sphere of mental functioning which includes the emotions themselves, moods, evaluations, and other feeling states, including fatigue or energy. Definitions of *emotional intelligence* should in some way connect emotions with intelligence if the meanings of the two terms are to be preserved. Recall that motivation is a third sphere of personality. It refers to biological urges or learned goal-seeking behavior. To the extent that it is involved in emotional intelligence, it should be thought of as secondary.

Not everything that connects cognition to emotion, however, is emotional intelligence. Over the past 15 years or so, a great deal of study has been devoted to the mutual interaction of feelings and thought. This general area of research is called *cognition and affect*. Emotion is known to alter thinking in many ways — but not necessarily in ways that would make a person smarter. For example, research indicates that moods generally bias people's thoughts: People in good moods think they are healthier than others, that the economy is improving, and that Paris is a better example of a city than Calcutta. People in bad moods tend to think they are sicker than others, that the economy is getting worse, and that Calcutta exemplifies the present-day urban condition fairly accurately.[6] This mood-biasing effect, termed mood-congruent judgment, occurs when "...an affective match between a person's moods and ideas increases the judged merit, broadly defined, of those ideas."[7] Note that with mood-congruent judgment, mood and cognition interact without anyone being more or less smart. The field of cognition and affect also includes studies of emotional self-control, such as when a person buries her anger. Note that this doesn't necessarily improve the quality of the person's emotions or intelligence. It may be smart to be angry at times.

Emotional intelligence, as opposed to more general research, should in some way refer to heightened emotional or mental abilities. Although this criterion seems straightforward, some definitions of emotional intelligence don't really adhere to it. For example, one popular definition of emotional intelligence says it involves, "self-control, zeal and persistence, and the ability to motivate oneself."[8] This definition focuses on motivational characteristics such as zeal and persistence rather than on emotion. The concept of a motivational intelligence has been proposed to incorporate such alternative definitions.[9]

A slightly abbreviated version of the definition of emotional intelligence that we prefer is: "the ability to perceive emotions, to access and generate emotions so as to assist thought, to understand emotions and emotional knowledge, and to reflectively regulate emotions so as to promote emotional and intellectual growth." This definition combines the ideas that emotion makes thinking more intelligent and that one thinks intelligently about emotions. Both connect intelligence and emotion.

The Development of the Concept of Emotional Intelligence

Initial Work Relating Emotional Intelligence to Intelligence

The logic for identifying an intelligence within psychology is: (a) to define it, (b) to develop a means for measuring it, (c) to document its partial or complete independence from known intelligences, and (d) to demonstrate that it predicts some real-world criteria. Very simply, one might define a "vocabulary" intelligence, measure it with a vocabulary test, show that vocabulary intelligence is different from previously discovered intelligences, and demonstrate that it predicts success at, say, studying

What is Emotional Intelligence?

literature. Each of these four steps is necessary. Because a great deal of research on intelligences exist, one of the most important steps in this series involves demonstrating that a new intelligence is different from those already known. Knowledge of vocabulary, for example, is typically indistinguishable from the already established verbal intelligence (to be discussed shortly).

Two intelligences are said to be the same if they are highly correlated with one another. A high correlation between two variables means that the two tend to rise and fall together. For example, the lengths of a person's right arm and left arm are highly correlated: some people have long right and left arms; some people have short right and left arms; and greatly dissimilar arms in the same person are unusual. Similarly, two intelligences are correlated if the intelligence levels correspond within each person: that is, both intelligences are high in person A, low in person B, medium in person C, and so forth. A complete lack of correlation would mean that one intelligence would tell you nothing about the level of the other. Most intelligences are moderately correlated with one another. That is, in a given individual, the intelligences will tend to operate at levels that are closer together than one would expect by chance. The correlation among intelligences is only moderate, as opposed to high (as in the arm length example), which allows for a moderate amount of difference among intelligences in the same person. This agrees with everyday experience, because we know people who are good at some mental tasks but less good at others.[10]

If two intelligences correlate highly then they are considered to represent the same intelligence. For example, vocabulary size and reading ability closely coincide in most people and as a consequence are usually considered part of one broader intelligence (in this case, *verbal-propositional* intelligence). Analogously, rather than discuss a person's right arm length and left arm length, one could refer simply to arm length. Ideally, a new intelligence should be low-to-moderately correlated with earlier intelligences. A low-moderate correlation (as opposed to a high one) means that the new intelligence is distinct from old ones and will tell you something new about a person; if it correlated too highly with the original intelligence, one might be overfishing the same water. At the same time, a low-to-moderate correlation is preferable to a nonexistent correlation; no correlation at all could suggest the new "intelligence" is so different that it is not an intelligence at all.

The idea of testing whether intelligences correlate (move up and down together) is the standard way of determining whether an intelligence exists; this method has been employed throughout the century.[11] A few alternative methods for establishing intelligence have been employed, and it is worth mentioning these before further returning to the more influential correlational approach. Some people have tried to establish the existence of intelligence primarily through theoretical analysis. J.P. Guilford and R. Hoepfner proposed that 120 intelligences existed, on the basis that there were roughly that number of combinations of basic mental processes. For example, they considered "memory for single words," as one such intelligence because it combined processes of memory, word recognition, and analyses of single units (i.e., words) —

each of which they considered to be a discrete processes. This potentially useful model lost favor because it was difficult to test with the correlational method (one problem was there were just too many intelligences to track).[12] More recently, Howard Gardner developed his elegant theory of multiple intelligences, including linguistic, musical, bodily-kinesthetic, and personal intelligences (one of which resembles emotional intelligence). Gardner argues that his intelligences exist on the basis of their cultural significance and their correspondence to human brain structures. He avoids the correlational approach: Although he admits its utility for studying observed, expressed abilities, he notes that it provides only an indirect measure of internal brain processes. This is true, but so little is known about brain structure that Gardner's own conception has only modest support beyond its original formulation.[13]

The exceptions of Guilford, Gardner, and some others aside, the twentieth century has relied on the correlational approach to identifying intelligences.[14] In fact, researchers have developed measures for as many intelligences as they could imagine, and there has been a free-for-all examination of different intelligences and their interrelations throughout the century. In the 1930's, Thurstone suggested the existence of about a dozen intelligences including verbal comprehension, word fluency, associative memory, and perceptual speed.[15] Later in the century, the Educational Testing Service published a reference kit that measured dozens of cognitive intelligences.[16] Careful examination of the intelligences suggests that although there is an overall moderate correlation among them, some intelligences are more independent of one another than others. One empirically supportable idea earlier in the century was that the intelligences seemed to divide into two or three subgroups. The first of these is a verbal-propositional intelligence, which includes measures of vocabulary, verbal fluency, the ability to perceive similarities and to think logically. The second of these is a spatial-performance intelligence, which includes abilities of assembling objects, and recognizing and constructing designs and patterns. The third, more controversial intelligence, social intelligence, is concerned with peoples' skills in relating to one another.

Historically, there were serious difficulties in developing the concept of social intelligence because it seemed so highly correlated with the first two intelligences as to be indistinguishable from them. That is, people's reasoning about social situations rises and falls so closely with their verbal-propositional and spatial-performance skills that the justification for treating social reasoning as a separate intelligence seemed uncertain. So, there appeared to be little need for studying this third, more purely social, variety of intelligence.[17] The major midcentury intelligence test, Wechsler's intelligence scales, measured only the verbal-propositional and spatial-performance portions of general intelligence. Although both the verbal and performance measures included social reasoning, social intelligence was not measured as a distinct entity.

At the outset of our work, we thought that it might make sense to exchange emotional for social intelligence in this proposed triumvirate of intelligences. Emotional intelligence would combine a group of skills that were more distinct from both verbal-propositional and spatial-performance intelligence than social intelligence had been and

What is Emotional Intelligence?

at the same time would still be close enough to the concept of an intelligence to belong to the triad. We therefore expect emotional reasoning to be correlated with but distinct from other intelligences; the evidence to date supports this position (as we will describe in the section on measuring emotional intelligence).

One final issue was important to defining emotional intelligence: it had to be distinguished from traits and talents. Traits can be defined as characteristic or preferred ways of behaving (e.g., extroversion, shyness); talents as non-intellectual abilities (e.g., skill at sports). Certain recently proposed intelligences seemed more like valued traits or talents than legitimate intelligences. Scarr has written:

> There are many human virtues that are not sufficiently rewarded in our society, such as goodness in human relationships.... To call them intelligence does not do justice either to theories of intelligence or to the personality traits and special talents that lie beyond the consensual definition of intelligence.[18]

We editorialized in the journal Intelligence that emotional intelligence could be considered an actual intelligence as opposed to, say, a highly valued social trait.[19] Scarr's "goodness in human relationships," might indeed be composed of the traits of sociability, trustworthiness, and warmth. But in addition there might exist actual abilities, such as knowing what another person is feeling, that may involve considerable thinking and consequently could be considered an intelligence. In this way, we distinguished a mental skill that could legitimately be called emotional intelligence (e.g., being able to figure out one's own and others' emotions) from preferred ways of behaving (e.g., being sociable, or warm).

Initial Work Relating Emotional Intelligence to the Emotions

The conceptual development of emotional intelligence required relating it not only to intelligence research but also to research on emotion. We began with the observation that emotion and intelligence have often been seen as adversaries, with emotions viewed as an intrinsically irrational and disruptive force.[20] For example, the idea that the mind is "hijacked" by intense emotional experiences — although true in some instances — emphasizes how emotions disrupt thought. In many instances, however, extreme emotional reactions promote intelligence by interrupting ongoing processing and directing attention toward what may be important. In this sense they prioritize cognition.[21] We view emotions of all sorts as potentially contributing to thought rather than disorganizing it.

Our concept of emotional intelligence is primarily focused on the complex, potentially intelligent tapestry of emotional reasoning in everyday life. For most healthy individuals, we assume that emotions convey knowledge about a person's relationships with the world.[22] For example, fear indicates that the person is facing a relatively powerful or uncontrollable threat. Happiness typically indicates one's harmonious relations with others, and anger often reflects a feeling of injustice. According to this view, there are certain generalities and laws of emotions. These general rules and laws can be employed in recognizing and reasoning with feelings. For example, certain universals of emotional expression exist and people should be able to recognize them.[23] Emotional reasoning therefore extends into questions about relationships. For example, an insulted person might feel anger, or if the person was insecure and nonassertive, might feel shame, humiliation — or repressed anger. Recognizing these reactions requires some form of intelligence.

What we are getting at here is that emotional intelligence requires at least some "right" answers as to feelings. Of course, some questions about emotions don't have right answers. For example, the question "What is the best emotional response to shouting?" has no answer. If one's parents plainly loved each other but often shouted at one another, then one may grow up comfortable with shouting. If one's parents first yelled at one another on the day they decided to get a divorce, one may be uncomfortable with it. To the first person, shouting reflects frustration in the context of a loving relationship. To the second person, shouting represents adult hatreds. So, no right response exists. An answer to the question *can* be given, however, if more information is provided (e.g., if we know something about the person's individual learning history). We also recognize the need to consider culture and subculture. For example, individuals in warmer climates are described and describe themselves as more emotionally demonstrative than those in colder climates.[24]

Examining more complex manifestations of emotional intelligence (beyond that of the simple identification of emotion) often requires understanding the individual's own cultural framework. Only by knowing the person's standards can certain "emotional reactions and models...be assessed according to their logical consistency, and hence, their intelligence."[25]

A Revised Definition of Emotional Intelligence

In our earlier work we defined emotional intelligence according to the abilities involved in it. One of our first definitions of emotional intelligence was "the ability to monitor one's own and others' feelings and emotions, to discriminate among them, and to use this information to guide one's thinking and action".[26] But this and other earlier definitions now seem vague in places and impoverished in the sense that they talk only about perceiving and regulating emotion, and omit thinking about feelings. A revision that corrects these problems is as follows:

> Emotional intelligence involves the ability to perceive accurately, appraise, and express emotion; the ability to access and/or generate feelings when they facilitate thought; the ability to understand emotion and emotional knowledge; and the ability to regulate emotions to promote emotional and intellectual growth.

We have diagrammed the skills in Figure 1. The four branches of the diagram are arranged from more basic psychological processes to higher, more psychologically integrated processes. For example, the lowest level branch concerns the (relatively) simple abilities of perceiving and expressing emotion. In contrast, the highest level branch concerns the conscious, reflective, regulation of emotion. Each branch has four representative abilities on it (in boxes). Abilities that emerge relatively early in development are to the left of a given branch; later-developing abilities to the right. Because the developmentally early skills (to the left) are usually poorly integrated with one another they most clearly illustrate the distinctions among branches. Later-developing abilities (to the right) emerge within a more integrated adult personality and are consequently less distinct. Each ability applies to emotions internally and in others except where otherwise noted. People high in emotional intelligence are expected to progress more quickly through the abilities designated, and to master more of them. In the discussion below we will examine each branch in turn, including the boxed abilities from left to right, referring to them as boxes 1 through 4, respectively.

The Perception, Appraisal, and Expression of Emotion

Figure 1's lowest branch concerns the accuracy with which individuals can identify emotions and emotional content. Infants and young children learn to identify their own and other's emotional states and to differentiate among those states. The infant distinguishes emotional facial expressions early on and responds to the parent's expressions. As she grows she will more accurately identify her own muscular and bodily sensations, and social surroundings (Branch 1, Box 1). A mature individual can carefully monitor internal feelings. If we ask a grown person who is staying up late how she feels she might respond that she is partly full of energy, partly fatigued, and anxious about whether or not her thinking is still clear.

Feelings can be recognized not only in oneself, but in other people and in other objects. As a child grows that child imaginatively attributes feelings to animate and inanimate objects. This imaginative thinking may help the child generalize from himself to others. For instance, he may connect times when he is personally anxious and has a constricted posture, to physical constriction observed in pets, other children, objects, and pictures, enabling him to recognize anxious expressions in other people and things (Box 2). Suitably developed and abstracted, the developing person begins to evaluate emotion wherever it might be expressed — in other people, in architecture, in artworks, and so on.[27] So, when we see Munch's well-known painting, *The Scream* (of a cartoonish figure howling), not only do we immediately recognize the face of anxiety but how right it is that in the painting's background, the world is dissolving into nothingness at the same time. The individual is also able to express feelings accurately and to express needs surrounding those feelings (Box 3). Because emotionally intelligent individuals know about the expression and manifestation of emotion, they are also sensitive to its false or manipulative expression (Box 4).

Figure 1

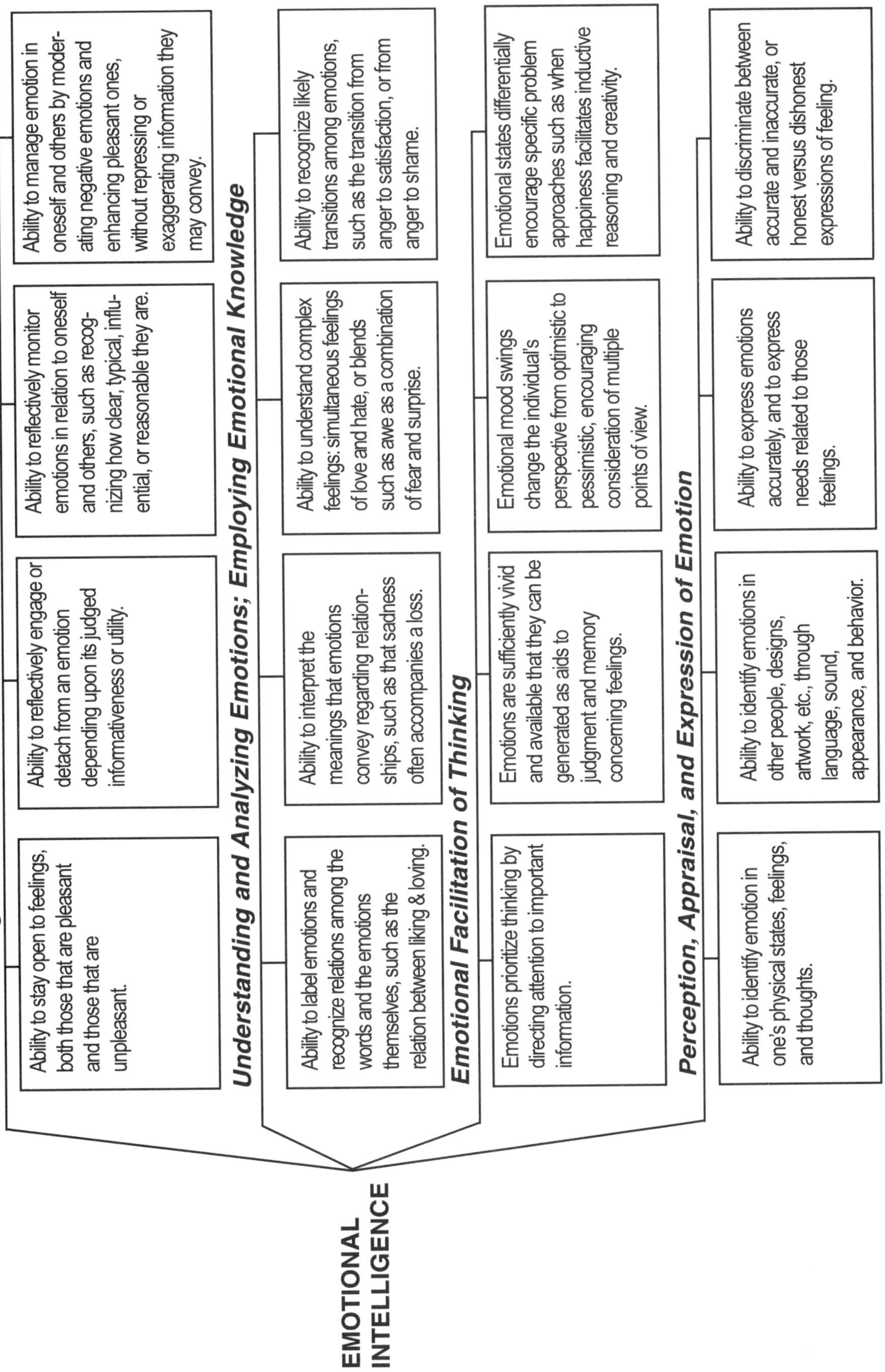

EMOTIONAL INTELLIGENCE

Reflective Regulation of Emotions to Promote Emotional and Intellectual Growth

- Ability to stay open to feelings, both those that are pleasant and those that are unpleasant.
- Ability to reflectively engage or detach from an emotion depending upon its judged informativeness or utility.
- Ability to reflectively monitor emotions in relation to oneself and others, such as recognizing how clear, typical, influential, or reasonable they are.
- Ability to manage emotion in oneself and others by moderating negative emotions and enhancing pleasant ones, without repressing or exaggerating information they may convey.

Understanding and Analyzing Emotions; Employing Emotional Knowledge

- Ability to label emotions and recognize relations among the words and the emotions themselves, such as the relation between liking & loving.
- Ability to interpret the meanings that emotions convey regarding relationships, such as that sadness often accompanies a loss.
- Ability to understand complex feelings: simultaneous feelings of love and hate, or blends such as awe as a combination of fear and surprise.
- Ability to recognize likely transitions among emotions, such as the transition from anger to satisfaction, or from anger to shame.

Emotional Facilitation of Thinking

- Emotions prioritize thinking by directing attention to important information.
- Emotions are sufficiently vivid and available that they can be generated as aids to judgment and memory concerning feelings.
- Emotional mood swings change the individual's perspective from optimistic to pessimistic, encouraging consideration of multiple points of view.
- Emotional states differentially encourage specific problem approaches such as when happiness facilitates inductive reasoning and creativity.

Perception, Appraisal, and Expression of Emotion

- Ability to identify emotion in one's physical states, feelings, and thoughts.
- Ability to identify emotions in other people, designs, artwork, etc., through language, sound, appearance, and behavior.
- Ability to express emotions accurately, and to express needs related to those feelings.
- Ability to discriminate between accurate and inaccurate, or honest versus dishonest expressions of feeling.

Emotion's Facilitation of Thinking

The next branch up, "Emotional Facilitation of Thinking," concerns emotion acting on intelligence; it describes emotional events that assist intellectual processing. Emotion serves as an alerting system essentially from birth. The infant cries when it needs milk, warmth, or other care, and laughs in response to smiles and other pleasures. Emotions thus operate from the start to signal important changes in the person and in the environment. As the person matures, emotions begin to shape and improve thinking by directing a person's attention to important changes. For example, a child worries about his homework while watching TV. A teacher becomes concerned about a lesson that needs to be completed for the next day. The teacher, with his better developed thinking, moves on to complete the task before his concern overtakes his enjoyment (Box 1).

A second contribution of emotion to thinking is to generate emotions "on demand" so that they can be better understood. When asked, "How does the character in a story feel," or when deciding how another person feels, children generate the feelings within themselves.[28] This permits an immediate, real-time, inspection of the feeling and its characteristics. In the growing person, the ability to generate feelings assists with planning. The individual can anticipate how entering a new school, taking a new job, or encountering a social criticism might feel. Anticipating such feelings can help a person decide whether to take a job or make a criticism. There exists, in other words, an "emotional theater of the mind," or more technically, a processing arena, in which emotions may be generated, felt, manipulated, and examined, so as to be better understood. The more accurately and realistically such an emotional theater operates, the more it can help the individual choose alternative life courses (Box 2).[29]

The remaining two abilities of Branch 2 are examples of a larger set of emotional contributions to more sophisticated, efficient thoughts. Emotionality may help people consider multiple perspectives. Recall that mood-congruent judgment involves good moods leading to optimistic thought; bad moods, to pessimistic thought. A sad high school senior may feel inadequate and consequently apply to a lot of colleges with easy admissions standards. Then, as her mood improves, she might apply to more selective colleges. This individual's shifting moods led her to consider more possibilities, which will be an advantage in conditions of uncertainty (Box 3). Close relatives of manic depressives are likely to have more mood swings than others, assisting them to change perspective often. This may explain why such relatives are rated as exhibiting higher creativity in both their occupational and nonoccupational activities.[30] The final ability on this branch recognizes that different kinds of work and different forms of reasoning (e.g., deductive versus inductive) may be facilitated by different kinds of moods (Box 4).[31]

Understanding and Analyzing Emotions; Employing Emotional Knowledge

The third branch up of Figure 1 concerns the ability to understand emotions and to utilize emotional knowledge. Soon after the child recognizes emotions he begins to label them and perceive relations among those labels. For example, many emotions form sets along continua of intensity. The child begins to recognize similarities and differences between liking and loving, annoyance and anger, and so on (Box 1).[32] The child is simultaneously learning what each feeling means in terms of relationships. Parents teach children about emotional reasoning by linking emotions to situations. For example, they teach the connection between sadness and loss by helping a child recognize she is sad because her best friend won't spend time with her any more. A formal philosophy of feelings has developed over the centuries. For example, Spinoza defined *shame* as "pain accompanied by the idea of some action of our own, which we believe to be blamed by others."[33] Some consensus exists as to these meanings, with anger frequently viewed as arising from the perception of injustice, sadness arising from loss, fear from threat, and so forth.[34] Emotional knowledge begins in childhood and grows throughout life, with increased understanding of these emotional meanings (Box 2).

The growing person also begins to recognize the existence of complex, contradictory emotions in certain circumstances. The child learns that it is possible to feel both love and hate toward the same person.[35] Probably also at this level of development, blends (or combinations) of emotions are acknowledged. For example, awe is sometimes viewed as a combination of fear and surprise; hope as a combination of faith and optimism (Box 3).[36] Emotions tend to occur in patterned chains: anger may intensify to rage, be expressed, and then transform to satisfaction or to guilt, depending upon the circumstance. The person goes on to reason about sequences of emotion: an individual who feels unlovable might reject another's care for fear of later rejection. Reasoning about the progression of feelings in interpersonal relationships is central to emotional intelligence (Box 4).

Reflective Regulation of Emotions to Promote Emotional and Intellectual Growth

The highest branch of Figure 1 concerns the conscious regulation of emotions to enhance emotional and intellectual growth. Emotional reactions must be tolerated—even welcomed— when they occur, somewhat independently of how pleasant or unpleasant they are. Only if a person attends to feelings can something be learned about them. For that reason, this highest level branch begins with openness to feelings (Box 1).

As the child grows, the parents teach her not to express certain feelings: to smile in public even if feeling sad, to go to her room if angry. Gradually, the child internalizes these divisions between feeling and acting: The child begins to learn that emotions can be separated from behavior.[37] Parents teach rudimentary emotion control strategies ("Count to 10 when you are angry"). As a consequence, the child learns to engage and disengage from emotion at appropriate times. Rage against another or against an injustice may be useful in reasoning about the situation, but probably less so when the feeling is at its climax. At those times the emotionally mature individual will know to draw back and discuss matters with more cool-headed confidants. Later, the emotional insight and energy provided by such experiences may be applied to the reasoning process, and may both motivate it, and provide a means by which to, for example, elicit others' anger in opposition to the injustice (Box 2). As the individual matures, there also emerges a consistently reflective or meta-experience of mood and emotion. These feelings involve experiences of mood such as, "I don't fully understand the way I'm feeling," or "This feeling is influencing how I'm thinking."[38] Such thoughts are conscious reflections on emotional responses, as opposed to simple perceptions of feelings. The meta-experience of mood seems divisible into two parts: meta-evaluation and meta-regulation. The evaluations include how much attention one pays to one's mood, and how clear, typical, acceptable, and influential one's mood is (Box 3). The regulation concerns whether the individual is trying to improve a bad mood, dampen a good one, or leave the mood alone. The meta-experiences of mood appear to be related to important phenomena, such as how long one dwells on traumatic experiences. The laws of meta-experiences are not as-of-yet well understood, but new measures have been developed to assess both its ongoing dynamics and dispositional qualities. One quality that seems important is that emotions are understood without exaggerating or minimizing their importance (Box 4).

Emotional Intelligence, Emotional Achievement, and Emotional Competencies

Up to now we have been discussing a concept of emotional intelligence that is reflected in a set of abilities. Consideration of emotional intelligence raises the issue of whether there exists emotional achievement and emotional competence, just as, say, academic intelligence can be compared to academic achievement and academic competence.[39] In the sphere of academic intelligence, intelligence is the aptitude, achievement represents what one has accomplished, and competency indicates that one's achievement meets a particular requirement. Analogous to such concepts, emotional intelligence represents the core aptitude or ability to reason with emotions. Emotional achievement represents the learning a person has attained about emotion or emotion-related information, and emotional competence exists when one has reached a required level of achievement. All things being equal, a person's emotional intelligence determines her emotional achievement. But things are rarely equal, and the family in which one grew up, the lessons about emotions one was taught, the life events one has undergone, all influence how much one has achieved in learning about emotions.

Many educational psychologists prefer speaking in terms of competencies rather than intelligences, and the idea of emotional competencies has already been introduced by Saarni.[40] It focuses on the knowledge and skills the individual can attain in order to function adequately across situations rather than on the more difficult to assess and, in some ways educationally less relevant, issue of emotional intelligence. Some advocates of competency testing view it as a safeguard against the misuse of haphazardly administered group intelligence tests.[41] It is plainly more focused on the educational process than on psychological aptitude. From at least a theoretical standpoint, it makes sense to develop the ideas of emotional intelligence, emotional achievement, and emotional competencies together.

At least part of the excitement with which the concept of emotional intelligence has been greeted, we think, has been the definite implication that we understand emotions so well that we can speak in terms of specific emotional abilities and competencies at those abilities. Without the concept of emotional intelligence, teaching about emotion must be geared toward the institutionally-sanctioned requirement of behaving "well" or "nicely." Emotional intelligence provides a more flexible (if less easily defined) criterion for emotional competence: one increases one's emotional abilities to an agreed upon level. Emotional intelligence is a good goal for a democratic culture. It does not dictate the outcome of a person's emotional behavior, but rather encourages a process of personal investigation that can occur in the context of the person's own politics, ethnicity, religion, and other characteristics.

The Assessment of Emotional Intelligence

Now that we have described emotional intelligence it is worth considering the evidence for it. As noted at the outset understanding the form emotional intelligence takes will require demonstrating that the abilities included under the term "emotional intelligence" are meaningfully different from general intelligence and yet related enough to it to qualify as an intelligence. The media depiction of a monolithic EQ is without question premature. The determination of whether emotional intelligence is, say, one true intelligence, or whether it is multiple skills unrelated to general intelligence, or something in between, will depend upon its measurement and assessment.

The Measurement of Emotional Intelligence

Earlier we reviewed a great deal of psychological literature that suggests that some of the abilities on the branches of Figure 1 can be measured.[42] When we turn to studies that actually speak to the existence of emotional intelligence, only a small minority of the studies directly inform us of its existence or nonexistence. This small number of studies must meet three criteria. First, an ability of the type described in Figure 1 must be measured. Note that this excludes a great number of important personal qualities, such as optimism and motivation, which do not specifically involve emotional contributions to intelligence, or intellectual understanding of emotion.[43] A second criterion is that the studies directly measure an ability rather than a person's self-description of how emotionally intelligent he or she is. Self-descriptions of intelligence can be of some research value but are not dependable to demonstrate that the concept exists. In the realm of academic intelligence, every instructor is familiar with the bright student who believes she isn't very smart, and the not-so-smart student who believes she is much smarter than she is. Asking people to actually solve a problem produces a more valid sample of behavior for study. The third criterion is that such studies should connect multiple abilities from Figure 1 to one another, or one or more emotionally intelligent abilities to an important criterion.

Only a few studies meet the above criteria. In one study with Maria DiPaolo,[44] we found evidence supporting the idea that there is a basic skill that accounts for individual differences in recognizing (consensual) emotion not only in faces, but in abstract designs, and even in colors. That is, skills at decoding faces, designs, and colors were either generally high, medium, or low in a given individual. Moreover, people higher in these skills also obtained higher scores on a scale of self-reported empathy, a skill also envisioned as a part of emotional intelligence. These findings argue for the existence of emotional intelligence as described in the first branch of the diagram (perception of emotion), in that they point to a unity of emotional recognition, in faces, colors, or designs. Mayer and Geher further found that emotional perception of characters in situations correlates with SAT scores (a measure of intelligence), with empathy, and with emotional openness (from the highest, "regulatory" branch).[45] At the time this chapter went to press, these findings were replicated and extended using a new scale that measures skills from all four branches of Figure 1.

Important additional information concerning the third, "understanding emotions," branch comes from work by Averill and Nunley on emotional creativity.[46] In one of their tasks, participants are asked to write a brief description of a situation in which they might feel three emotions together (e.g., joy, relief, and distress). As our conceptualization of emotional intelligence (or theirs of emotional creativity) would predict, success at this task appears related to but independent of general intelligence. These few studies suggest that at least some of the abilities in Figure 1 intercorrelate with one another, and are partly independent of general intelligence. Development of tasks requires caution because serious theoretical and empirical issues must be considered. These include, most pressingly, "How do we find the right answer to a test item in emotional intelligence?" — especially as those answers become more sophisticated. A more detailed discussion of this issue can be found in the article by Mayer and Geher (1996).

What Emotional Intelligence Predicts

Given that emotional intelligence has been studied so little, not much is known about what it predicts. Psychologists recognize that general intelligence predicts some aspects of success — defined as academic achievement and occupational status. General intelligence is often said to account for between 10 and 20% of such success, leaving about 80% to 90% of it to be explained by other factors.[47] So there is certainly room for emotional intelligence to predict a portion of such achievement. Generally speaking, a single personality factor explains only a small portion of life outcomes, so even a 10% contribution of emotional intelligence would be considered very large indeed. Some observers believe they have identified such contributions in the workplace. For example, some have argued that emotional intelligence contributed to success among engineers at Bell Laboratories, in particular, their ability to network effectively.[48] In the Bell Labs study "networking" meant that engineers found answers from one another by bartering with information. This meant:

> "...first becoming a technical expert in a particularly sought-after area, then letting people know of your expertise, then making yourself available to others. Once an engineer has developed his or her bargaining chips, it's possible to gain access to the rest of this knowledge network..."[49]

Such bartering seems to us to depend more on understanding the unwritten demands of the job than on emotional intelligence.[50] Although the bartering might involve emotional intelligence, we just do not know because no measures were taken of it. We do believe that emotional intelligence can contribute to success, at least when success is defined broadly.

More emotionally intelligent individuals might succeed at making their workers feel better, at communicating in interesting ways, and at designing projects that involve infusing products with feelings and aesthetics. Emotional intelligence may make the difference between constructing the Brooklyn Bridge, with its renowned beauty, and the more mundane Fifty-ninth Street Bridge.[51]

As more research is carried out, we can better evaluate what emotional intelligence contributes to achievement. In the meantime, the potential gains from teaching emotional intelligence will need to be considered with caution. It is to those applications we turn next.

Applications of Emotional Intelligence in the Schools and Beyond

Emotional intelligence as described here is expected to be involved in the home, in school, in work, and other settings. In many of these settings, emotional problems frequently are solved well. In the story that opened this chapter, about the boy who was given a coat, was resolved with emotional intelligence. At the end of the fight some of the teachers and staff were already saying something like, "There are often fights between middle class and poorer children in this school. Perhaps it was good that all this is out in the open because now it can be dealt with." The principal called in the boys who started the fight, talked to them, and had them write letters of apology to the boy who received the coat. The principal chose to have them write letters of apology, he said, because it required them to think about what happened for a while. He also decided to devote a staff development day to what had happened so that the teachers could further understand what was going on in the school. The boy with the new coat wrote a letter of thanks to the teacher and the nurse. When the teacher received it, she said, "...I understand it created some problems for you." The boy replied, "Oh, it's okay, they apologized...and I really like the coat." This doesn't totally take care of the problem, of course, but then, human problems are complex.

Acquiring Emotional Intelligence

If one wanted to improve emotional skills, how would that be done? Most skills can be improved through education and it is likely this will hold true for at least some of the skills related to emotional intelligence. Emotional skills begin in the home with good parent-child interaction. Parents help children identify and label their emotions, to respect their feelings, and to begin to connect them to social situations. This process may succeed to a greater or lesser degree in each home. We have come to realize over the course of our study that individuals operate from different emotional starting places. These can be considered their emotional knowledge base.[52] The opportunities for learning emotional skills are not always equal. Parents may suffer from psychological limitations so severe that they are unable to initiate an emotional-cognitive learning process. A child may learn incorrect lessons about emotions: Parents may avoid feelings, or a parent may deny he is angry even while behaving with hostility. As a consequence, children sometimes develop disorders in which they become far removed from their feelings or misunderstand them. Sometimes a psychotherapist will be

What is Emotional Intelligence?

necessary to correct the problem. Psychotherapists are trained in empathic listening, reflection of feeling, and searching for lost emotions that need to be constructed, recovered, or acted on in better ways. For example, a therapist may see a client who is consistently taken advantage of, exploited, and yet denies any anger. The therapist may inquire as to whether anger is there and help the individual to channel it productively for the purposes of self-protection and placing limits on others' inappropriate behavior. It is also possible for some remedial learning to take place in the schools. Some of the most important learning takes place in the informal relationships between child and teacher; teachers often serve in the role of an important and potentially wise adult model. Another place where emotionally intelligent skills are taught is in the standard curriculum — a point to which we turn next.

The Incorporation of Emotional Intelligence in the Standard Curriculum

Particularly useful, we believe, is the natural emotional teaching that comes with many of the liberal arts and with various value systems as well. In school reading lessons that involve more engaging stories, children begin to learn about feelings of characters. Story characters have an inescapable tendency to become happy, afraid, jealous, and so forth, and children can observe both what makes those characters feel as they do and also how the characters cope in response to the feelings. This learning proceeds throughout the educational system, and as stories become more complex, so does emotional learning. The ways in which the feelings of characters motivate their actions, which in turn moves forward the plot, is a lesson in emotional perception for young adults as much as it is in plot construction. In fact, one cannot evaluate a plot without asking "What does this character, with his history and personal style, feel in this situation," and then, "How reasonable is it that someone feeling this way would act as the character does?" Literature is probably the first home of the emotional intelligences. But so, too, are art programs, music, and theater.

Nor is the importance of values to be overlooked, as these determine in part the person's more conscious knowledge of the emotions. Values are often discussed and taught in such liberal arts subjects as history, citizenship, and (more often in private schools) religion. From these we learn about the value systems within which emotional responsivity occurs. Different styles of emotionality exist within different systems. One prevalent Western tradition esteems individual life, democracy, equality among individuals, and education, while it abhors destruction of life and property, discrimination, and ignorance. Such values define expected emotional responses. Cultural and/or religious observances further define expected emotions. The Jewish holiday of Yom Kippur requires those who worship to traverse cycles of repentance for sins during the year. The repentence begins with a critical self-appraisal with accompanying regret, guilt, and shame. Next, the person takes action to remedy those mistakes that can be repaired. After sincere repentance, there will follow solemnity, calmness, relief, and perhaps joyousness.[53] Making available these resources does not always work. The student may not read much, art courses may be curtailed, the student may reject religious, ethical, or national value systems. In such cases, should the school system step in directly with programs focused on emotional competencies?[54]

We think it is worth exploring this issue. We should keep in mind that courses directly focused on the topic should be approached cautiously, as there is little scientific guidance about how they should be designed. To discuss the "correct" response(s) to a complex social event seems to stretch our knowledge. We cannot be sure we know all the right answers. But some discussion of such issues seems reasonable.

Educational Programs Directly Concerning Emotional Intelligence

Emotions have been taught in the schools before the concept of emotional intelligence was developed. We are impressed with the inventive ways in which some instructors have arranged affective curricula, but we also have concerns about them. In some schools and some programs where such materials are carefully worked out and the staff is well trained, a unique and potentially valuable program is undoubtedly being implemented. Just the same, as we examine details of some programs, we are at times uncomfortable. For example, programs that seem to adopt an "emotions are good" philosophy untempered by the fact that emotions exist in the context of other personal characteristics and interpersonal relationships are troubling to us.

Presumably, those students who need emotional education most desperately have come from households in which emotional communication is skewed in some way or another. These individuals already employ maladaptive emotional responses. We are not sure such severely damaged children profit from, say, being required to share their emotions in a class discussion, or whether they will be overwhelmed by it, or feel coerced.

Another concern is that individuals from different subcultures approach emotions differently. Although most share Western values, some will have been taught to "let it all hang out," whereas others may take a more "stoical" view. Some may emphasize a Christian attitude of turning the other cheek when confronted, so as to emphasize peace; others may emphasize a more Jewish attitude of employing anger to expose injustice and hence repair the world. (These are simplifications that cannot do justice to the more complete religious teachings.) In some instances, individuals may be members of discriminated-against groups and the target of such serious but covert hatred as to feel unable to participate in exercises that assume a degree of interpersonal trust.

A more promising starting point is exemplified by some conflict resolution programs we have seen. For example, Linda Lantieri, who runs the Resolving Conflicts Creatively program in the New York City public school system, argues that conflict resolution is based on learning the skills of an emotionally intelligent person. Her program teaches how to identify the feelings of your adversary, your own feelings, and the feelings of others involved.[55] Violence reduction is an important and central goal in schools, where its threat is so salient as to greatly interfere with learning and concentration. It is more concrete and easier to agree upon implementing a conflict resolution curriculum (from our perspective) than a program devoted to increasing emotional intelligence (should such be possible) per se. The more focused goals of such a program also prevent it from being misinterpreted as teaching the "right" (or "best") way to feel.

Teaching basic social skills, or even basic socio emotional skills, if you prefer, is different than teaching an intelligence. Most beginning cooks who carefully follow a recipe can produce a good-tasting meal without necessarily knowing about all the ingredients. Similarly, any student enrolled in these programs can learn the social recipes without necessarily learning emotional intelligence. In our experience, many such school-based programs seem focused on these basic recipes and this is to their credit. It makes assessing their outcomes relatively easy, and it avoids difficult issues like whether emotional intelligence can be assessed or taught, and by which cultural or multicultural criterion it will be evaluated. Might these programs teach a bit of emotional intelligence? Perhaps; just as gaining experience around the kitchen might help someone begin to develop as a chef. But whether or not it occurs doesn't matter. If the program reduces maladaptive interpersonal distress, we are happy about it.

Conclusion

Emotional intelligence is the ability to perceive emotions, to access and generate emotions so as to assist thought, to understand emotions and emotional meanings, and to reflectively regulate emotions so as to promote both better emotion and thought. It is our belief that the adaptive use of emotion-laden information is a significant aspect of what is meant by anyone's definition of intelligence, yet it is not studied systematically by investigators of intelligence nor included in traditional school curricula. As we have argued, using the emotions as one basis for thinking, and thinking with emotions themselves, may be related to important social competencies and adaptive behavior. Presently, we are at the beginning of the learning curve about emotional intelligence; the coming years should bring exciting research that contributes to our understanding of the concept.

GLOSSARY

Achievement — The level at which a person has learned to perform a particular skill.

Affect — One of three traditional spheres of mental activity (along with motivation and cognition), involving emotions, moods, and other associated feelings states such as liveliness and tiredness.

Cognition — One of three traditional spheres of mental activity (along with motivation and affect), involving learning, thought, judgment, memory, and other forms of thinking.

Competence — The condition of meeting a standard of achievement.

Conation — see *Motivation*.

Correlation — A statistical measure of the degree to which two variables are related. Correlation coefficients typically take on values from 1.0 to -1.0. A correlation of 1.0 means that variables rise and fall together with an exact correspondence. When variables are said "to be correlated" it more often means they rise and fall together according to a loose pattern; this pattern is represented by a number between 0.0 and 1.0, where a higher value close to 1.0 indicates a stronger association. Negative correlations involve movements of the variables in opposite directions (i.e., one rises as the other falls) and are represented by numbers between 0.0 and -1.0.

Emotion — Short-term feeling states including happiness, anger, or fear, that mix varying amounts of pleasantness-unpleasantness and arousal-calm, among other sensations.

Emotion Intelligence — This intelligence involves the ability to perceive accurately, appraise, and express emotion; the ability to access and/or generate feelings when they facilitate thought; the ability to understand emotion and emotional knowledge; and the ability to reflectively regulate emotions in ways that promote emotional and intellectual growth.

Intelligence — Traditionally, a characterization of how well the cognitive sphere operates, e.g., how quickly someone can learn, how well they can judge and think, and so on.

Meta-Experience (or Meta-Mood Experience). A reflective thought or feeling about an emotion or mood, such as "I don't like this feeling."

Motivation (or Conation) — One of three traditional spheres of mental activity (along with affect and cognition) that concerns both basic urges such as hunger and thirst, and more complex goal-directed activities such as the pursuit of friendship, achievement, or power.

Talent (and Non-intellectual Talent) — A talent is any human skill or ability. A non-intellectual talent is an ability that does not involve (or only minimally involves) human cognition or intelligence, such as the ability to walk long distances, or to eat hot peppers, etc.

Trait — Any fairly consistent behavior or set of behaviors an individual tends to exhibit such as enjoying being with people, or being conscientious, or trying new things.

What is Emotional Intelligence?

References

Anastasi, A. (1967). Psychology, psychologists, and psychological testing. *American Psychologist,* 26, 1036-1037.

Anastasi, A. (1988). *Psychological testing.* New York: Macmillan Publishing Company.

Arnheim, R. (1954/1974). *Art and visual perception: A Psychology of the creative eye (the new version).* Berkeley, CA: University of California Press.

Averill, J.R., & Nunley, E.P. (1992). *Voyages of the heart: Living an emotionally creative life.* New York: Free Press.

Bower, G.H. (1981). Mood and memory. *American Psychologist,* 36, 129-148.

Buck, R. (1984). *The communication of emotion.* New York: The Guilford Press.

Clynes, M. (1977). *Sentics: The touch of emotions.* Garden City, NY: Doubleday.

Cronbach, L.J. (1960). *Essentials of psychological testing (2nd ed.)* New York: Harper and Row.

Detterman, D.K. (1982). Does *"g"* exist? *Intelligence,* 6, 99-108.

Ekman, P. (1985). *Telling lies: Clues to deceit in the marketplace, politics, and marriage.* New York: Norton.

Ekman, P., Friesen, W.V., O'Sullivan, M., Chan, A., Diacoyanni-Tarlatzis, I., Heider, K., Krause, R., LeCompte, W.A., Pitcairn, T., Ricci-Bitti, P.E., Scherer, K., Tomita, M., & Tzavaras, A. (1987). Universals and cultural differences in the judgments of facial expressions of emotion. *Journal of Personality and Social Psychology,* 53, 712-717.

Ekstrom, R.B., French, J.W., Harman, H.H., & Dermen, D. (1976). *Manual for kit of factor-referenced cognitive tests (3rd ed.)* Princeton, NJ: Educational Testing Service.

Emmons, R.A., & Colby, P.M. (1995). Emotional conflict and well-being: Relation to perceived availability, daily utilization, and observer reports of social support. *Journal of Personality and Social Psychology,* 68, 947-959.

Forgas, J.P. (1995). Mood and judgment: The Affect Infusion Model (AIM). <u>*Psychological Bulletin,*</u> 117, 39-66.

Frijda, N. H. (1988). The laws of emotion. *American Psychologist,* 43, 349-358.

Gardner, H. (1983). *Frames of mind: The theory of multiple intelligences,* New York: Basic Books.

Gardner, H. (1993). *Frames of mind: The theory of multiple intelligences (Tenth-Anniversary Edition),* New York: Basic Books.

Gardner, H. (1995). Cracking open the IQ box. In S. Fraser (Ed.) *The Bell Curve wars,* (pp. 23-35). New York: Basic Books.

Gerrig, R.J. (1993). *Experiencing narrative worlds: On the psychological activities of reading.* New Haven, CT: Yale University Press.

Gibbs, N. (1995, October 2). The EQ factor. S.E. Epperson, L. Mondi, J.L. Graff, & L.H. Towle (Reporters), *Time,* 146, 60-68.

Goleman, D. (1995a, September 10). Ideas and trends: The decline of the nice-guy quotient. *The New York Times (Sunday Week in Review)*, p. 6.

Goleman, D. (1995b). *Emotional intelligence*. New York: Bantam Books.

Guilford, J.P., & Hoepfner, R. (1971). *The analysis of intelligence*. New York: McGraw Hill.

Hilgard, E.R. (1980). The trilogy of mind: Cognition, affection, and conation. *Journal of the History of the Behavioral Sciences,* 16, 107-117.

Isen, A.M., Shalker, T.E., Clark, M., & Karp, L. (1978). Affect, accessibility of material in memory, and behavior: A cognitive loop? *Journal of Personality and Social Psychology,* 36, 1-12.

Kelley, R., & Caplan, J. (1993). How Bell Labs creates star performers. *Harvard Business Review,* 71, 128-139.

Lazarus, R.S. (1991). *Emotion and adaptation*. New York: Oxford University Press.

Mandler, G. (1984). *Mind and body: Psychology of emotion and stress*. New York: W.W. Norton & Co.

Mayer, J.D. (1986). How mood influences cognition. In N.E. Sharkey (Ed.), *Advances in cognitive science* (Vol. 1). Chichester, England: Ellis Horwood.

Mayer, J.D. (1995). A framework for the classification of personality components. *Journal of Personality*, 63, 819-877.

Mayer, J.D., DiPaolo, M.T., & Salovey, P. (1990). Perceiving affective content in ambiguous visual stimuli: A component of emotional intelligence. *Journal of Personality Assessment*, 54, 772-781.

Mayer, J.D., & Gaschke, Y.N. (1988). The experience and meta-experience of mood. *Journal of Personality and Social Psychology*, 55, 102-111.

Mayer, J.D., Gaschke, Y., Braverman, D.L., & Evans, T. (1992). Mood-congruent judgment is a general effect. *Journal of Personality and Social Psychology*, 63, 119-132.

Mayer, J.D., & Geher, G. (1996). Emotional intelligence and the identification of emotion. *Intelligence*, 22, 89-113.

Mayer, J.D. & Hanson, E. (1995). Mood-congruent judgment over time. *Personality and Social Psychology Bulletin*, 21, 237-244.

Mayer, J.D., & Mitchell, D.C. (in press). Intelligence as a subsystem of personality: From Spearman's *g* to contemporary models of hot-processing. In W. Tomic & J. Kingma (Eds). *Reflections on the concept of intelligence*. Greenwich, CT: JAI Press.

Mayer, J.D., & Salovey, P. (1988). Personality moderates the interaction of mood and cognition. In K. Fiedler and J. Forgas (Eds.), *Affect, cognition and social behavior: New evidence and integrative attempts.* (pp. 87-99). Toronto: C.J. Hogrefe.

Mayer, J.D., & Salovey, P. (1993). The intelligence of emotional intelligence. *Intelligence*, 17, 433-442.

Mayer, J.D., & Salovey, P. (1995). Emotional intelligence and the construction and regulation of feelings. *Applied and Preventive Psychology*, 4, 197-208.

Mayer, J.D., & Stevens, A. (1994). An emerging understanding of the reflective (meta-) experience of mood. *Journal of Research in Personality*, 28, 351-373.

Mayer, J.D., Caruso, D., & Salovey, P. (1997). A test of emotional intelligence. Manuscript in perparation.

Mayer, J.D., Salovey, P., & Caruso, D. (in press). *Emotional IQ test* (CD-ROM version). Needham, MA: Virtual Knowledge.

Mendelssohn, M. (1755/1971). *Moses Mendelssohn: Gesammelte Schriften Jubilaum Sausgabe* (Band 1: Schriften zur Philosophie und Asthetik). Stuttgart: Friedrich Frommann Verlag (Gunther Holzboog). (Original work published in 1755).

Miller, A. (1990). *The drama of the gifted child.* R. Ward (Trans.). New York: Basic Books.

Mischel, W., Shoda, Y., & Peake, P.K. (1988). The nature of adolescent competencies predicted by preschool delay of gratification. *Journal of Personality and Social Psychology*, 54, 687-696.

Mitchell, D., & Mayer, J.D. (1996). *Empathy and the identification of emotion.* Manuscript.

Nannis, E.D. (1988). Cognitive-developmental differences in emotional understanding. In E.D. Nannis, & PA. Cowan (eds.). *Developmental psychopathology and its treatment: New Directions for Child Development.* Vol 39 (pp. 31-49). San Francisco: Jossey-Bass.

Neisser, U., Boodoo, G., Bouchard, T.J., Boykin, A.W., Brody, N., Ceci, S.J., Halpern, D.F., Loehlin, J.C., Perloff, R., Sternberg, R.J., & Urbina, S. (1996). Intelligence: Knowns and unknowns. *American Psychologist*, 51, 77-101.

Palfai, T.P., & Salovey, P. (1993). The influence of depressed and elated mood on deductive and inductive reasoning. *Imagination, Cognition, and Personality*, 13, 57-71.

Peli, P. (1984). *Soloveitchik on repentence.* New York: Paulist Press.

Pennebaker, J.W., Rimé, B., & Blankenship, V.E. (1996). Stereotypes of emotional expressiveness of Northerners and Southerners: A cross-cultural test of Montesquieu's hypothesis. *Journal of Personality and Social Psychology*, 70, 272-280.

Piaget, J., & Inhelder, B. (1969). *The psychology of the child.* New York: Basic Books.

Plutchik, R. (1984). Emotions: A general psychoevolutionary theory. In K.R. Scherer and P. Ekman (Eds.) *Approaches to emotion* (pp. 197-219). Hillsdale, NJ: Erlbaum.

Richards, R., Kinney, D.K., Lunde, I., Benet, M., & Merzel, A.P.C. (1988). Creativity in manic-depressives, cyclothymes, their normal relatives, and control subjects. *Journal of Abnormal Psychology*, 89, 286-290.

Roseman, I.J. (1984). Cognitive determinants of emotion: A structural theory. *Review of Personality and Social Psychology*, 5, 11-36.

Saarni, C. (1988). Emotional competence: How emotions and relationships become integrated. In R.A. Thompson (Ed.), *Nebraska Symposium on Motivation* (vol. 36, pp. 115-182). Lincoln: University of Nebraska Press.

Salovey, P., & Birnbaum, D. (1989). Influence of mood on health-related cognitions. *Journal of Personality and Social Psychology, 57,* 539-551.

Salovey, P. & Mayer, J.D. (1990). Emotional intelligence. *Imagination, Cognition, and Personality, 9,* 185-211.

Salovey, P., Hsee, C., & Mayer, J.D. (1993). Emotional intelligence and the self-regulation of affect. In D.M. Wegner and J.W. Pennebaker (Eds.) *Handbook of mental control* (pp. 258-277). Englewood Cliffs, NJ: Prentice-Hall.

Salovey, P., Mayer, J.D., Goldman, S., Turvey, C., & Palfai, T. (1995). Emotional attention, clarity, and repair: Exploring emotional intelligence using the Trait Meta-Mood Scale. In J. W. Pennebaker (Ed.) *Emotion, disclosure, and health* (pp. 125-154). Washington, D.C.: American Psychological Association.

Sattler, J.M. (1982). *Assessment of children's intelligence and special abilities.* (2nd edition). Boston: Allyn and Bacon.

Scarr, S. (1989). Protecting general intelligence: Constructs and consequences for interventions. In R.L. Linn (Ed.), *Intelligence: Measurement, theory, and public policy.* Urbana, IL: University of Illinois Press.

Schaffer, L.F., Gilmer, B., & Schoen, M. (1940). *Psychology.* New York: Harper & Brothers.

Scherer, K.R. (1993). Studying the emotion-antecedent appraisal process: An expert system approach. *Cognition and Emotion, 7,* 325-355.

Shoda, Y., Mischel, W., & Peake, P.K. (1990). Predicting adolescent cognitive and self-regulatory competencies from preschool delay of gratification: Identifying diagnostic conditions. *Developmental Psychology, 26,* 978-986.

Smith, C.A., & Ellsworth, P.C. (1985). Patterns of cognitive appraisal in emotion. *Journal of Personality and Social Psychology, 48,* 813-838.

Spearman, C. (1927). *The abilities of man: Their nature and measurement.* New York: Macmillan.

Spinoza, B. (1984) "Ethics (Part III): On the origin and nature of the emotions," In Calhoun, C., & Solomon, R.C. (Eds.) *What is emotion?* Oxford: Oxford University Press. (Original work published in 1675).

Sternberg, R. J. (1988). *The triarchic mind: A new theory of human intelligence.* New York: Penguin.

Sternberg, R. J. (1994). Commentary: Reforming school reform: Comments on "Multiple intelligences: The theory in practice." *Teachers College Record, 95,* 561-569.

Sundberg, N.D., Snowden, L.R., & Reynolds, W.M. (1978). Toward assessment of personal competence and incompetence in life situations. *Annual Review of Psychology, 29,* 179-221.

What is Emotional Intelligence?

Thorndike, R.L., & Stein, S. (1937). An evaluation of the attempts to measure social intelligence. *Psychological Bulletin, 34,* 275-284.

Thurstone, L.L. (1938). *Primary mental abilities.* Chicago: University of Chicago Press.

Tice, D. & Baumeister, R.F. (1993). Controlling anger: Self-induced emotion change. In D.M. Wegner, & J.W. Pennebaker (Eds.) *Handbook of mental control* (pp. 393-409). Englewood Cliffs, NJ: Prentice Hall.

Wagner, R.K., & Sternberg, R.J. (1985). Practical intelligence in real-world pursuits: The role of tacit knowledge. *Journal of Personality and Social Psychology, 50,* 737-743.

Walsh, W.B., & Betz, N.E. (1995). *Tests and assessment (3rd ed.)* Englewood Cliffs, NJ: Prentice-Hall.

Wechsler, D. (1958). *The measurement and appraisal of adult intelligence (4th ed.)* Baltimore, MD: The Williams & Wilkins Company.

Young, P.T. (1936). *Motivation of behavior.* New York: John Wiley & Sons.

Young, P.T. (1943). *Emotion in man and animal: Its nature and relation to attitude and motive.* New York: John Wiley & Sons.

Endnotes

[1] This is a true story in which a few details have been changed to protect the privacy of those involved. Similarly, the aftermath reported later in the chapter is similarly what occurred.

[2] Discussion of the concept has occurred in academic research settings (Emmons & Colby, 1995), in popular news magazines such as TIME (Gibbs, 1995); and in a popular book (Goleman, 1995b).

[3] This three-part division is basic to the modern enterprise of psychology. Historical reviews can be found in Hilgard (1980) and in Mayer (1995); the origins of the system date from Mendelssohn (1755/1971).

[4] Wechsler (1958), for example, defined intelligence as related not only to cognition, but to general adaptation as well. In Mayer & Salovey (1995), we have examined the distinction between adaptation and intelligence. Although adaptation is plainly involved in intelligence, it is insufficient by itself to characterize what intelligence is. Many organisms, such as ants, are well adapted without necessarily being highly intelligent in the sense employed here.

[5] "The power to combine and separate," was suggested by the philosopher Thomas Aquinas, 1225-1274 (cited in Walsh & Betz, 1995); the importance of reasoning and judgment was evident in the early Binet tests (see Sattler, 1982); Spearman (1927) emphasized the importance of abstract reasoning.

[6] A number of research laboratories have examined mood-congruent judgement. A few key publications include: Bower (1981); Forgas (1995); Isen, Shalker, Clark, & Karp (1978); Mayer & Salovey (1988); Mayer, Gaschke, Braverman, & Evans (1992); Salovey & Birnbaum (1989).

[7] Mayer et al. (1992, p. 129).

[8] This brief definition forms one of the several definitions employed by Goleman (1995b, p. xii). A second definition is similar to ours; a third definition says that emotional intelligence is "character" (1995b, p. 285).

[9] Motivational intelligences are discussed briefly in the introduction to Mayer & Geher (1996). The view there is that intelligences might be divided into cognitive, affective, and motivational sets rather than the social (and intrapersonal) intelligences most recently popularized by Gardner, has been studied under different names by earlier researchers.

[10] When psychologists speak about intelligence they are keeping in mind the full range of the variable, from its lowest manifestations in the severely retarded, where most individuals possess very few skills, to the level of the extremely gifted, where individuals can do many things with at least some skill (For example, Einstein played the violin in a chamber group, although always a bit stiffly).

[11] Some psychologists were interested in interpreting this cohesion among the various intelligences (i.e., that they rose and fell together). For example, Spearman (1927) believed that their movement together occurred because they drew on a common mental resource that, if possessed in quantity, helped a person excel, and if possessed in poverty, limited a person's abilities. This general common resource, termed g for general intelligence, could be estimated for a person according to various mathematical models that were developed for that purpose. Although there exists consensus that all the intelligences are empirically interrelated (i.e., rise and fall together across individuals), the g model of intelligence was more controversial. Alternative explanations for this collective rise and fall of abilities exist (see, e.g., Detterman, 1982). Whether one believed in g, or not, the mathematical models developed with it provided an accurate and convenient means for keeping track of the degree to which the intelligences cohered.

[12] One of us recalls this critique of Guilford and Hoepfner's (1971) model: If everyone in the field of personality testing joined in, it could still take 100 years to establish so many intelligences. Although it attracted some attention in the 1970's, interest in the theory dropped off. In fact, we could find no coverage of their model in several contemporary volumes on psychological testing.

[13] Gardner's theory (1983; 1993) is beautifully described and intuitively compelling. Although he recognizes that all intelligences intercorrelate (Gardner, 1993,

p. xx), he wonders whether this may be an accident of the experimental methods employed (Gardner, 1993, p. xi). Other theorists join him in maintaining a skepticism concerning the obtained correlations among intelligences (e.g., Detterman, 1982). Still, it leaves no way to test the theory of multiple intelligences, and the theory is regarded by many experts in the field (including ourselves) as appealing but lacking in empirical support as of now (Sternberg, 1994).

[14] Another plausible exception is Sternberg's (1988) triarchic theory of intelligence. Sternberg does sometimes employ the correlational method, however. The centrality of correlational methods is supported by a recent task force summary of the status of intelligence research, reported in the American Psychologist (Neisser, et al., p. 78).

[15] Thurstone (1938).

[16] Ekstrom, French, Harman, & Dermer (1976).

[17] Thorndike & Stein (1937) contributed some of the empirical findings; Cronbach (1960) presented an influential review arguing that further examination of social intelligence was unwise.

[18] Scarr (1989, p. 78).

[19] Mayer & Salovey (1993).

[20] For example, Schaffer, Gilmer, & Schoen (1940, pp. xii, 521); Young (1936, pp. 457-458; 1943, p. 263).

[21] George Mandler (1984) first popularized this idea as a component of human information processing.

[22] Many philosophers and psychologists have said this before us; our reasoning is presented in Mayer & Salovey (1995).

[23] See Frijda (1988), for the lawfulness of emotions; also, see Ekman, Friesen, O'Sullivan, Chan, et al. (1987).

[24] The original hypothesis concerning this dates to Montesquieu; the modern test was conducted by Pennebaker, Rimé, and Blankenship (1996).

[25] Mayer & Salovey (1995, p. 197).

[26] For example, Salovey & Mayer (1990, p. 189).

[27] For example, Arnheim (1954/1974); Clynes (1977).

[28] For example, Piaget and Inhelder (1969, pp. 120-122) consider interpersonal perspective taking as emerging partially within the concrete-operations stage. See also Gerrig (1993).

[29] The *arena* is a memory location within which symbols are manipulated by one or more intelligences (Mayer & Mitchell, in press). In emotional intelligence, the individual would generate a feeling—sadness, for instance—on command so as to think about its facets, meanings, and associated thoughts. Having the emotions in this processing arena can presumably reduce the requirements on memory for processing.

[30] A more elaborate description of how mood swings affect the college planning process is outlined in Mayer (1986); relevant evidence for mood-congruent judgment over time is in Mayer & Hanson (1995); information about the first-degree relatives of manic-depressives can be found in Richards, Kinney, Lunde, Benet, & Merzel (1988).

[31] Palfai & Salovey (1993) present evidence that specific moods enhance specific forms of mental processing.

[32] Plutchik (1984)

[33] Spinoza, B. (1675/1984, p. 83).

[34] For recent reviews of these ideas, see Lazarus (1991); Plutchik (1984); Roseman (1984); Scherer (1993); Smith & Ellsworth (1985).

[35] Nannis (1988) considers full understanding of multiple feelings as requiring fairly sophisticated thoughts — that is, arising late in development.

[36] Plutchik (1984).

[37] The parent's ability to suppress feelings in the child is described in Alice Miller's (1990) book, "The Drama of the Gifted Child." Miller emphasizes, in terms somewhat different from the argument here, that some children will deny negative feelings in themselves altogether as a consequence of parental disapproval.

[38] Nannis (1988) refers to introspection and levels of consciousness concerning emotion as occurring very late in development. The original discussion of meta-experience can be found in Mayer & Gaschke (1988). The concept is developed more recently in both Mayer & Stevens (1994), and Salovey, Mayer, Goldman, Turvey, & Palfai (1995). Some actual approaches to mood regulation are examined by Tice & Baumeister (1993).

[39] Anastasi (1988) presents a good introduction to these concepts.

[40] Saarni (1988); this volume.

What is Emotional Intelligence?

[41] Anastasi (1988, p. 264); additional discussion can be found in Anastasi (1967) and Sundberg, Snowden, & Reynolds (1978).

[42] See in particular Salovey & Mayer (1990); Salovey, Hsee, & Mayer (1993).

[43] Research on delay of gratification, an example of which is the popularly reported "marshmallow test" (see Gibbs, 1995), is fascinating. We view it, however, as more closely related to motivation than emotion. The studies in question are by Mischel, Shoda, & Peake (1988) and Shoda, Mischel, & Peake (1990).

[44] Mayer, DiPaolo, & Salovey (1990).

[45] A replication and extension of the Mayer and Geher work using a new scale based on the Figure 1 model is reported in Mayer, Caruso, and Salovey (1997). The new scale is a computer-based testing instrument (Mayer, Salovey, & Caruso, in press). The Mayer and Geher (1996) article illustrates many of the complexities that will arise in measuring emotional intelligence and that tend to be swept aside in the present wave of enthusiasm for the concept. Several criteria were used for the "correct" answer as to what a character was feeling in a story. One criterion involved the character him or herself who was in the particular situation (real situations were used). A second criterion was the overall consensus of the participants in the study as to what the person was feeling. These two criteria behaved differently in the study. Interestingly, however, they both supported the existence of an actual emotional intelligence. A replication and extension of the work is described in Mitchell & Mayer (1996).

[46] Averill and Nunley (1992)

[47] Howard Gardner (1995, p. 26-27) has suggested this range, which seems consistent with the current literature.

[48] This was the central illustration employed in the New York Times coverage of the topic, and appeared in TIME and a popular book as well (Gibbs, 1995; Goleman, 1995a; 1995b). The original study was reported by Kelly and Caplan (1993) in the Harvard Business Review.

[49] Kelley & Caplan, 1993, p. 132.

[50] Incidentally, "tacit intelligence," refers to the ability to recognize the implicit demands of a job. It has been studied in some depth by Wagner and Sternberg (1985).

[51] We do recognize, however, that the 59th Street Bridge has inspired its own musical lore, notably, "The Fifty-ninth Street Bridge Song (Feelin' Groovy)," by Paul Simon of the musical group Simon & Garfunkel.

[52] See Mayer and Salovey (1995) for a more extensive discussion of the emotional knowledge base.

[53] Peli, 1984

[54] It does not seem, to our ear, appropriate usage to talk about teaching an intelligence. The definition of an ability is that it is a capacity rather than a topic to be taught. To teach intelligence sounds to us like exercising a person's sports ability. One exercises muscles to build strength; similarly, one teaches emotional skills to build emotional intelligence.

[55] This program is described in Goleman (1995b).

Educator's Commentary

Karol Defalco

Few would disagree that the purpose of schools is to promote academic skills and knowledge and to take students from one level to the next. However, that's difficult to accomplish if the student is absent; if the student is suspended or expelled; if the student is dropping out of school; if the student is dealing with a death; if the student believes that life is something that happens to him and he has no control over it. Although some students dealing with these issues are in our classrooms and doing fine, many are absent. Others are in our classrooms in body but not mind. Their minds are dealing with the above stressors of home, of community, of peers, of life. Although these young people are in our classrooms, their thoughts are on these social/emotional issues. They're often not paying attention, have low concentration, participate little, neglect the assignments, act out. For these kids, the parts of speech and the addition of mixed numbers are not high priorities. When standardized tests do not show improvement, school districts traditionally have responded by increasing the amount of time spent in class, choosing a new textbook, reassigning teachers, and reevaluating assessment tools. Each of these responses can provide benefits. However, they do not speak to the needs of students who are skipping school or are being suspended. They do not address the needs of those students who are in school in body only. Nor do they meet the needs of the students mentioned at the opening of this chapter: the boys who accused a fourth-grader of stealing the new coat he was wearing. In that vignette, it is easy to surmise that, after returning from recess, there was more than one student in that class who was not focused on academics. The victim of the tirade, the bullies, and the students who had witnessed the venomous attack may all be dealing with that social/emotional event rather than attending to the lesson. The young people in this account need skills not usually considered part of a school's core curriculum: impulse control, stress management, empathy, dealing with an accusation, and problem solving. To get these students to their next academic levels, we must meet them where they are and give them skills and resources to cope with stressors so that they will then be better able to attend to academics. Without these social/emotional skills, the stressors take over and prevent our students from living up to their academic potential. So, in addition to teaching emotional competencies for their own sake, we teach them in order to impact academics.

Let's talk about emotional competency programs. Some say that emotional competency programs teach "the best way to feel, the correct way to act." I am not an advocate of these values-based programs in public schools. I support curricula that teach social skills as part of a comprehensive, sequential program. Just as there are many math skills, there are many social skills, including:

impulse control
anger management
empathy
recognizing similarities and differences among people
complimenting
self-monitoring
communication
evaluating risks
positive self-talk
problem solving
decision making
goal setting
resisting peer pressure

Some educators implement emotional competency lessons in response to a problem in the cafeteria, hallway, gym, or on the playground (as in the opening story), and although there is a role for this type of intervention, I prefer a program that comes from a prevention point of view: one offered to all students - not just "problem kids" – to reduce the occurrence of antisocial or at-risk behaviors, one offered to all students so that when the stressors of life confront them, they will be able to cope. After all, which student will not have to resist impulses at some point in her life? Which student will not have to evaluate risks? Which student will not be in a situation needing anger management skills? Emotional competency programs for all!

How should social/emotional skills be taught? Well, think about the way other skills are taught. A math teacher might present the material, model the skills by doing an example on the board, give students a chance to practice, require students to apply the skill to a project, and reward the student for doing a good job – present, model, practice, apply, reward. Also, math skills are taught sequentially as part of a comprehensive K-12 program. They are taught every day to every child, every grade, every year.

Yet when social skills are taught, they are often introduced in a hit-or-miss fashion after a problem has occurred rather than as part of a planned program. Sometimes hundreds of students are called to the auditorium for a program that is supposed to address social competencies. After the program, the students return to their classrooms and adults hope that the 45-minute presentation will make a difference in student attitudes or behaviors. Would a 45-minute auditorium program be an appropriate way to teach math? Hardly. Neither does it work for social skills. Social skills should be taught in the same way as academic skills: sequentially, as part of a comprehensive program, to every child, every day, every year, using a present/model/practice/apply/reward format.

In New Haven, where I am a middle school teacher, there is a comprehensive K-12 Social Development Program. The curriculum includes social/emotional competencies for each grade. In kindergarten through grade 3, students work on self-awareness, relationships, and decision making. Fourth- and fifth-graders are focused on empathy training, impulse control, and anger management. In middle schools, students learn a problem-solving process using stress management, problem identification, goal setting, solution generating, consequential thinking, and planning. They also learn peer pressure resistance skills. Among other skills, high-schoolers learn decision making, which includes the consideration of others' points of view and recognizing risks/opportunities.

The boys involved in the stolen coat accusation were called to the office, talked to by the principal, and assigned letters of apology. The boy who received the new coat wrote a thank-you letter. These are all appropriate gestures. Are they enough? Have the bullies learned empathy skills? Have they learned to accept others? Have they learned to accurately express emotion? Has the victim learned stress management skills on problem-solving skills? Does he have the necessary skills to cope with similar situations as they arise in his life? Talking about emotions is a stare. Talking about story characters' feelings is a start. Building competencies is the goal.

As Mayer and Salovey point out, "We are at the beginning of the learning curve about emotional intelligence; the coming years should bring exciting research that contributes to our understanding of the concept." May I add: It will contribute to the way we work with kids.

What is Emotional Intelligence?

Used by permission of Oxford University Press, Inc.
Salovey, P., Mayer, J.D., & Caruso, D. (2002). The positive psychology of emotional intelligence. From *Handbook of positive psychology* (pp. 159-171). Edited by C.R. Snyder & Shane J. Lopez, 2001, by Oxford University Press Inc. New York: Oxford University Press.

The Positive Psychology of Emotional Intelligence

Peter Salovey, Yale University
John D. Mayer, University of New Hampshire
David Caruso, Work-Life Strategies

Acknowledgements

Preparation of this chapter was facilitated by grants from the National Cancer Institute (R01-CA68427), the National Institute of Mental Health (P01-MH/DA56826), and the Donaghue Women's Health Investigator Program at Yale University to Peter Salovey.

The Positive Psychology of Emotional Intelligence

Out of the marriage of reason with affect there issues clarity with passion. Reason without affect would be impotent, affect without reason would be blind (Tomkins, 1962, p. 112).

For psychologists, the 1990s were best known as the "Decade of the Brain." But there were moments during the last ten years when the popular press seemed ready to declare it the "Decade of the Heart," not so much for a popular interest in cardiovascular physiology, but rather as a reflection on the growing interest in emotions and emotional intelligence, in particular. During the second half of the 1990s, emotional intelligence and EQ (we much prefer the former term to the latter) were featured as the cover story in at least two national magazines (Gibbs, 1995; Goleman, 1995a), received extensive coverage in the international press (e.g., Alcade, 1996; Miketta, Gottschling, Wagner-Roos, & Gibbs, 1995; Thomas, 1995), were named the most useful new words or phrases for 1995 by the American Dialect Society (1995, 1999; Brodie, 1996), and made appearances in syndicated comic strips as diverse as Zippy the Pinhead and Dilbert.

What is this construct, and why has it been so appealing? Emotional intelligence represents the ability to perceive, appraise, and express emotion accurately and adaptively; the ability to understand emotion and emotional knowledge; the ability to access and/or generate feelings when they facilitate cognitive activities and adaptive action; and the ability to regulate emotions in oneself and others (Mayer & Salovey, 1997). In other words, emotional intelligence refers to the ability to process emotion-laden information competently and to use it to guide cognitive activities like problem-solving and to focus energy on required behaviors. The term suggested to some that there might be other ways of being intelligent than those emphasized by standard IQ tests, that one might be able to develop these abilities, and that an emotional intelligence could be an important predictor of success in personal relationships, family functioning, and the workplace. The term is one that instills hope and suggests promise, at least as compared to traditional notions of crystalized intelligence. For these very reasons, emotional intelligence belongs in positive psychology. The purpose of this chapter is to review the history of and current research on emotional intelligence and to determine whether our positive assessments are appropriate or misplaced.

History of the Concept

Turning to the field of psychology, there are two references to emotional intelligence prior to our work on this concept. First, Mowrer (1960, pp. 307-308) famously concluded that "the emotions. . . do not at all deserve being put into opposition with 'intelligence'. . . they are, it seems, themselves a high order of intelligence." Second, Payne (1983/1986) used the term in an unpublished dissertation. A framework for an emotional intelligence, a formal definition, and suggestions about its measurement were first described in two articles that we published in 1990 (Mayer, DiPaolo, & Salovey, 1990; Salovey & Mayer, 1990).

The tension between exclusively cognitive views of what it means to be intelligent and broader ones that include a positive role for the emotions can be traced back many centuries. For example, the Stoic philosophers of ancient Greece viewed emotion as too individualistic and self-absorbed to be a reliable guide for insight and wisdom. Later, the Romantic movement in late-18th century and early-19th century Europe stressed how emotion-rooted intuition and empathy could provide insights that were unavailable through logic alone.

The modern interest in emotional intelligence stems, perhaps, from a similar dialectic in the field of human abilities research. Although narrow, analytically-focused definitions of intelligence predominated much of this century, following Cronbach's (1960) often cited conclusion that a social intelligence was unlikely to be defined and had not been measured, cracks in the analytic intelligence edifice began to appear in the 1980's. For example, Sternberg (1985) challenged mental abilities researchers to pay more attention to creative and practical aspects of intelligence, and Gardner (1983/ 1993) even defined an intrapersonal intelligence that concerns access to one's feeling life, the capacity to represent feelings, and the ability to draw upon them as a means of understanding and guide for behavior. Shortly thereafter, in their controversial book, *The Bell Curve*, Herrnstein and Murray (1994) revived debate about the genetic basis for traditionally-defined intelligence and the degree to which intelligence is affected by environmental circumstances. Paradoxically, instead of crystallizing support for the genetic intelligence position, the effect of *The Bell Curve* was to energize many educators, investigators, and journalists to question whether the traditional view of intelligence was conceptualized too narrowly, and to embrace the notion that there might be other ways to be smart and succeed in the world.

It was in this context that we wrote our 1990 articles, introducing emotional intelligence as the ability to understand feelings in the self and others, and to use these feelings as informational guides for thinking and action (Salovey & Mayer, 1990). At that time, we described three core components of emotional intelligence – appraisal and expression, regulation, and utilization — based on our reading and organizing of the relevant literature rather than on empirical research. Since this original article, we have refined our conceptualization of emotional intelligence so that it now includes four dimensions (Mayer & Salovey, 1997), which we will discuss later in this chapter.

Our work was reinforced by neuroscientists' interest in showing that emotional responses were integral to "rational" decision making (e.g., Damasio, 1995). Through our theorizing, we also helped to stimulate the writing of the best-selling book, *Emotional Intelligence*, in which Goleman (1995b) promised that emotional intelligence rather than analytical intelligence predicts success in school, work, and home. Despite the lack of data to support some of Goleman's claims, interest in emotional intelligence soared, with books appearing monthly in which the authors touted the value of emotional intelligence in education (Schilling, 1996), child-rearing (Gottman & DeClaire, 1997; Shapiro, 1997), the workplace (Cooper & Sawaf, 1996; Goleman, 1998; Ryback, 1998; Simmons & Simmons, 1997; Weisinger, 1998), and personal growth (Epstein, 1998; Salerno, 1996; Segal, 1997; Steiner & Perry, 1997). Very little of this explosion of available resources on emotional intelligence represented empirically-oriented scholarship.

In the past five years, there also has been great interest in the development of measures to assess the competencies involved in emotional intelligence. Not surprisingly, a plethora of supposed emotional intelligence scales and batteries of varying psychometric properties appeared (e.g., Bar-On, 1997; Cooper & Sawaf, 1997; Schutte et al., 1998). In reality, these instruments tapped self-reported personality constructs, and they were disappointing in terms of their discriminant and construct validities (Davies, Stankov, & Roberts, 1998). As an alternative, we have been arguing for the value of conceptualizing emotional intelligence as a set of abilities and to measure it as such (Mayer, Salovey & Caruso, 2000, in press). We will describe this approach to measurement later in the chapter.

Current Model of Emotional Intelligence

What follows is a brief summary of our ability theory of emotional intelligence, displayed in Figure 1; more detailed presentations can be found elsewhere (e.g., Mayer, Caruso, & Salovey, 1999; Mayer & Salovey, 1997; Salovey, Bedell, Detweiler, & Mayer, 2000; Salovey & Mayer, 1990). Although there is sometimes empirical utility in considering emotional intelligence as a unitary construct, most of our work suggests that it can be divided into four branches. The first of these branches, <u>Emotional Perception and Expression</u>, involves recognizing and inputting verbal and nonverbal information from the emotion system. The second branch, <u>Emotional Facilitation of Thought</u> (sometimes referred to as <u>Using Emotional Intelligence</u>), refers to using emotions as part of cognitive processes such as creativity and problem-solving. The third branch, <u>Emotional Understanding</u>, involves cognitive processing of emotion, that is insight and knowledge brought to bear about one's feelings or the feelings of others. Our fourth branch, <u>Emotional Management</u>, concerns the regulation of emotions in oneself and in other people.

The first branch of emotional intelligence begins with the capacity to perceive and to express feelings. Emotional intelligence is impossible without the competencies involved in this first branch (see also Saarni, 1990, 1999). If each time unpleasant feelings emerged, people turned their attentions away, they would learn very little about feelings. Emotional perception involves registering, attending to, and deciphering emotional messages as they are expressed in facial expressions, voice tone, or cultural artifacts. A person who sees the fleeting expression of fear in the face of another understands much more about that other's emotions and thoughts than someone who misses such a signal.

The second branch of emotional intelligence concerns emotional facilitation of cognitive activities. Emotions are complex organizations of the various psychological subsystems – physiological, experiential, cognitive, and motivational. Emotions enter the cognitive system both as cognized feelings, as is the case when someone thinks, "I am a little sad now," and as altered cognitions, as when a sad person thinks, "I am no good." The Emotional Facilitation of Thought – Branch 2 – focuses on how emotion affects the cognitive system and, as such, can be harnessed for more effective problem-solving, reasoning, decision-making, and creative endeavors. Of course, cognition can be disrupted by emotions, such as anxiety and fear, but emotions also can prioritize the cognitive system to attend to what is important (Easterbrook, 1959; Mandler, 1975; Simon, 1982), and even to focus on what it does best in a given mood (e.g., Palfai & Salovey, 1993; Schwarz, 1990).

Figure 1. The Four Branch Model of Emotional Intelligence (after Mayer & Salovey, 1997)

Emotional Perception and Expression

    Ability to identify emotion in one's physical and psychological states.

    Ability to identify emotion in other people.

    Ability to express emotions accurately and to express needs related to them.

    Ability to discriminate between accurate/honest and inaccurate/dishonest feelings.

Emotional Facilitation of Thought (Using Emotional Intelligence)

    Ability to redirect and prioritize thinking on the basis of associated feelings.

    Ability to generate emotions to facilitate judgment and memory.

    Ability to capitalize on mood changes to appreciate multiple points of view.

    Ability to use emotional states to facilitate problem-solving and creativity.

Emotional Understanding

    Ability to understand relationships among various emotions.

    Ability to perceive the causes and consequences of emotions.

    Ability to understand complex feelings, emotional blends, and contradictory states.

    Ability to understand transitions among emotions.

Emotional Management

    Ability to be open to feelings, both pleasant and unpleasant.

    Ability to monitor and reflect on emotions.

    Ability to engage, prolong, or detach from an emotional state.

    Ability to manage emotions in onself.

    Ability to manage emotions in others.

Emotions also change cognitions, making them positive when a person is happy, and negative when the person is sad (e.g., Forgas, 1995; Mayer, Gaschke, Braverman, & Evans, 1992; Salovey & Birnbaum, 1989; Singer & Salovey, 1988). These changes force the cognitive system to view things from different perspectives, e.g., alternating between skeptical and accepting. The advantage of such alterations to thought are fairly apparent. When one's point of view shifts between skeptical and accepting, the individual can appreciate multiple vantage points and, as a consequence, think about a problem more deeply and creatively (e.g., Mayer, 1986; Mayer & Hanson, 1995). It is just such an effect that may lead people with mood swings toward greater creativity (Goodwin & Jamison, 1990; see also Simonton's chapter on creativity in this volume).

Branch 3 involves understanding emotion. Emotions form a rich and complexly interrelated symbol set. The most fundamental competency at this level concerns the ability to label emotions with words and to recognize the relationships among exemplars of the affective lexicon. The emotionally intelligent individual is able to recognize that the terms used to describe emotions are arranged into families and that groups of emotion terms form fuzzy sets (Ortony, Clore & Collins, 1988). Perhaps more importantly, the relations among these terms are deduced – that annoyance and irritation can lead to rage if the provocative stimulus is not eliminated, or that envy often is experienced in contexts that also evoke jealousy (Salovey & Rodin, 1986, 1989). The person who is able to understand emotions – their meanings, how they blend together, how they progress over time – is truly blessed with the capacity to understand important aspects of human nature and interpersonal relationships.

Partly as a consequence of various popularizations, and partly as a consequence of societal pressures to regulate emotions, many people primarily identify emotional intelligence with its fourth branch, Emotional Management (sometimes referred to as Emotional Regulation). They hope emotional intelligence will be a way of getting rid of troublesome emotions or emotional leakages into human relations, and rather, hope to control emotions. Although this is one possible outcome of the fourth branch, optimal levels of emotional regulation may be moderate ones; attempts to minimize or eliminate emotion completely may stifle emotional intelligence. Similarly, the regulation of emotion in other people is less likely to involve the suppressing of others' emotions but rather the harnessing of them, as when a persuasive speaker is said to "move" his or her audience.

Individuals use a broad range of techniques to regulate their moods. Thayer, Newman, and McClain (1994) believe that physical exercise is the single most effective strategy for changing a bad mood, among those under one's own control. Other commonly reported mood regulation strategies include listening to music, social interaction, and cognitive self-management (e.g., giving oneself a "pep talk"). Pleasant distractions (errands, hobbies, fun activities, shopping, reading, and writing) also are effective. Less effective (and, at times, counter-productive) strategies include passive mood management (e.g., television viewing, caffeine, food, and sleep), direct tension reduction (e.g., drugs, alcohol, and sex), spending time alone, and avoiding the person or thing that caused a bad mood. In general, the most successful regulation methods involve expenditure of energy; active mood management techniques that combine relaxation, stress management, cognitive effort, and exercise may be the most effective strategies for changing bad moods (reviewed by Thayer, Newman, & McClain, 1994). Central to emotional self-regulation is the ability to reflect upon and manage one's emotions; emotional disclosure provides one means of doing so. Pennebaker (1989, 1993, 1997) has studied the effects of disclosure extensively and finds that the act of disclosing emotional experiences in writing improves individuals' subsequent physical and mental health (see Niederhoffer & Pennebaker in this volume).

Measuring Emotional Intelligence

We believe that the only valid approach for assessing emotional intelligence is the use of task-based, ability measures. Although self-report inventories assessing various aspects of emotional intelligence have proliferated in recent years (e.g., Bagby, Parker, & Taylor, 1993a, 1993b; Bar-On, 1997; Catanzaro & Mearns, 1990; EQ Japan,

1998; Giuliano & Swinkels, 1992; Salovey, Mayer, Goldman, Turvey, & Palfai, 1995; Schutte et al., 1998; Swinkels & Giuliano, 1995; Wang et al., 1997), these constructs are difficult to distinguish from already-measured aspects of personality (Davies et al., 1998); moreover, whether emotional competency self-belief scores actually correlate systematically with those competencies per se has yet to be determined (Mayer, Caruso, & Salovey, 1999). We ask the reader to imagine whether he or she would be convinced of the analytic intelligence of another person based on the respondent's answer to a question such as, "Do you think you're smart?" We are not, and therefore since the beginning of our work on emotional intelligence, we have suggested that tasks that tap into the various competencies that underlie emotional intelligence are likely to have more validity than self-report measures (e.g., Mayer, DiPaolo, & Salovey, 1990).

Task-based measures of emotional abilities developed on the basis of other theoretical frameworks may be useful in the assessment of emotional intelligence. For example, in the Levels of Emotional Awareness Scale (LEAS) respondents are asked to describe their feelings about various stimuli and then these protocols are coded according to differentiations in the feeling language used (Lane, Quinlan, Schwartz, Walker, & Zeitlin, 1990). Another possibility is Averill and Nunley's (1992; see also Averill, 1999) test of emotional creativity in which participants are asked to write about situations in which they experience three different emotions simultaneously. Various measures of non-verbal emotional sending and receiving ability also have been explored over the years (e.g., Buck, 1976; Freedman, Prince, Riggio, & DiMatteo, 1980; Rosenthal, Hall, DiMatteo, Rogers, & Archer, 1979).

The first comprehensive, theory-based battery for assessing emotional intelligence as a set of abilities was the Multifactor Emotional Intelligence Scale (MEIS), which can be administered through interaction with a computer program or via pencil-and-paper (Mayer, Caruso, & Salovey, 1998, 1999). The MEIS comprises twelve ability measures that are divided into four branches, reflecting the model of emotional intelligence presented earlier: (a) perceiving and expressing emotions; (b) using emotions to facilitate thought and other cognitive activities; (c) understanding emotion; and (d) managing emotion in self and others (Mayer & Salovey, 1997). Branch 1 tasks measure emotional perception in Faces, Music, Designs, and Stories. The second branch measures Synesthesia Judgments (e.g., "How hot is anger?") and Feeling Biases (translating felt emotions into judgments about people). Branch 3's four tasks examine the understanding of emotion. Sample questions include, "Optimism most closely combines which two emotions?" A participant should choose "pleasure and anticipation" over less specific alternatives such as "pleasure and joy." Branch 4's two tests measure Emotion Management in the Self and in Others. These tasks ask participants to read scenarios and then rate four reactions to them according to how effective they are as emotion management strategies focused on the self or on others.

An issue that comes up in task-based tests of emotional intelligence concerns what constitutes the correct answer. We have experimented with three different criteria for determining the "correct" answer to questions such as identifying the emotions in

The Positive Psychology of Emotional Intelligence

facial expressions or making suggestions about the most adaptive way to handle emotions in difficult situations. The first, involves target criteria. Here, we would ask the person whose facial expression is depicted on our test item what he or she was feeling. To the extent that the respondent's answer matches the target's, the answer would be scored as correct. A second approach is to use expert criteria. In this strategy, experts on emotion such as psychotherapists or emotion researchers would read test items and provide answers. To the extent that the respondent's answers match the experts', they would be scored as correct. Lastly, the consensus criteria involves norming the test on a large, heterogeneous sample. The test-taker now receives credit for endorsing answers that match those of the larger group.

One might think that a consensus or a target criteria would not be an appropriate approach to scoring tasks measuring emotional competence. After all, aren't most people misguided about their true feelings? We were able to look at how the target, expert, and consensus criteria are interrelated across some of the MEIS ability tasks. The correlations were actually rather high; half were above $r = .52$ (Mayer, Caruso, & Salovey, 1999). In general, the consensus approach correlated more highly with the target criteria than did the expert criteria. At the moment, we are recommending a consensus-based approach to scoring the MEIS for several reasons. Targets sometimes minimize their own negative feelings when asked to report on them (Mayer & Geher, 1996), but large normative samples, when responses are pooled, tend to be reliable judges (Legree, 1995).

Investigations using the MEIS are in rather preliminary stages, but there are a few findings to report (Mayer, Caruso, & Salovey, 1999). In general, we found support for the theoretical model of emotional intelligence described earlier (Mayer & Salovey, 1997). In a sample of 503 adults, MEIS tasks were generally positively intercorrelated with one another, but not highly so (most were in the $r = .20$ to $.50$ range). As well, the test's factorial structure recommended two equally viable factorial models: (a) a three to four factor solution that separated out factors of emotional perception, understanding, management, and, at times, using emotions to facilitate cognitive activities; or (b) a hierarchical structure that first describes a general factor, g_{ei}. The internal consistency of the MEIS is reasonably high: using consensus scoring, most of the twelve subscales had Cronbach alphas in the .70 to .94 range, though the Branch 3 tasks, which are the shortest subscales, tended to have lower internal consistency (although two of these tasks had alphas of .78 and .94, respectively, two others were .49 and .51). In an independent investigation, the Cronbach alpha reported for the MEIS as a whole was .90 (Ciarrochi, Chan, & Caputi, 2000).

The MEIS as a whole correlates positively with verbal intelligence (but only in the $r = .35$ to $.45$ range), self-reported empathy, and parental warmth, and negatively with social anxiety and depression (Mayer, Caruso, & Salovey, 1999). The MEIS is not correlated with nonverbal measures of intelligence such as the Raven Progressive Matrices (Ciarrochi, Chan, & Caputi, 2000). Finally, and consistent with the idea that emotional intelligence is a set of abilities that are developed through learning and experience, scores on the MEIS improve with age (Mayer, Caruso, & Salovey, 1999).

A refined and better normed successor to the MEIS, called the Mayer, Salovey, and Caruso Emotional Intelligence Scales (MSCEIT) presently is being prepared for distribution (Mayer, Salovey, & Caruso, in preparation). We recommend this set of tasks for assessing emotional intelligence as an ability. Structured much like the MEIS, the MSCEIT is also based on the four-branch model of emotional intelligence, but allows for the assessment of emotional intelligence in less time than the MEIS. Poorly worded items have been eliminated, and extensive normative data will be available.

Current Research Findings

We have just started to publish research using ability-based measures of emotional intelligence, like the MEIS and the MSCEIT (see Salovey, Woolery, & Mayer, in press, for a summary). However, there are some findings to report that are promising with respect to the prediction of important behavioral outcomes. We note that many of the findings described below are as of yet unpublished and unreviewed by other scientists, so they should be viewed as suggestive.

Mayer and his colleagues have been developing measures of individuals' life space – a description of a person's environment in terms of discrete, externally verifiable responses (e.g., How many pairs of shows do you own? How many times have you attended the theater this year? see Mayer, Carlsmith, & Chabot, 1998). In these studies, higher scores on the MEIS are associated with lower self-reported, life-space measures of engagement in violent and antisocial behavior among college students; the correlations between the MEIS and these measures were in the $r = .40$ range. Other investigators have also reported that greater emotional intelligence is associated with lower levels of antisocial behavior. For example, Rubin (1999) found substantial negative correlations between a version of the MEIS developed for adolescents (the AMEIS) and peer ratings of their aggressiveness; prosocial behaviors rated by these schoolchildren's teachers were positively associated with emotional intelligence ($|r|$'s = .37 to .49).

Research focused on adolescents' substance use has been conducted by Trinidad and Johnson (1999). They collected data from 205 culturally diverse seventh and eight grade students using five subtests from the AMEIS. Those scoring high on overall emotional intelligence were significantly less likely to have ever tried smoking a cigarette or to have smoked recently. They were also less likely to report having had an alcoholic beverage in the past week. Emotional intelligence was positively correlated with endorsing the idea that doing well in school is important.

Emotional intelligence, as assessed with the MEIS, also appears to be important in workplace situations. In an intriguing study conducted with 164 employees of an insurance company assigned to 26 customer claim teams, Rice (1999) administered a shortened version of the MEIS to these employees and then asked a department manager to rate the effectiveness of these teams and their leaders. The MEIS scores were highly correlated with the manager's ratings of the team leaders' effectiveness, $r =$ .51. The average MEIS scores of each of the teams – the team emotional intelligence – also was related to the manager's ratings of the team performance in customer service, $r = .46$. However, emotional intelligence was negatively associated with the team's speed in handling customer complaints, $r = -.40$. It appears that emotional intelligence may help team leaders and their teams to be better at satisfying customers but not necessarily to increase the efficiency with which they perform these behaviors. Perhaps dealing with customers' feelings in an adaptive way takes time.

Interventions to Improve Emotional Intelligence
Despite the paucity of predictive validity data on emotional intelligence, interventions are being developed aimed at raising emotional intelligence in a variety of contexts.

Interventions in education. With the availability of materials suggesting how teachers can cultivate emotional intelligence in school children, there has been an increasing interest in the last decade in developing school-based programs focused on these abilities (Mayer & Cobb, in press; Salovey & Sluyter, 1997). For example, in guidebook for developing emotional intelligence curricula for elementary school students, Schilling (1996) recommends units on self-awareness, managing feelings, decision making, managing stress, personal responsibility, self-concept, empathy, communication, group dynamics, and conflict resolution. As should be obvious, the emotional intelligence rubric is being applied quite broadly to the development of a range of social-emotional skills. As a result, many of the school-based interventions designed to promote emotional intelligence are better classified under the more general label, Social and Emotional Learning (SEL) programs (Cohen, 1999a; Elias et al., 1997).

There are over 300 curriculum-based programs in the United States purporting to teach Social and Emotional Learning (Cohen, 1999b). These range from those based on very specific social problem-solving skills training (e.g., Elias & Tobias, 1996) to more general conflict resolution strategies (e.g., Lantieri & Patti, 1996), to very broad programs organized around themes like "character development" (Lickona, 1991). One of the oldest SEL programs that has a heavy dose of emotional intelligence development within it is the Social Development Curriculum in the New Haven, Connecticut Public Schools (Shriver, Schwab-Stone, & DeFalco, 1999; Weissberg, Shriver, Bose, & DeFalco, 1997). The New Haven Social Development Program is a Kindergarten through Grade 12 curriculum that integrates the development of social and emotional skills in the context of various prevention programs (e.g., AIDS prevention, drug use prevention, teen pregnancy prevention; see also Durlak, 1995). The curriculum provides 25-50 hours of highly structured classroom instruction at each grade level. Included in the early years of this curriculum are units on self-monitoring, feelings awareness, perspective taking (empathy), understanding nonverbal communication, anger management, and many other topics, some of which are loosely consistent with our model of emotional intelligence. Although this program has not been evaluated in a randomized, controlled trial, a substantial survey administered every two years to New Haven schoolchildren has revealed positive trends since implementation of the program. For example, one change has been reduced school violence and feelings of hopelessness (Shriver et al.,1999).

Another well known emotional intelligence curriculum is called Self Science, which was developed and field tested at the Nueva School in Hillsborough, California in the first through eighth grades (Stone-McCown, Jensen, Freedman, & Rideout, 1998). The Self Science program begins with three assumptions: there is no thinking without feeling and no feeling without thinking; the more conscious one is of what one is experiencing, the more learning is possible; and, self-knowledge is integral to learning. The Self Science curriculum is a flexible one, although it is organized around 54 lessons grouped into ten goals. For example, Goal 3 is called "Becoming More Aware of Multiple Feelings," and it includes lessons such as Naming Feelings, What are Feelings?, Reading Body Language, Emotional Symbolism, Evoking Emotions, Acting on Emotions, Sources of Feelings, and Responsibility for Feelings. The Self Science approach directly focuses on emotions in about half of the lessons. The goals of the Self Science curriculum include: talking about feelings and needs; listening, sharing, and comforting others; learning to grow from conflict and adversity; prioritizing and setting goals; including others; making conscious decisions; and giving time and resources to the larger community (Stone-McCown et al., 1998).

Finally, many emotional intelligence interventions for school children take place within other more specific prevention programs. A good example is the Resolving Conflict Creatively Program (RCCP) that began in the New York City public schools (Lantieri & Patti, 1996). The program goals include increasing awareness of the different choices available to children for dealing with conflicts; developing skills for making these choices; encouraging children's respect for their own cultural background and the backgrounds of others; teaching children how to identify and stand against prejudice; and increasing children's awareness of their role in creating a more peaceful world. These goals are addressed in a 25-hour teacher's training program, and a program emphasizing peer mediation for children in grades 4-6. A follow-up program, Peace in the Family, trains parents in conflict resolution strategies. RCCP training programs emphasize identifying one's own feelings in conflict situations and taking the perspective of and empathizing with others' feelings. In an evaluation that included 5,000 children participating in the RCCP program in New York City, hostile attributions and teacher-reported aggressive behavior dropped as a function of the number of conflict resolution lessons that the children had received, and academic achievement was highest among those children who received the most lessons (Aber, Brown, & Henrich, 1999; Aber, Jones, Brown, Chaudry, & Samples, 1998).

Although increasing numbers of Social and Emotional Learning programs are being evaluated formally (e.g., Elias, Gere, Schuyler Branden-Muller, & Sayette, 1991; Greenberg, Kushe, Cook, & Quamma, 1995), many still have not been subjected to empirical scrutiny. There is virtually no reported research on whether these programs are effective by enhancing the kinds of skills delineated in our model of emotional intelligence

Interventions in the workplace. Possible interventions to increase emotional intelligence can also be found in the workplace (e.g., Caruso, Mayer, & Salovey, in press; Cherniss & Goleman, 1998; Goleman, 1998). These workplace programs, however, are at a much earlier stage of development than those designed for the classroom. Furthermore, many of these workplace "emotional intelligence" programs are really old and familiar training sessions on human relations, achievement motivation, stress management, and conflict resolution.

One promising approach to workplace emotional intelligence is the Weatherhead MBA Program at Case Western Reserve University, where training in social and emotional competency is incorporated into the curriculum for future business leaders (Boyatzis, Cowen, & Kolb, 1995). Although not focused explicitly on emotions per se, these MBA students receive experiences designed to promote initiative, flexibility, achievement drive, empathy, self-confidence, persuasiveness, networking, self-control, and group management. Communication and emotion-related skills also are increasingly being incorporated into physician training (Kramer, Ber, & Moores, 1989).

Perhaps the workplace program that addresses itself to emotional intelligence most explicitly is the Emotional Competency Training Program at American Express Financial Advisors. The goal of the program is to assist managers in becoming "emotional coaches" for their employees. The training focuses on the role of emotion in the workplace and gaining an awareness of how one's own emotional reactions and the emotions of others affect management practices. Although systematic evaluation of this program has yet to be published, a higher business growth rate (money under management) has been found for the financial advisors whose managers had taken the training program as compared to those who had not (reported in Cherniss, 1999).

Directions for Future Research

Despite the rapid growth of interest in emotional intelligence, the measurement of emotional intelligence using ability-based indices is still in an early stage. Recently, as is inevitable for a new concept, emotional intelligence has received some criticism. In particular, using an array of available and, for the most part, poorly validated instruments as the basis for analysis, the construct validity of emotional intelligence has been questioned (Davis et al., 1998). It simply is premature to draw any such conclusions until investigators in our laboratory and other laboratories have completed and validated the appropriate ability-based measures of emotional intelligence.

The area of emotional intelligence is in need of energetic investigators interested in helping to refine the ability-based assessment of emotional intelligence, and, subsequently, studying the predictive validity of emotional intelligence (over and above other constructs) in accounting for important outcomes in school, workplace, family, and social relationships. Given the present status of instrument development and validation, we would encourage investigators to focus their energies on the refinement of ability measures of emotional intelligence. Although we have been pleased with the MEIS and are confident that its successor, the MSCEIT, will be the measurement instrument of choice for assessing emotional intelligence as an ability, research needs to be conducted to measure emotional intelligence with even greater precision and with more easily administered and briefer tests. Further work also will be needed before we can confidently claim that one method of scoring – expert, target, or consensus – is clearly more valid that the others. And it will be necessary to investigate whether tests of emotional intelligence are culture-bound or not. The fact is, we are in the early phase of research on emotional intelligence, both in terms of measuring it as an ability and in showing that such measures predict significant outcomes.

After refining the measurement of emotional intelligence, we are hoping that many investigators will join us in exploring what this construct predicts, both as an overall ability and in terms of an individual's profile of strengths and weaknesses. The domains in which emotional intelligence may play an important part are limited only by the imagination of the investigators studying these abilities, and we are hoping to see an explosion of research in the near future establishing when emotional intelligence is important – perhaps more so than conventional intelligence – and, of course, when it is not.

Finally, and reflecting the theme of this volume, Positive Psychology, attention will need to be focused on how emotional intelligence can be developed through the life span. We suspect that work on the teaching and learning of emotion-related abilities might prove to be a useful counterpoint to the nihilistic conclusions of books like The Bell Curve and may, instead, suggest all kinds of ways in which emotionally enriching experiences could be incorporated into one's life. We need to remind ourselves, however, that work on emotional intelligence is still in its infancy, and that what the field and general public need are more investigators treating it with serious empirical attention.

References

Aber, J. L., Brown, J. L., & Henrich, C. C. (1999). Teaching conflict resolution: An effective school-based approach to violence prevention. New York: National Center for Children in Poverty, The Joseph L. Mailman School of Public Health, Columbia University.

Aber, J. L., Jones, S. M., Brown, J. L., Chaudry, N., & Samples, F. (1998). Resolving conflict creatively: Evaluating the developmental effects of a school-based violence prevention program in neighborhood and classroom context. Development and Psychopathology 10, 187-213.

Alcalde, J. (1996, December). Inteligencia emocional? Muy Interesante, p. 41-46.

American Dialect Society (1995). American Dialect Society: e-mail from Allan Metcalf. http://www.americandialect.org/excite/collections/adsl/011272.shtml.

American Dialect Society (1999). American Dialect Society: Words of the Year.

Averill, J. R. (1999). Individual differences in emotional creativity: Structure and correlates. Journal of Personality, 67, 331-371.

Averill, J. R., & Nunley, E. P. (1992). Voyages of the heart: Living an emotionally creative life. New York: Free Press.

Bagby, R. M., Parker, J. D. A., & Taylor, G. J. (1993a). The twenty-item Toronto Alexithymia Scale: I. Item selection and cross-validation of the factor structure. Journal of Psychosomatic Research, 38, 23-32.

Bagby, R. M., Parker, J. D. A., & Taylor, G. J. (1993b). The twenty-item Toronto Alexithymia Scale: II. Convergent, discriminant, and concurrent validity. Journal of Psychosomatic Research, 38, 33-40.

Bar-On, R. (1997). BarOn Emotional Quotient Inventory: A measure of emotional intelligence. Toronto, ON: Multi-Health Systems, Inc.

Boyatzis, R. E., Cowen, S. S., & Kolb, D. A. (1995). Innovation in professional education: Steps on a journey to learning. San Francisco: Jossey-Bass.

Brodie, I. (1996, January 5). Newtron bomb fall-out changes slang. The Times (Overseas News Section). Times Newspapers Limited, p. 26.

Buck, R. (1976). A test of nonverbal receiving ability: Preliminary studies. Human Communication Research, 2, 162-171.

Caruso, D. R., Mayer, J. D., & Salovey, P. (in press). Emotional intelligence and emotional leadership. In R. Riggio & S. Murphy (Eds.), Multiple intelligences and leadership. Mahwah, NJ: Lawrence Erlbaum Associates.

Catanzaro, S. J., & Mearns, J. (1990). Measuring generalized expectancies for negative mood regulation: Initial scale development and implications. Journal of Personality Assessment, 54, 546-563.

Cherniss, C. (1999). Model program summaries. A technical report issued by the Consortium for Research on Emotional Intelligence in Organizations (available at www.eiconsortium.org).

Cherniss, C., & Goleman, D. (1998). Bringing emotional intelligence to the workplace. A technical report issued by the Consortium for Research on Emotional Intelligence in Organizations (available at www.eiconsortium.org)

Ciarrochi, J. V., Chan, A. Y. C., & Caputi, P. (2000). A critical evaluation of the emotional intelligence construct. Personality and Individual Differences, 3, 539561.

Cohen, J. (Ed.) (1999a). Educating minds and hearts: Social emotional learning and the passage into adolescence. New York: Teachers College Press.

Cohen, J. (1999b). Social and emotional learning past and present: A sychoeducational dialogue. In J. Cohen (Ed.), Educating minds and hearts: Social emotional learning and the passage into adolescence (pp. 2-23). New York: Teachers College Press.

Cooper, R. K., & Sawaf, A. (1996). Executive EQ: Emotional intelligence in leadership and organizations. New York: Grosset/Putnam.

Cronbach, L. J. (1960). Essentials of psychological testing. New York: Harper and Row.

Damasio, A. R. (1995). Descartes' error : Emotion, reason, and the human brain. New York: Avon.

Davies, M., Stankov, L., & Roberts, R. D. (1998). Emotional Intelligence: In search of an elusive construct. Journal of Personality and Social Psychology, 75, 989-1015.

Durlak, J. A. (1995). Schoolbased prevention programs for children and adolescents. Thousand Oaks, CA: Sage Publications.

Easterbrook, J. A. (1959). The effects of emotion on cue utilization and the organization of behavior. Psychological Review, 66, 183-200.

Elias, M. J., Gere M. A., Schuyler, T. F., Branden-Muller, L. R., & Sayette, M. A. (1991). The promotion of social competence: Longitudinal study of a preventive schoolbased program. American Journal of Orthopsychiatry, 61, 409417.

Elias, M. J., & Tobias, S. E. (1996). Social problem solving interventions in the schools. New York: Guilford Press.

Elias, M. J., Zins, J. E., Weissberg, R. P., Frey, K. S., Greenberg, M. T., Haynes, N. M., Kessler, R., Schwab-Stone, M. E., & Shriver, T. P. (1997). Promoting social and emotional learning: Guidelines for educators. Alexandria, VA: Association for Supervision and Curriculum Development.

Epstein, S. (1998). Constructive thinking: The key to emotional intelligence. Praeger, Westport, CT.

EQ Japan, Inc. (1998). Emotional Quotient Inventory. Tokyo, Japan: Author.

Forgas, J. P. (1995). Mood and judgment: The affect infusion model (AIM). Psychological Bulletin, 117, 39-66.

Freedman, H. S., Prince, L. M., Riggio, R. E., & DiMatteo, M. R. (1980). Understanding and assessing nonverbal expressiveness: The Affective Communication Test. Journal of Personality and Social Psychology, 39, 333-351.

Gardner, H. (1983/1993). Frames of mind: The theory of multiple intelligences. (10th Anniversary Edition). New York: Basic Books.

Gibbs, N. (1995, October 2). The EQ factor. Time, p. 60-68.

Giuliano, T., & Swinkels, A. (1992, August). Development and validation of the Mood Awareness Scale. Paper presented at the annual meeting of the American Psychological Association, Washington, D.C.

Goleman, D. (1995a, September 10). Why your emotional intelligence quotient can matter more than IQ. USA Weekend, p. 4-8.

*Goleman, D. (1995b). Emotional intelligence. New York: Bantam.

Goleman, D. (1998). Working with emotional intelligence. New York: Bantam.

Goodwin, F. K., & Jamison, K. R. (1990). Manic-depressive illness. New York: Oxford University Press.

Gottman, J., & DeClaire, J. (1997). The heart of parenting: Raising an emotionally intelligent child. New York: Simon and Schuster.

Greenberg, M. T., Kushe, C. A., Cook, E. T., & Quamma, J. P. (1995). Promoting emotional competence in schoolaged children: The effects of the PATHS curriculum. Development and Psychopathology, 7, 117136.

Herrnstein, R. J., & Murray, C. (1994). The bell curve: Intelligence and class in American life. New York: Free Press.

Kramer, D., Ber, R., & Moores, M. (1989). Increasing empathy among medical students. Medical Education, 23, 168-173.

Lane, R. D., Quinlan, D. M., Schwartz, G. E., Walker, P., & Zeitlin, S. B. (1990). The levels of emotional awareness scale: A cognitive-developmental measure of emotion. Journal of Personality Assessment, 55, 124-134.

Lantieri, L., & Patti, J. (1996). Waging peace in our schools. Boston: Beacon Press.

Legree, P. J. (1995). Evidence for an oblique social intelligence factor established with a Likert-based testing procedure. Intelligence, 21, 247-266.

Lickona, T. (1991). Educating for character: How our schools can teach respect and responsibility. New York: Bantam.

Mandler, G. (1975). Mind and emotion. New York: Wiley.

Mayer, J. D. (1986). How mood influences cognition. In N. E. Sharkey (Ed.), Advances in cognitive science (pp. 290-314). Chichester, West Sussex: Ellis Horwood Limited.

Mayer, J. D., Carlsmith, K. M., & Chabot, H. F. (1998). Describing the person's external environment: Conceptualizing and measuring the life space. Journal of Research in Personality, 32, 253-296.

Mayer, J. D., Caruso, D. R., & Salovey, P. (1998). Multifactor Emotional Intelligence Test (MEIS). (Available from John D. Mayer, Department of Psychology, University of New Hampshire, Conant Hall, Durham, NH 03824.)

*Mayer, J. D., Caruso, D. R., & Salovey, P. (1999). Emotional intelligence meets standards for a traditional intelligence. Intelligence, 27, 267-298.

Mayer, J. D., & Cobb, C. D. (in press). Educational policy on emotional intelligence: Does it make sense? Review of Educational Psychology.

Mayer, J. D., DiPaolo, M. T., & Salovey, P. (1990). Perceiving affective content in ambiguous visual stimuli: A component of emotional intelligence. Journal of Personality Assessment, 54, 772-781.

Mayer, J. D., Gaschke, Y., Braverman, D. L., & Evans, T. (1992). Mood-congruent judgment is a general effect. Journal of Personality and Social Psychology, 63, 119-132.

Mayer, J. D. & Geher, G. (1996). Emotional intelligence and the identification of emotion. Intelligence, 22, 89-113.

Mayer, J. D., & Hanson, E. (1995). Mood-congruent judgment over time. Personality and Social Psychology Bulletin, 21, 237-244.

*Mayer, J. D. & Salovey, P. (1997). What is emotional intelligence? In P. Salovey & D. Sluyter (Eds)., Emotional development and emotional intelligence: Implications for educators (pp. 3-31). New York: Basic Books.

*Mayer, J. D., Salovey, P., & Caruso, D. (2000). Models of emotional intelligence. In R. J. Sternberg (Ed.), The handbook of intelligence (2nd edition, pp. 396-420). New York: Cambridge University Press.

*Mayer, J. D., Salovey, P., & Caruso, D. (in press). Emotional intelligence as Zeitgeist, as personality, and as a mental ability. In R. Bar-On & J. D. A. Parker (Eds.), The handbook of emotional intelligence. New York: Jossey-Bass.

Mayer, J. D., Salovey, P., & Caruso, D. (in preparation). Mayer, Salovey, and Caruso Emotional Intelligence Test (MSCEIT). Toronto, ON: Multi-Health Systems, Inc.

Miketta, G., Gottschling, C., Wagner-Roos, L., & Gibbs, N. (1995, October 9). Die neue Erfolgsformel: EQ. Focus, p. 194-202.

Mowrer, O. H. (1960). Learning theory and behavior. New York: Wiley.

Ortony, A., Clore, G. L., & Collins, A. (1988). The cognitive structure of emotions. Cambridge: Cambridge University Press.

Palfai, T. P., & Salovey, P. (1993). The influence of depressed and elated mood on deductive and inductive reasoning. Imagination, Cognition, and Personality, 13, 57-71.

Payne, W. L. (1983/1986). A study of emotion: Developing emotional intelligence; self-integration; relating to fear, pain and desire. Dissertation Abstracts International, 47, p. 203A. (University Microfilms No. AAC 8605928). [Doctoral Dissertation at the Union Graduate School, Cincinnati, OH. Original dissertation work submitted and accepted, May, 1983].

Pennebaker, J. W. (1989). Confession, inhibition, and disease. In L. Berkowitz (Ed.), Advances in experimental social psychology (Vol. 22, pp. 211-244). New York: Academic Press.

Pennebaker, J. W. (1993). Putting stress into words: Health, linguistic, and therapeutic implications. Behavior Research and Therapy, 31, 539-548.

Pennebaker, J. W. (1997). Writing about emotional experiences as a therapeutic process. Psychological Science, 9, 162-166.

Rice, C.L. (1999). A quantitative study of emotional intelligence and its impact on team performance. Unpublished master's thesis, Pepperdine University, Los Angeles, CA.

Rosenthal, R., Hall, J. A., DiMatteo, M. R., Rogers, P., & Archer, D. (1979). Sensitivity to nonverbal communication: A profile approach to the measurement of individual differences. Baltimore: Johns Hopkins University Press.

Rubin, M. M. (1999). Emotional intelligence and its role in mitigating aggression: A correlational study of the relationship between emotional intelligence and aggression in urban adolescents. Unpublished manuscript, Immaculata College, Immaculata, PA.

Ryback, D. (1998). Putting emotional intelligence to work: Successful leadership is more than IQ. Boston: Butterworth-Heinemann.

Saarni, C. (1990). Emotional competence: How emotions and relationships become integrated. In R. A. Thompson (Ed.), Socioemotional development: Nebraska symposium on motivation. (Vol. 36, pp. 115-182). Lincoln, NE: University of Nebraska Press.

*Saarni, C. (1999). Developing emotional competence. New York: Guilford.

Salerno, J. G. (1996). Emotional quotient (EQ): Are you ready for it? Oakbank, Australia: Noble House of Australia.

*Salovey, P., Bedell, B., Detweiler, J. B., & Mayer, J. D. (1999). Coping intelligently: Emotional intelligence and the coping process. In C. R. Snyder (Ed.), Coping: The psychology of what works (pp. 141-164). New York: Oxford University Press.

*Salovey, P., Bedell, B. T., Detweiler, J. B., & Mayer, J. D. (2000). Current directions in emotional intelligence research. In M. Lewis & J. M. Haviland-Jones (Eds.), Handbook of emotions (2nd edition, pp. 504-520). New York: Guilford Press.

Salovey, P., & Birnbaum, D. (1989). The influence of mood on health-relevant cognitions. Journal of Personality and Social Psychology, 57, 539-551.

*Salovey, P., & Mayer, J. D. (1990). Emotional intelligence. Imagination, Cognition, and Personality, 9, 185-211.

Salovey, P., Mayer, J.D., Goldman, S.L., Turvey, C., & Palfai, T.P. (1995). Emotional attention, clarity, and repair: Exploring emotional intelligence using the Trait Meta-Mood Scale. In J. W. Pennebaker (Ed.), Emotion, disclosure, and health (pp. 125-154). Washington, D.C.: American Psychological Association.

Salovey, P., & Rodin, J. (1986). Differentiation of social-comparison jealousy and romantic jealousy. Journal of Personality and Social Psychology, 50, 1100-1112.

Salovey, P., & Rodin, J. (1989). Envy and jealousy in close relationships. Review of Personality and Social Psychology, 10, 221-246.

Salovey, P., & Sluyter, D. (Eds). (1997). Emotional development and emotional intelligence: Implications for educators. New York: Basic Books.

*Salovey, P., Woolery, A., & Mayer, J. D. (in press). Emotional intelligence: Conceptualization and measurement. In G. Fletcher & M. Clark (Eds.). The Blackwell handbook of social psychology. London: Blackwell.

Shriver, T. P., Schwab-Stone, M., & DeFalco, K. (1999). Why SEL is the better way: The New Haven Social Development Program. In J. Cohen (Ed.), Educating minds and hearts: Social emotional learning and the passage into adolescence (pp. 43-60). New York: Teachers College Press.

Schilling, D. (1996). Fifty activities for teaching emotional intelligence: Level I: Elementary. Torrance, CA: Innerchoice Publishing.

Schutte, N. S., Malouff, J. M., Hall, L. E., Haggerty, D. J., Copper, J. T., Golden, C. J., & Dornheim, L. (1998). Development and validation of a measure of emotional intelligence. Personality and Individual Differences, 25, 167-177.

*Schwarz, N. (1990). Feelings as information: Informational and motivational functions of affective states. In E. T. Higgins & E. M. Sorrentino (Eds.), Handbook of motivation and cognition (Vol. 2, pp. 527-561). New York: Guilford Press.

Segal, J. (1997). Raising your emotional intelligence: A practical guide. New York: Holt.

Shapiro, L. E. (1997). How to raise a child with a high EQ: A parents' guide to emotional intelligence. New York: HarperCollins.

The Positive Psychology of Emotional Intelligence

Simon, H. A. (1982). Comments. In M. S. Clark & S. T. Fiske (Eds.), Affect and cognition (pp. 333-342). Hillsdale, NJ: Erlbaum.

Singer, J. A., & Salovey, P. (1988). Mood and memory: Evaluating the Network Theory of Affect. Clinical Psychology Review, 8, 211-251.

Simmons, S., & Simmons, J. C. (1997). Measuring emotional intelligence. Arlington, TX: Summit Publishing Group.

Steiner, C., & Perry, P. (1997). Achieving emotional literacy: A personal program to increase your emotional intelligence. New York: Avon.

Sternberg, R. J. (1985). The triarchic mind: A new theory of human intelligence. New York: Penguin.

Stone-McCown, K., Jensen, A. L., Freedman, J. M., & Rideout, M. C. (1998). Self-science: The emotional intelligence curriculum (2nd edition). San Mateo, CA: Six Seconds.

Swinkels, A., & Giuliano, T. A. (1995). The measurement and conceptualization of mood awareness: Monitoring and labeling one's mood states. Personality and Social Psychology Bulletin, 21, 934-939.

Thayer, R. E., Newman, J. R., & McClain, T. M. (1994). Self-regulation of mood: Strategies for changing a bad mood, raising energy, and reducing tension. Journal of Personality and Social Psychology, 67, 910-925.

Thomas, B. (1995, December 13). A la recherche du QE perdu. Le Canard Enchaîné, p. 5.

Tomkins, S. S. (1962). Affect, imagery, and consciousness (Vol. 1: The positive affects). New York: Springer.

Trinidad, D. R., & Johnson, C.A. (1999). Unpublished data, University of Southern California. Personal communication, 2 November 1999.

Wang, A. Y., Tett, R. P., Fisher, R., Griebler, J. G., & Martinez, A.M. (1997). Testing a model of emotional intelligence. Manuscript in preparation, University of Central Florida.

Weisinger, H. (1998). Emotional intelligence at work: The untapped edge for success. San Francisco: Jossey-Bass.

Weissberg, R. P., Shriver, T. P., Bose, S., & DeFalco, K. (1997). Creating a district wide social development project. Educational Leadership, 54, 37-39.

The Positive Psychology of Emotional Intelligence

Reprinted with permission of Cambridge University Press.
Mayer, J.D., Salovey, P., & Caruso, D. (2000). *Models of emotional intelligence.* In R.J. Sternberg (Ed.), The handbook of intelligence (pp. 396-420). New York: Cambridge University Press.

Models of Emotional Intelligence

John D. Mayer, University of New Hampshire
Peter Salovey, Yale University
David Caruso, Work-Life Strategies

Acknowledgements

The authors wish to acknowledge the others who assisted us with this chapter. Tamara L. Bress, and Tracey A. Martin conducted library research that greatly enriched this review. Tracey A. Martin and Sherry Palmer critiqued and helped clarify the figures. Sherry Palmer generated the computer figures. We are grateful for all their help.

Preparation of this manuscript was supported in part by a University of New Hampshire Faculty Scholar Award to John D. Mayer and by the grants SBR-9058020 from NSF, PBR-84B from ACS, and R01-CA68427 and P01-MH/DA56826 from NIH to Peter Salovey.

Competing Models of Emotional Intelligence

Studies of emotional intelligence initially appeared in academic articles beginning in the early 1990's.[1] By mid decade, the concept had attracted considerable popular attention and powerful claims were made concerning its importance for predicting success. Emotional intelligence is the set of abilities that account for how people's emotional reports vary in their accuracy and how the more accurate understanding of emotion leads to better problem solving in an individual's emotional life. More formally, we define emotional intelligence as the ability to perceive and express emotion, assimilate emotion in thought, understand and reason with emotion, and regulate emotion in the self and others (Mayer & Salovey, 1997). As of now, the academic concept has been developed over several theoretical articles (e.g., Mayer & Salovey, 1997; Salovey & Mayer, 1990), and is based on a growing body of relevant research (e.g., Averill & Nunley, 1992; Buck, 1984; Lane, Sechrest, Reidel, et al., 1996; Mayer, DiPaolo, & Salovey, 1990; Mayer & Geher, 1996; Mayer & Stevens, 1994; Rosenthal, Hall, DiMatteo, Rogers, & Archer, 1979; Salovey, Mayer, Goldman, Turvey, & Palfai, 1995; see also, Salovey & Sluyter, 1997).

Shortly after the academic work had begun, a popular book on the subject appeared (Goleman, 1995a). The book covered much of the literature reviewed in the aforementioned articles, as well as considerable additional research on emotions and the brain, emotions and social behavior, and school-based programs designed to help children develop emotional and social skills. The book emphasized earlier comments we had made concerning how people with emotional intelligence might be more socially effective than others in certain respects (Salovey & Mayer, 1990). Particularly strong claims were made as to emotional intelligence's contribution to the individual and society (Goleman, 1995a, p. xii). This combination of science and human potential attracted extensive media coverage, culminating, perhaps, when TIME magazine asked the question "What's your EQ?," on its cover, and stated: "It's not your IQ. It's not even a number. But emotional intelligence may be the best predictor of success in life, redefining what it means to be smart." (TIME, 1995)

In short order, the general notion of emotional intelligence became widely known, appearing in many magazine and newspaper articles (e.g., Bennetts, 1996; Henig, 1996; Peterson, 1997), popular books (e.g., Cooper & Sawaf, 1997; Gottman, 1997; Salerno, 1996; Segal, 1997; Shapiro, 1997; Simmons & Simmons, 1997; Steiner & Perry, 1997; Weisinger, 1997), and even two popular comic strips, Dilbert (Adams, 1997) and Zippy the Pinhead (Griffith, 1996).[2]

The first portion of this chapter will review several competing concepts of emotional intelligence. Some attention will be paid to what is meant by the terms "emotion," "intelligence," and "emotional intelligence." A distinction will be drawn between models of emotional intelligence that focus on mental abilities and those that mix together mental abilities with personality attributes such as persistence, zeal and optimism. Measures of emotional intelligence will be examined in the chapter's second section. Research work increasingly supports the existence of a mental-ability emotional intelligence that is somewhat distinct from standard, analytical intelligence. Research work on mixed models of emotional intelligence are more preliminary to-date, but show some progress. In the Discussion we will address in greater detail the claims about what emotional intelligence might predict, and discuss the opportunities, real and imagined, that exist more generally in the fields of intelligence and personality, for studying an individual's success.

Theoretical Considerations Regarding Emotional Intelligence

The Terms "Emotion" and "Intelligence"

Theories should be internally consistent, make meaningful use of technical language, and make important predictions. One issue in studying emotional intelligence is that some theories pertain to emotions and intelligence, whereas others seem far broader. Therefore, it is worth examining the constituent terms, emotion, intelligence, and their combination at the outset.

Conceptions of Emotion

Emotions are recognized as one of three or four fundamental classes of mental operations These classes include motivation, emotion, cognition, and, (less frequently) consciousness (Bain, 1855/1977; Izard, 1993; MacLean, 1973; Mayer, 1995a; 1995b; Plutchik, 1984; Tomkins, 1962; see Hilgard, 1980; Mayer, Chabot, & Carlsmith, 1997, for reviews). Among the triad of motivation, emotion, and cognition, basic motivations arise in response to internal bodily states and include drives such as hunger, thirst, need for social contact, and sexual desires. Motivations are responsible for directing the organism to carry out simple acts so as to satisfy survival and reproductive needs. In their basic form, motivations follow a relatively determined time course (e.g., thirst rises until quenched), and are typically satisfied in a specific fashion (e.g., thirst is satisfied by drinking).

Emotions form the second class of this triad. Emotions appear to have evolved across mammalian species so as to signal and respond to changes in relationships between the individual and the environment (including one's imagined place within it). For example, anger arises in response to threat or injustice; fear arises in response to danger. Emotions follow no rigid time course but instead respond to external changes in relationships (or internal perceptions of them). Moreover, each emotion organizes several basic behavioral responses to the relationship; for example, fear organizes fighting or fleeing. Emotions are therefore more flexible than motivations, though not quite so flexible as cognition.

Cognition, the third member of the triad, allows the organism to learn from the environment and to solve problems in novel situations. This is often in service to satisfying motives or keeping emotions positive. Cognition includes learning, memory, and problem solving. It is ongoing, and involves flexible, intentional information processing based on learning and memory (see Mayer, et al., 1997, for a review of these concepts). These three basic classes of personality components are illustrated in the lower portion of Figure 1.

The next level up in Figure 1 depicts the interaction between motivation and emotion (on the left) and emotion and cognition (on the right). A great deal of research addresses both how motivations interact with emotions, and how emotions interact with cognition. For example, motives interact with emotion when frustrated needs lead to increased anger and aggression. And emotion interacts with cognition when good moods lead a person to think positively. One would expect that the interaction of emotion and cognition would also give rise to emotional intelligence.

Although it makes sense to distinguish among basic motivation, emotion, and cognition, and their interactions, as the three areas are integrated in more complex personality functioning, we no longer speak of emotional, motivational, or cognitive elements separately. Rather, the focus turns to more general personality or social processes, which blend the three. For example, the self-concept involves a blended-together representation of oneself involving all three areas or modes of processing. The top of Figure 1 includes components that focus on these more general intra- and inter-personal qualities.

The term "emotional intelligence," then, implies something having to do with the intersection of emotion and cognition. From our perspective, evaluating theories of and related to emotional intelligence requires an assessment of the degree to which the theory pertains to this intersection.

Figure 1

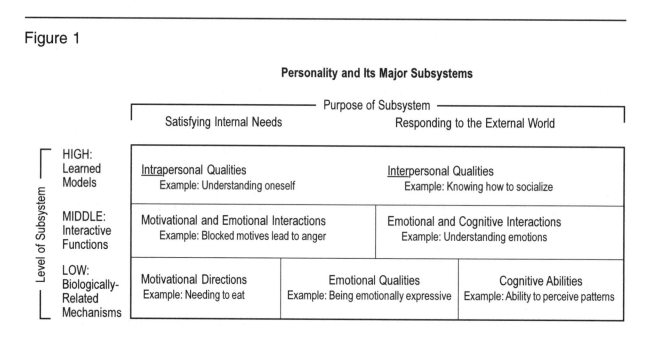

Personality and Its Major Subsystems

Figure 1. *An Overview of Personality and Its Major Subsystems.* A representation of personality components primarily according to lower versus higher-levels of processing (adapted from Mayer, 1995b; in press). Components at lower levels are generally divisible into motivational, emotional, and cognitive groups. For example, an urge to eat is motivational, whereas a feeling of generalized fear is emotional. Mid-level components, such as emotional intelligence, involve the interaction between lower level groups, such as the interactions between internal emotional feelings and cognitive understanding. High level components, such as self-esteem, are representations of the personal and social worlds that synthesize the lower-levels of processing in more complex, integrated fashions.

Models of Emotional Intelligence

Conceptions of Intelligence

An intelligence researcher was invited mistakenly to a conference on military intelligence by someone who noticed he was an expert on intelligence — but did not notice the kinds of intelligence he studied.[33] The problem of intelligence's meaning is an old one in the field and should not discourage us. Spearman (1927, p. 24) noted:

> Gardner (1997) uses this true story about himself to make the point that *intelligence* is used differently by different people. Although we acknowledge different meanings of the term, we also believe intelligence possesses a core meaning in the sciences. Artificial intelligence, human intelligence, even Offices of Military Intelligence, all imply gathering information, learning about that information, and reasoning with it — they all imply mental ability associated with the cognitive operations. The mental ability model was represented in pure form by Terman (1921, p. 128), who stated that, "An individual is intelligent in proportion as he is able to carry on abstract thinking." In fact, symposia on intelligence over the years repeatedly conclude that the first hallmark of intelligence is high-level mental ability such as abstract reasoning (Sternberg, 1997).

Intelligence, conceptualized as abstract thinking, has often been demonstrated to predict one or another type of success, particularly academic success. But although it is a potent predictor, it is far from a perfect one, leaving the vast amount of variance unexplained. As Wechsler (1940, p. 444) put it, "individuals with identical IQs may differ very markedly in regard to their effective ability to cope with the environment." One way to regard this limitation is to view human life as naturally complex and subject both to chance events and complicated interactions. A second approach is to search for better ways to assess intelligence (e.g., Sternberg, 1997). A third approach is to attribute the difference to a combination of nonintellective factors, such as personality traits. These approaches are all complementary and have all been used with different degrees of effectiveness in enhancing psychological predictions of positive outcomes.

A fourth alternative to dealing with IQ's limited predictive ability is to redefine intelligence itself as a combination of mental ability and personality traits. Thus, Wechsler (1943, p. 103) wondered, "whether non-intellective, that is, affective and conative [motivational] abilities are admissible as factors in general intelligence." In his next sentence, he concluded they were. A few sentences thereafter, however, he qualifies the notion: they predict intelligent *behavior* (as opposed to being a part of intelligence). Wechsler remained straddling the fence, as it were. On the one hand, he at times defined intelligence as involving "...the aggregate or global capacity of the individual to act purposefully, to think rationally and to *deal effectively with his environment.*" (italics added; Wechsler, 1958, p. 7). On the other hand, the intelligence tests that carried his name focused on measuring mental ability.

Although most (if not all) intelligence researchers agree that traits other than intelligence predict success, many are quite vocal in their objections to considering those other characteristics *to be* intelligence. As noted above, there is a long theoretical tradition that distinguishes mental ability (i.e., cognition) from motivation and emotion. Labeling non-intellectual characteristics intelligence potentially obscures their meaning (cf., Salovey & Mayer, 1994; Sternberg, 1997). Goodness in human relationships, athletic ability (i.e., kinesthetic ability), and certain talents in music, dance, and painting, have all been labeled intelligence at one time or another. Scarr (1989, p. 78) cautions, however, that, "[t]o call them intelligence does not do justice either to theories of intelligence or to the personality traits and special talents that lie beyond the consensual definition of intelligence." Empirical findings illustrate repeatedly that mental abilities are generally unrelated to (i.e., uncorrelated with) personality traits in any simple, strong fashion (although some modest and more complex connections are found; see, for example, Mayer, Caruso, Zigler, & Dreyden, 1989; Sternberg & Ruzgis, 1994).

Some models of emotional intelligence covered in this chapter do define emotional intelligence as a mixture of abilities and personality dispositions and traits. The motivation for this appears to be the desire to label as a single entity what appear to be, in fact, a diverse group of things that predict success. Although we realize we cannot prevent such usage, it presents considerable difficulty for us. For example, does it make sense to label a trait such as optimism an "intelligence" because it predicts success (like intelligence)? We wonder whether this makes any more sense than labeling sleepiness an "alcoholic beverage" because, like alcohol, it leads to traffic accidents. Despite such reservations, we will cover all noteworthy models that use the term emotional intelligence. We will distinguish, however, between *ability models* of emotional intelligence, which focus on the interplay of emotion and intelligence as traditionally defined, and *mixed models*, which describe a compound conception of intelligence that includes mental abilities, dispositions, and traits.

Competing Models Labeled "Emotional Intelligence"

Ability Models of Emotional Intelligence

Both in Western history and in psychology, emotions and reasoning sometimes have been viewed in opposition to one another (e.g., Schaffer, Gilmer, & Schoen, 1940; Publilius Syrus, 100 B.C.E./1961; Woodworth, 1940; Young, 1936). The contemporary view that emotions convey information about relationships, however, suggests that emotions and intelligence can work hand in hand. Emotions reflect relationships between a person and a friend, a family, the situation, a society, or more internally, between a person and a reflection or memory. For example, joy might indicate one's identification with a friend's success; sadness might indicate disappointment with one's self. Emotional intelligence refers in part to an ability to recognize the meanings of such emotional patterns and to reason and problem solve on the basis of them (Mayer & Salovey, 1997; Salovey & Mayer, 1990).

The domain of emotional intelligence describes a number of discrete emotional abilities. As we now view it,[4] these emotional abilities can be divided into four classes or branches, as shown in Table 1, Column 1. (The specific skills listed in Column 1 are meant to be representative; there are other skills that could be included on each branch as well as the ones shown). The most basic skills involve the perception and appraisal of emotion. For example, early on, the infant learns about facial expressions of emotion. The infant watches its cries of distress, or joy, mirrored in the parent's face, as the parent empathically reflects those feelings. As the child grows, he or she discriminates more finely among genuine versus merely polite smiles and other gradations of expression. Also importantly, people generalize emotional experience to objects, interpreting the expansiveness of a dining hall, or the stoicism of a Shaker chair (cf., Arnheim, 1974).

The second set of skills involve assimilating basic emotional experiences into mental life, including weighing emotions against one another and against other sensations and thoughts, and allowing emotions to direct attention. For example, we might hold an emotional state in consciousness so as to compare it to a similar sensation in sound, color, or taste.

The third level involves understanding and reasoning about emotions. The experience of specific emotions — happiness, anger, fear, and the like — is rule-governed. Anger generally rises when justice is denied; fear often changes to relief; dejection may separate us from others. Sadness and anger move according to their own characteristic rules, just as the knight and bishop on a chessboard move in different ways. Consider a woman who is extremely angry and an hour later ashamed. It is likely that only certain events might have intervened. For example, she might have expressed her anger inappropriately, or discovered she falsely believed that a friend betrayed her. Emotional intelligence involves the ability to recognize the emotions, to know how they unfold, and to reason about them accordingly.

The fourth, highest level, of emotional intelligence involves the management and regulation of emotion in oneself and others, such as knowing how to calm down after feeling angry or being able to alleviate the anxiety of another person. Tasks defining these four levels are described in greater detail in the section concerning scale development below.

The mental ability model of emotional intelligence makes predictions about the internal structure of the intelligence, and also its implications for a person's life. The theory predicts that emotional intelligence is, in fact, an intelligence like other intelligences in that it will meet three empirical criteria. First, mental problems have right or wrong answers, as assessed by the convergence of alternative scoring methods. Second, the measured skills correlate with other measures of mental ability (because mental abilities tend to intercorrelate), as well as with self-reported empathy (for more complex reasons; see Mayer, DiPaolo, & Salovey, 1990). Third, the absolute ability level rises with age.

The model further predicts that emotionally intelligent individuals are more likely to: (a) have grown up in biosocially adaptive households (i.e., have had emotionally sensitive parenting), (b) be non-defensive, (c) be able to reframe emotions effectively (i.e., be realistically optimistic and appreciative), (d) choose good emotional role models, (e) be able to communicate and discuss feelings, and (f) develop expert knowledge in a particular emotional area such as aesthetics, moral or ethical feeling, social problem-solving, leadership, or spiritual feeling (Mayer & Salovey, 1995).

Table 1: Three Competing Models, all Labeled "Emotional Intelligence"

Mayer & Salovey (1997)	Bar-On (1997)	Goleman (1995a)
Overall Definition	Overall Definition	Overall Definition(s)
"Emotional intelligence is the set of abilities that account for how people's emotional perception and understanding vary in their accuracy. More formally, we define emotional intelligence as the ability to perceive and express emotion, assimilate emotion in thought, understand and reason with emotion, and regulate emotion in the self and others (after Mayer & Salovey, 1997)."	"Emotional intelligence is...an array of noncognitive capabilities, competencies, and skills that influence one's ability to succeed in coping with environmental demands and pressures." (Bar-On, 1997, p. 14).	"The abilities called here *emotional intelligence*, which include self-control, zeal and persistence, and the ability to motivate oneself." (Goleman, 1995a, p. xii). [...and...] "There is an old-fashioned word for the body of skills that emotional intelligence represents: *character*." (Goleman, 1995a, p. 28).
Major Areas of Skills and Specific Examples	Major Areas of Skills and Specific Skills	Major Areas of Skills and Specific Examples
Perception and Expression of Emotion *identifying and expressing emotions in one's physical states, feelings, and thoughts. *identifying and expressing emotions in other people, artwork, language, etc. *Assimilating Emotion in Thought* *Emotions prioritize thinking in productive ways. *Emotions generated as aids to judgment and memory *Understanding and Analyzing Emotion* *Ability to label emotions, including complex emotions and simultaneous feelings *Ability to understand relationships associated with shifts of emotion. *Reflective Regulation of Emotion* *Ability to stay open to feelings *Ability to reflectively monitor and regulate emotions to promote emotional and intellectual growth. (after Mayer & Salovey, 1997, p. 11)	*Intrapersonal Skills:* *Emotional self-awareness, *Assertiveness, *Self-Regard, *Self-Actualization, *Independence *Interpersonal Skills:* *Interpersonal relationships *Social responsibility *Empathy *Adapatability Scales:* *Problem Solving, *Reality Testing, *Flexibility *Stress-Management Scales:* *Stress Tolerance, *Impulse, *Control *General Mood:* *Happiness, *Optimism	*Knowing One's Emotions* *recognizing a feeling *as it happens* *monitoring feelings from moment to moment. *Managing Emotions* *handling feelings so they are appropriate *ability to soothe oneself *ability to shake off rampant anxiety, gloom, or irritability *Motivating Oneself* *marshalling emotions in the service of a goal *delaying gratification and stifling impulsiveness *being able to get into the "flow" state *Recognizing Emotions in Others* *empathic awareness *attunement to what others need or want *Handling Relationships* *skill in managing emotions in others *interacting smoothly with others
Model Type	Model Type	Model Type
Ability	*Mixed*	*Mixed*

Mixed Models of Emotional Intelligence

Mixed models of emotional intelligence are substantially different than the mental ability models. In one sense, both kinds of models were proposed in the first academic articles on emotional intelligence (e.g., Mayer, DiPaolo, & Salovey, 1990; Salovey & Mayer, 1990). Although these articles set out a mental ability conception of emotional intelligence, they also freely described personality characteristics that might accompany such intelligence. Thus, emotional intelligence was said to distinguish those who are "genuine and warm...[from those who] appear oblivious and boorish." Emotionally intelligent individuals were also said to "generate a larger number of future plans...and [better]...take advantage of future opportunities (p. 199)...., exhibit "...persistence at challenging tasks..."" (p. 200); and have "positive attitudes toward life...that lead to better outcomes and greater rewards for themselves and others...(Salovey & Mayer, 1990, pp. 199-200)."

Almost immediately after these initial articles on emotional intelligence appeared, we recognized that our own theoretical work would be more useful if we constrained emotional intelligence to a mental ability concept and separated it from the very important traits of warmth, outgoingness, and similarly desirable virtues. By keeping them separate, it would be possible to analyze the degree to which they independently contributed to a person's behavior and general life competence. Although traits such as warmth and persistence are important, we believe they are better addressed directly, and as distinct from emotional intelligence (Mayer & Salovey, 1993; 1997).

In contrast to honing this core conception of emotional intelligence, others expanded the meaning of emotional intelligence by explicitly mixing in non-ability traits. For example, Bar-On's (1997) model of emotional intelligence was intended to answer the question of "Why are some individuals more able to succeed in life than others?" Bar-On reviewed the psychological literature for personality characteristics that appeared related to life success, and identified five broad areas of functioning relevant to success. These are listed in Column 2 of Table 1, and include (a) intrapersonal skills, (b) interpersonal skills, (c) adaptability, (d) stress management, and (e) general mood. Each broad area is further subdivided. For example, intrapersonal skills are divided into emotional self-awareness, assertiveness, self-regard, self-actualization, and independence. Bar-On offered the following rationale for his use of the term emotional intelligence:

> *Intelligence* describes the aggregate of abilities, competencies, and skills...
> that...represent a *collection of knowledge used to cope with life effectively*.
> The adjective *emotional* is employed to emphasize that this specific type of
> intelligence differs from cognitive intelligence...(Bar-On, 1997, p. 15).

Bar-On's theoretical work combines what may possibly qualify as mental abilities (e.g., emotional self-awareness) with other characteristics that are considered separable from mental ability, such as personal independence, self-regard, and mood; this makes it a mixed model. (There is generally no consistent correlation between mood and intelligence, for example; Watson, 1930; Wessman & Ricks, 1966, p. 123).

Despite the breadth of his model, Bar-On (1997) is relatively cautious in his claims for his model of emotional intelligence. Although his model predicts success, this success is "the end-product of that which one strives to achieve and accomplish..." Moreover, his Emotional Quotient Inventory (EQ, reviewed below) relates to "the potential to succeed rather than success itself." At a broader level, he believes that EQ, along with IQ, can provide a more balanced picture of a person's general intelligence (Bar-On, 1997, p. 19).

A third view of emotional intelligence was popularized by Goleman (1995a). Goleman created a model that also was mixed, with five broad areas depicted in Column 3 of Table 1, including: (a) knowing one's emotions, (b) managing emotions, (c) motivating oneself, (d) recognizing emotions in others, and (e) handling relationships. His list of specific attributes under motivation, for example, include, marshalling emotions, delaying gratification and stifling impulsiveness, and entering flow states (Goleman, 1995a, p. 43). Goleman recognized that he was moving from emotional intelligence to something far broader. He states that "'ego resilience,'...is quite similar to [this model of] emotional intelligence" in that it includes social (and emotional) competencies (Goleman, 1995a, p. 44). He goes so far as to note that, "There is an old-fashioned word for the body of skills that emotional intelligence represents: *character*." (Goleman, 1995a, p. 285).

Goleman (1995a) makes extraordinary claims for the predictive validity of his mixed model. He states that emotional intelligence will account for success at home, at school, and at work. Among youth, he says, emotional intelligence will lead to less rudeness or aggressiveness, and more popularity, as well as improved learning (Goleman, 1995a, p. 192), and better decisions about "drugs, smoking, and sex" (Goleman, 1995a, p. 268). At work, emotional intelligence will assist people "in teamwork, in cooperation, in helping learn together how to work more effectively." (Goleman, 1995a, p. 163). More generally, emotional intelligence will confer:

> ...an advantage in any domain in life, whether in romance and intimate relationships or picking up the unspoken rules that govern success in organizational politics (Goleman, 1995a, p. 36).

Goleman notes that "At best, IQ contributes about 20% to the factors that determine life success, which leaves 80% to other factors." (Goleman, 1995a, p. 34). That 20% figure, with which we agree, is obtained (by mathematical means) from the fact that IQ correlates with various criteria at about the $r = .45$ level.[5] "...[W]hat data exist," Goleman writes of emotional intelligence, "suggest it can be as powerful, and at times more powerful, than IQ." With this statement, Goleman predicts that emotional intelligence should predict success at many life tasks at levels higher than $r = .45$. It is hard not to conclude that at least part of the popular excitement surrounding emotional intelligence is due to this very strong claim. If there were truly a single psychological entity that could predict widespread success at such levels, it would exceed any finding in a century of research in applied psychology.

Summary

There are both mental ability models and mixed models of emotional intelligence. The mental ability model focuses on emotions themselves and their interactions with thought (Mayer & Salovey, 1997; Salovey & Mayer, 1990). The mixed models treat both mental abilities and a variety of other characteristics such as motivation, states of consciousness (e.g., "flow") and social activity as a single entity (Bar-On, 1997; Goleman, 1995a). Figure 2 projects the different makeup of emotional intelligence as described by these models onto the earlier diagram of personality components. There, as in Figure 1, personality components are divided among those primarily concerned with lower level, specific processing (motivation, emotion, cognition), mid-level functioning that concerns interactions between the lower level areas, and those that represent upper-level, synthetic models of the intrapersonal self, and interpersonal social world.

In this diagram, the three models represent emotional intelligence in different ways. Both the Bar-On (1997) and Goleman (1995a) models are distributed across the

Figure 2

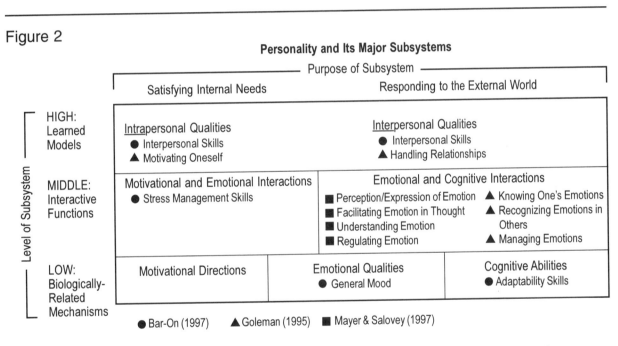

Personality and Its Major Subsystems

Figure 2. *An Overview of Personality and Its Major Subsystems with Three Models of Emotional Intelligence Embedded Within It.* Figure 2 retains the general arrangement of personality components depicted in Figure 1. Added to the picture, however, are specific personality components said (by three different theories) to be a part of emotional intelligence. Goleman's (1995) five-part model is split between both intrapersonal and interpersonal qualities (e.g., motivating oneself; handling relationships) as well as interactions between emotion and cognition (e.g., recognizing emotions in others). Bar-On's (1997) five-part model is similarly divided among intrapersonal qualities (e.g., intrapersonal skills), emotional states (e.g., general mood), and other areas. Mayer & Salovey's (1997) four-part model is located within the area of emotional-cognitive interactions (e.g., perceiving emotions; understanding emotions).

various levels. For example, Bar-On's adaptability skills (problem-solving, reality testing, and flexibility) primarily represent cognitive skills (lower right) whereas his interpersonal skills (interpersonal relationships, social responsibility, and empathy) primarily represent more synthetic interpersonal relatedness (upper right). By way of contrast, the Mayer & Salovey (1997) model fits within the emotion and cognitive interactions area. The diagram shows in yet another way that a central difference among models is that the mental ability models operate in a region defined by emotion and cognition whereas mixed models label a multitude of components as emotional intelligence.

Other-Named Concepts Related to Emotional Intelligence

The mental ability and mixed models of emotional intelligence overlap to some degree with other concepts. The ability model of emotional intelligence overlaps with several other hypothesized intelligences. Mixed models, because of their breadth, overlap with dozens of other concepts.

<u>Concepts Primarily Related to the Mental Ability Model of Emotional Intelligence</u>
Some concepts related to the mental ability emotional intelligence focus on one or another of its specific skills such as non-verbal perception (e.g., Buck, 1984; Rosenthal, et al., 1979) or empathic accuracy (Ickes, 1997). Other related concepts appear to be similar or complementary to emotional intelligence. For example, Saarni's emotional competence (Saarni, 1990; 1997; in press), is defined as the demonstration of capacity and skills in emotion-eliciting social transactions (e.g., Saarni, 1997, p. 38). Emotional creativity (Averill & Nunley, 1992) emphasizes the divergent, unexpected, creative elements in thinking about feelings. Finally, there are intelligences that are defined in such a way as to partially overlap emotional intelligence. These include personal intelligence (Gardner, 1993), social intelligence (Cantor & Kihlstrom, 1987; Sternberg & Smith, 1985; Thorndike & Stein, 1937), and even Jung's feeling function (Jung, 1921/1971, p. 354).

Of the partly overlapping intelligences, only social intelligence has been operationalized satisfactorily as a mental ability (e.g., Legree, 1995; Sternberg & Smith, 1985; Wong, Day, Maxwell, & Meara, 1995). Others among the forgoing concepts have been operationalized in more limited fashion, such as emotional creativity (Averill & Nunley, 1992). Still other intelligences, such as Gardner's (1993) personal intelligences or Jung's (1921, p. 354) feeling function have been left virtually unoperationalized (as mental abilities; Sternberg, 1994).

Given the partial theoretical overlap among some of these concepts, there is likely to be some empirical overlap among them as well. The key to selecting which of these intelligences is "best" is to some degree a matter of personal theoretical preference. Ultimately, each may do the job of describing abilities that presently are omitted from intelligence tests. Emotional intelligence (as a mental ability) is our preferred theory because we believe it is theoretically defined as more distinct from traditional (i.e., verbal and performance) intelligences than some of these alternatives.

For example, compared to social intelligence, emotional intelligence is broader in including internal, private emotions that are important for personal (as opposed to social) growth. On the other hand, emotional intelligence is also more focused than social intelligence in pertaining primarily to the emotional (as opposed to the social or political) aspects of problems. This makes it distinct from the social knowledge questions already found in many of today's tests of verbal intelligence (e.g., "Who was President Kennedy?"), although admittedly, social intelligence shows good psychometric distinctness from traditional intelligence measures (e.g., Sternberg & Smith, 1985). This increased theoretical breadth and focus of emotional intelligence means that it may make a very good counterpart to traditional measurement scales when compared to the alternatives.

<u>Concepts Related to the Mixed Models of Emotional Intelligence</u>

The family of overlapping concepts for the mixed models of emotional intelligence is larger than that of the mental ability model. Like the mental ability model, the mixed models are a member of a family of concepts (e.g., Davies, Stankov, & Roberts, 1998; Feist, 1996; Goleman, 1995a). There are, first of all, often vast literatures on each of the parts of mixed models of emotional intelligence. These include literatures on achievement motivation (McClelland, Atkinson, Clark, & Lowell, 1953), alexithymia (Bagby, Parker, & Taylor, 1994), emotional-responsiveness empathy (Mehrabian & Epstein, 1972), openness (Costa & McCrae, 1985), optimism (Scheier & Carver, 1985), pleasant-unpleasant affectivity (Green, Goldman, & Salovey, 1993; Mayer & Gaschke, 1988; Russell, 1979), practical intelligence (Sternberg & Caruso, 1985; Sternberg, Wagner, Williams, & Horvath, 1995; Wagner & Sternberg, 1985), self-esteem (e.g., Blascovich & Tomaka, 1991), and subjective well-being (Andrews & Robinson, 1991).

Other concepts partially overlap the mixed models of emotional intelligence, because, like them, they are composites of many characteristics thought to lead to life success. Recall that Goleman (1995a) acknowledges that his model is little different than Block and Block's (1980) model of ego-strength. Other related concepts include general intelligence itself, and also practical and creative intelligence (e.g., Sternberg, 1997; Sternberg & Caruso, 1985; Sternberg & Lubart; 1995a; 1995b; Wagner & Sternberg, 1985), constructive thinking (Epstein & Meier, 1989), the aforementioned ego strength (Block & Block, 1980), the motivation toward social desirability, (Paulhus, 1991) and social insight (Chapin, 1967). Moreover, the individual aspects of the mixed models overlap considerably with the specific areas of Big Five personality dimensions (e.g., McCrae & Costa, 1985), including such Big Five subscales as warmth, assertiveness, trust, self-discipline, and others. (This overlap tells us a great deal about the mixed models' potential for predicting success, which will be considered in the Discussion). It will be desirable in the future for the mixed model theorists to compare and distinguish their own versions of emotional intelligence from these related concepts.

The Measurement of Emotional Intelligence

Mental ability models of emotional intelligence, as well as mixed models, have prompted the construction of instruments to measure emotional intelligence. These measures will be examined in this section of the chapter. Mental ability models of emotional intelligence are most directly assessed by ability measures, but self-reported ability provides an alternative approach. Ability measures have the advantage of representing an individual's performance level on a task. By contrast, self-report measures are filtered through a person's self-concept and impression management motives. For example, a bright student with low self-esteem might believe she isn't very smart, and a not-so-bright student who needs to impress others might claim she is smarter than she is. Mental ability measures are typically both reliable and valid, and often intercorrelate at the $r = .80$ level or better. Self-report measures seem far less valid, correlating rather poorly with actual performance levels. For example, in one study, people's scores on a self-report scale of problem solving skills (e.g., "When trying to solve a problem, I look at each possibility and then decide on the best way") correlated only $r = .15$ with an actual test of mental ability (Bar-On, 1997, p. 138).[6] We begin by examining the ability measures of emotional intelligence, move to the self-report, and then look at the relation between the two.

Emotional Intelligence as a Mental Ability Measured with Ability Measures
Emotional Intelligence Measurement before Emotional Intelligence Theory

Recall that emotional intelligence, as we define it, consists of four broad areas of specific tasks: emotional perception, assimilation, understanding, and management. As of 1990, there were a number of studies describing measures of emotional (or, more accurately, nonverbal) perception but fewer or no ability-task studies related to the other areas. Concerning such emotional perception tests, the Affect Sensitivity Test presented videotaped interactions between pairs of individuals; respondents indicated the emotions and thoughts that targets are expressing (Campbell, Kagan, & Krathwohl, 1971; Kagan, 1978). Other tests existed as well (e.g., the Profile of Nonverbal Sensitivity; PONS; Rosenthal et al., 1979; the CARAT; Buck, 1976).

Three methods were commonly employed to assess the participants' responses to these tests. The first, consensus method, compared a participant's answers to the remainder of the group (or to a prior criterion sample), and individuals received credit according to their agreement with the group consensus. The second, expert method, compared participants' answers to an expert criterion (e.g., Ekman's Facial Coding System). The third criterion, target method, compared participants' answers to that of the target they were judging. For example, members of a couple might be asked to identify what their partners reported feeling during videotaped conversation (Ickes, Stinson, Bissonette, & Garcia, 1990); other participants have been asked to predict what an actor was asked to portray (Buck, Miller, & Caul, 1974).

These early scales provided little evidence for an actual emotional intelligence. The scales themselves seemed to be unrelated to one another; the tests intercorrelated only slightly, leading one reviewer to conclude that either the early tests were sensitive to different aspects of nonverbal receiving ability, or, non-verbal receiving ability was not a unidimensional construct. (Buck, 1984, pp. 277, 282-283). Some interesting patterns emerged, however, including the existence of low correlations among socioemotional perception, intelligence scales, and self-reports of empathy, as well as the finding that women sometimes performed slightly better than men.

Early Research Explicitly Directed Toward Emotional Intelligence

In our initial work on measuring aspects of emotional intelligence, we suggested that emotional perception might be similar across a variety of stimuli that had been studied before in isolation (faces, abstract designs, and colors), and that prior tests may have masked a general emotion perception factor by using overly simplistic response scales (Mayer, DiPaolo, & Salovey, 1990). For example, on the PONS, participants viewed a brief videotape and then were asked only one or two questions such as how pleasant or unpleasant the video character was. We reasoned that scales would be more reliable if the response alternatives were increased in number and specificity. For example, given a face, how angry is it?...sad?...happy? and so on. One hundred thirty-nine participants judged the specific emotional content of 18 stimuli including faces, abstract designs, and colors. Consensual accuracy in identifying emotion was reliable, and there was a single factor of emotional perception common to all those stimuli.

Davies, Stankov, and Roberts (1998, Study 1) replicated and extended these findings. They correlated four emotion perception measures: faces, colors, music, and sound intervals, and found they were unifactorial. In their study, emotional perception showed nonsignificant positive correlations with measures of analytical intelligence (crystalized intelligence, $r = .05$, fluid intelligence, $r = .15$), as measured by Cattell's matrices and letter cancellation tasks (Roberts, Beh, Spilsbury, & Stankov, 1991). Davies et al., also expressed serious reservation about the reliability of these individual performance tasks. This criticism has been addressed in more recent measures, as will be seen below.

The early 1990's also saw work related to the higher level skills of emotional intelligence: understanding emotions and managing them. For example, Mayer and Geher (1996) studied emotional perception in complex story passages. Preliminary to the main study, eight targets each described their thoughts in a brief passage. For example, one target wrote:

> My best friend's father died this weekend. He had diabetes for a long time, and as he got older his health grew worse and worse. I went to his funeral on Monday. Many of my friends from high school were also there because we all wanted to be there for our friend and because we all knew and liked her father. It made me realize how lucky I am to have younger, healthy parents when I saw my friend standing there crying. Just watching her huge family come pouring into the synagogue also made me sad. (Mayer & Geher, 1996, p.98).

Participants in the main study were asked to identify the targets' emotions or emotion-related thoughts in the passage by making a series of forced choices between two alternatives. (e.g. be by myself — kick something; fearful — apart from others.) Skill at this task, measured by agreement with the group consensus, correlated significantly with self-reported SAT scores (a proxy measure of verbal intelligence), and with self-reports of trait empathy. Target agreement showed similar but weaker results. A closely related task was developed by Lane et al. (1996). In that study, participants read a sentence (e.g., "I want to hit someone") and were asked to match it to one of seven emotion words (e.g., happiness, sadness, fear, anger, surprise, disgust, and neutral).[7] In other parts of the task, they matched sentences to emotional faces, or emotional faces to emotion words, and so forth. Regrettably, no measures of intelligence or empathy were included in the latter study. A study using similar tasks to Lane et al.s', however, did find a correlation between task performance and intelligence among a group of mentally retarded adults (Simon, Rosen, & Ponpipom, 1996).

In another test of emotional understanding, Averill and Nunley (1992) presented participants with three emotions and asked them to write a brief description of a situation in which they would feel the three emotions together. For example, in response to the emotional triad "joy/relief/distress;" one participant wrote about the joy of being on a mountain-top, the distress at imagining falling off, and the relief of not actually falling. Scoring was according to an expert criterion. Success at this task appears moderately correlated with general intelligence, as well as with measures of creativity.

Another task that measured something between understanding and management (or at least, awareness) was also designed by Lane, Quinlan, Schwartz, Walker, and Zeitlin (1990). In this test, participants read stories such as:

> You and your best friend are in the same line of work. There is a prize given annually to the best performance of the year. The two of you work hard to win the prize. One night the winner is announced: your friend. How would you feel?

The test-taker provides an open-ended response that is then compared, and matched, if possible, with various alternatives. For example, a low awareness response to the above is "I'd probably feel bad about it for a few days and try to figure out what went wrong. I'm sure my friend would be feeling really good." A high awareness response, by contrast, is "I'd feel disappointed that I didn't win but glad that if someone else did, that person was my friend. My friend probably deserved it! My friend would feel happy and proud but slightly worried that my feelings might be hurt."

Better performance at this task correlated positively with the emotional perception task developed by the same authors (see above), and negatively with the Toronto Alexithymia Scale (Taylor, Ryan, & Bagby, 1985), a self-report measure of difficulty at expressing emotion.

More Recent Measurement Work With Emotional Intelligence

The Multifactor Emotional Intelligence Scale (MEIS) study. Our current research program has been devoted primarily to developing a full-fledged test of emotional intelligence as a set of mental abilities (Mayer, Caruso, & Salovey, 1998). We have designed a Multifactor Emotional Intelligence Scale (MEIS) that consists of twelve ability measures of emotinal intelligence divided into 4 classes or "branches" of abilities including (a) perceiving, (b) assimilating, (c) understanding, and (d) managing emotion (Mayer & Salovey, 1997; Mayer, Caruso, & Salovey, 1998; Mayer, Salovey, & Caruso, 1997). Branch 1 tasks measure emotional perception in Faces, Music, Designs, and Stories. The first three of these were similar to the emotional perception tasks described above (Mayer, DiPaolo, & Salovey, 1990), and the fourth Stories task, which is equally an understanding task, was also discussed above (Mayer & Geher, 1996). The second, Facilitation branch, contains two tests that measure Synesthesia Judgments (e.g., "How hot is anger?") and Feeling Biases. Briefly, these tasks were expected to measure emotion's facilitation of cognition but resulted in a weaker factor than the others and may be dropped for some purposes. Branch 3's four tasks examined the understanding of emotion. For example, one question asked, "Optimism most closely combines which two emotions?" and a participant had to choose "pleasure and anticipation" over less specific alternatives such as "pleasure and joy."

Branch 4's two tests measured Emotion Management in (a) the Self and (b) Others. These tasks asked participants to read a scenario such as the following and then rate five reactions to it according to how good they were. For example:

> One of your colleagues at work looks upset and asks if you will eat lunch with him. At the cafeteria, he motions for you to sit away from the other diners. After a few minutes of slow conversation he says that he wants to talk to you about what's on his mind. He tells you that he lied on his resume about having a college degree. Without the degree, he wouldn't have gotten the job.

(Please judge the value of the following reaction:)

Ask him how he feels about it so you can understand what's going on. Offer to help him, but don't push yourself on him if he really doesn't want any of your help.

Five hundred and three adults completed all the tasks as well as several criterion scales. An additional 229 adolescents also completed a slightly abbreviated version of the scales.

Findings with the MEIS. Work with the MEIS yielded a number of important findings. First, consensus, expert, and target scoring methods for the same tasks converged on correct answers to a degree anticipated by theory. This adds confidence to any of the scoring approaches. Of these, consensus scoring appeared to be the best all-around method. As noted earlier, Davies et al. (1998) worried about early mental ability tasks in the area because they exhibited only modest reliabilities. The MEIS achieved a full-scale alpha reliability of $r = .96$.

The second major finding concerned the structure of emotional intelligence as represented by these 12 tasks. First, the tasks were generally positively intercorrelated with one another. A study of the test's factorial structure recommended two equally viable factorial models. The first was a three-factor solution that separated out factors of (a) emotional perception, (b) emotional understanding, and (c) emotional management. The second was a hierarchical factor analysis based on those three factors (equally well represented by the first unrotated factor of the whole test) that describes a general factor of emotional intelligence, g_{ei}.

The same study indicated that general emotional intelligence, g_{ei}, correlated both with measures of verbal intelligence ($r = .36$) and with measures of self-reported empathy ($r = .33$). Few other criterion scales were administered, but the same general factor also correlated with parental warmth ($r = .23$). The fourth major finding was that ability at emotional intelligence was age dependent, increasing between young adolescence and early adulthood.

Findings from the MEIS indicate that emotional intelligence may qualify as a conventional intelligence operationalized as a mental ability (Mayer & Salovey, 1993; Neisser, Boodoo, Bouchard, Boykin, Brody, Ceci, Halpern, Loehlin, Perloff, Sternberg, & Urbina, 1996; Scarr, 1989). Emotional intelligence, like other well-operationalized intelligences, shows convergence among criteria for scoring correct answers. Emotional intelligence also "looks like" other intelligences, in that its tasks are intercorrelated. Findings also indicate that emotional intelligence is related to more traditional intelligence (i.e., analytical intelligence), but sufficiently distinct from it to represent new and unique variance. And finally, emotional intelligence, like other standard intelligences, develops with age (Binet & Simon, 1905, p. 320-321; Brown, 1997; Fancher, 1985, p. 71). Certain of these findings have now been replicated in other laboratories (Ciarrochi, Chan, & Caputi, in press).

Emotional Intelligence as a Mental Ability but Measured with Self-Report Measures

The mental ability model of emotional intelligence can be measured by self-report scales as well as by mental ability tasks. Self-report is a less direct way of assessing performance. It has its own merits, though, including being relatively easy to administer, tapping internal experiences difficult to obtain with performance measures, and assessing ongoing conscious processes related to emotional thinking. As with ability measures, there are a number of self-report scales that examine individual aspects of emotional intelligence, particularly Branch 1 (perception) and Branch 4 (management).

One of the most original and interesting approaches to measuring emotional perception (Branch 1) is the "BB" (based on body) scale of Bernet's (1996) Style in the Perception of Affect Scale (SIPOAS). The BB scale is intended to assess real connectedness to the (sometimes) slight bodily changes that accompany feelings and emotions. It is contrasted to two other ways of thinking about emotion. The "Emphasis on Evaluation" (EE) scale reflects effortful attempts to understand one's own emotions in terms of outsiders, ideals, or expectations, and is related to neuroticism. The "Looking to Logic" (LL) scale involves favoring intellect and avoiding feeling. Bernet (1996) has found that (self-reported) gains in psychotherapy are highest among high BB scorers who experience a variety of treatment modalities including talking therapies, but also physically-oriented therapies and spiritual approaches to difficulties. The exact relation of the SIPOAS scores to emotional intelligence is not yet clear, but it appears to be an interesting measure worthy of further study.

A number of scales also measure the management of emotion (Branch 4). Mayer and Gaschke (1988) described a reflective experience of mood they termed meta-experience. This reflective experience is measured with such questions as, "I know exactly how I am feeling," or "I am confused about how I feel." Since then, a large number of both state and trait measures of emotional meta-experience have been developed and studied. Findings with such scales indicate, for example, that people higher in mood attention and clarity are better able to reduce their rumination over negative material (Salovey et al., 1995). Further details on the measurement properties and results obtained with such scales may be found in several recent articles and chapters (e.g., Mayer & Stevens, 1994; Salovey et al., 1995; Salovey, Bedell, Detweiler, & Mayer, in press). For that reason we will not repeat those reviews here. Instead, we will focus on a full self-report operationalization of the emotional intelligence model.

Tett and his colleagues (Tett, Wang, Fisher, Martinez, Griebler, & Linkovich, 1997; Tett, Wang, Gribler, & Martinez, 1997) developed 10 scales based on the original model of emotional intelligence (Salovey & Mayer, 1990). Emotional appraisal was divided into four scales (a) Emotional Perception of the Self — Verbal, (b) Emotional Perception in the Self — Nonverbal, (c) Emotion in Others — Nonverbal, and (d) Empathy. The regulation of emotion was divided into two: (e) Regulation of Emotion in the Self, and (f) Regulation of Emotion in Others. Lastly, the utilization of emotion was divided into four additional scales: (g) Flexible Thinking, (h) Creative Thinking, (i) Mood Redirected Attention, and (j) Motivating Emotions. Each of the scales was internally consistent, with coefficient alphas ranging between "= .60 and .86. A factor analysis of these scales yielded four factors: (a) recognition and regulation of emotion in others, (b) the recognition of emotion in the self and the expression of emotion, (c) emotional stability, and (d) high self-reported intuition coupled with poor delay of gratification. This self-report measure plainly yielded results somewhat different from those obtained with the MEIS. The Tett et al. measures have not yet been correlated with other criteria.

Emotional Intelligence As a Mixed Model Measured by Self-Report

Just as the ability model of emotional intelligence can be operationalized and measured, so too can the mixed models. To date, all mixed models have been measured via self-report approaches. A first test of mixed-model emotional intelligence drew its organization from Salovey and Mayer (1990). Schutte, Malouff, Hall, Haggerty, Cooper, Golden, and Dornheim (1997) purposefully interpreted the 1990 model as a mixed model so that it would inlcude diverse attributes defined as emotional intelligence in popular works (specifically, Cooper & Sawaf, 1997; Goleman, 1995a). Using factor analytic techniques, the authors extracted four factors from 62 initial test items they examined, but settled on a single factor solution because their factors 2 through 4 loaded few of those items. Items from all the areas of the 1990 model were fairly evenly represented on this single, first, factor, which had an alpha coefficient of " = .90, and a test-retest reliability of $r = .78$.

A correlational analysis between their final 33-item scale and other measures suggested its overlap with positive affectivity and openness (Schutte et al., 1997). For example, the scale correlated highly (and negatively) with the Toronto Alexithymia Scale ($r(24) = -.65$) and positively with attention and clarity subscales of the Trait Meta-Mood Scale ($r(47) = .63, .52$, respectively), as well as in expected directions with a number of scales that overlap with generally positive affect (e.g., Life Orientation Test/Pessimism, $r(23) = -.43$, Zung Depression, $r(37) = -.37$, Trait Meta-Mood Mood/Repair, $r(47) = .68$). It also correlated $r(22) = .54$ with Openness on the NEO scale (and at lower levels, positively with Extraversion and negatively with Neuroticism).

The work by Schutte et al. (1997) tests a uniquely important behavioral prediction. In their studies, 64 first-year college students completed the 33-item emotional intelligence scale at the outset of the academic year; SAT or ACT scores were also available for 42 of the participants. The emotional intelligence scale predicted end-of-year GPA for the students ($r(63) = .32$) even though scores on the emotional intelligence scale were not related to SATs ($r(41) = -.06$). This study provides some initial support for the idea that mixed models of emotional intelligence may predict academic success beyond that of general cognitive measures. Other research, however, has indicated that happier college students obtain higher grades in general (Wessman & Ricks, 1966, p. 123). Because the Schutte et al.scale (and other self-report measures of emotional intelligence) correlate highly with positive affect, future research will need to partial out the influence of general mood level from those self-report scales.

Bar-On's mixed model of emotional intelligence was designed and operationalized as his Emotional Quotient Inventory (EQ_i). A factor analysis of his EQ_i scale (Bar-On, 1997, pp. 98-108) yielded 13 factors, more or less consistent with the individual attributes listed in Table 1 (column 3) of this chapter. For example, a first, self-contentment factor, was measured by such items as "I feel sure of myself in most situations." The second, social responsibility factor was measured by such items as "I like helping people," and a third impulse control factor was measured by, "When I start talking it is hard to stop." The first three factors represented about 23%, 5%, and 4% of the variance, respectively. The remaining factors explained from between 3% to 1% of the test variance. The 13 subscales have intercorrelations hovering around $r = .50$, and not surprisingly given such interdependence, a one-factor solution of the test is also possible (Bar-On, 1997).

The overall test correlates negatively and highly (in the $r = .50$ to .75 range) with measures of negative affect such as the Beck Depression Inventory and the Zung Self-Rating Depression Scale. It also correlates positively with traits related to positive affect. A cross-national administration of the Bar-On and the 16PF indicated that the Bar-On was consistently positively correlated (mostly between $r = .40$ and .60) with emotional stability, and with components of extraversion including social boldness and social warmth; Bar-On, 1997, p. 110-111). Notably, neither the overall scale, nor any of its subscales ever showed a significant correlation with the mental ability intelligence test — Scale B — embedded in the 16PF. Consistent with that, a study correlating the EQ_i with the WAIS-R yielded a negligible correlation of $r = .12$; Bar-On, 1997, p. 137-138).

The EQ_i has been correlated with a number of other scales as well (see Bar-On, 1997), but there are few reported predictions of actual behavioral outcomes. The closest to such a study concerns job performance and work satisfaction in which the EQ_i predicted a self-report measure of "sense of competence" on the job ($r = .51$). It is difficult to interpret this finding because the EQ_i and sense of competence scale were given at the same time and would seem to share content and error variance. Hence, the correlation could reflect a general sense of positive affectivity and self-esteem at the time of testing; on the other hand, something more might be involved. Further research is needed in order to clarify the findings.

Finally, Goleman (1995b) also compiled a test of emotional intelligence for an article in the Utne Reader. The Goleman scale was composed of 10 items; for each item, people must state their response to a hypothetical situation. One item reads, for example:

Assume you're a college student who had hoped to get an A in a course, but you have just found out you got a C- on the mid term. What do you do?

   a. Sketch out a specific plan for ways to improve your grade and resolve to follow through on your plans.
   b. Resolve to do better in the future.
   c. Tell yourself it really doesn't matter much how you do in the course, and concentrate instead on other classes where your grades are higher.
   d. Go to see the professor and try to talk her into giving you a better grade.

We doubted Goleman ever intended that this scale would be used for serious purposes, which he recently confirmed for us (D. Goleman, personal communication, July 22, 1999). Nonetheless, Goleman's scale does bear some content overlap with the third factor of the MEIS (which loads emotional management tasks) and has been studied by Davies, Stankov, & Roberts (1998). Goleman's scale, like the third MEIS factor, correlates highly with self-reported empathy (Davies, Stankov, & Roberts, 1998). Davies et al. found that the Goleman scale also correlated with a measure of emotional control (Roger & Najarian, 1989). The same authors also concluded, however, that the Goleman test has unacceptably low reliability ($a = .18$; Davies, Stankov, & Roberts, 1998, pp. 33, 55).

Summary

Several self-report measures of the mixed models of emotional intelligence exist. As a group, the scales tend to be strongly related to both positive affect (and negatively to negative affect), as well as to emotional openness. Whether these self-report scales of emotional intelligence add unique variance above and beyond already-existing measures of personality has not yet been answered, but their item content seems sufficiently distinct that it is possible they do. In this regard, the findings by Schutte et al. (1998) that their measure may predict academic achievement independently of traditional measures of analytic intelligence is provocative.

Discussion

This chapter first covered several competing models of emotional intelligence and compared them. The concepts of "emotion," "intelligence," and their combination were examined. A distinction was made between mental ability conceptions of emotional intelligence, and mixed conceptions that combine abilities with non-ability components of personality.

The chapter next reviewed some of the current research on emotional intelligence, which was quite supportive of the mental ability model of emotional intelligence. Some key findings include that (a) different methods for finding the correct answers to emotional intelligence questions appear to converge, (b) there is a clear general factor of emotional intelligence, and (c) this general factor breaks down into three specific subfactors concerned with emotional perception, understanding, and management. Moreover, (d) findings from several different laboratories indicate that emotional intelligence correlates (low-to-moderately) with general intelligence and empathy. Finally, (e) the abilities involved appear to grow with age. There are further hints that emotional intelligence is related to self-report of warm parenting.

Matters with the mixed models are less clear. The Schutte et al. (1998) report suggests that emotional intelligence measured by their scale might predict the grades obtained by incoming college students, somewhat independently of predictions made from SAT scores. The Bar-On EQ_i has been normed, factor analyzed, and correlated with many tests, but its predictions to academic or career success have not yet been ascertained. The Goleman scale has not been used much by researchers, and it appears to be unreliable.

Several issues remain to be concluded. A very central issue is whether, as some have claimed, emotional intelligence is a better predictor of success than intelligence. Is this claim serious and can it be supported? If not, what is the real excitement of emotional intelligence? What are its challenges (if any) to contemporary approaches to intelligence. And, finally, what will future research tell us?

Excitement over Emotional Intelligence: What is Real and What is Unreal?

At the outset of this chapter, we noted that emotional intelligence had attracted a great deal of attention and had generated a great deal of excitement. Although we are great fans of emotional intelligence, and we believe some of the enthusiasm is deserved, we must also say that some of the enthusiasm appears to be misplaced.

Misplaced Excitement over Emotional Intelligence

Earlier in the chapter, for example, we considered the popular claim that emotional intelligence predicted a variety of successful behaviors: among children, at home, and at work, at a level at or exceeding that of general intelligence. Such a claim appears misleading in several ways. The first way it is misleading is as to how strong a prediction can be made. According to popular writing, if intelligence predicts 20% of the variance of some success, emotional intelligence can help fill in the 80% gap. To the unsophisticated reader, bringing up the "80% unaccounted-for variance" figure suggests that there might indeed be a heretofore overlooked variable that truly could predict huge portions of life success. Although that is desirable, no variable studied in a century of psychology has made much such huge contributions.

The unexplained 80% of success appears to be in large part the consequence of complex, possibly chaotic interactions among hundreds of variables playing out over time. Predicting a person's future success shares much in common with intermediate or long range forecasts of such outcomes as earthquakes, hurricanes, stock market rallies, election outcomes, and geopolitics. For example, a person's career success is a product not only of personality components themselves, but also economic forces (e.g., real estate booms), political forces (e.g., pork-barrel projects), scientific advances (e.g., automation of customer service), and swings in public sentiment (e.g., demand for Peruvian coffee). We can predict such outcomes at levels that are recognizably greater than chance but far less than certainty. For these reasons, a new variable's value for predicting success is more realistically compared to how much variance new variables typically explain rather than how much unexplained variance is yet to be explained. The best new variables typically increment predictions, for instance, of job performance by between 1% to 4%. That 1% to 4% can mean great savings when scientific methods of selection are employed for thousands of people, but it is far different than what was claimed for emotional intelligence.

A second way that such popular claims are misleading is that they suggest there is an integrated, single, psychological entity that combines such entities as "persistence," "zeal," "emotional perceptiveness," and "good social skills." There is nothing wrong with studying such assorted variables together and seeing how they collectively predict some criterion. But to call them a single entity, i.e., "emotional intelligence," — or even parts of a single entity, leaves the mistaken impression that all those different attributes come together as a package, when in fact, they are more-or-less independent entities (recall how they are spread out in Figure 2). In addition, calling them a single entity suggests that the "package" is somehow new and mysteriously powerful when, in fact, many of its elements have been studied for years and have no special predictive powers. Finally such claims suggest that this highly desirable package can be acquired or learned as a whole, when in fact it consists of many different — perhaps even opposing — qualities.

Consider this analogy: It is perfectly acceptable, and even desirable, to study variables that cause car accidents together: alcoholism, poor eyesight, suicide-proneness, lead-footedness, and sleep-deprivation. It is also justifiable to create mathematical composites of such variables to predict car accidents. To claim, however, that alcoholism, poor eyesight, suicide-proneness, and so forth are all part of a *unitary syndrome* of "car-accident-proneness" that some unfortunate people have and some lucky ones do not, is misrepresentation. Poor eyesight, alcoholism, and other unrelated variables each arise from different causes and are treated by different methods. Claiming that they are a single syndrome that defines a radical new understanding of driving skill is sensationalism, not science.

Finally, the most serious way that these popular claims are misleading is in seeming to present scientific studies that support their powerful claims, while in fact failing to do so. For instance, Goleman (1995a; 1995c) referred to a study of Bell Laboratory engineers in which the top performers were equivalent in IQ to other engineers. The key difference, he claims, is that the top performers were more emotionally intelligent than were their peers. Unfortunately, this is conjecture, as the engineers were not tested for emotional intelligence explicitly using either mental ability or mixed model approaches to measurement (see Kelley & Caplan, 1993).

Extravagant claims as to the power of emotional intelligence to predict success in the workplace appear to fly in the face of our existing research base. For instance, Barrick and Mount (1991) conducted a meta-analysis of 117 criterion-related validity studies of how the Big Five personality dimensions predict on the job behavior. The 117 studies yielded 162 samples with a total N of 23,994 individuals. The Big Five dimensions include Emotionality, Extraversion, Openness, Agreeableness, and Neuroticism. Each dimension is a composite that itself includes several highly correlated sub-factors or facets. Interestingly, many of these factors overlap with what Goleman and Bar-On describe as emotional intelligence. For example, Agreeableness overlaps in part with such mixed models in its facets of (a) trust, (b) straightforwardness, (c) altruism, (d) compliance, (e) modesty, and (f) tendermindedness. What did Agreeableness predict among the 23,994 individuals who were studied? Agreeableness, the authors conclude, "is not an important predictor of job performance, even in those jobs containing a large social component (e.g., sales or management)" (Barrick & Mount, 1991 p. 21).

Extraversion also contains mixed-model elements such as (a) warmth, (b) gregariousness, (c) assertiveness, (d) activity, (e) excitement-seeking, and (f) positive emotions. Extraversion fared a bit better, validly predicting success for people in management and sales, although not for those in professions (e.g., lawyers, accountants, teachers), in police work, or in skilled or semi-skilled occupations (e.g., plumbers, farm workers, factory workers). And, a third dimension, Conscientiousness, overlaps with mixed models a bit as well, including (a) competence, (b) order, (c) dutifulness, (d) achievement striving, (e) self-discipline, and (f) deliberation. Conscientiousness was found to be the best predictor, showing consistent predictions across all occupational groups (Barrick & Mount, 1991, pp. 17-18). What was the strength of such predictions? The overall correlations topped out at $r = .15$, or 2% to 3% of the variance — rather less than the 20% to 80% suggested in popular writings.

Justifiable Excitement over Emotional Intelligence

Real excitement intrinsic to emotional intelligence. If emotional intelligence is not what Gibbs (1995, p. 60) referred to as the "true measure of intelligence," is it worth getting excited about? We certainly think so. The rigorous search for new intelligences can result in important, incremental predictive power over current measures of intelligence. We believe that emotional intelligence — as mental ability — identifies a previously overlooked area of ability critical to certain human functioning. These emotionally intelligent skills lay hidden in the boundary area between mental ability and non-cognitive dispositions. Many intelligence researchers were relieved when Scarr (1989) came to the defense of traditional intelligence with the statement that "human virtues...such as goodness in human relationships, and talents in music, dance, and painting" should not be called intelligent. Yet there is a borderland between the two. Musical ability, after all, is related to mathematical ability. Bar-On's (1997) search for "non-cognitive competencies" represents this intuition that ability sometimes lurks amidst everyday traits and tendencies. Our own intuition was that there was something more than simple hyper-emotionality among those sometimes labeled as touchy-feely, bleeding hearts, sensitive, or empathic souls. Emotional intelligence is the mental ability that lurks amidst the emotions.

"There is no right way to feel," is a battle cry of the human potential movement, and it obscures the fact that there may indeed be right ways to feel. Emotions are certainly evolved as a part of natural selection; consistent signal systems provide evolutionary advantages to those organisms that develop them over others (Darwin, 1872/1965; Ekman, 1973). Once evolved, these emotions are modified by culture as necessary. Thus, the correct feeling(s) to have at a funeral or elsewhere are the joint product of evolutionary developments in emotion and socially constructed rules of how to feel and behave.

A mental ability test of emotional intelligence will be the optimal tool for identifying people who truly understand emotions. Mental ability tests best distinguish between the person who is aesthetically minded but doesn't really understand feelings from the person who does really understand. Ability-based emotional intelligence measures can distinguish best the people who truly understand their own emotions from those who get lost in them. It is such ability-based emotional intelligence measures that can identify optimally those who may be mismatched with a given career (e.g., counseling and psychotherapy) because they lack the understanding of feelings necessary to listen empathically and to behave sensitively.

There is a social implication of this finding as well as an individual differences/ career selection implication. Scarr (1989) believes that identifying an intelligence adjusts social behavior so as to value the entity more than before. She suspects this is one reason some have labeled non-intelligences such as warmth, as intelligence. Identifying an actual intelligence, therefore, might possibly readjust values. For example, people who have different skills and know it often can communicate more smoothly about their abilities and limitations. We have often noticed that people in cars readily say, "Oh, I can't read maps, you tell me where to go" (low spatial intelligence) and pass the map over to someone else. We look forward to the day when, rather than dismiss someone else as a "bleeding heart," or a "touchy feely type," or "oversensitive," a person feels comfortable to exclaim, "Oh, I can't read emotions, you help me understand how to make my spouse feel better." Passing the job of emotional reading over to the individual who can perform it would be readjusting social values in a way that might make good sense for both parties.

Real excitement about emotional intelligence and success. The concept of emotional intelligence has also raised the issue of how success might be predicted. Although success may not be optimally predicted by emotional intelligence alone, the prediction of success is a relevant aspect of intelligence research, and more generally, personality psychology (Ford, 1994; Sternberg, 1996). A headlong rush to predict success was unleashed by the concept of emotional intelligence. Thus far, the science of prediction has been overwhelmed by wild claims and popular self-help writings. If this interest in success can be channeled more seriously, however, much good may come of the enthusiasm.

To us, studying personal success involves collecting measurable characteristics of personality and using them to predict measurable outcomes. Within the realm of cognition this may mean measuring a broader variety of intelligences than has been the case in the past (e.g., Gardner, 1993; Sternberg, 1996); more generally it means examining any part of personality that may contribute to a good life — as well as better defining what a successful life is. To some extent, the mixed models of emotional intelligence have initiated such a search. If we superimpose the predictive elements of these mixed models on a generic model of personality as was done in Figure 2, however, it is apparent that the features selected do not cover intelligence or personality in a comprehensive or balanced fashion. Those studying success, in other words, might do better to sample variables from a broader and more balanced fashion across the personality system. Over 400 parts of personality are commonly discussed in personality psychology (Mayer, 1995b) and these are unevenly included. Once variables are collected, it is necessary to remember that a systems' elements have unexpected and non-linear relations with one another. High self-esteem may seem perfectly wonderful in itself, but in some personalities that are disconnected from normal human relations — e.g., Adolph Hitler, Joseph Stalin — such self-esteem can lead to evil behavior (Baumeister, 1997; Mayer, 1993).

In addition to better variable selection, more attention needs to be paid to what kind of success we are talking about. There are many different sorts of success, a point that can be made quite clearly if we represent personality amidst its neighboring systems. Personality and its neighboring systems can be arranged according to two dimensions we employed earlier to arrange its internal components: the molecular-molar dimension, which separated basic level emotional and cognitive processing from more synthetic processing, and the internal-external dimension, which separated the intrapersonal from the interpersonal. Extending these two dimensions, as in Figure 3, we see personality surrounded by its own neurological underpinnings (below), its external situation (to the right), and the groups to which it belongs (above; Mayer, 1995a; in press).

Looked at this way, success depends upon which system we are observing. Internal personality may attain success in the form of happiness or other private positive feelings. Biological success involves good health and longevity, situational success involves being treated well, and group-based success involves being a well-accepted member of a loving family and other desirable social organizations. Looked at this way, it seems unlikely that there will be a one-personality-fits-all sort of success. Rather some personality features will assist with some sorts of success, and other features will assist with other sorts of success. We share the desire with others to understand what leads to human success — that is one motive (among several) that turned us to the study of emotional intelligence in the first place. There is no reason that good scientific research should not have important practical applications in that regard; but it needs to take a more thoughtful turn than has been the case thus far.

Charting New Ground

Once upon a time in our discipline, there was a fairly active search for characteristics other than traditional analytical intelligence that predicted success in life (e.g., McClelland et al., 1953). Some of these searches yielded mixed results but were forgotten; many other searches failed, or appeared to do so. To avoid unnecessary disappointments, we must look at what will be realistic and worthwhile — additional prediction over existing constructs in the 1%-5% range should satisfy us for the time being. If we find variables that predict somewhat above that, all the better.

Figure 3

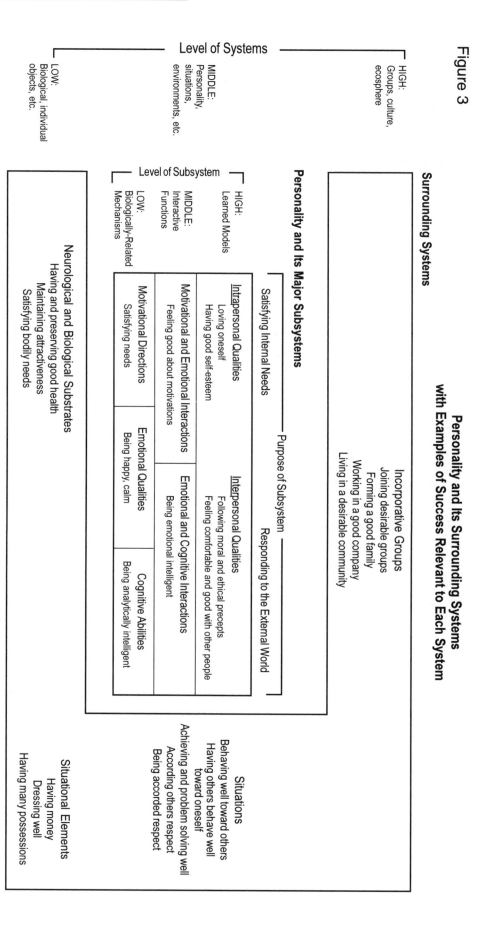

Figure 3. *Personality and Its Surrounding Systems With Examples of Success Releveant to Each System.* In Figure 3, personality is placed amidst its neighboring systems: biology (below), situations (to the right), and groups (above) so as to illustrate the multifaceted nature of success (modified from Mayer, in press). Personal success is an aspect of personality and all its adjoining systems. For example, personal success might include good health (biology), a calm, happy mood (internal emotions), plenty of money (situational elements), or respect from others (situations), as well as success in forming a rewarding family environment (social groups).

We must define success, and then we must develop good criteria for success carefully. As we only have come to understand in the last decade, measures of traditional intelligence look like wonderful predictors in part because the school performance they predict so well is a powerful criterion. People care about school performance, of course, but school performance is also unique as a variable because it aggregates so many behavioral observations. Consider: a person's grade point average is a reflection of her or his behavior over hundreds of days, over hundreds of quizzes, tests, and other assignments, as assessed by multiple independent observers (teachers). We now know that it is far more possible to predict records of aggregated behavior than it is to predict individual instances of behavior (Epstein, 1979).

What will be the aggregated criteria for emotional intelligence or other types of success? We need to find new such criteria to chart the predictors of success. There will be many directions to pursue. Perhaps certain emotional disorders (i.e., psychiatric diagnoses) will distinguish otherwise emotionally intelligent individuals from the emotionally unintelligent. Perhaps the quality of social networks will be an important criterion, or retrospective reports of parenting. To aggregate such outcomes, some personality psychologists have been working on scales that aggregate external, behavioral or life space measures (e.g., Buss & Craik, 1983; Mayer, Carlsmith, & Chabot, in press; Stokes, Mumford, & Owens, 1994). For example, life space scales are basically a means of aggregating a wide variety of outcome variables, all external to personality, (e.g., "How many jars of vitamins do you own?" "Do you belong to the Young Republicans?") so as to create new more powerful descriptions of a person's environment, and for those interested in it, new measures of their success.

So, there are reasons to be excited both about emotional intelligence and the search for variables that predict success. Naive approaches will, we suspect, run headlong into the disappointments of predicting success that have arisen in the past. There is, however, room for further sophisticated studies of intelligence, personality, and their predictions of success.

Conclusion

There now are two general models of emotional intelligence: a mental ability model and a mixed model that includes various personality dispositions. The mental ability model is probably the only one that is aptly called emotional intelligence. The other is somewhat more general than the meanings of "emotional" and "intelligence" would suggest. The use of the term "intelligence" to depict all varieties of human endeavor aside from mental ability is not new, however, and has merely reasserted itself in the present context.

Current research suggests that mental ability models of emotional intelligence can be described as a standard intelligence, and empirically meet the criteria for a standard intelligence. This means that certain people previously called emotional may be carrying out sophisticated information processing. Emotional intelligence, carefully considered, also illuminates a boundary between cognitive intelligence and non-intellective dispositions. For example, emotional intelligence makes clear that socializing involves both intellective and non-intellective aspects; only the intellective, we argue, should be referred to as intelligent.

The concept of emotional intelligence as ability is distinct from mixed models of emotional intelligence. Both may be useful in the study of human effectiveness and success in life. We believe it is useful to take a reasoned, thoughtful approach to studying human effectiveness under various conditions, and indeed much research does so. Calling any human variable related to personal success, "emotional intelligence," however, is likely to impede rather than promote progress in either area. More serious undertakings than can be orchestrated from the popular press are required.

The first mental ability measures of emotional intelligence now exist and they appear reliable, content-valid, and structurally valid. To some extent, the fate of emotional intelligence measures is connected to advances in personality psychology wherein better criteria of life activities (including success) are specified. There are few ready made real-life criteria with which to correlate emotional intelligence at present. Questions such as "What is an effective emotional life?" or "What is an effective, successful life?" have only begun to be addressed in measurement psychology. Answering such questions will require a great deal of ingenuity on the part of both theorists and researchers. Clarification of the spheres of life activity will profit not only research on emotional intelligence, but research on the intelligences and personality psychology more broadly.

References

Adams, S. (4/7/1997). Dilbert. In The Boston Globe. Boston, MA.

Andrews, F. M., & Robinson, J. P. (1991). Measures of subjective well-being. In J. P. Robinson, P. R. Shaver, & L. S. Wrightsman (Eds.). Measures of personality and social psychological attitudes (pp. 61-114). New York: Academic Press/Harcourt Brace Jovanovich.

Arnheim, R. (1974). Art and visual perception (The new version). Berkeley, CA: University of California Press.

Averill, J.R., & Nunley, E.P. (1992). Voyages of the heart: Living an emotionally creative life. New York: Free Press.

Bagby, R. M., Parker, J. D., & Taylor, G. J. (1994). The twenty-item Toronto Alexithymia Scale — I. Item selection and cross-validation of the factor structure. Journal of Psychosomatic Research, 38, 23-32.

Bain, A. (1855/1977). The senses and the intellect. London: John W. Parker & Son. [Reprinted in D. N. Robinson (Ed..), Significant contributions to the history of psychology: 1750-1920 [Series A: Orientations; Vol. 4]. Washington, DC: University Publications of America.

Bar-On, R. (1997). The Emotional Quotient Inventory (EQ-i): Technical Manual. Toronto, Canada: Multi-Health Systems.

Barrick, M. R., & Mount, M. K. (1991). The Big Five personality dimensions and job performance: A meta-analysis. Personnel Psychology, 44, 1-26.

Baumeister, R. F. (1997). Evil: Inside human violence and cruelty. New York: W. H. Freeman & Company.

Bennetts, L. (March, 1996). Emotional Savvy. Parents, 56-61.

Bernet, M. (1996). Emotional intelligence: Components and correlates. In Symposium #4057, "Emotional health and emotional intelligence." Presentation at the 104th Annual Convention of the American Psychological Association. Toronto, Canada, August 9-13th.

Binet, A., & Simon, T. (1905). Applications des méthodes nouvelles au diognostic du niveau intellectuel chez des enfants normaux et anormaux d'hospice et d'école primaire. L'Année Psychologique, 11, 245-336.

Blascovich, J., & Tomaka, J. (1991). Measures of self esteem. In J. P. Robinson, P. R. Shaver, & L. S. Wrightsman (Eds.). Measures of personality and social psychological attitudes (pp. 115-160). New York: Academic Press/Harcourt Brace Jovanovich.

Block, J., & Block, J. H. (1980). The role of ego-control and ego resiliency in the organization of behavior. In W. A. Collins (Ed.), The Minnesota symposium on child psychology (Vol. 13, pp. 33-101). Hillsdale, NJ: Erlbaum.

Brown, B. (June, 1997). Raw scores of cognitive ability are real psychological variables: IQ is a hyperspace variable. In V. C. Shipman (Chair). IQ or cognitive ability? Symposium presented to the 95th annual convention of the American Psychological Society. Washington, DC.

Buck, R. (1976). A test of nonverbal receiving ability: Preliminary studies. Human Communication Research, 2, 162-171.

Buck, R. (1984). The communication of emotion. New York: The Guilford Press.

Buck, R., Miller, R. E., & Caul, D. F. (1974). Sex, personality, and physiological variables in the communication of emotion via facial expression. Journal of Personality and Social Psychology, 30, 587-596.

Buss, D. M., & Craik, K. H. (1983). The act frequency approach to personality. Psychological Review, 90, 105-126.

Campbell, R.J., Kagan, N.I., & Krathwohl, D.R. (1971). The development and validation of a scale to measure affective sensitivity (empathy). Journal of Counseling Psychology, 18, 407-412.

Cantor, N., & Kihlstrom, J. F. (1987). Personality and social intelligence. Englewood Cliffs, NJ: Prentice-Hall.

Chapin, F. S. (1967). The social insight test. Palo Alto, CA: Consulting Psychologists Press.

Costa, P. T., & McCrae, R. R. (1985). The NEO Personality Inventory Manual. Odessa, FL: Psychological Assessment Resources, Inc.

Cooper, R. K., & Sawaf, A. (1997). Executive EQ: Emotional intelligence in leadership and organizations. New York: Grosset/Putnum.

Davies, M., Stankov, L., & Roberts, R.D. (1998). What remains of emotional intelligence? Unpublished manuscript.

Darwin, C. (1872/1965). The expression of emotions in man and animals. Chicago: University of Chicago Press.

Ekman, P. (1973). Darwin and facial expression: A century of research in review. New York: Academic Press.

Epstein, S. (1979). The stability of human behavior: On predicting most of the people most of the time. Journal of Personality and Social Psychology, 37, 179-184.

Epstein, S., & Meier, P. (1989). Constructive thinking: A broad coping variable with specific components. Journal of Personality and Social Psychology, 54, 332-350.

Fancher, R. E. (1985). The intelligence men: Makers of the IQ controversy. New York: W. W. Norton.

Feist, G. J. (1996). Academic versus emotional intelligence as predictors of career success and life satisfaction. Poster presented at the 00th annual convention of the American Psychological Society. San Francisco, CA: June, 1996.

Ford, M. E. (1994). A living systems approach to the integration of personality and | intelligence. In Sternberg, R.J., & Ruzgis, P. (1994). Personality and intelligence. Cambridge, England: Cambridge University Press.

Gardner, H. (1993). Frames of Mind (10th Anniversary Edition). New York: Basic Books.

Gardner, H. (March, 1997). "Who owns 'Intelligence?'" Invited talk, in G. Sinatra (Chair) and C. Bereiter (Discussant) Expanding our concept of intelligence: What's missing and what could we gain? Symposium at the 00th Annual Meeting of the American Educational Research Association. Chicago, IL.

Gibbs, N. (1995, October 2). The EQ factor. Time, pp. 60-68.

Goleman, D. (1995a). Emotional intelligence. New York: Bantam Books.

Goleman, D. (1995b). What's your EQ. The Utne Lens, Utne Reader. http://www.utne.com/lens/bms/eq.htm/.

Goleman, D. (1995c, September 10). Ideas and trends: The decline of the nice-guy quotient. New York Times (Sunday Week in Review), p. 6.

Gottman, J. (1997). The heart of parenting: How to raise an emotionally intelligent child. New York: Simon & Schuster.

Green, D. P., Goldman, S. L. & Salovey, P. (1993). Measurement error masks bipolarity in affect ratings. Journal of Personality and Social Psychology, 64, 1029-1041.

Greenspan, S. I. (1989). Emotional intelligence. In Field, K., Cohler, B. J., & Wool, G. (Eds.). Learning and education: Psychoanalytic perspectives. Madison, CT: International Universities Press.

Griffith, B. (11/17/1996). Zippy the pinhead. The Boston Globe (Comics section). Boston: MA.

Henig, R. M. (June, 1996). Are you smarter than you think? McCall's. 84-91.

Hilgard, E. R. (1980). The trilogy of mind: Cognition, affection, and conation. Journal of the History of the Behavioral Sciences, 16, 107-117.

Ickes, W. (1997). Empathic accuracy. New York: Guilford.

Ickes, W., Stinson, L., Bissonette, V., & Garcia, S. (1990). Naturalistic social cognition: Empathic accuracy in mixed-sex dyads. Journal of Personality and Social Psychology, 54, 730-742.

Izard, C. E. (1993). Four systems for emotion activation: Cognitive and noncognitive processes. Psychological Review, 100, 68-90.

Jung, C. (1921/1971). Psychological types. H. G. Baynes (Trans.), R. F. C. Hull (Rev. Trans.). Princeton, NJ: Princeton University Press. [Original work published 1921].

Kagan, N. (1978). Affective sensitivity test: Validity and reliability. Paper presented at the 00th meeting of the American Psychological Association, San Francisco.

Kelley, R. & Caplan, J. (1993). How Bell Labs creates star performers. Harvard Business Review, 71, 128-139.

Lane, R.D., Quinlan, D. M., Schwartz, G.E., Walker, P.A., Zeitlin, S. B. (1990). The Levels of Emotional Awareness Scale: A cognitive-developmental measure of emotion. Journal of Personality Assessment, 55, 124-134.

Lane, R. D., Sechrest, L., Reidel, R., Weldon, V., Weldon, V., Kaszniak, A., & Schwartz, G. E. (1996). Impaired verbal and nonverbal emotion recognition in alexithymia. Psychosomatic Medicine, 58, 203-210.

Legree, P. J. (1995). Evidence for an oblique social intelligence factor established with a likert-based testing procedure. Intelligence, 21, 247-266.

Leuner, B. (1966). Emotional intelligence and emancipation. Praxis der Kinderpsychologie und Kinderpsychiatie, 15, 193-203.

MacLean, P. D. (1973). A triune concept of the brain and behavior. Toronto: University of Toronto Press.

Mayer, J. D. (1993). The emotional madness of the dangerous leader. Journal of Psychohistory, 20, 331-348.

Mayer, J. D. (1995a). The System-Topics Framework and the structural arrangement of systems within and around personality. Journal of Personality, 63, 459-493.

Mayer, J. D. (1995b). A framework for the classification of personality components. Journal of Personality, 63, 819-877.

Mayer, J. D. (in press). A systems framework for the field of personality psychology. Psychological Inquiry.

Mayer, J.D., Caruso, D., Zigler, E., Dreyden, J. (1989). Intelligence and intelligence-related personality traits. Intelligence, 13, 119-133.

Mayer, J. D., Caruso, D., & Salovey, P. (1998). Emotional intelligence meets traditional standards for an intelligence. Manuscript under review.

Mayer, J. D., Chabot, H. F., & Carlsmith, K. M. (1997). Conation, affect, and cognition in personality. In G. Matthews (Ed.). Cognitive science perspectives on personality and emotion (pp. 31-63). New York: Elsevier.

Mayer, J.D., Carlsmith, K. M., Chabot, H. F. (in press). Describing the person's external environment: Conceptualizing and measuring the life space. Journal of Research in Personality.

Mayer, J.D., DiPaolo, M.T., & Salovey, P. (1990). Perceiving affective content in ambiguous visual stimuli: A component of emotional intelligence. Journal of Personality Assessment, 54, 772-781.

Mayer, J.D., & Gaschke, Y.N. (1988). The experience and meta-experience of mood. Journal of Personality and Social Psychology, 55, 102-111.

Mayer, J.D., & Geher, G. (1996). Emotional intelligence and the identification of emotion. Intelligence, 22, 89-113.

Mayer, J.D., & Salovey, P. (1993). The intelligence of emotional intelligence. Intelligence, 17, 433-442.

Mayer, J.D., & Salovey, P. (1995). Emotional intelligence and the construction and regulation of feelings. Applied and Preventive Psychology, 4, 197-208.

Mayer, J. D. & Salovey, P. (1997). What is emotional intelligence? In P. Salovey & D. Sluyter (Eds). Emotional Development and Emotional Intelligence: Implications for Educators (pp. 3-31). New York: Basic Books.

Mayer, J. D., Salovey, P., & Caruso, D. (1997). Emotional IQ test (CD ROM). Needham, MA: Virtual Knowledge.

Mayer, J.D., & Stevens, A. (1994). An emerging understanding of the reflective (meta-) experience of mood. Journal of Research in Personality, 28, 351-373.

McClelland, D. C., Atkinson, J. W., Clark, R. W., & Lowell, E. L. (1953) The achievement motive. New York: Appleton-Century-Crofts.

McCrae, R. R. & Costa, P. T., Jr. (1985). Updating Norman's "adequate taxonomy": Intelligence and personality dimensions in natural language and in questionnaires. Journal of Personality and Social Psychology, 49, 710-721.

Mehrabian, A., & Epstein, N. (1972). A measure of emotional empathy. Journal of Personality, 40, 525-543.

Neisser, U., Boodoo, G., Bouchard, T. J., Boykin, A. W., Brody, N., Ceci, S. J., Halpern, D. F., Loehlin, J. C., Perloff, R., Sternberg, R. J., & Urbina, S. (1996). Intelligence: Knowns and unknowns. American Psychologist, 51, 77-101.

Paulhus, D. L. (1991). Measurement and control of response bias. In J. P. Robinson, P. R. Shaver, & L. S. Wrightsman (Eds.). Measures of personality and social psychological attitudes (pp. 17-60). New York: Academic Press/Harcourt Brace Jovanovich.

Payne, W. L. (1986). A study of emotion: Developing emotional intelligence; Self-integration; relating to fear, pain and desire. <u>Dissertation Abstracts International, 47,</u> (01), p. 203A. (University Microfilms No. AAC 8605928).

Peterson, K. S. (Feb. 18, 1997). Signs of intelligence: Do new definitions of smart dilute meaning? <u>USA Today</u> Section D, p. 1.

Plutchik, R. (1984). Emotions: A general psychoevolutionary theory. In K. R. Scherer & P. Ekman (Eds.), <u>Approaches to emotion.</u> Hillsdale, NJ: Lawrence Erlbaum.

Publilius Syrus (1961). "Sententiae" in J. W. Duff & A. M. Duff (eds.) <u>Minor Latin poets.</u> Cambridge, MA: Harvard University Press. [Original work published c. 100 B.C.E.].

Roberts, R. D. Beh, H. C., Spilsbury, G., & Stankov, L. (1991). Evidence for an attentional model of human intelligence using the competing task paradigm. <u>Personality and Individual Differences, 12,</u> 445-555.

Roger, D., & Najarian, B. (1989). The construction and validation of a new scale for measuring emotional control. <u>Personality and Individual Differences, 10,</u> 845-853.

Rosenthal, R., Hall, J. A., DiMatteo, M. R., Rogers, P. L., & Archer, D (1979). <u>Sensitivity to nonverbal communication: The PONS Test.</u> Baltimore, MD: Johns Hopkins University Press.

Russell, J. A. (1979). Affective space is bipolar. <u>Journal of Personality and Social Psychology, 37,</u> 1161-1178.

Saarni, C. (1990). Emotional competence: How emotions and relationships become integrated. In R. A. Thompson (Ed.), <u>Socioemotional development, Nebraska symposium on motivation.</u> (Vol. 36, pp. 115-182). Lincoln, NE: University of Nebraska Press.

Saarni, C. (1997). Emotional competence and self-regulation in childhood. In P. Salovey, & D. J. Sluyter, <u>Emotional development and emotional intelligence (pp.35-66).</u> New York: Basic Books.

Saarni, C. (in press). <u>Developing emotional competence.</u> New York: Guilford.

Salerno, J. G., (1996). <u>The whole intelligence: Emotional quotient (EQ).</u> Oakbank, South Australia: Noble House of Australia.

Salovey, P., Bedell, B., Detweiler, J., & Mayer, J. D. (in press). Coping intelligently: Emotional intelligence and the coping process. In C. R. Snyder (ed.), <u>The psychology of coping.</u> New York: Oxford University Press.

Salovey, P. & Mayer, J.D. (1990). Emotional intelligence. <u>Imagination, Cognition, and Personality, 9,</u> 185-211.

Salovey, P., Mayer, J.D., Goldman, S., Turvey, C., & Palfai, T. (1995). Emotional attention, clarity, and repair: Exploring emotional intelligence using the Trait Meta-Mood Scale. In J. W. Pennebaker (Ed.) <u>Emotion, disclosure, and health</u> (pp. 125-154). Washington, D.C.: American Psychological Association.

Salovey, P., & Mayer, J. D. (1994). Some final thoughts about personality and intelligence. In R. J. Sternberg, & P. Ruzgis (Eds.) Personality and intelligence (303-318). Cambridge, England: Cambridge University Press.

Salovey, P., & Sluyter, D. J. (1997). Emotional development and emotional intelligence. New York: Basic Books.

Scarr, S. (1989). Protecting general intelligence: Constructs and consequences for intervention. In R. L. Linn (Ed.), Intelligence: Measurement, theory, and public policy. Urbana, IL: University of Illinois Press.

Schaffer, L.F., Gilmer, B., & Schoen, M. (1940). Psychology (pp. xii). New York: Harper & Brothers.

Scheier, M. F., & Carver, C. S. (1985). Optimism, coping, and health: Assessment and implications of generalized outcome expectancies. Health Psychology, 4, 219-247.

Schutte, N. S., Malouff, J. M., Hall, L. E., Haggerty, D. J., Cooper, J. T., Golden, C. J., & Dornheim, L. (1998). Development and validation of a measure of emotional | intelligence. Personality and Individual Differences, 25, 167-177.

Segal, J. (1997). Raising your emotional intelligence. New York: Holt.

Shapiro, L. E. (1997) How to raise a child with a high E.Q: A parents' guide to Emotional Intelligence. New York: HarperCollins Publishers.

Simmons, S., & Simmons, J. C. (1997). Measuring emotional intelligence with techniques for self-improvement. Arlington, TX: Summit Publishing Group.

Simon, E. W., Rosen, M., & Ponpipom, A. (1996). Age and IQ as predictors of emotion identification in adults with mental retardation. Research in Developmental Disabilities, 17, 383-389.

Spearman, C. (1927). The abilities of man. New York: The Macmillan Company.

Steiner, C. & Perry, P. (1997). Achieving emotional literacy: A program to increase your emotional intelligence. New York: Avon.

Sternberg, R. J. (1988). The triarchic mind: A new theory of human intelligence. New York: Penguin Books.

Sternberg, R. J. (1994). Commentary: Reforming school reform: Comments on "Multiple intelligences: The theory in practice." Teachers College Record, 95, 561-569.

Sternberg, R. J. (1996). Successful intelligence: How practical and creative intelligence determine success in life. New York: Simon & Schuster.

Sternberg, R. J. (1997). The concept of intelligence and its role in lifelong learning and success. American Psychologist, 52, 1030-1045.

Sternberg, R. J. & Caruso, D. R. (1985). Practical modes of knowing. In E. Eisner (Ed.) Eighty-fourth Yearbook of the National Society for the Study of Education (Part II) (pp. 133-158) Chicago: University of Chicago Press.

Sternberg, R. J., & Lubart, T. I. (1995a). An investment perspective on creative insight. In R. J. Sternberg & J. E. Davidson (Eds.). The nature of insight. Cambridge, MA: MIT Press.

Sternberg, R. J., & Lubart, T. I. (1995b). Defying the crowd: Cultivating creativity in a culture of conformity. New York: Free Press.

Sternberg, R. J., & Ruzgis, P. (1994). Personality and Intelligence. New York: Cambridge University Press.

Sternberg, R. J., & Smith, C (1985). Social intelligence and decoding skills in nonverbal communication. Social Cognition, 3, 168-192.

Sternberg, R. J., Wagner, R. K., Williams, W. M., & Horvath, J. A. (1995). Testing common sense. American Psychologist, 50, 912-927.

Stokes, G. S., Mumford, M. D., & Owens, W. A. (1994). Biodata handbook: Theory, research, and use of biographical information in selection and performance prediction. Palo Alto, CA: Consulting Psychologists Press.

Taylor, G. J., Ryan, D., & Bagby, R. M. (1985). Toward the development of a new self-report alexithymia scale. Psychotherapy and psychosomatics, 44, 191-199.

Terman, L. M. (1921). II. [Second contribution to "Intelligence and its measurement: A symposium"] Journal of Educational Psychology, 12, 127-133.

Tett, R., Wang, A., Fisher, R., Martinez, A., Griebler, J., & Linkovich, T. (April 4, 1997). Testing a model of emotional intelligence. Paper presented at the 1997 Annual Convention of the Southeastern Psychological Association, Atlanta, GA.

Tett, R., Wang, A., Thomas, M., Griebler, J., & Martinez, A. (April 4, 1997). Development of Self-Report Measures of Emotional Intelligence. Paper presented at the 1997 Annual Convention of the Southeastern Psychological Association, Atlanta, GA.

Thorndike, R. L. & Stein, S. (1937). An evaluation of the attempts to measure social intelligence. Psychological Bulletin, 34, 275-284.

TIME (October 2, 1995). [Cover]. New York: Time Warner.

Tomkins, S. S. (1962). Affect, imagery, consciousness. Vol. 1: The positive affects. New York: Springer.

Wagner, R. K., & Sternberg, R. J. (1985). Practical intelligence in real-world pursuits: The role of tacit knowledge. Journal of Personality and Social Psychology, 50, 737-743.

Watson, G. (1930). Happiness among adult students of education. Journal of Educational Psychology, 21, 79-109.

Wechsler, D. (1940). Nonintellective factors in general intelligence. Psychological Bulletin, 37, 444-445.

Wechsler, D. (1943). Non-intellective factors in general intelligence. Journal of Abnormal Social Psychology, 38, 100-104.

Wechsler, D. (1958). The measurement and appraisal of adult intelligence (4th ed.). Baltimore, MD: The Williams & Wilkins Company.

Weisinger, H. (1997). Emotional intelligence at work. New York: Jossey-Bass.

Wessman, A. E., & Ricks, D. F. (1966). Mood and personality. New York: Holt, Rinehart, & Winston, Inc.

Wong, C. T., Day, J. D., Maxwell, S. E., Meara, N. M. (1995). A multitrait-multimethod study of academic and social intelligence in college students. Journal of Educational Psychology, 87, 117-133.

Woodworth, R. S. (1940). Psychology, 4th ed.. New York: Henry Holt.

Young, P. T. (1936). Motivation of behavior. New York: John Wiley & Sons.

Footnotes

[1] The term, "emotional intelligence" has been used for several decades at least before the present set of articles. Some use of the term stems from a Piagetian tradition (e.g., his book on affect and intelligence). Articles focused on Piaget's work, although noteworthy, are generally focused on a Piagetian stage or concept relatively unrelated to the present work (e.g., Leuner, 1966; Greenspan, 1989). Probably the most interesting development prior to 1990 was in a dissertation by Payne (1986) who writes, in his abstract, that "the mass suppression of emotion throughout the civilized world has stifled our growth emotionally," and who reports the development of a rigorous theoretical and philosophical framework to explore and address this problem. To the best of our knowledge, however, the research we cite from 1990 forward marks the first development of the concept as an empirical research area of study.

[2] We could not resist entering the popular arena as well, with an educational CD-ROM version of an emotional intelligence test. We experienced first hand the lengths marketers will go to capture people's attention. Our publisher put the quote, "The true measure of intelligence!" from Gibbs' (1995) Time Magazine article on the box: even though (as the CD-ROM itself makes clear) we do not view this as accurate.

[3] The most enthusiastic advocates of intelligence become doubtful of it themselves. From having naively assumed that its nature is straightway conveyed by its name, they now set out to discover what this nature really is. In the last act, the truth stands revealed, that the name really has no definite meaning at all; it shows itself to be nothing more than a hypostatized word, applied indiscriminately to all sorts of things.

[4] For example, since our original theory was proposed we have more carefully distinguished between the intelligence and human effectiveness portions of our model, and each has been developed in important ways. The intelligence model has been clarified by (a) describing how and in what sense emotions convey information, and by (b) adding explicit discussion of the fact that a central portion of emotional intelligence involves reasoning with or understanding of emotion (neither our own nor any other theory had mentioned this until recently (Mayer & Salovey, 1995). In addition, we have focussed our social adaptiveness model so that it deals specifically with emotional effectiveness.

[5] The correlation is the square root of the proportion of variance accounted for (i.e., r = .447 is the square root of .20 — 20% of the variance) under standard assumptions of linearity, homoscedasticity, and so forth..

[6] This correlation may underestimate the relation a bit as it did not directly ask people how intelligent they believed themselves to be.

[7] No examples are presented in the original study; we infer the sentences were similar to this.

Part II

Measuring Emotional Intelligence as a Mental Ability with the Mayer-Salovey-Caruso Emotional Intelligence Test (MSCEIT)

In this section, we present four articles that introduce and discuss ability tests of EI that are now being used in our and others' research. The first article, *Emotional intelligence meets traditional standards for an intelligence* by Mayer, Caruso, and Salovey (1999) empirically demonstrated that EI, measured by the MEIS (the precursor to the published MSCEIT), meets three classical criteria of a standard intelligence. The article also described the different tasks that are used to measure each branch of EI.

The second and third articles, both by Mayer, Salovey, Caruso, and Sitarenios (2002, 2003) pertain to the measurement of EI with the MSCEIT. The first article, *Emotional intelligence as a standard intelligence*, is in part, a response to researchers in the field who questioned the psychometric properties of the MEIS and whether EI is a real intelligence. The authors present arguments for the reasonableness of measuring EI as an ability.

In the third article, *Measuring emotional intelligence with the MSCEIT V2.0*, the authors examined the psychometric properties of the MSCEIT and demonstrated that (a) the scoring of the test is sound, (b) the test has adequate reliability, and (c) the factor structure of the test supports the theoretical model of EI.

The fourth article is titled, *Convergent, discriminant, and incremental validity of competing measures of emotional intelligence.* Here, Brackett and Mayer (2003) conducted an empirical investigation that compared EI measured as a mental ability with the MSCEIT to two self-report tests of EI. Their research demonstrated that ability models have discriminant validity, i.e., they are relatively unrelated to well-established measures of personality and well-being, whereas self-report tests of EI overlap greatly with these measures. This article also presents a glance at the predictive and incremental validity of both ability and self-report measures of EI.

Reprinted from *Intelligence*, Vol. 27, No. 4, pp. 267-298, by Mayer, J.D., Caruso, D., & Salovey, P. (1999). Emotional intelligence meets traditional standards for an intelligence, with permission from Elsevier.

Emotional Intelligence Meets Traditional Standards for an Intelligence

John D. Mayer, University of New Hampshire
David Caruso, Work-Life Strategies
Peter Salovey, Yale University

Acknowledgements

The research reported here was supported in part by the University of New Hampshire. We are grateful for the assistance we received from a number of individuals. Peter Legree read and commented on this manuscript several times and contributed substantially to its quality. Scott Formica was also instrumental in identifying several ambiguities in the near-final manuscript that we were able to correct. In respect to developing the MEIS test itself, the music selections used in the test were composed and recorded by Richard Viard. Graphic designs used in the test were created by David Silverman and Jeremiah Washburn. Finally, Amy Van Buren and Heather Chabot conducted a portion of the data collection. To these and all others who contributed to this work, we extend our heartfelt thanks.

An intelligence must meet several standard criteria before it can be considered scientifically legitimate. First, it should be capable of being operationalized as a set of abilities. Second, it should meet certain correlational criteria: the abilities defined by the intelligence should form a related set (i.e., be intercorrelated), and be related to pre-existing intelligences, while also showing some unique variance. Third, the abilities of the intelligence should develop with age and experience. In two studies, adults (N = 503) and adolescents (N = 229) took a new, 12 sub-scale ability test of emotional intelligence: the Multifactor Emotional Intelligence Scale (MEIS). The present studies show that emotional intelligence, as measured by the MEIS, meets the above three classical criteria of a standard intelligence.

Emotions are internal events that coordinate many psychological subsystems including physiological responses, cognitions, and conscious awareness. Emotions typically arise in response to a person's changing relationships. When a person's relationship to a memory, to his family, or to all of humanity changes, that person's emotions will change as well. For example, a person who recalls a happy childhood memory may find the world appears brighter and more joyous (e.g., Bower, 1981). Because emotions track relationships in this sense, they convey meaning about relationships (Schwarz & Clore, 1983). Emotional intelligence refers to an ability to recognize the meanings of emotions and their relationships, and to reason and problem solve on the basis of them. Emotional intelligence is involved in the capacity to perceive emotions, assimilate emotion-related feelings, understand the information of those emotions, and manage them (Mayer & Salovey, 1997; Salovey & Mayer, 1990).

Emotional intelligence can be assessed most directly by asking a person to solve emotional problems, such as identifying the emotion in a story or painting, and then evaluating the person's answer against criteria of accuracy (Mayer, DiPaolo, & Salovey, 1990; Mayer & Geher, 1996). It is worth noting, however, that emotional intelligence, as an ability, is often measured in other ways. Some approaches have asked people their personal, self-reported beliefs about their emotional intelligence. Test items such as, "I'm in touch with my emotions," or "I am a sensitive person," assess such self understanding (e.g., Mayer & Stevens, 1994; Salovey, Mayer, Goldman, Turvey, & Palfai, 1995). Self-reports of ability and actual ability, however, are only minimally correlated in the realm of intelligence research (e.g., $r = .20$; Paulhus, Lysy, & Yik, 1998) and that appears to hold in the area of emotional intelligence as well (Davies, Stankov, & Roberts, 1998).[1] Self-concept is important, of course, because people often act on their beliefs about their abilities as opposed to their actual abilities (Bandura, 1977). Emotional intelligence as a domain of human performance, however, is best studied with ability measures.

Emotional intelligence has often been conceptualized (particularly in popular literature) as involving much more than ability at perceiving, assimilating, understanding, and managing emotions. These alternative conceptions include not only emotion and intelligence per se, but also motivation, non-ability dispositions and traits, and global personal and social functioning (e.g., Bar-On, 1997; Goleman, 1995). Such broadening seems to undercut the utility of the terms under consideration. We call these *mixed* conceptions because they combine together so many diverse ideas. For example, the Bar-On Emotional Quotient Inventory (EQ$_i$) includes fifteen self-report

Emotional Intelligence Meets Traditional Standards for an Intelligence

scales that measure a persons' self-regard, independence, problem solving, reality-testing, and other attributes (Bar-On, 1997). Such qualities as problem solving and reality testing seem more closely related to ego strength or social competence than to emotional intelligence. Mixed models must be analyzed carefully so as to distinguish the concepts that are a part of emotional intelligence from the concepts that are mixed in, or confounded, with it.

General intelligence serves as an umbrella concept that includes dozens of related groups of mental abilities. Most of the smaller subskills studied in this century are related to verbal, spatial, and related logical information processing (see Carroll, 1993, for an authoritative review). Such processing is sometimes referred to as "cold" to denote that its ego- or self-involvement is minimal (Abelson, 1963; Mayer & Mitchell, 1998; Zajonc, 1980). Information processing, however, also deals with "hot," self-related, emotional processing. Emotional intelligence is a hot intelligence. It can be thought of as one member of an emerging group of potential hot intelligences that include social intelligence (Sternberg & Smith, 1985; Thorndike, 1920), practical intelligence (Sternberg & Caruso, 1985; Wagner & Sternberg, 1985), personal intelligence (Gardner, 1993), non-verbal perception skills (Buck, 1984; Rosenthal, Hall, DiMatteo, Rogers, & Archer, 1979), and emotional creativity (Averill & Nunley, 1992). Each of these forgoing concepts form coherent domains that partly overlap with emotional intelligence, but that divide human abilities in somewhat different ways.

The ability conception of emotional intelligence was developed in a series of articles in the early 1990's (Mayer, et al., 1990; Mayer & Salovey, 1993; Salovey & Mayer, 1990). For example, the first empirical study in the area demonstrated that people's abilities to identify emotion in three types of stimuli: colors, faces, and designs, could be accounted for by a single ability factor — which we supposed was emotional intelligence (Mayer, et al., 1990). Another study examined the understanding of emotion in stories (Mayer & Geher, 1996); this latter study provided further indications that the underlying factor "looked like" an intelligence. Simultaneous with this empirical work, we have honed our definition of emotional intelligence and the abilities involved (e.g., Mayer & Salovey, 1997). The present article represents a culmination of this work, testing our most highly developed conception of emotional intelligence, by operationalizing it according to 12 ability tests of emotional intelligence. The present study can help answer important questions about emotional intelligence, among them: whether emotional intelligence is a single ability or many, and how it relates to traditional measures of general intelligence and other criteria.

Figure 1

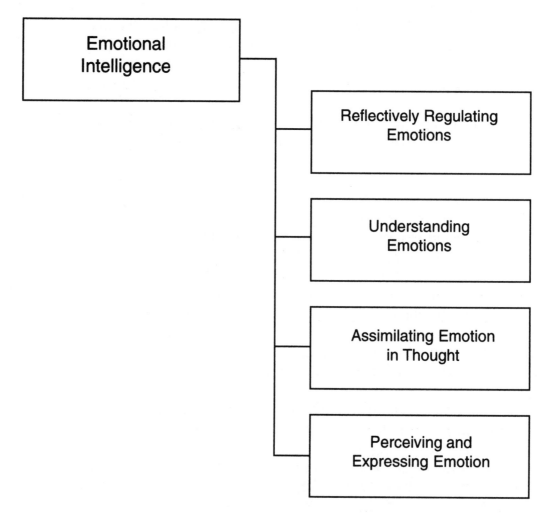

Figure 1. A four-branch model of the skills involved in emotional intelligence (after Mayer & Salovey, 1997).

Standard Criteria for an Intelligence

Three Criteria for an Intelligence

An intelligence such as emotional intelligence must meet stringent criteria in order to be judged as a true intelligence. For the purposes here, these criteria can be divided into three fairly distinct groups: conceptual, correlational, and developmental. The first, conceptual criteria, includes that intelligence must reflect mental performance rather than simply preferred ways of behaving, or a person's self-esteem, or non-intellectual attainments (Carroll, 1993; Mayer & Salovey, 1993; Scarr, 1989); moreover, mental performance should plainly measure the concept in question, i.e., emotion-related abilities. The second, correlational criteria, describe empirical standards:

specifically, that an intelligence should describe a set of closely related abilities that are similar to, but distinct from, mental abilities described by already-established intelligences (Carroll, 1993; Neisser, et al., 1996).[2] The third, developmental criterion, states that intelligence develops with age and experience, and is based on the groundbreaking work by Binet and Simon at the beginning of century (as reviewed in Fancher, 1985, p. 71; see also, Brown, 1997). These three criteria will be examined in greater detail.

Conceptual Criteria for an Intelligence
        We have argued elsewhere that emotional intelligence does indeed describe actual abilities rather than preferred courses of behavior. These four broad classes of abilities can be arranged from lower, more molecular, skills to higher, more molar, skills, as is done in Figure 1 (Mayer & Salovey, 1993; 1997). The lowest level skills involve the perception and appraisal of emotion, e.g., in a facial expression or artwork. The next level up involves assimilating basic emotional experiences into mental life, including weighing emotions against one another and against other sensations and thoughts, and allowing emotions to direct attention. An example includes holding an emotional state in consciousness long enough to compare its correspondences to similar sensations in sound, color, and taste. The third level involves understanding and reasoning about emotions. Each emotion — happiness, anger, fear, and the like — follows its own specific rules. Anger rises when justice is denied; fear often changes to relief; sadness separates us from others. Each emotion moves according to its own characteristic rules, like the different pieces on a chessboard. Emotional intelligence involves the ability to see the pieces, know how they move, and reason about emotions accordingly. The fourth, highest level, involves the management and regulation of emotion, such as knowing how to calm down after feeling angry or being able to alleviate the anxiety of another person. Tasks defining these four levels or branches are described in greater detail in the section concerning scale development below.

        In considering tasks for an emotional intelligence test, how are we to discriminate right from wrong answers? One common approach drawn from emotions research has been to look for group *consensus* as to the emotional content of stimuli (e.g., Mayer, et al., 1990; Wagner, MacDonald, & Manstead, 1986). If the group agrees that a face is happy, say, then that becomes the correct answer. A second possibility is to use *expert* criteria for emotional meanings. An expert could bring a history of philosophy and empirical psychology to bear on judgments about emotional meanings (e.g., Darwin, 1872/1965; Ortony, Clore, & Collins, 1988; Plutchik, 1984; Spinoza, 1675/1984), and this might provide answers similar to or different from a consensus criterion. On the other hand, it has been argued that experts simply provide estimates of group consensus, and those estimates are fallible (Legree, 1995). Finally, a *target* criterion is applicable in selected circumstances in which a target individual's emotions or emotional creations are being judged. In such cases, the target can report the emotion he or she was feeling or expressing at the time. The group's consensus, the expert, and the target criteria, represent somewhat different perspectives, and it is therefore unlikely that they would be in complete agreement. For example, target individuals sometimes report pleasant feelings, perhaps to be socially conforming, when in fact they are perceived by a group as experiencing less pleasant feelings (Mayer & Geher, 1996). Such differences in perspective do not necessarily rule out a general convergence toward a criterion. Such a rough convergence would substantiate the view that emotions convey information, and that emotional intelligence is, in fact, an intelligence.

Correlational Criteria for an Intelligence

The Logic of Correlational Criteria for Intelligence. Emotional intelligence should define a set of abilities that are moderately intercorrelated with one another. There are many excellent overviews of mental abilities and the criteria for defining their class (e.g., Carroll, 1993, Flanagan, Genshaft, & Harrison, 1997). This logic can be illustrated with an example drawn from the clinical assessment of intelligence. The original Wechsler Adult Intelligence Scales (i.e., WAIS, WAIS-R, WAIS-II; Wechsler, 1958; see Anastasi & Urbina, 1997, for a review of later tests) contained a set of verbal intelligence scales. These consisted of many related mental tests including identifying similarities among concepts, recognizing word meanings (vocabulary), general information, comprehension, and arithmetic. The abilities measured, e.g., vocabulary and information, are moderately intercorrelated — they rise and fall across people at about the $r = 0.40$ level. The tasks can be summarized by a verbal IQ, where the IQ is based on a person's overall performance on those tasks compared to the performance of other people their age (because ability-levels change with age).

The Wechsler tests from mid-century to 1998 typically paired verbal intelligence with a performance intelligence. Performance abilities, such as assembling puzzles, identifying missing elements in visual depictions, and ordering picture sequences, also correlate highly with each other. These can be summarized by a performance IQ, similarly based on the person's overall performance on the tasks. The verbal and performance tasks correlate less highly with each other; i.e., the verbal and performance tasks are related to each other, but not quite as closely as skills within each group.[3] They are also related, however, and can be combined to form an overall IQ, which represents the individual's average performance on a broader range of mental tasks.

The Establishment of New Intelligences. The possibility that there exists one or more additional classes of intelligence, beyond verbal and performance intelligence, has long intrigued researchers. The identification of a new class of intelligence would broaden our contemporary concepts of intelligences. Moreover, adding missing intelligences to an omnibus IQ test can increase the test's fairness by more accurately representing individuals whose abilities were higher on unknowingly omitted tests than on the tests that were present.

The identification of a class of intelligence, such as the verbal or performance, however, does not occur all at once. Usually, there proceeds a painstaking process of developing candidate tasks for the intelligence, finding a rationale for correct answers (if not obvious), and then examining their intercorrelations with existing measures of

Emotional Intelligence Meets Traditional Standards for an Intelligence

intelligences. For example, social intelligence was proposed as a third member of the verbal/performance grouping earlier in the century; it was defined as "the ability to understand men and women, boys and girls, to act wisely in human relations" (Thorndike, 1920). Measures of verbal intelligence, however, already incorporate much social thinking; in fact, normal verbal communication is so social that it is difficult to come up with vocabulary ("What is democracy?") or general knowledge questions ("Who was John F. Kennedy?") that do not contain social information. In part for such reasons, Cronbach (1960) concluded that social intelligence could not be distinguished from verbal intelligence. The search for a third broad intelligence abated for the next several decades, although a number of alternative intelligences have been discussed as possible candidates.

Research on social intelligence has continued, with important work by Sternberg and Smith (1985), Cantor and Kihlstrom (1987), Legree (1995) and others. Much of that work represented important conceptual development of social intelligence; little of that work, however, concerned itself with actual ability measurement in relation to other intelligences (some exceptions are Legree, 1995; Wagner & Sternberg, 1985). In addition, other intelligences have been proposed, e.g., the multiple intelligences of Gardner (1993), which included personal, musical, and other intelligences. Here, too, research on individual differences and their relations to already-existing intelligences was de-emphasized (Sternberg, 1994).

Emotional intelligence represents an alternative grouping of tasks to social intelligence. On the one hand, emotional intelligence is broader than social intelligence, including not only reasoning about the emotions in social relationships, but also reasoning about internal emotions that are important for personal (as opposed to social) growth. On the other hand, emotional intelligence is more focused than social intelligence in that it pertains primarily to the emotional (but not necessarily verbal) problems embedded in personal and social problems. For example, reasoning about a sequence of internal feelings, or about the feelings in a relationship, can be readily distinguished from general questions about democracy, or John F. Kennedy, as described above. This increased focus means that emotional intelligence may be more distinct from traditional verbal intelligence than is social intelligence.

The Developmental Criterion for an Intelligence

There remains a third criterion an intelligence must meet: that it develops with age and experience, from childhood to adulthood. That third criterion will be discussed at the outset of Study 2, which is focused on studying developmental issues in emotional intelligence.

Introduction to the Present Studies

Widely accepted intelligences share certain features in common: they are abilities, they manifest specific correlational patterns among themselves and in relation to other intelligences, and they develop with age and experience. The two studies described here operationalize emotional intelligence as a set of abilities, study the intercorrelational pattern among those abilities, and examine evidence for their growth between adolescence and early adulthood.

In Study 1, we constructed a set of 12 ability measures drawn from each of the four defined areas of emotional intelligence including perceiving, assimilating, understanding, and managing emotion (Mayer, Salovey, & Caruso, 1997). The test was administered to a large group of adults. We predicted moderate correlations among the 12 tasks, and that a group factor, i.e., one that loads all 12 tasks, can be derived. As in our earlier work, we predicted that a combination of these tasks correlates with traditional forms of intelligence such as verbal intelligence at such a level as to be distinct from such traditional intelligences. Study 1 also examines evidence of whether this emotional intelligence predicts empathy, parental warmth, and cultural pursuits.

Study 2 focused more specifically on whether emotional intelligence meets the developmental criterion for an intelligence. An adolescent sample was given a reduced set of the same group of tasks. The adolescent data are then compared to a subset of the adult data from Study 1 so as to test the hypothesis that adults outperform adolescents on the tasks.

STUDY 1

Method

Participants

Participants were 503 adults (164 men and 333 women, six unreported) with a mean age of 23 years (range: 17-70), drawn from several sources. One group of individuals (47%, N = 235) was comprised of full-time college students who participated to fulfill an introductory psychology course research requirement, or who were paid (US $15) for their participation. The remainder (53%, 268) were part-time college students, corporate employees, career workshop attendees, and executives in an outplacement setting, who volunteered. The full sample was roughly representative of the ethnic composition of the United States census (Self-identified ethnicity/race: African-American, 12% (58), Asian or Asian-American, 6% (31), Hispanic, 6% (32), Native American, 1% (4); White: 68% (340); Other/Not Reported: 7% (38)). The sample was above average in education: less than 1% (2) had no college, 80% (401) were in college or had been, 12% (59) were college graduates, 7% (34) had advanced degrees; information on the remainder 1% (7) was unreported.

The Multifactor Emotional Intelligence Scale (MEIS)

Overview of Test Organization. The MEIS consists of 12 tasks, divided into 4 classes or "branches" of abilities including (a) perceiving, (b) assimilating, (c) understanding, and (d) managing emotion (Mayer & Salovey, 1997; Mayer, Salovey & Caruso, 1997). Branch 1's four tests measured emotional perception in Faces, Music, Designs, and Stories. Branch 2's two tests measured Synesthesia Judgments and Feeling Biases. Branch 3's four tests examined the understanding of emotion, including in Blends, Progressions, and Transitions between and among emotions, and Relativity

Emotional Intelligence Meets Traditional Standards for an Intelligence

in emotional perception. Branch 4's two tests examined Emotion Management in the Self and Others. The content of the subtests and their scoring is described below, as are the three scoring methods employed: consensus, expert, and target.

Branch 1: Perceiving Emotion

Branch 1 tasks concerned the ability to perceive and identify the emotional content of a variety of stimuli.

Faces (Eight stimuli; 48 items). The first Branch 1 task, Faces, used as stimuli eight faces from a CD-ROM photographic library and from personal photos, chosen to represent a variety of emotions, and for their authenticity in representing those emotions. Each face was followed by six emotions: *happiness*, *anger*, *fear*, *sadness*, *disgust*, and *surprise*. The test-taker was to answer on a five point scale whether a given emotion (e.g., anger) was "Definitely Not Present" (1) or "Definitely Present" (5). The responses were scored according to two criteria: consensus and expert.

Consensus scoring. The group consensus served as the criterion for this scoring approach. Each participant response was scored according to its agreement with the proportion of the participant group who endorsed the same alternative. For example, if 0.51 of the participant group reported that anger was somewhat present ("4" on the scale) then a participant who chose "4" would receive 0.51 for the item. If the participant believed anger was definitely not present ("1" on the scale), and only 0.06 of the sample agreed, then the individual would receive a 0.06 for the item.

Expert scoring. The first two authors served as experts for the tasks, and went through the test answering questions by bringing to bear, as much as possible, their reading of Western philosophical treatments of emotion, and their reading of contemporary psychological models of emotion. For example, in deciding questions about emotional blends, reference was made to the theory of emotional blends by Plutchik (1984). For each item, the authors identified the best alternative (from 1 to 5) for each response; general agreement with this best response (choosing the selected value, or the integer on either side of it) was scored "1;" otherwise the individual received a "0."[4]

Music (Eight stimuli; 48 items). The second Branch 1 task, Music, was similar to the Faces task. The stimuli consisted of eight brief (5-10 s) original pieces of music composed for this project. Participants heard each piece of music and then rated each one as to its emotional content on a series of mood adjective scales. Each mood adjective was rated from 1 ("Definitely Not Present") to 5 ("Definitely Present"). The same six mood adjectives were employed as in Faces.

Target scoring. The music test was scored according to the consensus and expert methods used above. In addition, the target scoring method was employed here. Target scoring made use of an additional data set. As the composer-musician worked, he was requested to think about his feelings and the feelings his music conveyed, which he then recorded on a mood scale. Target scoring was scored for agreement with the target's feelings (in this case, the composer-musician). It was scored as the expert scoring was, with a "1" for a match (give or take 1) and "0" for a non-match. Indeed, the target can be thought of as a second type of expert.

Designs (Eight stimuli; 48 items). The third Branch 1 task, Designs, was identical to the above except that eight original computer-generated graphic designs served as the stimuli. The designer was requested to create graphics that portrayed a variety of feelings. As the designer worked, he recorded his feelings on the six-adjective mood scale about what he expressed in the design. Consensus, expert, and target scoring were employed for this task.

Stories (six stimuli; 42 items). The fourth Branch 1 task, Stories, was identical to the above tasks except that six stories were employed. The stories were obtained as in Mayer and Geher (1996). Fifteen adult acquaintances of the authors were asked to report on situations or thoughts affecting their moods, including (a) "What led up to the situation?", (b) "What is the situation, or what you are thinking about?, and (c) "What happened in this situation which made you feel the way you do?" Immediately thereafter, these 15 supplemental participants recorded their moods on a 30 item mood-adjective checklist, using the five-point rating scale described above (see Faces). The passages were then edited lightly. The six passages were then presented to participants in the main study. An example was as follows:

> *This story comes from a middle-aged man.* Everything has been piling up at work and I am falling behind. I have been working late many nights and as a result, my wife and daughter are feeling left out. My relationship with them is being stressed. I feel that I am letting them down emotionally. I feel guilty not spending time with them. At the same time, a close family member moved in with us after his divorce and job loss. We have no privacy and I finally told him he has to move out. It was very difficult for me, especially since in the way I was raised you don't treat a guest this way.

Each story was followed by a seven-adjective mood scale; the adjectives varied from story to story. They were selected so as to balance adjectives that were applicable to the story and those that were not, as well as to balance positive and negative-toned adjectives. For the above story, the seven adjectives were, "depressed, frustrated, guilty, energetic, liking, joyous, and happy." The participant's job was to identify the emotion in the story. The responses were scored by consensus, expert, and target criteria.

Branch 2: Assimilating Emotions

Branch 2 tasks concerned the ability to assimilate emotions into perceptual and cognitive processes.

Synesthesia (six stimuli; 60 items). The first Branch 2 task, Emotional Synesthesia, measured people's ability to describe emotional sensations and their parallels to other sensory modalities. The analysis of emotions often involves

Emotional Intelligence Meets Traditional Standards for an Intelligence

describing their composition in regard to other sense modalities, including movement, touch, pace, and color (Clynes, 1977; de Rivera, 1977). In this task, people imagined an event that could make them feel a particular feeling, which they then described on 10 semantic differential scales. For example, one item asked, "Imagine an event that could make you feel both somewhat surprised and somewhat displeased...Now describe your feelings on," each of 10, five-point semantic differential scales, including "warm 1 2 3 4 5 cold," and other scales involving color (yellow or purple) touch (sharp or dull) and so forth; the scales were invariant across stimuli. This task was scored by consensus and expert criteria.

Feeling Biases (four stimuli; 28 items). The second Branch 2 task, Feeling Biases, asked people to assimilate their present mood into their judgments of *how they felt toward* a [fictional] *person at the moment*. Thus, one task instructed participants to:

> Imagine that Jonathan is one of your relatives. He is a tall, muscular person. Jonathan said something to you that made you feel both guilty and afraid. Feeling both guilty and afraid about Jonathan, how does he seem?

The seven traits following each passage varied so as to be relevant to each passage; in the above example, traits included "sad, trusting, tense, cynical, aggressive, controlling, and hasty." The traits were rated on a five-point scale ("Definitely Does Not Describe" (1) to "Definitely Does Describe" (5)). The rationale for this task was that people who use their emotions in thinking do so in part by analyzing judgmental transformations that occur with mood. This task was scored according to consensus and expert criteria.

Branch 3: Understanding Emotions

Branch 3's tasks concerned reasoning about and understanding emotions.

Blends (eight stimuli; eight items). The first Branch 3 task, Blends, concerned the ability to analyze blended or complex emotions. Items were of the following form:

> Optimism most closely combines which two emotions?
> (a) pleasure and anticipation   (b) acceptance and joy
> (c) surprise and joy   (d) pleasure and joy.

Participants were instructed to select the single best answer. The eight items covered blends of two emotions (four items), blends of three emotions (two items), and blends of four emotions (two items). Scoring was by consensus and expert criteria.

Progressions (eight stimuli; eight items). The second Branch 3 task, Progressions, concerned people's understanding of how emotional reactions proceed over time, with a special focus on the intensification of feelings. A sample item read:

Emotional Intelligence Meets Traditional Standards for an Intelligence

If you feel angrier and angrier toward someone so that you are losing control, it would result in (choose one):

      (a) gloating   (b) resentment   (c) hate   (d) rage

Participants were instructed to identify the single best answer. Items were scored according to consensus and expert criteria.

Transitions (four stimuli; 24 items). The third Branch 3 task, Transitions, concerned people's understanding of how emotions (and implicitly, the situations eliciting them) follow upon one another. Items were of the following form:

> A person is afraid and later is calm. In between, what are the likely ways the person might feel?

Each item was followed by six alternative feelings. Alternatives for the above item were acceptance, fear, anger, anticipation, surprise, and disappointment. The participant rated each item as "Extremely Unlikely" (1) to have occurred, or as "Extremely Likely" (5). The remaining three items followed the same form.

Relativity (4 stimuli; 40 items). The fourth Branch 3 task, Relativity, was composed of items depicting conflictual social encounters between two characters. The participant's task was to estimate the feelings of both those characters. One item read:

> A dog is chasing sticks outside when he runs out in the street and gets hit by a car. The driver stops when the dog's owner dashes over to check on the dog.

The first items concern the dog-owner's feelings. Participants must decide to what extent the dog owner feels each of five ways, including, "ashamed about not being able to have better trained the dog," or "challenged to protect other dogs from mishaps." Each alternative was rated according to how likely a feeling-reaction was, from "Extremely Unlikely" (1) to "Extremely Likely" (5). Next, the participant made similar judgments as to the second character (the driver, above). In the above example, participants judged whether the driver felt "relief that it was only a dog," or "guilty for not being a more cautious driver," and so on, on the same response scale.

Branch 4: Managing Emotions

Branch 4 concerns the ability to manage emotions.

Managing Feelings of Others (six stimuli; 24 items). The first Branch 4 task, Social Regulation examines how participants manage the emotions of others. Participants were asked to evaluate plans of action in response to fictional people, described in brief vignettes, who needed assistance. The task consisted of six vignettes, each followed by four possible courses of action. For example:

One of your colleagues at work looks upset and asks if you will eat lunch with him. At the cafeteria, he motions for you to sit away from the other diners. After a few minutes of slow conversation he says that he wants to talk to you about what's on his mind. He tells you that he lied on his resume about having a college degree. Without the degree, he wouldn't have gotten the job.

Participants were to rate alternatives such as (for the above vignette):

Ask him how he feels about it so you can understand what's going on. Offer to help him, but don't push yourself on him if he really doesn't want any of your help.

Participants rated responses from "Extremely Ineffective (1)" to "Extremely Effective (5)." Tasks were scored according to consensus and expert criteria.

Managing Feelings of the Self (six stimuli; 24 items). The second Branch 4 task, Managing Feelings of the Self, concerns how a person would regulate his own emotions. This task consisted of six vignettes, each one describing a particular emotional problem. For example:

You have been dating the same person for several months and feel very comfortable. Lately, you are thinking that this relationship may be the one and although marriage hasn't been discussed, you are assuming that it is a real possibility. The last thing you expected was the phone call you received saying that the relationship is over. You have lost the love of your life.

Participants were instructed that not every situation is equally applicable to everyone but to imagine, if in that situation, the effectiveness of given responses. One such response to the above situation was:

The best way to cope with this terrible blow is to do whatever you can to block it out and not let it get to you any more than it has. You would throw yourself into your work or some activity and then try to put it behind you.

Participants rated each response from "Extremely Ineffective (1)" to "Extremely Effective (5)." Tasks were scored according to consensus and expert criteria.

Criterion Scales

Two classes of criterion scales were employed along with the MEIS. Primary criteria included measures of intelligence and self-reported empathic feeling, both of which have been predicted to correlate with emotional intelligence in the past (Mayer, et al., 1990; Salovey & Mayer, 1990). Secondary criteria included measures of several areas in which emotionally intelligent individuals are thought to differ from others.

These include higher life satisfaction, a family environment that encourages learning about feelings, and aesthetic perception and participation (Mayer & Salovey, 1990; 1995; Salovey & Mayer, 1990).

Primary Criteria

Intelligence Measure. The intelligence criterion was adapted from the Army Alpha test of intelligence (Yerkes, 1921). The Army Alpha was employed because its validity is well-established and its form is ideal for group testing of the sort carried out here. The vocabulary scale was used because that subtest is the strongest component of verbal intelligence (e.g., Morrison, 1976, p. 318-325; Wechsler, 1958). Thirty of the more difficult vocabulary items from the 50 were selected; more difficult items were favored so as to tailor the test to the participant population, which included mostly college-educated individuals. The Army Alpha vocabulary scale employs four response options for each word to be defined (e.g., "Reply: (1) make (2) do (3) answer (4) come"). Participants were instructed to select the alternative from the list that most nearly meant the same as the target word. The scale had an alpha reliability of $a = 0.88$ in this data set.

Empathy Measure. A 30-item empathy scale (Caruso & Mayer, 1999) was developed with content coverage similar to the Epstein-Mehrabian scale (Mehrabian & Epstein, 1972), but with identifiable factor-based subscales. This newer scale was employed so that overall self-reported empathy and also its subcomponents could be compared to emotional intelligence. The scale's overall self-reported empathy score has an alpha reliability of $a = 0.86$. Because of content overlap with the Epstein-Mehrabian scale, it is likely to perform similarly to it. In contrast to the Epstein-Mehrabian, however, the present scale can be divided into five more specific factor-based scales. The five subscales, their reliabilities, and a sample item from each are: (a) Empathic Suffering, $a = 0.79$, "The suffering of others deeply disturbs me;" (b) Positive Sharing, $a = 0.72$, "Seeing other people smile makes me smile;" (c) Responsive Crying, ($a = 0.74$), e.g., "I cry easily when seeing a sad movie;" (d) Avoidance, $a = 0.72$, "I find it annoying when other people cry in public;" and (e) Feeling for Others, $a = 0.61$, "If someone is upset, I get upset too."

Secondary Criteria

Life Satisfaction. Each person was asked about their satisfaction with his Relationships, Academic Status, and Career and Work Situation, to be reported on a five-point rating scale (from "Not at All Satisfied" to "Extremely Satisfied"). A factor analysis indicated the items were unifactorial although they were only moderately intercorrelated. A single life satisfaction score ($a = 0.59$) was employed, representing the sum of each person's responses.

Artistic Skills. Participants also reported their degree of artistic skill in eight areas (from "1" no or little talent to "3" very talented). A unifactorial "Artistic Skill" score ($a = 0.71$) indicated overall self-reported artistic skill in those areas, which included sculpture, music, and writing.

Emotional Intelligence Meets Traditional Standards for an Intelligence

Parental Warmth. Participants also described their parents' behaviors on a seven-item scale. A unifactorial parental "Parental Warmth" factor ($a = 0.81$) included items reporting that parents were warm, listened, were non-abusive, and, (reversed) yelled and were strict.

Psychotherapy. Psychotherapy was scored as the number of months a person had psychotherapy (which for some people was zero) multiplied by the number of sessions of psychotherapy per month.

Life-Space Leisure. Life space scales consist of items that record a person's environment in terms of discrete, externally verifiable, responses (e.g., "How many pairs of shoes do you own?" "How many times have you attended the theater in the last year?"; Mayer, 1998; Mayer, Carlsmith, & Chabot, 1998). Certain life activities, particularly those involving aesthetic appreciation, have been predicted to involve more emotional intelligence than others (Mayer, et al., 1990). Thirty-three items concerning leisure activities were administered to participants covering books read, television watched, and cultural events observed. These items yielded three factor-based scales of leisure activities, based on an unrotated, principal components analysis, using all items loading on a given factor $r > +/- 0.45$. The first, Culture-Seeking, factor scale ($a = 0.78$) loaded the following items: listening to classical music, attending concerts, listening to soul, listening to gospel, listening to country, listening to rap, listening to new-age music, listening to bluegrass, listening to rock, and attending museums. The second, Improvement-Seeking, scale ($a = 0.60$), loaded reading self-help books, how-to books, medical books, business books, and short-stories. The third, Entertainment-Seeking, factor scale ($a = 0.67$), loaded watching action television programs, watching comedy programs, listening to punk music, listening to blues music, and watching televised sports.

Procedure

Participants completed the study in small groups or individually. Each participant received an item and answer booklet that contained all necessary instructions, test items and responses. The test was not timed and the test materials were self-administered, with the exception of the music task, for which a tape of instructions and music was played by the experimenter in group settings.

Results

This section is divided into three parts. First, scoring methods for emotional intelligence are compared. Second, the emotional intelligence tasks are intercorrelated and factor analyzed. Third, emotional intelligence is correlated with various external criteria.

Scoring for Emotional Intelligence

Consensus, Expert, and Target Criteria for Correct Answers

Emotional intelligence depends on the idea that certain emotional problems have answers that can be judged correct and incorrect. Convergence among different scoring criteria provides a foundation for such assumptions. The data analysis began by comparing the three different methods for identifying a correct answer: according to (a) the group consensus, (b) expert's identification, and, (c) a target's assessment (for three tasks only). We began by examining the degree to which these three methods converged toward a correct response. To the extent that the group consensus (as identified by the modal response) and experts agree as to the best answer, their selections should intercorrelate over the items of a given test. For example, if both the group consensus and experts agree that anger is high in one story ("4" or "5"), but low in another ("1" or "2"), then the correlations should be high.

To test the relation between consensus and expert ratings, we selected four tasks, each drawn randomly from one of the four branches, and calculated the intercorrelation between ratings. The four tasks collectively contain 127 items, representing each branch, and provide a good estimate of the test's overall pattern. For

Table 1
Means, Standard Deviations, and Reliabilities (Coefficient Alpha) of the Agreement with Consensus, Expert, and Target Criteria.

Branch and Task	Scoring Method								
	Consensus			Expert			Target		
	M	S	a	M	S	a	M	S	a
Emotional Identification									
1: Faces	0.40	0.08	0.89	0.64	0.11	0.74	—	—	—
1: Music	0.44	0.11	0.94	0.73	0.10	0.86	0.75	0.12	0.88
1: Designs	0.36	0.08	0.90	0.69	0.11	0.74	0.65	0.14	0.81
1: Stories	0.38	0.07	0.85	0.72	0.11	0.72	0.66	0.10	0.61
Assimilating Emotions									
2: Synesthesia	0.31	0.04	0.86	0.69	0.09	0.66	—	—	—
2: Feeling Biases	0.30	0.05	0.70	0.72	0.12	0.60	—	—	—
Understanding Emotions									
3: Blends	0.49	0.10	0.49	0.60	0.19	0.35	—	—	—
3: Progressions	0.58	0.10	0.51	0 83	0.16	0.50	—	—	—
3: Transitions	0.30	0.04	0.94	0.56	0.11	0.85	—	—	—
3: Relativity	0.30	0.04	0.78	0.56	0.11	0.63	—	—	—
Managing Emotions									
4: Managing Others	0.28	0.04	0.72	0.60	0.12	0.42	—	—	—
4: Managing Self	0.27	0.04	0.70	0.55	0.12	0.40	—	—	—

Emotional Intelligence Meets Traditional Standards for an Intelligence

each item, we paired the modal consensus choice with the specific expert selection. In fact, the consensus and expert ratings were fairly highly intercorrelated across tasks: Stories (Branch 1) $r = 0.70$, Feeling Bias (Branch 2) $r = 0.64$, Relativity (Branch 3) $r = 0.61$, and Managing Feelings of Others (Branch 4) $r = 0.80$. (All r's were significant, $p < 0.0001$ level). This suggests that the two criteria are closely related.

The third, Target criterion was available only for three Branch 1 tasks. This criterion involves reports by the Targets of their actual feelings as they were creating their artistry (Music and Designs) or telling how they felt (Stories). In general, Consensus correlated a bit more highly with the Target criteria than did the Expert criterion (Music task: $r = 0.61$ for consensus, $r = 0.52$ for expert; Designs, $r = 0.70$ and 0.60; Stories, $r = 0.80$ and 0.69).

Generally speaking, the three criteria appeared to correlate moderately highly, indicating that some answers were "more correct" than others, according to any and all of the scoring methods used: consensus, expert, and target.

Agreement Scoring for Consensus, Expert, and Target Criteria

A given participant's performance can be assessed in relation to each of the above three scores: Consensus, Expert, and Target. These agreement scores represent the degree to which a given participant's responses coincided with those of the criteria. The means, standard deviations, and reliabilities of the participants' performance, broken down by the three scoring methods, can be seen in Table 1. The means are not directly comparable across consensus, expert, and target because of their substantially different scoring approaches (see above). The figures do indicate, however, the average performance level of the sample, and also that there were no problems of floor or ceiling effects in any of the three scoring methods.

The reliabilities of the agreement scores are also promising, with individual tasks having reliabilities most often between $a = 0.70$ to 0.94, for consensus, and a bit lower for expert agreement. The first two tasks of Branch 3, which were also the shortest, had lower reliabilities, $a = 0.35$ to 0.51; the Branch 4 management tasks were also low, but for expert scoring only. All the reliabilities are satisfactory for this exploratory study concerning the factorial structure of emotional intelligence and what it predicts.

Sex Differences in Performance

Women performed somewhat higher than men on the 12 tasks, according to all the scoring procedures. The difference was .5 standard deviations for consensus agreement ($M_{women} = 0.376$; $SD_{women} = 0.029$; $M_{men} = 0.358$; $SD_{men} = 0.036$; Hotelling's $F(12, 409) = 4.0$, $p < 0.001$.), and about 0.1 standard deviations for each of expert agreement ($M_{women} = 0.664$; $SD_{women} = 0.048$; $M_{men} = 0.657$; $SD_{men} = 0.061$; Hotelling's $F(12, 408) = 4.7$, $p < 0.001$), and target agreement ($M_{women} = 0.689$; $SD_{women} = 0.093$; $M_{men} = 0.676$; $SD_{men} = 0.079$; Hotelling's $F(3, 482) = 1.34$, n.s.). This replicates earlier similar findings (Mayer & Geher, 1996; cf. Buck, 1984). We endeavored to understand more about this difference by focusing on the Story task in particular, which was representative of the full test according to subsequent factor analyses (see below). The Story task also showed the greatest sex differences, and contained all three scoring criteria. It is possible that women outperformed men using consensus scoring because the women were using a women's criterion which was different than the men, and the larger number of women in the sample (N = 333 versus 164) meant that the women's choices were scored with higher values than the men's. This, however, did not account for the women's slightly better performance. Women and men seemed to be employing close to the same criterion. The correlation between women's and men's choices for the emotional content across the 42 story items (six stories, seven items each) was $r(42) = 0.993$, indicating a high level of agreement. (Nor was there any difference in the average emotion-level perceived on an item: $M_{women} = 2.67$; $SD_{women} = 1.19$; $M_{men} = 2.69$; $SD_{men} = 1.04$; $t(41) = 0.77$, n.s.).

We further examined women and men's performance by employing a two (male participant/female participant) by two (male story character/female story character) by two (male-selected consensus/female-selected consensus) MANOVA on the story data. The MANOVA yielded a main effect representing the women's better consensual accuracy ($F(1,495) = 20.08$, $p < 0.001$). Women outperformed men under all conditions, even using male-chosen consensus across stories ($M_{women} = 0.37$; $SD_{women} = 0.056$; $M_{men} = 0.35$; $SD_{men} = 0.059$; $t(495) = 3.68$, $p < 0.001$). A second main effect indicated that the participants, as a whole, were more accurate when using women's consensus criteria over men's ($F(1,495) = 928.7$, $p < 0.001$). A sex by consensus interaction indicated that women did slightly better using their own consensus criterion ($F(1,495) = 67.3$, $p < 0.001$). There was also a sex-of-target effect that favored judgments concerning male targets ($F(1,495) = 696.3$, $p < 0.001$). Collectively, these results indicate that women generally do better than men on these tasks and that the results are not caused by any simple bias in the test materials or how they are scored. Moreover, if one judges by the consensus scoring (which may be fairest, as the expert's criteria were developed by the male authors), the difference between women and men's performance is a moderate .5 standard deviation in size.

Correlations Among Consensus, Expert, and Target-Scored Tasks

Consensus and Expert Scoring Considered Individually. One correlational standard for an intelligence is that it defines a cluster of interrelated abilities (Guttman & Levy, 1991). The following analyses examine the intercorrelations among the 12 tasks to see if they show a "positive manifold" — i.e., a correlation matrix in which most tasks correlate positively with one another. Correlations among the 12 emotional intelligence tasks were calculated using all three scoring methods. In each case, a positive manifold was evident. Scored by the consensus method, the tasks mostly correlated with one another between $r = 0.20$ and 0.50, with the full range spanning $r = 0.07$ to 0.68. Scored by the expert method, the tasks mostly correlated with one another $r = 0.10$ to 0.40, with a full range from $r = 0.00$ to 0.54. In either case, the matrix possesses a positive manifold; almost all the tasks are positively intercorrelated, as expected in regard to a unified intelligence. The consensus-scored tasks (with alpha reliabilities on the diagonal) can be seen in Table 2.

Emotional Intelligence Meets Traditional Standards for an Intelligence

Table 2
Intercorrelations of the Consensus Scored Tasks with Reliabilities (Coefficient Alpha) on the Diagonal*

Branch and Task	1				2		3				4	
	Fa	Mu	De	St	Sy	Fe	Bl	Pr	Tr	Re	Mo	Ms
Emotional Identification												
1: Faces	*0.89*											
1: Music	0.61	*0.94*										
1: Designs	0.68	0.60	*0.90*									
1: Stories	0.54	0.47	0.54	*0.85*								
Assimilating Emotions												
2: Synesthesia	0.24	0.24	0.26	0.38	*0.86*							
2: Feeling biases	0.30	0.24	0.35	0.47	0.39	*0.71*						
Understanding Emotions												
3: Blends	0.07	0.13	0.09	0.24	0.22	0.26	*0.49*					
3: Progressions	0.10	0.15	0.14	0.25	0.34	0.35	0.41	*0.51*				
3: Transitions	0.25	0.29	0.29	0.37	0.26	0.34	0.19	0.17	*0.94*			
3: Relativity	0.30	0.35	0.32	0.41	0.32	0.38	0.30	0.34	0.43	*0.78*		
Managing Emotions												
4: Managing Others	0.20	0.21	0.20	0.28	0.25	0.24	0.16	0.22	0.18	0.37	*0.72*	
4: Managing Self	0.19	0.15	0.14	0.30	0.27	0.22	0.20	0.23	0.17	0.25	0.54	*0.70*

*$N = 500$. Note that correlations above $\tilde{r} = 0.08$ are significant at beyond the $p < .01$ level.

Comparisons among Consensus, Expert, and Target Scoring. To further compare scoring methods, we examined participants' performance on each of the 12 tasks, scored according to a consensus, expert-scoring, or target criterion. For consensus and expert scoring (which were available for all 12 tasks), participants' performance, scored each way correlated between $r = -0.16$ and 0.95, with half the tasks above $r = 0.52$. The only negative correlation ($r = -0.16$), which occurred for faces, and other low correlations for the Designs task ($r = 0.24$) may have been a consequence of different color photocopying employed to reproduce the stimuli for the groups and the experts.

The convergence for participant's consensus and target scores for the Music, Designs, and Stories tasks (where target scoring was available) were $r = 0.81$, 0.22, and 0.43 respectively; the same values for expert and target scoring were $r = 0.67$, 0.46, and 0.16. Subsequent analyses indicated the general superiority of the consensus scoring method in relation to the other alternatives. It yielded higher alpha test reliabilities for every task without exception, clearer factor results, (which were, nonetheless, highly similar to expert scoring), and higher correlations with criteria. The superiority of consensus scoring has been argued persuasively elsewhere (e.g., Legree, 1995). For that reason, the subsequent analyses focus on the consensus scoring.

Table 3
Three-Factor Solutions for the Emotional Intelligence Test Scored According to Consensus and According to Expert Criteria, in Unrotated and Rotated Solutions: Principal Components Factoring[a]

		Unrotated			Oblique Rotated (Pattern Matrix)[b]		
Solution	Branch/Task	I	II	III	I	II	III
Unrotated Solution							
Emotional Identification							
	1: Faces	**0.67**	**-0.48**	-0.11	-0.10	**0.86**	0.04
	1: Music	**0.63**	**-0.34**	-0.04	0.02	**0.70**	0.02
	1: Design	**0.69**	**-0.44**	-0.02	0.01	**0.82**	-0.03
	1: Stories	**0.73**	-0.09	0.05	0.30	**0.52**	0.08
Assimilating Emotions							
	2: Synesthesia	**0.51**	0.19	0.10	**0.43**	-0.12	0.10
	2: Feeling biases	**0.59**	0.13	0.21	**0.53**	-0.20	-0.00
Understanding Emotions							
	3: Blends	**0.35**	**0.32**	0.24	**0.57**	-0.10	-0.01
	3: Progressions	**0.43**	**0.38**	**0.25**	**0.64**	-0.11	0.02
	3: Transitions	**0.48**	0.04	0.12	**0.35**	0.23	0.00
	3: Relativity	**0.61**	0.18	0.09	**0.45**	0.20	0.14
Managing Emotions							
	4: Managing Others	**0.49**	**0.36**	**-0.49**	-0.05	0.00	**0.81**
	4: Managing Self	**0.44**	**0.36**	**-0.38**	0.03	-0.03	**0.68**

[a]Loadings above +/- .25 are in bold typeface for clarity
[b]Loadings indicated that all three factors were unipolar (that is, loadings on a factor above +/-.25 all shared the same sign). Rotated factors II and III, however, were negative. To clarify results and facilitate discussion, loadings on rotated Factors II and III were reversed in sign here and in subsequent analyses.

Emotional Intelligence Meets Traditional Standards for an Intelligence

The Structure of Emotional Intelligence

Factor Structure of the MEIS

Our next question was whether emotional intelligence is best characterized as one or many abilities. Although a highly developed theory of emotional intelligence motivates this article, this represented our own first empirical examination of so many tasks. For that reason, we employed exploratory factor analysis at the outset. We therefore applied principal axis factoring (with communalities on the matrix diagonal) to scores on the 12 MEIS subscales. A joint scree/meaningfulness criterion yielded a three factor solution (first six eigenvalues: 4.3, 1.6, 1.1, 0.9, 0.8, 0.6). Table 3 (left columns) show the three-factor, unrotated solution for the 12 consensus-scored subscales. We then further analyzed this three-factor solution by rotating it according to an oblique criterion (using an oblimin procedure). The right columns of Table 3 show this result.

In the unrotated solution, the first factor may be interpreted as a general emotional intelligence (g_{ei}) because it loads all the tasks without exception. This g_{ei} apparently represents a group factor of emotional intelligence tasks, suggesting their interrelatedness (below, we explore this question further). The second factor, Managing vs. Perceiving Emotions, discriminates tasks high in reasoning from those high in simple emotional perception. And the third factor, Managing Emotions, describes the two Branch 4 tasks concerning regulating emotions in oneself and others.

The rotated version of this three-factor solution tells the same story from a different angle. The first factor, Emotional Understanding, loads most of the tasks on Branch 3 (Understanding), along with tasks on Branch 2 (Assimilation). The second factor, Emotional Perception, loads most of the tasks on Branch 1 (Perception). The third, Managing Emotion factor, loads the two Branch 4 (Regulation) tasks, as in the unrotated solution. In this analysis, oblimin factors 2 and 3 had uniformly negative loadings. We reversed the loadings in sign so that a higher score indicated a higher level of ability across tasks. We similarly changed the sign of factor scores and scales based on these two factors. This procedure simplifies the presentation and discussion of results while remaining consistent with the substantive findings.

As a pattern matrix should do, this solution "turns up the contrast" on the loadings, separating the test into three portions: perception, understanding, and managing. This is done in part by transferring the common variance shared among the individual tasks to the three factors underlying them. As a consequence the three factors intercorrelate fairly substantially. Perception correlated $r = 0.39$ with Understanding and $r = .49$ with Management; the latter two intercorrelated $r = 0.33$.

The above results provide strong empirical support for a three factor model of the MEIS. Recall that our theoretical model involves a four branch model. We wondered whether there was also evidence for a four-factor model. To fully investigate this possibility, we modeled the data as a four-factor solution using covariance structural modeling. We used a stringent model in which each task was forced to load only on its hypothesized factor and no other (e.g., Arbuckle, 1997, p. 396). The factors themselves, however, were allowed to intercorrelate as above. The model fit was sufficiently good to be informative, with a Root Mean Square Error of Approximation (RMSEA) of .09 with no relaxation of parameters[5] (one rule of thumb is that a RMSEA .05 indicates a close fit; Browne & Cudeck, 1993). As appealing as this four-factor model is to us, the drawback is that the model estimates two of the factors, Assimilation and Understanding, to intercorrelate $r = .87$, which makes them difficult to distinguish from one another. For that reason, we continue to focus on the three-factor model in our analyses, while acknowledging that the four-factor model remains viable.

Hierarchical Relations Among Factors and the Creation of MEIS Scales

The first unrotated factor of the MEIS was earlier said to represent a g_{ei}, or general factor of the test. Such general factors sometimes can arise spuriously due to the nature of principal axis factoring. For that reason, it is often recommended that a hierarchical factor analysis be employed as a secondary check of the existence of a hierarchical factor (e.g., Carroll, 1993; Jensen & Weng, 1994). Obtaining a hierarchical (second-order) factor that loads all the primary factors is generally considered stronger evidence for a general factor because it is based solely on the covariances among the primary factors. A new factor analysis was therefore conducted on the Perception, Understanding, and Managing factor scores. A single hierarchical factor was extracted that loaded Perception, Understanding, and Management at substantial levels ($r = 0.50$, 0.86, and 0.75 respectively).[6] This hierarchical factor correlated with the unrotated first factor of the principal axis factoring at $r = 0.94$. This final result indicates that general emotional intelligence can be reasonably represented by the first unrotated principal axis factor, and that it loads all the scales studied here.

The Construction of Factor-Based Scales

For our further analyses, we first constructed factor scales for Perception, Understanding, and Managing Emotions factors (and for General Emotional Intelligence, g_{ei}, based on the first unrotated factor). The scales were constructed by summing z-scored subscale scores from tasks that loaded on the factors above $r = +/- 0.35$. The resulting factor-based scales were then correlated with the original factor scales (based on a weighted sum of all 12 scales) to ensure that they represented the original scales adequately. The three factor-based scales representing perception, understanding, and managing, correlated very highly with their respective factor scales ($r = 0.98$, 0.97, and 0.98, respectively), and were highly reliable ($a = 0.96$, 0.92, and 0.81). The three factor-based scales were moderately intercorrelated (Perception with Understanding, $r = 0.44$; Perception with Managing, $r = 0.29$; Understanding with Managing, $r = 0.43$). The overall general emotional intelligence factor-based scale also correlated with its original factor scale $r = 0.97$, and had a reliability of $a = 0.96$. These are the scales reported in the rest of the article.

Researchers wishing to retain the four branch theoretical model (modestly supported by covariance structural modeling, above) may wish to employ four, rather than three, factor-based scales. The above three scales may be transformed into four

Emotional Intelligence Meets Traditional Standards for an Intelligence

by (a) retaining the Perception and Managing scales as calculated above, and (b) splitting the Understanding scale, above, into two scales. The first of these two scales, the revised Understanding scale, is calculated as the sum of the z-scores of the Blends, Progressions, Transitions, and Relativity tasks. The second of these two scales, the new Assimilation scale, is calculated as the sum of the z-scores of the Synesthesia and Feeling Biases tasks.[7] The reliabilities of the (unchanged) perception, (new) Assimilation, (revised) Understanding, and (unchanged) Management factor-based scales are, respectively, $a = 0.96$, 0.86, 0.89, and 0.81. The Understanding factor-based scale still correlates with the original factor scale $r = 0.89$. The new, Assimilation factor-based scale, correlates with Understanding $r = 0.65$.

Relation of the Emotional Intelligence Factors to Criterion Measures

The final correlational criterion for an intelligence is that it correlates moderately with intelligences in other domains. The correlation should be high enough to indicate that the new skill is an intelligence, but low enough to illustrate that it says something new about human abilities. Aside from emotional intelligence's correlation with verbal intelligence, emotional intelligence will be important to the degree that it predicts other criteria as well.

Table 4 shows the correlation of the emotional intelligence factors with various criteria. The central correlations to examine are those with the g_{ei} factor (first column). General emotional intelligence is then divided into subfactors of perception, understanding, and management; correlations with those subfactors are shown in the next three columns.

The correlation between the General Emotional-Intelligence factor-based scale and verbal intelligence is $r = 0.36$, $p < 0.001$. This is the moderate level at which one would hope that a new domain of intelligence would be correlated with existing domains. In addition, emotional intelligence has a number of interesting correlations with other variables. The g_{ei} factor-based scale correlates $r = 0.33$, $p < 0.001$ with overall empathy, also as expected (Mayer, et al., 1990; Mayer & Geher, 1996; Salovey & Mayer, 1990), and possesses a number of significant correlations with subtypes of empathy as well, correlating positively and at similar levels with Suffering, Positive Sharing, and negatively with Avoidance. Emotional intelligence had a positive correlation with parental warmth, $r = 0.23$, $p < 0.01$, and a negative correlation with pragmatic attempts at self-improvement $r = -0.16$, $p < 0.01$, including reading self-help books, books on business methods, and the like. The subfactor scales further qualify the relations, suggesting that Understanding is most closely related to verbal intelligence among the three subfactors, and that Management most accounts for empathy; all three subfactors are related to Parental Warmth.

An extremely stringent test would partial verbal IQ and self-reported empathy out of the correlation between emotional intelligence and the six secondary criteria. Doing this may remove variance that legitimately belongs to emotional intelligence, but it also ensures that emotional intelligence contributes unique variance in predicting criteria.

Partialing out the influence of intelligence and empathy yielded a g_{ei} that maintained its significant negative correlation with attempted self-improvement ($r = -0.10$, $p < 0.05$), and added a negative relation to culture-seeking ($r = -0.09$, $p < 0.05$), although it no longer correlated with life satisfaction or parenting.

Although the statistical relations between emotional intelligence and the life space criteria may seem low, two things are worth noting about them. First, our central focus has been on understanding the structure of emotional intelligence. The few secondary criterion scales included here were exploratory and brief. Even these crude measures, however, demonstrate that emotional intelligence predicts criteria

Table 4
Correlations Between Individual Tasks and Selected Criterion Variables.

Criterion Variables	Overall Score	Subfactor Scores		
	g_{ei}	perception	understand.	management
Primary Criteria				
Ability				
Verbal IQ	0.36**	0.16**	0.40**	0.20**
Empathy				
Overall	0.33**	0.20**	0.25**	0.34**
Suffering	0.35*	0.18**	0.28**	0.37**
Positive Feelings	0.26**	0.12**	0.16*	0.36**
Crying	0.14**	0.10*	0.10*	0.13**
Avoidance	-0.26**	-0.20**	-0.23**	-0.15**
Feel for Others	0.16**	0.08	0.09*	0.24**
Secondary Criteria				
Life Satisfaction	0.11*	0.01	0.11*	0.13**
Artistic Skills	0.05	0.03	0.07	0.00
Parental Warmth	0.23**	0.20**	0.18**	0.15**
Psychotherapy	0.03	0.04	0.14*	0.02
Leisure (Life Space)				
Culture-Seeking	0.00	-0.07	0.01	0.03
Self-Improvement	-0.16**	-0.07	-0.22**	-0.05
Entertainment	-.002	0.09*	-0.04	0.05

*$p < 0.05$ level; **$p < 0.01$ level, two tailed tests.

Emotional Intelligence Meets Traditional Standards for an Intelligence

independent of the influence of both verbal intelligence and empathy. Second, it is worth recalling that personality relations tend to be small but consistent over the years. This small but consistent influence can substantially change a person's position in life, just like a slow but steady current can move a boat a considerable distance across a lake over time.

Summary and Discussion of Study 1

The results from Study 1 indicate that emotional intelligence shows a pattern that is consistent with a new domain of intelligence. Emotional intelligence can be operationalized as sets of abilities, and better answers can be distinguished from worse answers, as indicated by the convergence of three scoring methods. The 12 tasks also intercorrelate with one another, independent of which scoring method is employed. The scale yields four scores: A first, superordinate factor of general emotional intelligence that provides one excellent and economical method for representing the concept. The General Emotional Intelligence factor can be divided in turn into three subscales: Perception, Understanding, and Managing (thus reducing our four-branch model to a three-branch model). Finally, emotional intelligence correlates moderately with a measure of verbal intelligence, indicating that it is related to other intelligences without being the same as them. Emotional intelligence shows promise as a predictor of other qualities such as empathy, (retrospective) parenting style, and life activities.

STUDY 2

Thus far, emotional intelligence has met two of three important criteria of a traditional intelligence. First it has been operationalized as a set of abilities. Second, it has shown a pattern of correlations consistent with the existence of such an intelligence. The third criterion is that intellectual capacities grow with age and experience from childhood to early adulthood (Brown, 1997; Fancher, 1985). The importance of age to intelligence was first recognized by Binet. As Fancher (1985, p. 71) describes it:

> Gradually...a key insight developed — one which seemed perfectly obvious once recognized, but which nevertheless had previously eluded Binet and other investigators of intelligence. *Age* was a crucial factor to be considered: both subnormal and normal children might learn to pass the same tests, but normal children did so at a younger age.

Fancher attributes Binet's success in measuring intelligence, in comparison to the failures of his contemporaries, to the realization that mental abilities grow with age and experience.

For emotional intelligence to behave as does a standard intelligence, it should be shown to increase with age. To test whether this actually occurs, several portions of the scale employed in Study 1 were administered to a young adolescent sample (Ages 12-

16) in Study 2. The performance of the adolescents was then compared to the performance of an adult subsample drawn from Study 1. The use of two samples close in age ensures that the same test items can be used and understood by both groups. It also provides a challenging test of the developmental hypothesis because proximity in age should yield only small differences in performance between the two groups. We hypothesized that the adult sample would significantly out-perform the adolescents on the scale.

Method
Adolescent Sample
Participants were 229 adolescents (125 young men, 101 young women; 3 unidentified) with a mean age of 13.4 (range 12-16) who were recruited from two independent secondary schools and a religious youth group. These were split among 35% (81) 7th graders, 36% (83) 8th graders, 9% (20) 9th graders, 12% (27) 10th graders, 6% (13) 11th graders, and 1% (2) 12th graders; (percentages add to 99% due to rounding error). The sample deviated somewhat from the ethnic composition of the United States census in under-representing minority groups (Self-identified ethnicity/ race: African-American, 5% (12), Asian or Asian-American, 3% (6), Hispanic, 3% (7), Native American, 0% (0), White: 79% (177), Other/Not Reported: 9% (27).

Adult Sample
The adult sample from Study 1 was again used in Study 2. Here, however, the adult sample was divided on the basis of subject number into two equal-sized samples: the "Independent Adult Sample" and the "Consensus Sample." The Independent Adult Sample served as the comparison group for the adolescent group. The Consensus Sample was used to calculate a consensus score to which the first, "Independent Sample" had not contributed.

Materials
For reasons of time and age-appropriateness, only a subset of the scales administered to adults were administered to the developmental sample. These included Faces, Music, Designs, and (age-appropriate portions of) Stories from Branch 1,[8] Synesthesia from Branch 2, and Blends and Relativity from Branch 3. In addition, the Army Alpha Vocabulary scale and the Empathy scale were administered as criteria.[9]

Procedure
Parental consent was first obtained for each participant in the adolescent group, and then informed consent obtained from each subject. All data were collected anonymously; no names were requested. Furthermore, subjects were explicitly instructed not to answer any questions that made them uncomfortable.

Participants in the developmental sample were tested in a similar manner to the adults. They completed the materials in small groups. Each participant received an item and answer booklet that contained all necessary instructions, test items and responses. For the music task, a researcher (or a classroom teacher), played the cassette tape that included all necessary instructions as well as the musical selections. Students required 45 to 75 minutes to complete the test booklet.

Table 5
A Test of the Developmental Hypothesis: Means (and Standard Deviations) of Adult versus Adolescent Performance on Selected Consensus-Scored Scales of Emotional Intelligence

Branch/Task	Adult		Adolescent		
	M	SD	M	SD	F
Emotional Identification					
1: Faces	0.400	0.078	0.384	0.075	5.2*
1: Music	0.445	0.092	0.438	0.074	0.5
1: Design	0.359	0.086	0.353	0.077	0.7
1: Stories	0.328	0.069	0.323	0.061	1.5
Assimilating Emotions					
2: Synesthesia	0.306	0.045	0.295	0.047	7.8**
Understanding Emotions					
3: Blends	0.491	0.087	0.424	0.105	52.2**
3: Relativity	0.307	0.053	0.304	0.058	0.2
Combined Tests	0.378	0.046	0.359	0.048	25.6**

* $p < 0.05$; ** $p < 0.01$

Results

Scoring

Three scoring procedures were employed as in Study 1: agreement with consensus, expert ratings, and target reports. Some modifications in the consensus scoring were necessary for this study. Using the adult consensus as in Study 1 would plainly favor adults because each adult's score contributed to the consensus. To control for this, the adult sample was divided in half (on the basis of odd/even subject number). Next, new adult consensus scores were calculated for the even half of the sample only (the consensus sample). This left the odd half of the adult sample with responses that were independent of the adult consensus (the independent sample). It was this "independent" adult sample whose consensus scores were compared to the adolescent's consensus scores. Expert-scoring and target-scoring were the same as in Study 1.

<u>Adult-Adolescent Comparisons</u>

The central purpose of Study 2 was to examine whether adults functioned at a higher level of emotional intelligence than adolescents. This hypothesis was tested via a two (Age-Group) by seven (Task) ANOVA, where the seven tasks were within-subjects variables. As the developmental hypothesis predicted, scores were higher for adults than for adolescents for consensus agreement (Grand Mean = 0.38 versus 0.36; $F(1, 713) = 23.8$, $p < 0.001$), for expert agreement (Grand Mean = 0.66 versus 0.64; $F(1, 709) = 22.3$, $p < 0.001$), and for target agreement (Grand Mean = 0.69 versus 0.67; Hotelling's $F(1, 718) = 8.0$, $p < 0.01$). Significant Task and Age X Task effects were also present for all three scoring methods. Focusing on consensus scoring, there was a significant Age-Group X Task interaction for consensus ($F(6, 708) = 12.5$, $p < 0.01$). Table 5 shows a more detailed comparison between the adult and adolescent groups for consensus scoring on the individual tasks they both received, and which tasks showed significant differences in the predicted direction on their own. We did not examine age-performance correlations beyond demonstrating these average differences. First, the two samples were not strictly comparable, as the adolescents were of slightly higher social class (and therefore would be expected to perform more highly than average). More seriously, the restriction of age-range in both samples would render the correlation impossible to assess. We did, however, determine that the adolescents' scores showed the same pattern of correlations with verbal intelligence ($r(220) = .45$, $p < 0.001$) and empathy ($r(227) = 0.37$, $p < 0.001$) as did the adults.

Discussion of Study 2

Study 2 tested whether emotional intelligence met the third of three criteria for a standard, conventional intelligence: whether ability levels increase with age. As predicted, adults performed at higher ability levels than do adolescents. In addition, emotional intelligence in adolescence shows the same relations to verbal intelligence and empathy as with adults.

General Discussion

Three major criteria for a standard intelligence are that it consists of mental abilities, that those abilities meet certain correlational criteria, and that the abilities develop with age. In the tests conducted here, emotional intelligence met all three criteria. First, emotional intelligence could be operationalized as a set of ability tests. Second, performance on those ability tests were intercorrelated and partly distinct from verbal intelligence, against which they were compared. Third, emotional intelligence was shown to grow from early adolescence to young adulthood. Collectively, these findings bring us a major step forward toward demonstrating a plausible case for the existence of this intelligence. The data also tell us about the structure of emotional intelligence, and what it might predict.

Emotional Intelligence Meets Traditional Standards for an Intelligence

The Nature of Emotional Intelligence and Its Measurement

Our factor analyses of the 12 MEIS tasks suggest that one can best conceptualize emotional intelligence as involving three primary factors, and a higher order, General Emotional Intelligence factor that combines the three. The three primary factors involve Perception, Understanding, and Managing of emotion. Perception skills include those drawn from the first branch of the model, including recognizing emotions in Faces, Music, Designs, and Stories. Understanding skills include those drawn from the Assimilation and Understanding branches of the model, including Synesthesia, Feeling Biases, Blends, Progressions, Transitions, and Relativity. Finally, Managing emotions represent skills drawn from the fourth branch of the model, including Managing Others and Managing the Self. The three primary factors, in other words, could be said to capture the four branches of our most recent model of emotional intelligence (Mayer & Salovey, 1997): The Perception branch was captured by the Perception factor scale, the Assimilation and Understanding branches were combined into a single Understanding Factor Scale, and the Managing Branch was captured by the Managing factor scale. This three-branch measurement approach is also broader than our original 1990 model (which omitted the Understanding branch). The three primary facets of Perception, Understanding, and Management, clearly emerged from the data, and although one still might possibly develop a four-branch measure, it would apparently require developing substantially different Branch 2 tasks than the ones employed here, so as to better distinguish them from the Understanding branch.

The three primary abilities appear to be differentially related to traditional intelligence, with Perception least related ($r = 0.16$), Management moderately related, and Understanding most related ($r = 0.40$). This is consistent with other findings that scales of non-verbal perception, such as the PONS (Profile of Nonverbal States; Rosenthal, et al., 1979), which appear to be loaded on emotional perception, are relatively unrelated to intelligence, whereas problem solving of the sort covered on the Understanding branch plainly resembles traditional test items for intelligence more closely. Thus, skills representing emotional intelligence can be ordered along a continuum from those least to those most related to general intelligence. At the same time, the three tasks apparently share a common core of emotionally intelligent processing, as indicated by a more general, overall emotional intelligence factor.

As just noted, a single factor of emotional intelligence incorporates all the tasks studied here. This factor arises as a hierarchical factor obtained from factor analyzing the three primary factor-based scales of Perception, Understanding, and Management (which are obtained by an oblimin rotation of the 12 tasks). Those three primary scales are fairly intercorrelated and factor analyzing them yields a single overall factor that summarizes performance across them all. This hierarchical factor is essentially identical to the first, unrotated principal factor of the 12 scales (their $r = .94$). The global factor indicates that it makes sense to talk about a single, unified emotional intelligence and a single emotional intelligence score. Such a score provides a reasonable first approximation of a person's ability level in the domain of emotional intelligence. As with any generalization, however, this overall score neglects variations in three subsidiary aspects of emotional intelligence, which can provide further clarification of any overall score.

Alternative representations. It should be noted that the 12 tasks employed here do not exhaust the universe of emotionally intelligent abilities. As other tasks are developed, it is possible that more factors will be identified. One sort of task in particular that does not lend itself to group testing but that may form a separate factor, is ability at expressing emotion (Branch 1 skills). It may also be that a factor better encompassing assimilating emotions (Branch 2 of our model, which merged into Branch 3) might still emerge as a more independent factor were it operationalized in tasks different than the ones used here.

Sex Differences

The identification of a new intelligence should increase the fairness of mental ability tests on average. That is because measures of the new intelligence help assess more of the total domain of intelligence, thereby giving any previously-neglected capacities their fair consideration. Women and men appear to perform about the same on most intelligence-related mental tests, with most mean differences between 0.15 and 0.30 of an estimated population standard deviation (Hedges & Nowell, 1995). There are, however, some regular differences in the profiles of the two groups. Women are somewhat better on tests of reading comprehension, perceptual speed, associative memory, and composition. Men are somewhat better in mathematics, social studies, and in scientific knowledge.

To the list of tasks at which women are somewhat better may be added emotional intelligence. Women performed about 0.5 standard deviation higher than men in the present study. The fact that women are slightly superior to men in perceiving emotion has been known for some time, through tests of nonverbal perception (that include emotion) such as the PONS (Rosenthal, et al., 1979), as well as earlier-developed tests of emotional intelligence (Mayer & Geher, 1996). One possible explanation for this is that women must read emotions more carefully because they possess less power in society than do men (LaFrance & Hecht, in press). It is women in more powerful positions rather than less, however, who exhibit the greater emotional accuracy (Hall & Halberstadt, 1994). Such findings suggest that emotional intelligence operates like other areas of intelligence, potentially raising the occupational status of an individual. Issues of power and status aside, women may be socialized to pay more attention to emotions, or they may be better biologically prepared to perform at such tasks; our research does not address the relative contributions of the two (cf., LaFrance & Banaji, 1992).

Emotional Intelligence, Intelligence, and Empathy

The findings here also concern what emotional intelligence predicts. From the outset, emotional intelligence has been hypothesized to correlate with both intelligence and self-reported empathy (Mayer, et al., 1990; Salovey & Mayer, 1990). Overall

Emotional Intelligence Meets Traditional Standards for an Intelligence

emotional intelligence, g_{ei}, correlated with verbal intelligence at a low-to-moderate level, as predicted. This replicates some of our earlier work as well (Mayer & Geher, 1996).

Overall emotional intelligence, g_{ei}, also correlates with self-reported empathy. This, too, replicates earlier studies (Mayer, et al., 1990; Mayer & Geher, 1996). Emotional intelligence appears to correlate reliably with self-report empathy scales that share content overlap with the Epstein-Mehrabian scale (Mehrabian & Epstein, 1972). Such scales, including the one used here and the Davis (1983) empathy subscales of "empathic concern" and "emotion-related fantasy," involve a view of oneself as emotionally responsive and concerned about the feelings of others. The new scale employed here divides that same content domain into a variety of subfactors including Empathetic Suffering, Positive Sharing, Responsive Crying, (reversed) Avoidance, and Feeling For Others. Emotional Intelligence correlated with each of these criteria in the expected direction.

Emotional Intelligence and Other Intelligences

The above demonstrations indicate that Emotional Intelligence, as measured by the MEIS, meets the most essential criteria for a standard intelligence. Our results illustrated that emotional intelligence does relate to general intelligence (via its proxy, verbal intelligence). The results, however, provide only the roughest idea of the relation between emotional intelligence and other intelligences. For example, traditional, academic intelligences can be divided into fluid and crystallized intelligences, or verbal and performance intelligences, or divided in many other ways (e.g., Carroll, 1993; Horn & Noll, 1994; Flanagan et al., 1997). Intelligence researchers will want to examine emotional intelligence and those various breakdowns in greater detail. The relation between emotional intelligence and other potentially similar intelligences such as social intelligence and personal intelligence, and the like, are similarly yet-to-be explored. As stated at the outset, any final choice between emotional intelligence and such alternatives as social intelligence, will depend upon the relative clarity of their operationalizations, their relative relations to general intelligence, and what criteria they predict. It is too early to make this comparison as of yet. Only one of the competing intelligences (social intelligence) has been operationalized well enough (e.g., a minimum of three or four ability tasks) to compare to emotional intelligence. Other alternative intelligences, however, such as personal intelligence, could move in that direction in the future. As alternative intelligences become operationalized, it will be of interest to see how they compare. Finally, emotional creativity (Averill & Nunley, 1992) emphasizes generative, divergent thinking rather than the reasoning and problem solving of emotional intelligence. Emotional intelligence can be thought of as bearing the same relation to emotional creativity as general intelligence bears to general creativity. The intelligence-creativity relations are likely to be complex, but the retention of both concepts likely will be useful.

Emotional Intelligence and Other Criteria

A crucial job of the field is to relate internal characteristics of personality — including abilities such as emotional intelligence — to other psychological tests, and ultimately, to criteria in the life space (Mayer, 1998; Mayer, Carlsmith, & Chabot, 1998). The test developed here has not yet been correlated with other personality scales such as the Big Five (McCrae & Costa, 1997), and that would be a desirable future direction. Instead, we moved modestly into comparing these internal abilities with actual life criteria: parental warmth, life satisfaction, psychotherapy, artistic ability, and leisure activities related to culture. The findings indicate that emotional intelligence is related to (self-reported) parental warmth and support, and, to a lesser extent, to life satisfaction. Emotional intelligence was also related to leisure pursuits including, negatively, to reading a large number of self-help books. Although these findings are preliminary, and better criteria are desirable, they are suggestive of the fact that emotional intelligence will be of use in predicting particular life criteria.

Future Research

We are presently at the beginning of the learning curve about emotional intelligence. Many questions remain unanswered. Some still concern the factorial structure of emotional intelligence: With the development of more tasks, will there be an additional factor of emotional expressiveness, or of assimilating emotion? Are there non-verbal tests that should be developed? Other questions concern the relation between emotional intelligence and other intelligences: How highly does emotional intelligence correlate with social intelligence, or with performance intelligence, or with spatial intelligence? More generally, how will it relate to the multitude of traditional cognitive abilities reviewed by Carroll (1993) and Horn & Noll (1994)?

Many of the questions of greatest interest to people, however, are those raised (as claims, rather than questions) by members of the press (e.g., Gibbs, 1995; Goleman, 1995). Specifically, these claims included that emotional intelligence accounts in some large part for an individual's success, perhaps more so than conventional analytic intelligence (IQ). Despite the fact that certain among these claims appeared in reputable magazines and newspapers, there has been little or no direct evidence to support them (Mayer & Salovey, 1997; Mayer, Salovey, & Caruso, in press). Until the present article, in fact, there has been no widespread, systematic attempt to understand the measurement of emotional intelligence as an ability, although self-report mixed-model scales are proliferating (e.g., Bar-On, 1997). The present results indicate that emotional intelligence does play some role in everyday life. It is our hope that the field can move forward employing measures such as the MEIS. Measures such as the MEIS can provide serious answers to the questions above, as well as those that will arise in the future.

There are some matters that are clearly important about emotional intelligence already. Although emotions often have been regarded with respect in the West, there also exists a widespread negative view of people who think emotionally (Payne, 1986). Emotional thinkers have been referred to over the centuries variously as "overly emotional," romantics (or hopeless romantics), people who think with their hearts (instead of their heads), people "swayed" by emotions, or "biased" by emotions. Such labeling does accurately capture a kind of person who is overwrought with unthinking

Emotional Intelligence Meets Traditional Standards for an Intelligence

emotionality. What the existence of emotional intelligence tells us, however, is that there exists another type as well: the emotional, romantic, thinker-with-a-heart, who is engaged in sophisticated information processing, and who, in such a manner, contributes importantly to our lives and culture.

Conclusion

Measures of intelligence focused on verbal and performance intelligence have been developed over the century. Although verbal, performance, and other similar intelligences have taken us far (cf., Ree & Earles, 1992), there has also been a dissatisfaction with such limited conceptions of mental abilities. Over the century, many have sought out broader sets of mental capacities (e.g., Gardner, 1993; Guilford, 1967; Sternberg, 1988; Thorndike, 1920), or depicted a system of mental abilities (Detterman, 1986). Emotional intelligence represents, to us, an important candidate to enlarge the group on which general intelligence is based. Perhaps a general intelligence that includes emotional intelligence will be a more powerful predictor of important life outcomes than one that does not.

References

Abelson, R. P. (1963). Computer simulation of "hot cognitions." In S. Tomkins & S. Messick (Eds.), Computer simulation of personality (pp. 277-298). New York: Wiley.

Anastasi, A., & Urbina, S. (1997). Psychological Testing. Upper Saddle River, NJ: Prentice Hall.

Arbuckle, J. L. (1997). Amos Users' Guide (Version 3.6). Chicago, IL: SmallWaters Corporation.

Averill, J.R., & Nunley, E.P. (1992). Voyages of the heart: Living an emotionally creative life. New York: Free Press.

Bandura, A. (1977). Self-efficacy: Toward a unified theory of behavioral change. Psychological Review, 84, 191-215.

Bar-On, R. (1997). Bar-On emotional quotient inventory: A measure of emotional intelligence. Toronto, ON: Multi-Health Systems, Inc.

Bower, G.H. (1981). Mood and memory. American Psychologist, 36, 129-148.

Brown, B. (1997). Raw scores of cognitive ability are real psychological variables: IQ is a hyperspace variable. In V.C. Shipman (Chair). IQ or cognitive ability? Symposium presented to the 9th Annual Convention of the American Psychological Society. Washington, DC.

Browne, M.W., & Cudeck, R. (1993). Alternative ways of assessing model fit. In K.A. Bollen, & J.S. Long, (Eds.). Testing structural equation models (pp. 136-162). Newbury Park, CA: Sage.

Buck, R. (1984). The communication of emotion. New York: The Guilford Press.

Cantor, N., & Kihlstrom, J.F. (1987). Personality and social intelligence. Englewood Cliffs, NJ: Prentice-Hall.

Carroll, J. B. (1993). Human cognitive abilities: A survey of factor-analytic studies. New York: Cambridge University Press.

Caruso, D.R., & Mayer, J.D. (1999). A quick scale of empathy. Manuscript in preparation.

Caruso, D.R., Van Buren, A., & Mayer, J. D., Salovey, P. (1998). An extension of the emotional intelligence test to an adolescent sample. Manuscript in preparation.

Clynes, M. (1977). Sentics: The touch of emotions. Garden City, NY: Anchor Press/ Doubleday.

Cronbach, L. J. (1960). Essentials of psychological testing (2nd ed.). New York: Harper and Row.

Darwin, C. (1965). The expression of emotions in man and animals. Chicago: University of Chicago Pres. (Original work published 1872).

Davies, M., Stankov, L., & Roberts, R.D. (1998). Emotional intelligence: In search of an elusive construct. Journal of Personality and Social Psychology, 75, 989-1015.

Davis, M. H. (1983). Measuring individual differences in empathy: Evidence for a multidimensional approach. Journal of Personality and Social Psychology, 44, 113-126.

de Rivera, J. (1977). A structural theory of the emotions. New York: International Universities Press.

Detterman, D.K. (1986). Human intelligence is a complex system of separate processes. In R. J. Sternberg & D. K. Detterman (Eds.), What is intelligence? Contemporary viewpoints on its nature and definition (pp. 57-61). Norwood, NJ: Ablex.

Fancher, R. E. (1985). The intelligence men: Makers of the IQ controversy. New York: W. W. Norton.

Flanagan, D. P., Genshaft, J. L., & Harrison, P. L. (1997). Contemporary intellectual assessment: theories, tests, and issues. New York: Guilford Press.

Gardner, H. (1993). Frames of mind: The theory of multiple intelligences. (10th Anniversary Edition). New York: Basic Books.

Gibbs, N. (1995, October 2). The EQ factor. Time, pp. 60-68.

Goleman, D. (1995). Emotional intelligence. New York: Bantam.

Guilford, J. P. (1967). The nature of human intelligence. New York: McGraw-Hill.

Guttman, L. & Levy, S. (1991). Two structural laws for intelligence. Intelligence, 15, 79-103.

Hall, J. A., & Halberstadt, A. G. (1994). "Subordination" and sensitivity to nonverbal cues: A study of married working women. Sex Roles, 31, 149-165.

Hedges, L.V., & Nowell, A. (1995). Sex differences in mental test scores, variability, and numbers of high-scoring individuals. Science, 269, 41-45.

Horn, J., & Noll, J. (1994). A system for understanding cognitive capacities: A theory and the evidence on which it is based. In D. K. Detterman (Ed.). Current topics in human intelligence, Theories, tests, and issues (Vol 4). New York: Guilford Press.

Jensen, A.R., & Weng, L. (1994). What is good *g*? Intelligence, 18, 231-258.

LaFrance, M. & Banaji, M. (1992). Towards a reconsideration of the gender-emotion relationship. Review of Personality and Social Psychology, 14, 178-201.

LaFrance, M. & Hecht, M.A. (in press). Option or obligation to smile: The effects of power and gender on facial expression. In P. Philippot, R. Feldman, & E. Coates (Eds.), The social context of non-verbal behavior. Cambridge: Cambridge University Press.

Legree, P.J. (1995). Evidence for an oblique social intelligence factor established with a Likert-based testing procedure. Intelligence, 21, 247-266.

Mayer, J. D. (1998). A systems framework for the field of personality. Psychological Inquiry, 9, 118-144.

Mayer, J.D., Carlsmith, K.M., & Chabot, H.F. (1998). Describing the person's external environment: Conceptualizing and measuring the life space. Journal of Research in Personality, 32, 253-296.

Mayer, J. D., DiPaolo, M.T., & Salovey, P. (1990). Perceiving affective content in ambiguous visual stimuli: A component of emotional intelligence. Journal of Personality Assessment, 54, 772-781.

Mayer, J.D., & Geher, G. (1996). Emotional intelligence and the identification of emotion. Intelligence, 22, 89-113.

Mayer, J.D., & Salovey, P. (1993). The intelligence of emotional intelligence. Intelligence, 17(4), 433-442.

Mayer, J.D., & Stevens, A. (1994). An emerging understanding of the reflective (meta-) experience of mood. Journal of Research in Personality, 28, 351-373.

Mayer, J.D., & Salovey, P. (1995). Emotional intelligence and the construction and regulation of feelings. Applied and Preventive Psychology, 4, 197-208.

Mayer, J.D., Salovey, P., & Caruso, D.R. (1997). Emotional intelligence test. Needham, MA: Virtual Knowledge [Producer and Distributor]. [CD-ROM].

Mayer, J.D., & Mitchell, D.C. (1998). Intelligence as a subsystem of personality: From Spearman's *g* to contemporary models of hot-processing. In W. Tomic & J. Kingma (Eds). Advances in cognition and educational practice. Conceptual issues in research on intelligence (pp. 43-75) Vol. 5. Greenwich, CT: JAI Press.

Mayer, J.D. & Salovey, P. (1997). What is emotional intelligence? In P. Salovey & D. Sluyter (Eds). Emotional development and emotional intelligence: Implications for educators (pp. 3-31). New York: Basic Books.

Mayer, J. D., Salovey, P., & Caruso, D. R. (in press). Competing models of emotional intelligence. In R. J. Sternberg (Ed.). Handbook of Human Intelligence (2nd ed.). New York: Cambridge.

McCrae, R. R. & Costa, P. T. (1997). Personality trait structure as a human universal. American Psychologist, 52, 509-516.

Mehrabian, A., & Epstein, N. (1972). A measure of emotional empathy. Journal of Personality, 40, 525-543.

Morrison, D. F. (1976). Multivariate statistical methods (2nd ed.). New York: McGraw-Hill.

Neisser, U., Boodoo, G., Bouchard, T.J., Boykin, A.W., Brody, N., Ceci, S.J., Halpern, D.F., Loehlin, J.C., Perloff, R., Sternberg, R.J., & Urbina, S. (1996). Intelligence: Knowns and unknowns. American Psychologist, 51, 77-101.

Ortony, A., Clore, G. L., & Collins, A. (1988). The cognitive structure of emotions. Cambridge: Cambridge University Press.

Paulhus, D.L., Lysy, D.C., Yik, M.S.M. (1998). Self-report measures of intelligence: Are they useful as proxy IQ tests? Journal of Personality, 66, 525-554.

Payne, W.L. (1986). A study of emotion: developing emotional intelligence; self-integration; relating to fear, pain and desire. Dissertation Abstracts International, (University Microfilms No. AAD9-5947), 47, (1-A), 203A.

Plutchik, R. (1984). Emotions: A general psychoevolutionary theory. In K. R. Scherer and P. Ekman (Eds.), Approaches to emotion (pp. 197-219). Hillsdale, NJ: Erlbaum.

Ree, M. J., & Earles, J. A. (1992). Intelligence is the best predictor of job performance. Current Directions in Psychological Science, 1, 86-89.

Rosenthal, R., Hall, J.A., DiMatteo, M.R., Rogers, P., & Archer, D. (1979). Sensitivity to nonverbal communication: A profile approach to the measurement of individual differences. Baltimore: Johns Hopkins University Press.

Salovey, P. & Mayer, J.D. (1990). Emotional intelligence. Imagination, Cognition, and Personality, 9, 185-211.

Salovey, P., Mayer, J.D., Goldman, S., Turvey, C, & Palfai, T. (1995). Emotional attention, clarity, and repair: Exploring emotional intelligence using the Trait Meta-Mood Scale. In J. W. Pennebaker (Ed.) Emotion, disclosure, and health (pp. 125-154). Washington, D.C.: American Psychological Association.

Scarr, S. (1989). Protecting general intelligence: Constructs and consequences for interventions. In R. L. Linn (Ed.). Intelligence: Measurement, theory, and public policy. Urbana: University of Illinois Press.

Schwarz, N., & Clore, G. L. (1983). Mood, misattribution, and judgments of well-being: Informative and directive functions of affective states. Journal of Personality and Social Psychology, 45, 513-523.

Spinoza, B. (1984) "Ethics (Part III): On the origin and nature of emotions," reprinted in Calhoun, C., & R.C. Solomon, (Eds.) What is emotion? Oxford: Oxford University Press.

Sternberg, R. J. (1988). The triarchic mind: A new theory of human intelligence. New York: Penguin Books.

Emotional Intelligence Meets Traditional Standards for an Intelligence

Sternberg, R. J. (1994). Commentary: Reforming school reform: Comments on "Multiple intelligences: The theory in practice." Teachers College Record, 95, 561-569.

Sternberg, R. J., & Caruso, D. R. (1985). Practical modes of knowing. In E. Eisner (Ed.). Learning and teaching the ways of knowing: 84th Yearbook of the National Society for the Study of Education (Part II, pp. 133-158). Chicago: University of Chicago Press.

Sternberg, R.J., & Smith, C. (1985). Social intelligence and decoding skills in nonverbal communication. Social Cognition, 3, 168-192.

Thorndike, E. L. (1920). Intelligence and its uses. Harper's Magazine, 140, 227-235.

Wagner, H. L., MacDonald, C. J., & Manstead, A. S. R. (1986). Communication of individual emotions by spontaneous facial expression. Journal of Personality and Social Psychology, 50, 737-743.

Wagner, R. K. & Sternberg, R. J. (1985). Practical intelligence in real-world pursuits: The role of tacit knowledge. Journal of Personality and Social Psychology, 49, 436-458.

Wechsler, D. (1958). The measurement and appraisal of adult intelligence (4th ed.) Baltimore, MD: Williams & Wilkins.

Yerkes, R. M. (1921). Psychological examining in the United States. Memoirs of the National Academy of Sciences (15:890 pp. entire).

Zajonc, R.B. (1980). Feeling and thinking: Preferences need no inferences. American Psychologist, 35, 151-175.

Footnotes

[1] The Davies et al. (1998) article critiques early scales in the emotional intelligence literature. The present article was essentially completed before the Davies et al. work was published, and so we do not comment specifically on those authors' criticisms of emotional intelligence scales developed before this one. Nonetheless, it is our hope that the test results here will put to rest certain of the Davies et al. concerns, such as those related to the reliability of emotional intelligence tests.

[2] One very different set of criteria, suggested by Howard Gardner, includes requirements that an intelligence be identified with a specific brain region or structure and be a culturally valued mental characteristic. Intelligences that are valid according to Gardner's criteria alone are definitely worth studying and may provide information for a next generation of intelligence tests. Still, intelligences that fit his criteria but that are indistinguishable from general intelligence at a behavioral level plainly cannot assist in predicting criteria such as academic success. For that reason, correlational approaches remain of the greatest pragmatic concerns for now.

[3] If two intelligences are entirely unrelated, however, we may want to raise the question as to whether one of them is a real intelligence, because mental abilities are

generally related to one another. In fact, the "First Law of Intelligence," of Guttman and Levy's (1991) states that all mental ability measures are positively correlated.

[4] If the expert-selected value was "3" on the five-point scale, responses from 2-4 were assigned the value of 1 (correct). If the expert-selected value was "1," then 1-2 would be correct; if the expert value was "5", then 4-5 would be correct, etc..

[5] Simply allowing the Stories task to load on the Understanding (as well as Perception) moves the RMSEA index to 0.077.

[6] As with Oblique factors II and III, we reversed the sign of the hierarchical factor so that a higher score reflected better ability.

[7] These two tasks had estimated loadings of 0.51 and 0.59, respectively, on the assimilation factor, of the oblique four-factor model.

[8] Adults and adolescents were compared on two of the eight stories as six stories were deemed potentially unsuitable to adolescents, using extremely cautious criteria, due to their content.

[9] Several additional scales were administered that had been rewritten for a younger age group. Reports on the downward extension of the emotional intelligence test can be found elsewhere (see Caruso, Van Buren, & Mayer, 1998). Only those tests that were identical across groups are examined here because only those are relevant to the developmental hypothesis examined here.

Emotional Intelligence Meets Traditional Standards for an Intelligence

Emotional Intelligence as a Standard Intelligence

John D. Mayer, University of New Hampshire
Peter Salovey, Yale University
David R. Caruso, Work-Life Strategies
Gill Sitarenios, Multi-Health Systems, Inc.

Abstract

The authors have claimed that emotional intelligence (EI) meets traditional standards for an intelligence (Mayer, Caruso, & Salovey, 1999). R. D. Roberts, M. Zeidner, and G. Matthews (2001) questioned whether that claim was warranted. The central issue raised by Roberts et al. concerning Mayer et al. (1999) is whether there are correct answers to questions on tests purporting to measure emotional intelligence as a set of abilities. To address this issue (and others), the present authors briefly restate their view of intelligence, of emotion, and EI. They then present arguments for the reasonableness of measuring EI as an ability, indicate that correct answers exist, and summarize recent data suggesting that such measures are, indeed, reliable.

In 1999, we published, "Emotional Intelligence Meets Traditional Standards for an Intelligence" in the journal Intelligence (Mayer et al., 1999). In that article, we presented a new scale of emotional intelligence (EI): The Multifactor Emotional Intelligence Scale (MEIS) based on a decade of theoretical and empirical work. We argued, on the basis of the MEIS and findings with it, that EI was a lot like a traditional intelligence: First, it could be measured as an ability for which there were correct answers. Second, the domain of EI was sizeable in that we could come up with 12 fairly diverse tasks to measure it – everything from recognizing emotion in faces to understanding how emotions might combine to form other emotional experiences. Third, after administering the test to 503 adults and 229 adolescents, we found that performance on those 12 diverse tasks was correlated positively across samples. A factor analysis of those tasks indicated that they could be defined by one general factor, and that they also fell into three or four subgroups of skills roughly corresponding to our model of emotional intelligence (Mayer & Salovey, 1997). Finally, EI ability increased with age, at least across the age ranges that we explored in cross-sectional studies.

Roberts, Zeidner, and Matthews (2001) have questioned what kind of an intelligence EI might be – if it is an intelligence at all. One should start with the fact that there is a great deal of agreement between their findings and our own. In their words (ms. p. 54):

> Some features of the psychometric analyses support Mayer, Caruso and Salovey's (1999) claim that EI meets criteria for an intelligence. We replicated the finding of a positive manifold between subtests of the MEIS, and, generally, the pattern of correlations corresponded well to the Mayer, Caruso, and Salovey (1999) findings. Exploratory and confirmatory factor analyses showed broad similarities with Mayer et al.'s factor solutions, although there were some differences in detail, and, in exploratory analyses, subscale communalities were often low. In fact, the confirmatory analyses tend to support Mayer et al.'s initial conception of four branches of EI, rather than the three-factor model that has subsequently been derived.

In fact, the MEIS represented a great step forward for us in relation to our earlier ability scales (e.g., Mayer, DiPaolo, & Salovey, 1990; Mayer & Geher, 1996). It included many tasks that Roberts et al., and we, found intercorrelated well. The overall Cronbach's alpha of the factor-based scale representing the entire test was .96 (Mayer et al., 1999, p. 286). And, one of the great advances of the MEIS over our earlier, more limited ability measures, was the first attempt to introduce an "expert" criterion for deciding on a correct answer, although at the time, we only had two such experts. In earlier studies, we had relied on general consensus scoring: basically, the degree to which the individual agreed with the response of the general group was the index of correctness. In expert scoring, two of the authors provided their own estimation of the optimal answers to the test. (We also examined a Target form of scoring, in which, say, a person whose face was being examined regarding the emotions expressed on it, reported how she or he felt).

Still, in reviewing the psychometrics of the MEIS, Roberts et al. (2001) found much to be concerned about. Again, in their words (ms. pp.54-55):

...other aspects of the data render many of the EI concepts more problematic than is acceptable of ability measures...In particular, the reliability of subtests that form the highest branches of the model, and are thus probably the most important components of the MEIS for prediction of real-world social behaviors (e.g., Progressions, Managing Others), are among the poorest in this battery. In addition intercorrelations between subtests, while resulting in 'positive manifold', are notably lower than is common in research involving cognitive ability measures (compare for example data presented here with various data sets presented in Carroll 1993). Further, various factor analyses indicate a structure that is relatively unstable, certainly when compared to similar analyses that have been conducted with intelligence and personality measures.

Perhaps the most severe psychometric difficulty is the lack of convergence between expert- and consensus-scored dimensions. There are instances of agreement, especially for the Blends and Progressions tests, but in general, cross-correlations are too small to suggest convergence. The correlation between the general factors extracted from each of the two data sets was only 0.26.

Their findings led them to several conceptual points of importance, raised mostly in their discussion. Roberts et al. (2001) concluded that there may be no objective answers to EI tests, and because correct answers are scored on the basis of group consensus, EI does not qualify as an intelligence. Perhaps, the authors suggest, EI actually measures some form of conformity in relation to the group. As previously noted, they were also concerned about the reliability of such scales. We first briefly restate our view of EI. Then, we address Roberts et al.'s concerns by considering the following: (a) Are there really correct answers on tests of EI? (b) If, as we argue, consensus scoring is ideal, is emotional intelligence merely a measure of conventionality? And, (c) are the tests reliable, and if not, can they be made to be reliable? We continue to assert that EI is, indeed, a traditional intelligence. Some of our arguments are theoretical, others rely on further findings from new studies we have conducted (Mayer, Salovey, Caruso, & Sitaraneos, 2001).

An Overview of the Concept of EI

The Nature of Intelligence

Symposia on intelligence over the years repeatedly conclude that the first hallmark of intelligence is high-level mental ability such as abstract reasoning (Sternberg, 1997). That is, intelligence involves such capacities as seeing the similarities and differences among objects, being able to analyze parts and see their relation to each other and as a whole, and generally, being able to reason validly within and across content domains. Abstract reasoning, although the core aspect, is assisted by several other functions. Several such adjunct areas are of relevance here: an input, a knowledge base, and meta-strategies (for a more detailed view, see Mayer & Mitchell, 1998). These are enumerated in Table 1.

Table 1

A Summary Overview of Parts of Intelligence (after Mayer & Mitchell, 1998, Table 1).

Aspect of Intelligence	Examples from Verbal Intelligence	Examples from Emotional Intelligence
Meta-processing (adjunct)	Knowing that writing something down can help one remember it.	Knowing that helping someone may make oneself feel better.
Abstract understanding and reasoning (core)	Being able to identify the protagonist of a story and compare the individual to other people.	Being able to analyze an emotion and identify its parts and how they combine.
Knowledge base processing (adjunct)	Having knowledge (and remembering analyses) of prior instances of stories.	Having knowledge (and remembering analyses) of prior instances of feelings.
Input processing (adjunct)	Being able to keep long sentences in memory.	Being able to perceive emotions in faces.

Note. This summary overview follows Mayer & Mitchell, 1998; Table 1.

Abstract reasoning cannot take place without an "input" function. Different intelligences are often defined according to what is input and processed. For example, verbal intelligence pertains to reasoning about language; spatial intelligence pertains to reasoning about the position and movement of objects in space. Whatever the area, something must get the information, be it verbal, spatial, or emotional, into the system. Second, abstract reasoning is assisted by a well-organized, related body of knowledge: the knowledge base. This was what Cattell originally referred to as crystallized intelligence (Ackerman, 1997; Cattell, 1943). Thirdly, there are 'meta-cognitions' – basically, strategies for operating with an intelligence in the context of broader mental life. A meta-cognition might be that it helps, in analyzing a problem, to write down portions of the problem so that not everything needs to be kept in short-term memory.

The Nature of Emotion and Emotional Information

There is considerable diversity of opinion as to what emotion is (Frijda, 2000; Solomon, 2000). A reasonably canonical definition, however, might be that an emotion is an organized mental response to an event that includes physiological, experiential, and cognitive aspects, among others. Of particular importance to us, is that emotions typically occur in response to relationships (cf., Lazarus, 1991). One is angry if blocked from attaining a goal, happy if loved by someone who one loves in return, afraid when threatened, and the like. These relationships may be entirely internal, as when one is afraid of what one might do, or external, as when one admires another person. If emotions often arise in relationships, then emotional information is information about certain forms of these relationships.

One critical aspect of emotional information is its consistency across people. Compelling cross-cultural research by Ekman (1973) has supported Darwin's hypothesis that emotional expression has evolved across species (Darwin, 1872/1965). This strongly implies that emotional information – and the capacity to read it – would show some universals across human beings and even closely related mammalian species. Ekman argued that recognition of facial emotional expression was universal. Any apparent differences in human emotional expression from culture to culture could be attributed to the fact that different societies taught different display rules about appropriate moments to express certain feelings. Additional evidence for the regularity of emotional information can be found in the area of artificial intelligence, where cognitive scientists created expert systems that could understand emotions in rudimentary stories (Dyer, 1983). We deal with the nature of emotional information in greater detail, below, as we discuss the issue of the "correct answer" to an EI test item.

The Nature of Emotional Intelligence

Our model of emotional intelligence begins with the idea that emotions contain information about relationships. (Other models of EI exist as well, see Mayer, Salovey, & Caruso, 2000b, for a review). When a person's relationship with another person or an object changes, so do their emotions toward that person or object. A person who is viewed as threatening is feared, an object that is expected is liked. Whether these relationships are actual, remembered, or even imagined, they are accompanied by the felt signals called emotions. EI, in turn, refers to an ability to recognize the meanings of emotions and their relationships, and to use them as a basis in reasoning and problem solving. It further involves using emotions to enhance cognitive activities (Mayer et al., 1999).

Our own analysis of emotion-related abilities led us to divide EI into four areas of skills (e.g., Mayer & Salovey, 1995; Mayer & Salovey, 1997; Salovey & Mayer, 1990.). We call these areas "branches" in reference to the diagrams in which they were first introduced. The four branch model which we now use divides EI into four areas: accuracy in (a) perceiving emotions, (b) using emotions to facilitate thought, (c) understanding emotions, and (d) managing emotions in a way that enhances personal growth and social relations. We view a distinction between the second branch (using emotions) and the other three. Whereas Branches 1, 3, and 4 involve reasoning about emotions, Branch 2 uniquely involves using emotions to enhance reasoning. Finally, we view the four branches as forming a hierarchy, with emotional perception at the "bottom" and "management" at the top. This four branch model serves as a basis of our current reviews of the field (e.g., Mayer, 2001; Salovey, Bedell, & Detweiler, 2000; Salovey, Mayer, & Caruso, in press; Salovey, Woolery, & Mayer, 2001). With this thumb-nail sketch of our model, let us proceed to Roberts et al.'s (this issue) concerns.

Which Areas of EI Should Correlate Highest with Cognitive Intelligence?

A clarification of one aspect of our EI model can explain a result obtained by Roberts et al., which they found to be unexpected. Recall that our four branch model of EI is hierarchical in the context of an individual's personality. The four branches are briefly described in Table 2. There, emotional understanding is most allied with cognitive processing and abstract reasoning; it is most cognitively saturated. emotion management, although the "highest" branch, creates an interface between the cognitive system and the more general personality system. As such, emotion management is actually less cognitive than emotional understanding, because it must balance many factors including the motivational, emotional, and cognitive (Mayer, 2001). Roberts et al. had expected the MEIS's emotion management score to have the highest correlation with general IQ, because it should be "most cognitive." In fact, however, our model supposes that the third, understanding, branch is most cognitive and should have the highest relation to abstract reasoning. That, in fact, is what the data show; the third branch does correlate most highly with IQ.

Are There Correct Answers to Our EI Tests?

Roberts et al. identified "the most severe psychometric difficulty," with our work to be "the lack of convergence between expert- and consensus-scored dimensions." (ms. p. 55). Let us begin in earnest with this issue for two reasons: First, it is primary to whether there can be a correct answer to a test of EI, and hence, whether emotional intelligence is a standard intelligence. Second, it is, by their own description, their most important criticism. As their own concern began with the empirical finding that consensus and expert data correlated only $r = .26$ (ms. p. 56) in their sample, let us start with the empirical issue. Roberts et al. note that "The discrepancies are sufficiently large that they imply that one or other scoring method should be discarded, in that it is hard to envisage modifications that would bring factors that are correlated at less than 0.50 into alignment (p. 61)."

Empirical Concerns

Roberts et al.'s findings suggest the unlikelihood of any eventual convergence between these scoring methods. At the same time, the MEIS was an experimental measure, a first attempt to operationalize our full model of EI. The addition of rudimentary expert scoring was intended as an exploration of the possibility of another criterion of correctness and was not intended as a final expert criterion. We recognized that two authors answering a long test would be unlikely to create the most optimal version of the expert criterion possible. Indeed, Legree has pointed out that individual experts are typically unreliable. His own research indicated that as experts are aggregated they might be expected to approach the general consensus in this domain (Legree, 1995). At the time our first paper on the MEIS appeared, we argued that expert scoring and consensus scoring converged to some degree, and that because the general group consensus appeared more reliable, and yielded better test factor structure, it should be employed (Mayer et al., 1999, pp. 283-284).

Emotional Intelligence as a Standard Intelligence

Table 2

Overview of the Four-Branch Model of Emotional Intelligence, with a Focus on Its Relation to Intelligence and Personality

Branch	Description of Measure	Relation to Intelligence and Personality
4: Managing Emotion	Ability to manage emotions and emotional relationships for personal and interpersonal growth	Interface with personality and personal goals
3: Understanding Emotion	Ability to comprehend emotional information about relationships, transitions from one emotion to another, linguistic information about emotions	Central locus of abstract processing and reasoning about emotions and emotional information
2: Facilitating Thought with Emotion	Ability to harness emotional information and directionality to enhance thinking	Calibrates and adjusts thinking so that cognitive tasks make use of emotional information
1: Perceiving Emotion	Ability to identify emotions in faces, pictures	Inputs information to intelligence

More recently, we have developed a new test of EI, the Mayer-Salovey-Caruso Emotional Intelligence Test (MSCEIT) that attempts to improve on the psychometric qualities of the MEIS. Findings from this new scale are reported in an unpublished manuscript presently under review at this journal (Mayer et al., under review). That manuscript, which is currently available from the authors, reports two large-sample psychometric studies. The second study concerns the MSCEIT V2.0, a 141 item ability scale that uses tasks similar to those of the MEIS to measure the four branches of EI. Like the MEIS, the MSCEIT can be scored according to a general consensus criterion. That is, if .56 of the sample says that there is a moderate amount of happiness in a face, and a participant agrees, his score is incremented by .56.

Also like the MEIS, we used expert scoring for the MSCEIT. Rather than use two authors as experts, however, we asked 21 members of the International Society of Research in Emotion (ISRE) to answer the MSCEIT questions. We then scored the

MSCEIT according to an expert-consensus criterion, based on the proportion of experts from ISRE who answered each item in a particular way. As reported in the manuscript, when over 2,000 participants' scores on the MSCEIT were calculated by general- and by expert- consensus scoring, the intercorrelation between the two sets of scores was $r = .98$. That figure is, obviously, well above the $r = .26$ figure Roberts et al. feature in their discussion. Perhaps it is less surprising when one realizes that the convergence between general consensus and expert scoring on the MEIS was between $r = .43$ to $.78$ for three of the four branches in their data set, with Branch 1's poor convergence ($r = .02$) bringing down the rest to an overall convergence of $r = .48$ (ms. p. 40). (The $r = .26$ figure they feature in their discussion was apparently a consequence of further transformation of the data into factor scales; see ms. p. 44).

Theoretical Concerns

The finding that general and expert consensus scoring effectively converge does not, by itself, solve whether there are correct answers to questions assessing EI. The finding does, however, greatly simplify the issue. If expert scoring is very close – or even the same as — consensus scoring the question can now be refocused on: "What does that consensus mean?" And, is this form of determining a correct answer much different than that used in cognitive intelligence tests?

It is worth noting at the outset, that cognitive IQ tests have items that are "objectively scored" freely intermixed with tests that are scored by a (presumably expert) consensus. An objectively scored test would be something like "digits forward" on the WAIS-III, for which participants hear a series of digits (3...5...2) and simply must repeat them. Other WAIS subtests, however, require some discussion to arrive at the correct answer. As the WAIS-III manual puts it:

> To refine the scoring criteria of those subtests for which many acceptable responses are possible (Vocabulary, Similarities, Information, and Comprehension on the WAIS-III...), the development team conducted several scoring studies...Two team members independently coded each response, identified discrepancies between the code assignments, and resolved the differences so that each response had only one code. At this point, team members had to agree on the grouping of responses and the assignment of codes but not on what score value to assign a code...After the codes were assigned, the team evaluated the quality of the responses and assigned a score value (0, 1, or 2) to each code on the basis of the accuracy of the response." (Psychological Corporation, 1997, p. 37)

The issue then, is not whether experts need to be used, but rather, the nature of emotional versus cognitive information, and the nature of emotional versus cognitive experts.

Similarities and Differences Between Emotional and Cognitive Information

When thinking about general and expert consensus scoring of emotional and cognitive tasks, there seem to be three issues that come into play: (a) domain of application, (b) general consensus versus expert consensus convergence, and (c) systematization of knowledge.

Differences in domain of application. Emotional and cognitive information differ in regard to their domain of application. Emotional information pertains to the human world: the relations of people (and animals) to one another, and their relation to cultural institutions, ideas, artifacts, and socio-emotional contracts, including rules of behavior. Put another way, emotional information applies primarily to matters of how human beings and their evolutionary ancestors survive and interact with the immediate living, world. Human beings have likely come to a general consensus about many emotional meanings. This does not imply that there is only one way to feel, or interpret feelings, but rather, that it helps to know how an individual's reactions compare to how most people would respond emotionally to a situation. Such knowledge helps define the general meaning of emotions in regard to relationships: for example, that happiness arises in harmonious environments, fear in response to threat, and anger to goal blockage, and so on.

Cognitive information, in contrast, describes rules that have areas of application far beyond our immediate living world. Although the child's mathematical world may begin in part with counting fingers and toes, the world of mathematics refers to a sometimes imaginary but often useful numerical world of equations, arithmetical functions, and physically possible and impossible spaces, created both for their beauty and their application. Laws that draw on mathematics to describe gravity, acceleration, and the like, apply as much to rocks, stars, and other galaxies, as they do to human beings.

Differences in expertise. This difference in domain of application has implications for the type of expertise in each area. Whereas in the general cognitive realm, objects are studied, in the emotional realm, the object of study is people. This gives rise to the second difference, what we refer to as the issue of (b) general versus expert convergence. Given that emotional information is bio-social – i.e., biological and learned, the expert becomes the expert to some extent by studying the group consensus, and becoming, as it were, more accurate about the group consensus than other individuals or small groups. For example, in the area of emotions, experts can reliably distinguish sincere or real, from false, tense smiles (cf., Ekman, 1985). It is likely, however, that the general consensus can do this as well. The decisive contribution of expertise is probably to identify and distinguish between the two sorts of smiles more cleanly and expertly than the average person can, and to elucidate how people do this naturally. That is, the general group will be "messier" in identifying the consensus than experts should be. General-expert convergence occurs in the domain of emotions, however, because experts look for the correct answer by paying attention to the consensual information of the group.

It is easy to come up with instances, in teaching physics, for example, where the group consensus is simply wrong and the expert opinion is correct. In fact, physicists refer to "lay physics" to represent the sometimes incorrect but consensual notions that people hold about the physical qualities and motions of objects. A well-known example of this is the common misconception (at least among young children) that heavier objects fall faster than lighter ones. Here is a case where expert knowledge plainly trumps lay knowledge, as, since Galileo's famous experiments, it has been known that the two sorts of objects fall at the same rate. The difference here is that the expert in physics, say, conducts experimental research in areas (i.e., the behavior of objects) of which the general person has no innate or pragmatic experience.

It is likely possible to come up with parallel instances of emotional expertise as the lay physics example. Suppose we ask: "Why did Billy beat up Bobby?" Because Billy (a) was unhappy about himself, (b) felt very good about himself, (c)was afraid. The lay answer is likely to be "a," based on early psychological theories about bullying. More recent evidence, however, has suggested that "b" may be the correct answer, as bullies tend to have high self-esteem (e.g., Baumeister, 1997, pp. 149-153). Making such a claim, however, troubles emotions researchers more so, we suspect, than it would physicists. This is part because discoveries in psychology are fraught with contention and have often been reversed as more knowledge is accumulated. This, of course, is also true of physics – after all, in the ancient Greek period, the expert answer to the problem of what sort of objects fell faster, was that heavier objects fell faster. In addition, however, part of the problem relates to what we would call systematization.

Differences in systematization and institutionalization. The third difference between information (and hence, expertise) in the emotional and the cognitive domain is systematization and institutionalization of knowledge. By systematization, we refer to authoritative dictionaries, manuals, descriptions of operations, and other texts dealing from a consistent viewpoint with the subject matter. Emotional information certainly has been systematized to some degree, but there is less than universal agreement as to the systematizations. For example, one can trace various enumerations of the meanings of emotions through philosophy, psychology, and now, artificial intelligence programs that decipher emotions in stories. Still, these authoritative manuals have not yet gained widespread cultural currency, are not well known, and are only beginning to be taught in schools. In short, they are not entirely culturally sanctioned. Cultural reasons for this lag are described elsewhere (Mayer, Salovey, & Caruso, 2000a).

There has been a higher level of systematization of certain areas of cognitive information than areas of emotional information. Western schools, colleges, and universities focus on areas such as language, literature, and mathematics, in ways that they simply do not in emotions. In part for that reason, more focus has been placed on creating canonical resource materials in literacy, mathematical, and similar areas. With resources such as dictionaries and textbooks, fields such as language, history, and mathematics appear more fixed, certain, and objective than does the emotions area. Imagine, for a moment, that investigators in the field of emotions were required to establish a high school curriculum for teaching about the emotions and their meanings (Cohen, 1997, 2001; Elias et al., 1997). Committees would meet, commissions would be established, and, ultimately, an authoritative expert body of knowledge would be produced. Biologists, chemists, and physicists have been doing this for years, with the tacit understanding that the body of expert knowledge will change over the years, but that each iteration represents a further approximation of some, ultimate, truth. When this begins happening in emotions, it is likely that the divergence between experts and the general consensus will be easier to describe and detect.

Do the Tests Measure EI or Emotional Conformity?

If emotional information turns out to be the general consensus, and is little different from the expert-consensus, then, have we, as Roberts et al. wonder, created a test of conformity? In their words:

> A conformity construct is of real-world relevance, but it is highly misleading to label it as an 'intelligence', because it relates to person-environment fit, rather than to any characteristic of the individual. Indeed, in some instances it is the nonconformist who should be deemed emotionally intelligent: for example, a writer or artist who finds a new and original way of expressing an emotion. (Roberts et al., this issue, p. 62).

Let us begin by drawing a distinction between convergent thinking and conformist or conventional thinking. Convergent thinking is the capacity to pinpoint a correct answer or answers. Conventional thinking is the limitation of one's perspective. Guilford (1959) noted that most exist in intelligence tests measure convergent thinking. For example, in reading comprehension, the correct answer is getting the same point as everybody else (or as the established experts have). In this sense, our test of EI is also convergent. But that does not mean that high scorers on the MEIS are conventional, any more than high scorers on the WAIS-III are necessarily conventional. High scorers typically can reason well beyond the designated answers they provide.

Our theory of EI states that emotional reasoning begins with perceiving emotions accurately. We do not see this as much different than saying that literacy analysis begins with comprehending the basic content in stories or that spatial relations begins with being able to name shapes. No one argues that such simple identification of basic linguistic meanings or basic shapes is conformity. EI continues with abstract reasoning about emotions. This includes analyzing linguistic terms relevant to emotion, and analyzing alterations in emotional sequences that are likely to occur (e.g., that delay turns frustration into anger). This is full-fledged reasoning, different perhaps, but still arguably on a par conceptually with, say, understanding the proper order of an argument. If the examples of such emotional reasoning are, perhaps, a bit more limited than those found in linguistic or spatial reasoning, it is probably in large part due to the relative paucity of systematization in the emotions area. We expect more such systematization in the future, however, as people continue to come to grips with the importance of the area of emotion. Even with such systematization that presently exists, we have been able to come up with enough items to write two entirely different EI tests of hundreds of items, each of which works fairly well (i.e., the MEIS and MSCEIT series).

If we believe the test involves intelligence, then where does creativity enter in? Does it not depend on idiosyncratic emotional reactions? As Roberts et al. asked, should the nonconformist — a writer or artist who finds a new and original way of expressing an emotion — be deemed emotionally intelligent? Absolutely, but note that discovering a new way of expressing an emotion doesn't necessarily involve inventing new emotional rules, or having idiosyncratic emotional reactions. In music, for example, it may involve arranging musical tones in a new way to elicit old or new emotions and their blends. In fact, it is the very capacity of the writer or artist to portray relations among people and to describe things so as to come up with new blends of feelings or transitions among emotions, that in part marks the creative process. A composer rarely exercises creativity in writing music by playing consistently off key; a writer rarely creates deep, new feelings in a reader by failing to understand how a reader would react emotionally in a similar situation to the character.

Consider Averill and Thompson-Knowles' (1991) triad task of emotional creativity. In that task, participants are asked to create a story in which there are relationships that represent particular triads of emotions. In response to the emotions "serene, bewildered, and impulsive," one participant, who was rated quite highly on creativity, wrote:

> The clouds are few, the sky is clear. I'm at the top of the cliff. It's real peaceful up here. Suddenly, I want to jump. I don't know why, I just want to. Calmly, I look down at what would be my unquestioned doom. It looks peaceful; warm and friendly. But why, why do I want to dive into the hands of the grim reaper? What does this mean? I hesitate, then motion to jump, something strange pulls me back. It is the peacefulness of the cliff. I can't destroy the peacefulness. The wind feels like velvet against my skin as I slowly shake my head. Why? (Averill & Thompson-Knowles, 1991, p. 280).

The above passage was rated high in novelty, authenticity, and creativity. And yet what makes it work is that its anonymous author did understand the meanings of emotion in a convergent sense. What was novel was the creation of a new situation to elicit the feelings.

Are the Tests Reliable?

Reliability at the Full-Scale, Branch, and Individual Task Level

The MEIS, and our subsequent tests, the MSCEIT RV1.0 and V 2.0 are all reliable tests at the full-scale level (where they all possess split-half reliabilities above r = .90). Our aforementioned manuscript (Mayer et al.,2001), reports MSCEIT V. 2.0 reliabilities at the branch level ranging from r = .79 to .91 using consensus scoring and r = .77 to .90 using expert scoring. The progression of tests: from MEIS, studied by Roberts et al. (2001), to our newer tests the MSCEIT RV 1.1 and MSCEIT V 2.0 also showed a gradual rise in reliability at the level of their individual tasks. Whereas using general consensus scoring on the 12 tasks of the MEIS yielded individual task reliabilities ranging from alphas of .49 to .94 (Mayer et al., 1999), the same scoring for the MSCEIT V2.0 yield individual task alphas from r = .64 to .88 (Mayer et al., 2001 review).

Davies, Stankov, and Roberts (1998) raised concerns regarding reliability of an early 1990 ability test, which measured one aspect of EI. That test provided an empirical demonstration of the possibility of EI rather than a fully operationalized test (Mayer et al., 1990). Given our primary focus at that time, which was to demonstrate the existence of EI psychometrically, we were not too worried about the admittedly modest, alpha of .63, of this rather constrained 1990 measure. To us, if EI existed, it is theoretically important, in part because it brings a new perspective to the field's view of both emotion and intelligence. After all, almost any test's reliability can be enhanced simply by making it longer (e.g., the Spearman-Brown prophecy formula; Nunnally, 1978, pp. 210-211). That said, we of course wanted tests to be used by others in the research and applied worlds. For that reason, we worked hard to ensure that the MEIS and MSCEIT all had full-scale reliabilities over .90, and succeeded.

Roberts and his colleagues were presumably satisfied with the MEIS full-scale reliability of r = .96 that we reported in the 1999 article. Their focus, however, is almost exclusively, or entirely, on the reliability of the smallest components of the test, that is, individual subtests, rather than on the branch scores and total test levels, where reliabilities range from very good to excellent. Roberts et al. expect all the subcomponents of the test, even at the level of individual tasks, to be of uniformly high reliability. It is important to note that this has little to do with whether or not EI exists. Rather, it appears to be, for them, an issue of utility. Their perspective, as it is clarified in their article in this issue, appears to be applied. They wanted to be assured that when people are tested, the scores those individuals obtain (i.e., are told about) at the individual task level are legitimate and accurate reflections of their ability. This is an obviously legitimate concern on their part. We recognize it to be of growing importance as tests such as the MSCEIT are prepared for general use.

Reliability or Accessibility?

Given that test reliability can be improved simply by lengthening the test, why did we not heed Davies et al.'s criticisms early on and make a test longer than the MEIS that was highly reliable even at the level of the individual task? We could have taken the MEIS (or the MSCEIT tests) and added items to them to make them longer and more reliable. Instead, we chose to shorten our tests, and build up reliability at the task level through careful item selection. Investigators have begun to, and will need to, correlate the test with real-life criteria. A short, efficient test that provides reliable scores at the branch and total-test level, like MSCEIT V2.0, can stimulate research better and faster than can a longer, more unwieldy and inefficient test that has optimized reliability for every individual task. Through careful item selection, we have actually improved reliability at the task level (this was accomplished in part by dropping four tasks). To adopt Roberts et al.'s perspective for a moment, it is worth comparing the present MSCEIT V2.0 with the original Wechsler Adult Intelligence Scale (WAIS), used until

1981. That scale was written after roughly 4 decades of intelligence testing, and itself replaced the earlier Wechsler-Bellevue Intelligence Test. The 11 WAIS subscale scores ranged in reliability from $r = .60$ to $.96$, not so different from the MSCEIT V2.0. (Matarazzo, 1972, p. 239).

Ongoing Issues

There are a few issues we are not yet prepared to address in this commentary due to the fact that they are empirical questions that are as-of-yet unresolved. To many people, the most important of these issues would probably concern whether the general and expert consensuses are uniform or cultural-bound in Western and non-Western societies. There are several additional issues that will chiefly be of interest to intelligence researchers. For example, why does emotional perception load most highly on factors of general EI? Here, our current work suggests that this finding may not hold up with our newer tests and therefore we have not commented on it. Another item chiefly of psychometric interest concerns whether the average interrelation among EI tasks are lower than that for general cognitive IQ, and if so why? This is an interesting question for which we have no answer at this time. We address concerns about the factor structure of the area in our aforementioned manuscript under review. Finally, we continue to believe that developmental aspects of intelligence are a defining feature of them but have not commented on that due to limitations of space.

Summary and Conclusions

In this commentary, we have restated our conceptual approach to intelligence, emotions, and emotional intelligence. Roberts et al. had discussed certain concerns about our theory and measurement of emotional intelligence. Those concerns centered to a large degree on the low correlation between two methods of scoring the MEIS (general consensus and expert). In particular, they raised the issue of whether, given the divergence of the scoring procedures, one could decide on correct answers for a test of emotional intelligence. We are appreciative of the fact that Roberts, Zeidner, and Mathews are engaged in this research and have raised these issues. Their work has encouraged us to present new data, and to present a further consideration of the theoretical issues involved in scoring such tests. We have referred to important findings indicating that different scoring methods converge at the $r = .98$ level rather than the $r = .26$ level suggested by Roberts et al.'s analyses. In addition, we provided a plausible theoretical explanation of the basis on which correct answers to EI tests can be determined.

In addition, we considered some other concerns of Roberts et al., including test reliability. Although the reliability for the full MEIS is .96, it is lower at the level of the 12, individual tasks. We have argued that the reliability issue raised by Roberts et al. is a limited problem, and one that is addressed by our new scale, the MSCEIT V2.0, which is now available for research.

With such an assessment tool, it is now possible to ask not only whether emotional intelligence exists, but whether it is important in various realms of our lives. We expect emotional intelligence to be an important predictor of significant outcomes, at levels that are typically found in psychological research. What research does exist suggests that emotional intelligence is likely to take its place alongside other important psychological variables as a predictor of various outcomes at school, home, and work. For example, higher EI may predict reduced levels of problem behavior such as drug use and interpersonal violence (Brackett, 2001; Formica, 1998; Mayer, Perkins, Caruso, & Salovey, 2001; Rubin, 1999; Salovey, Mayer, Caruso, & Lopez, in press; Trinidad & Johnson, in press).

The development and understanding of an intelligence requires a number of years of careful scrutiny and research. The most widely used cognitive scales of intelligence, the Wechsler Intelligence scales, are the product of 60 years of research. Moreover, that research itself was initiated after an earlier 40 years of work on the clinical assessment of intelligence. If the history of the study of intelligence is any guide, there is little question that there is much still to be learned about emotional intelligence. The first 10 years of emotional intelligence research have been frustrating but also immensely rewarding and full of promise. We look forward to continued research in the area and to learning more about what EI predicts.

References

Ackerman, P. L. (1997). Personality, self-concept, interests, and intelligence: Which concept doesn't fit? Journal of Personality, 65, 171-204.

Averill, J. R., & Thompson-Knowles. (1991). Emotional creativity. In K. T. Strongman (Ed.), International review of studies on emotion (Vol. 1, pp. 269-299). London: Wiley.

Baumeister, R. F. (1997). Evil: Inside human violence and cruelty. New York: W. H. Freeman & Company.

Brackett, M. (2001). Emotional intelligence and the life space. Unpublished Master's Thesis, University of New Hampshire, Durham, NH.

Cattell, R. B. (1943). The measurement of adult intelligence. Psychological Bulletin, 40, 153-193.

Cohen, J. (Ed.). (1997). Educating minds and hearts: Social emotional learning and the passage into adolescence. New York: Teachers College Press.

Cohen, J. (Ed.). (2001). Caring classrooms/intelligent schools: The social emotional education of young children. New York: Teachers College Press.

Darwin, C. (1872/1965). Expression of the emotions in man and animals. New York: Philosophical Library.

Davies, M., Stankov, L., & Roberts, R. D. (1998). Emotional intelligence: In search of an elusive construct. Journal of Personality and Social Psychology, 75, 989-1015.

Dyer, M. G. (1983). The role of affect in narratives. Cognitive Science, 7, 211-242.

Ekman, P. (1973). Darwin and facial expression: A century of research in review. New York: Academic Press.

Ekman, P. (1985). Telling lies. New York: Norton.

Elias, M. J., Zins, J. E., Weissberg, R. P., Frey, K. S., Greenberg, M. T., Haynes, N. M., Kessler, R., Schwab-Stone, M. E., & Shriver, T. P. (1997). Promoting social and emotional learning: Guidelines for educators. Alexandria, VA: Association for Supervision and Curriculum Development.

Formica, S. (1998). Description of the socio-emotional life space: Life qualties and activities related to emotional intelligence. Unpublished Senior Honors Thesis, University of New Hampshire, Durham, NH.

Frijda, N. H. (2000). The psychologist's point of view. In M. Lewis & J. M. Haviland-Jones (Eds.), Handbook of emotions (pp. 59-74). New York: Guilford Press.

Lazarus, R. (1991). Emotions and adaptation. New York: Oxford University Press.

Legree, P. I. (1995). Evidence for an oblique social intelligence factor established with a Likert-based testing procedure. Intelligence, 21, 247-266.

Matarazzo, J. D. (1972). Wechsler's measurement and appraisal of adult intelligence (5th ed.). New York: Oxford University Press.

Mayer, J. D. (2001). A field guide for emotional intelligence. In J. Ciarrochi & J. P. Forgas & J. D. Mayer (Eds.), Emotional intelligence and everday life. (pp. 3-24). New York: Psychology Press.

Mayer, J. D., Caruso, D. R., & Salovey, P. (1999). Emotional intelligence meets traditional standards for an intelligence. Intelligence, 27, 267-298.

Mayer, J. D., DiPaolo, M. T., & Salovey, P. (1990). Perceiving affective content in ambiguous visual stimuli: A component of emotional intelligence. Journal of Personality Assessment, 54, 772-781.

Mayer, J. D., & Geher, G. (1996). Emotional intelligence and the identification of emotion. Intelligence, 17, 89-113.

Mayer, J. D., & Mitchell, D. C. (1998). Intelligence as a subsystem of personality: From Spearman's g to contemporary models of hot processing. In W. Tomic & J. Kingma (Eds.), Advances in cognition and educational practice (Vol. 5, pp. 43-75). Greenwich, CT: JAI Press.

Mayer, J. D., Perkins, D., Caruso, D. R., & Salovey, P. (2001). Emotional intelligence and giftedness. Roeper Review, 23, 131-137.

Mayer, J. D., & Salovey, P. (1995). Emotional intelligence and the construction and regulation of feelings. Applied and Preventive Psychology, 4, 197-208.

Mayer, J. D., & Salovey, P. (1997). What is emotional intelligence? In P. Salovey & D. Sluyter (Eds.), Emotional development and emotional intelligence: Implications for educators (pp. 3-31). New York: Basic Books.

Mayer, J. D., Salovey, P., & Caruso, D. R. (2000a). Emotional intelligence as zeitgeist, as personality, and as a standard intelligence. In R. Bar-On & J. D. A. Parker (Eds.), Handbook of emotional intelligence (pp. 92-117). New York: Jossey-Bass.

Mayer, J. D., Salovey, P., & Caruso, D. R. (2000b). Models of emotional intelligence. In R. J. Sternberg (Ed.), Handbook of intelligence (pp. 396-420). Cambridge, England: Cambridge University Press.

Mayer, J. D., Salovey, P., Caruso, D. R., & Sitaraneos, G. (under review). Emotional intelligence meets traditional standards for an intelligence again: Findings from the MSCEIT.

Psychological Corporation. (1997). WAIS-III, WMS-III Technical Manual. San Antonio, TX: Author.

Roberts, R. D., Zeidner, M., & Matthews, G. (this issue). Does emotional intelligence meet traditional standards for an intelligence? Some new data and conclusions.

Rubin, M. M. (1999). Emotional intelligence and its role in mitigating aggression: A correlational study of the relationship between emotional intelligence and aggression in urban adolescents. Unpublished Dissertation, Immaculata College, Immaculata, Pennsylvania.

Salovey, P., Bedell, B., & Detweiler, J. B. (2000). Current directions in emotional intelligence research. In M. Lewis & Haviland-Jones (Eds.), Handbook of emotions (2nd ed., pp. 504-520). New York: Guildford Press.

Salovey, P., & Mayer, J. D. (1990.). Emotional intelligence. Imagination, Cognition, and Personality, 9, 185-211.

Salovey, P., Mayer, J. D., & Caruso, D. R. (in press). The positive psychology of emotional intelligence. In S. J. L. C. R. Snyder (Ed.), The handbook of positive psychology. New York: Oxford University Press.

Salovey, P., Mayer, J. D., Caruso, D. R., & Lopez, P. N. (in press). Measuring emotional intelligence as a set of abilities with the MSCEIT. In S. J. Lopez & C. R. Snyder (Eds.), Handbook of positive psychology assessment. Washington, DC: American Psychological Association.

Salovey, P., Woolery, A., & Mayer, J. D. (2001). Emotional intelligence: Conceptualization and measurement. In G. J. O. Fletcher & M. S. Clark (Eds.), Blackwell handbook of social psychology: Interpersonal processes (pp. 279-307). Malden, MA: Blackwell.

Solomon, R. C. (2000). The philosophy of emotions. In M. Lewis & J. M. Haviland-Jones (Eds.), Handbook of emotions (pp. 3-15). New York: Guilford.

Sternberg, R. J. (1997). The concept of intelligence and its role in lifelong learning and success. American Psychologist, 52, 1030-1045.

Trinidad, D. R., & Johnson, C. A. (in press). The association between emotional intelligence and early adolescent tobacco and alcohol use. Personality and Individual Differences.

Wechsler, D. (1955). Wechsler Adult Intelligence Scale. New York: Psychological Corporation.

Measuring Emotional Intelligence With the MSCEIT V2.0

John D. Mayer, University of New Hampshire
Peter Salovey, Yale University
David R. Caruso, Work-Life Strategies
Gill Sitarenios, Multi-Health Systems, Inc.

Abstract

Does a recently introduced ability scale adequately measure emotional
intelligence (EI) skills? Using the Mayer-Salovey-Caruso Emotional
Intelligence Test (MSCEIT; J.D. Mayer, P.Salovey, & D.R. Caruso, 2002b),
we examined (a) whether members of a general standardization sample
and emotions experts identified the same test answers as correct, (b) the
test's reliability, and (c) the possible factor structures of EI. Twenty-one
emotions experts endorsed many of the same answers as did 2112
members of the standardization sample, and exhibited superior
agreement particularly when research provides clearer answers to test
questions (e.g., emotional perception in faces). The MSCEIT achieved
reasonable reliability, and confirmatory factor analysis supported
theoretical models of EI. These findings help clarify issues raised in
earlier articles published in <u>Emotion.</u>

Modeling and Measuring Emotional Intelligence with the MSCEIT V2.0

The past 12 years have seen a growing interest in emotional intelligence (EI), defined as a set of skills concerned with the processing of emotion-relevant information, and measured with ability-based scales. A new ability test of EI, the Mayer-Salovey-Caruso Emotional Intelligence Test, Version 2.0 (MSCEIT), potentially improves upon earlier measures, and can inform the debate over the scoring, reliability, and factor validity of such scales (Mayer, Salovey, & Caruso, 2002b). The MSCEIT is intended to measure four branches, or skill groups, of emotional intelligence: (a) perceiving emotion accurately, (b) using emotion to facilitate cognitive activities, (c) understanding emotion, and (d) managing emotion (Mayer & Salovey, 1997).

The MSCEIT is the most recent of a series of ability scales of emotional intelligence. Its immediate predecessor was the MSCEIT Research Version 1.1 (MSCEIT RV1.1), and before that, the Multifactor Emotional Intelligence Scale (MEIS, Mayer, Caruso, & Salovey, 1999; Mayer et al., 2002b). Those tests, in turn, evolved out of earlier scales measuring related constructs such as emotional creativity, social intelligence, and non-verbal perception (e.g., Averill & Nunley, 1992; Kaufman & Kaufman, 2001; O'Sullivan & Guilford, 1976; Rosenthal, Hall, DiMatteo, Rogers, & Archer, 1979). The MSCEIT and its predecessors are based on the idea that emotional intelligence involves problem solving with and about emotions. Such ability tests measure something relatively different from, say, self-report scales of emotional intelligence, with which correlations are rather low (Mayer et al., 2002b). The ability to solve emotional problems is a necessary, although not sufficient, ingredient to behaving in an emotionally adaptive way.

The MSCEIT V2.0 standardization process required collecting data sets relevant to the several issues concerning emotional intelligence. For example, in a recent exchange of papers in this journal, Roberts, Zeidner, and Mathews (2001), raised concerns about the earlier-developed MEIS test of emotional intelligence. These concerns included whether there is one set of correct answers for an emotional intelligence test or whether expert and general (e.g., lay) opinions about answers diverge too much, whether such tests could be reliable, and whether the factor structure of such tests was fully understood and consistent with theory. In that same issue of the journal we, and others, responded (Izard, 2001; Kaufman & Kaufman, 2001; Mayer, Salovey, Caruso, & Sitaraneos, 2001; Schaie, 2001; Zeidner, Mathews, & Roberts, 2001). Findings from the MSCEIT standardization data reported here have the promise of more directly informing the debate, through empirical findings. The analyses we present address three questions: (a) Do general and expert criteria for correct answers to emotional intelligence test items converge? (b) What is the reliability of such tests? (c) And, is the factor structure of such tests consistent with theoretical models of EI?

Three Issues about Emotional Intelligence
Addressed in the Present Study

The Criteria for Correct Answers

One must know how to score a test's items before one can settle such issues as the test's reliability and factor structure. Our model of EI hypothesizes that emotional knowledge is embedded within a general, evolved, social context of communication and interaction (Mayer et al., 2001). Consequently, correct test answers often can be identified according to the consensus response of a group of unselected test-takers. For example, if the respondents identify a face as predominantly angry, then that can be scored as a correct answer. We have further hypothesized that emotions experts will identify correct answers with greater reliability than average, particularly when research provides relatively good methods for identifying correct alternatives, as in the case of facial expressions of emotion, and the meaning of emotion terms (Mayer et al., 2001).

If the general and the expert consensus diverge too far as to the correct answers on a test, a complication arises, because the two methods yield potentially different scores for each person. Roberts et al. (2001) used an expert criterion that we had developed based on only two experts, and a general consensus method to score the earlier MEIS measure, and found those methods did not always converge. Some aggregation of experts beyond two is necessary, however, to achieve a reliable identification of answers (Legree, 1995). Twenty-one emotions experts were employed in the present study.

Issues of Reliability

The MSCEIT V2.0 must exhibit adequate levels of reliability, as did the MEIS, MSCEIT RV1.0, and comparable psychological tests (see Mayer et al., 2001, 239-240). As with its predecessor tests, the four MSCEIT V2.0 branch scores (e.g., Perception, Facilitating, Understanding, Management) draw on different tasks that include different item forms; that is, the items are non-homogeneous. Under such conditions, split-half reliability coefficients are the statistic of choice (relative to coefficient alphas), as they involve the orderly allocation of different item types to the two different halves of the test (Nunnally, 1978). The test-retest reliability of the total MSCEIT score has been reported elsewhere, at $r(60) = .86$ (Brackett & Mayer, 2001).

Issues of Factor Structure

The factor structure of a test indicates how many entities it plausibly measures. It is important to any debate over whether EI is a coherent, unified, concept. In this specific case, it indicates how many dimensions of EI the test is "picking up" — one unified dimension, many related dimensions, or something else. We believe that the domain of EI is well described by 1-, 2-, and 4- oblique (correlated) factor models, as well as other equivalent models. If the MSCEIT V2.0 shows similar structure to the MEIS for both expert and general scoring, it would strengthen the argument that the theory of EI we employ works across tests. Using the standardization sample, we performed confirmatory factor analyses of the full scale MSCEIT V2.0, testing 1-, 2-,

Measuring Emotional Intelligence With the MSCEIT V2.0

and 4- factor models to examine the range of permissible factor structures for representing the EI domain.

Method

Participants

General Sample. The present sample consisted of 2,112 adult respondents, age 18 or older, who completed the MSCEIT V 2.0 in booklet or online forms prior to May, 2001. The sample was composed of individuals tested by independent investigators in 36 separate academic settings from several countries. The investigators had requested pre-release versions of the MSCEIT booklet or online forms (depending on Internet availability and other criteria), and had submitted documentation of their research qualifications and of approval of their research from their sponsoring institution. Only basic demographic data were collected across samples due to the diverse nature of the research sites.

Of those reporting gender, 1,217 (58.6%) were women and 859 (41.4%) were men. The mean age of the sample was M = 26.25; S = 10.51, with roughly half the sample college-aged (52.9%), and the rest ranging upward to 69 years old. The participants were educationally diverse, with 0.6% reporting not completing high school, 10.3% having completed only high school, 39.2% having some college or university courses, 33.7% having completed college, and 16.1% holding Masters level or higher degrees. The group was ethnically diverse as well, with 34.0% Asian, 3.4% Black, 2.0% Hispanic, 57.9% White, and 2.3% other or mixed ethnicity. Most participants came from the United States (1240), with others from South Africa (231), India (194), the Philippines (170), the United Kingdom (115), Scotland (122), and Canada (37); all testing was in English.

Expert Sample. The expert sample was drawn from volunteer members of the International Society for Research on Emotions (ISRE) at its 2000 meeting. The Society was founded in 1984 with the purpose of fostering interdisciplinary scientific study of emotion. Membership is open to researchers and scholars who can demonstrate a serious commitment to the investigation of the emotions. Twenty-one experts, 10 male and 11 female, from eight Western countries, participated. The sample of experts had a mean age of 39.38 (S = 6.44; Range =30 to 52); no data about their ethnicity were collected.

The MSCEIT V2.0

The MSCEIT V2.0 is a newly developed, 141-item scale designed to measure four branches (specific skills) of emotional intelligence: (a) Perceiving Emotions, (b) Using Emotions to Facilitate Thought, (c) Understanding Emotions, and (d) Managing Emotions. Each of the four branches is measured with two tasks. Perceiving Emotions is measured with the Faces and Pictures tasks; Facilitating Thought is measured with the Sensations and Facilitation tasks; Understanding Emotions is measured with Blends and Changes; and Managing Emotions is measured with Emotion Management and Emotional Relationships tasks.

Each of the eight MSCEIT tasks is made up of a number of item parcels or individual items. A parcel structure occurs, for example, when a participant is shown a face (in the Faces task), and asked about different emotions in the face in five subsequent items. The five items make up an item parcel because they are related to the same face, albeit each asks about a different emotion (Cattell & Burdsal, 1975). Other items involve one response per stimulus, and are, in that sense, free-standing. Response formats were intentionally varied across tasks so as to ensure that results generalized across response methods, and to reduce correlated measurement error. Thus, some tasks, such as Pictures, employed 5-point rating scales, whereas other tasks, such as Blends, employed a multiple-choice response format.

Briefly, in the faces task (four item parcels; five responses each), participants view a series of faces and for each, respond on a five point scale indicating the degree to which a specific emotion is present in a face. The pictures task (six parcels; five responses each) is the same as faces except that landscapes and abstract designs form the target stimuli, and the response scale consists of cartoon faces (rather than words) of specific emotions. In the sensations task (five parcels; three responses each), respondents generate an emotion and match sensations to them. For example, they might generate a feeling of envy and decide how hot or cold it is. In the facilitations task (five item parcels; three responses each), respondents judge the moods that best accompany or assist specific cognitive tasks and behaviors, for example, whether joy might assist planning a party. In the blends task (12 free-standing items), respondents identify emotions that could be combined to form other emotions. They might conclude, for example, that malice is a combination of envy and aggression. In the changes task (20 free-standing items), respondents select an emotion that results from the intensification of another feeling. For example, they might identify depression as the most likely consequence of intensified sadness and fatigue. Respondents in the emotion management task (five parcels; four responses each) judge the actions that are most effective in obtaining the specified emotional outcome for an individual in a story. They are asked to decide, for example, what a character might do to reduce her anger, or prolong her joy. Finally, in the emotional relationships task (three item parcels; three responses each), respondents judge the actions that are most effective for one person to use in the management of another person's feelings. See the test itself, and its manual, for more specific task information (Mayer, Salovey, & Caruso, 2002a; Mayer et al., 2002b, p. 20).

General and Expert Consensus Scoring . The MSCEIT yields a total score, two area scores (experiential and strategic), four branch scores corresponding to the four-branch model, and eight task scores. Each score can be calculated according to a general consensus method. In that method, each one of a respondent's answers is scored against the proportion of the sample who endorsed the same MSCEIT answer. For example, if a respondent indicated that surprise was "definitely present" in a face, and the same alternative was chosen by 45% of the sample, the individual's score would be incremented by the proportion, .45. The respondent's total raw score is the sum of those proportions across the 141 items of the test. The other way to score the

Measuring Emotional Intelligence With the MSCEIT V2.0

test is according to an expert scoring method. That method is the same, except that the each of the respondent's scores is evaluated against the criterion formed by proportional responding of an expert group (in this case, the 21 ISRE members). One of the purposes of this study was to compare the convergence of these two methods.

Procedure. The MSCEIT administration varied depending upon the research site at which the data were collected (see the *General sample* section). The MSCEIT was given to participants to complete in large or small groups, or individually. Of the 2,112 participants, 1,368 took the test in a written form and 744 took the test in an on-line form that presented the exact same questions and response scales, by accessing a web-page. Those taking the pencil and paper version completed scannable answer sheets that were entered into a database. Web page answers were transmitted electronically. Prior research has suggested that booklet and on-line forms of tests are often indistinguishable (Buchanan & Smith, 1999).

Results

Comparison of Test-Booklet versus On-Line Administration Groups. We first compared the MSCEIT V2.0 booklet and on-line tests. For each, there are 705 responses to the test (141 items; x five responses each). The correlation between response frequencies for each alternative across the two methods was $r(705) = .987$. By comparison, a random split of the booklet sample alone, for which one would predict there would be no differences, yields almost exactly the same correlation between samples of $r(705) = .998$. In each case, a scatterplot of the data indicated that points fell close to the regression line throughout the full range of the joint distribution, and that the points were spread through the entire range (with more points between .00 and .50, than above .50). Even deleting 30 zero-response alternatives from the 705 lowered the correlation by only .001 (in the random split case). The booklet and on-line tests were, therefore, equivalent, and the samples were combined.

Comparison of General vs. Expert Consensus Scoring Criteria. We next examined the differences between answers identified by the experts and by the general consensus. We correlated the frequencies of endorsements to the 705 responses (141 items x 5 responses) separately for the general consensus group and the expert consensus group, and obtained an $r(705) = .908$ that, although quite high, was significantly lower than the $r = .998$ correlation for the random split ($z(703) = 34.2$, $p < .01$). The absolute difference in proportional responding for each of the 705 alternatives also was calculated. The mean value of the average absolute difference between the expert and general groups was $\div M_D(705)| = .08$; $S = .086$, which also was significantly greater than the difference between the booklet and on-line samples of $\div M_D(705)| = .025$; $S = .027$; $z(705) = 16.3$, $p < .01$.

We hypothesized that emotions experts would be more likely than others to possess an accurate shared social representation of correct test answers; their expertise, in turn, could provide an important criterion for the test. If that were the case, then experts should exhibit higher inter-rater agreement than the general group. To assess inter-rater agreement, we divided the expert group randomly into two subgroups of 10 and of 11 experts each, and computed the modal response for each of the 705 responses for the two subgroup of experts. The Kappa representing agreement controlling for chance across the two expert subgroups for the 5 responses of the 141 items was k(110) = .84. We then repeated this process for two groups of 21 individuals, randomly drawn from the standardization (general) samples and matched to the expert group exactly on gender and age. Two control groups, rather than one, were used to enhance our confidence in the results; the education level of the comparison groups was comparable to that of the rest of the general sample. When we repeated our reliability analysis for the two matched control groups, we obtained somewhat lower Kappas of k(110) = .71 and .79.

The same superiority of the expert group exists at an individual level as well, where disaggregated agreement will be lower (Legree, 1995) . The average inter-rater Kappa coefficients of agreement across the 5 responses of the 141 items, for every pair of raters within the expert group, was k(210) = .43, which significantly exceeded the average Kappas of the two control groups k = .31; SD = .082; k = .38, SD = .098l zs(418) = 4.8, 1.85, p < .05 —.01, one-tailed test).

Because general and expert groups both chose similar response alternatives as correct, and experts have higher inter-rater reliability in identifying such correct alternatives, members of the standardization sample should obtain somewhat higher test scores when the experts' criterion is used (before normative scaling corrections are applied). Moreover, the expert group should obtain the largest score advantages on skill branches where the experts most agree, owing to the experts' greater convergence for those responses. For example, one might expect increased expert convergence for Branches 1 (emotional perception) and 3 (emotional understanding) because emotions experts have long focused on the principles of coding emotional expressions (e.g., Ekman & Friesen, 1975; Scherer, Banse, & Wallbott, 2001), as well as on delineating emotional understanding (e.g., Ortony, Clore, & Collins, 1988). By contrast, research on Branches 2 (emotional facilitation of thought) and 4 (emotion management) is newer and has yielded less consensus, and so experts might be more similar to the general sample in such domains.

To test this idea, we conducted a 4 (branch) X 2 (consensus versus expert scoring criterion) ANOVA on MSCEIT scores. The main effect for scoring criterion was significant (F(1,1984) = 3464, p < .001), indicating, as hypothesized, that participants obtained higher raw scores overall when scored against the expert criteria. The main effect for branch was significant as well (F(3,5952) = 1418, p < .001), indicating, unsurprisingly, that items on some branches were harder than others. Finally, there was a branch by scoring criterion interaction (F(3,5952) = 2611, p < .001).

Orthogonal contrasts indicated that participants scored according to the expert criterion on Branches 1 and 3 obtained significantly higher scores than when scored against the general consensus (see Table 1; F(1,1984) = 1631 and 5968, respectively;

p's < .001). Branch 2 (using emotions to facilitate thought) showed a significant difference favoring general consensus ($F_{(1,1984)} = 711$, p's < .001), and Branch 4 showed no difference ($F_{(1,1984)} = 1.57$, n.s.). The advantage for expert convergence on Branches 1 and 3 may reflect the greater institutionalization of emotion knowledge among experts in these two areas.

In a final comparison of the two scoring criteria, participants' tests were scored using the general criterion, on the one hand, and the expert criterion, on the other. The correlation between the two score sets ranged from $r(2004\text{-}2028) = .96$ to .98 across the Branches, Areas, and Total EIQ scores.

The evidence from this study reflects that experts are more reliable judges, and converge on correct answers where research has established clear criteria for answers. If further studies bear out these results, the expert criteria may prove superior to the general consensus.

Reliability of the MSCEIT V2.0. The MSCEIT has two sets of reliabilities depending upon whether a general or expert scoring criterion is employed. That is because reliability analyses are based on participants' scored responses at the item-level, and scores at the item-level vary depending upon whether responses are compared against the general or expert criterion. The MSCEIT full-test split-half reliability is $r(1985) = .93$ for general and .91 for expert consensus scoring. The two Experiencing and Strategic Area score reliabilities are $r(1998) = .90$ and .90, and $r(2003) = .88$ and .86 for general and expert scoring, respectively. The four branch scores of Perceiving, Facilitating, Understanding, and Managing range between $r(2004\text{-}2028) = .76$ to .91 for both types of reliabilities (see Table 1). The individual task reliabilities ranged from a low of "$(2004\text{-}2111) = .55$ to a high of .88. However scored, reliability at the total scale and area levels was excellent. Reliability at the branch level was very good, especially given the brevity of the test. Compared to the MEIS, reliabilities were overall higher at the task level (e.g., Mayer et al., 1999; Mayer et al., 2002b) but were sometimes lower than is desirable. We therefore recommend test interpretation at the total scale, area, and branch levels, with cautious interpretations at the task level, if at all.

Correlational and Factorial Structure of the MSCEIT V2.0. As seen in Table 2, all tasks were positively intercorrelated using both general (reported below the diagonal) and expert consensus scoring (above the diagonal). The intercorrelations among tasks ranged from $r(1995\text{-}2111) = .17$ to .59, p's < .01, but with many correlations in the mid .30's.

Measuring Emotional Intelligence With the MSCEIT V2.0

Table 1
Unscaled Score Means and Standard Deviations, Reliabilities, and Intercorrelations for the MSCEIT V 2.0 for General and Expert Scoring

Area score	Branch score	Subtest score	Descriptive statistic[a,b]				Reliability[b,c]	
			General		Expert		General	Expert
			M	SD	M	SD		
Total MSCEIT V2.0			.48	.07	.50	.08	.93	.91
Experimental			.49	.08	.50	.09	.90	.90
	Perceiving		.50	.10	.54	.13	.91	.90
		Faces	.50	.12	.57	.18	.80	.82
		Pictures	.50	.13	.50	.13	.88	.87
	Facilitating		.47	.09	.45	.08	.79	.76
		Facilitation	.44	.09	.41	.07	.64	.63
		Sensations	.50	.12	.50	.12	.65	.55
Strategic			.47	.08	.51	.10	.88	.86
	Understanding		.53	.10	.60	.13	.80	.77
		Changes	.56	.10	.63	.14	.70	.68
		Blends	.50	.12	.57	.16	.66	.62
	Managing		.42	.10	.42	.09	.83	.81
		Emotion manag.	.41	.09	.40	.09	.69	.64
		Emotional rel.	.43	.12	.43	.12	.67	.64

Note. MSCEIT V2.0 = Mayer-Salovey-Caruso Emotional Intelligence Test, Version 2.0; manag. = management; rel. = relationships.
[a] Final MSCEIT test scores for both general and expert scoring are converted to a standard IQ scale, where $M = 100$ and $SD = 15$.
[b] The *N* for the overall scale was 2,112; *ns* for the branch scores were Perceiving; 2,015, with task *ns* between 2,018 and 2,108; Facilitating: 2,028, with individual task ns between 2,034 and 2,103; Understanding: 2,015, with individual task *ns* between 2,016 and 2,111; Managing: 2,088, with individual task *ns* from 2,004 to 2,008.
[c] Split-half reliabilities are reported at the total test, area, and branch score levels due to item heterogeneity. Coefficient alpha reliabilities are reported at the subtest level due to item homogeneity.

Table 2
Intercorrelations for MSCEIT V2.0 General and Expert Scoring

Scale	1	2	3	4	5	6	7	8
Branch 1: Perceiving								
1. Faces	1.000	.356	.300	.315	.191	.157	.191	.179
2. Pictures	.347	1.000	.288	.400	.286	.263	.282	.271
Branch 2: Facilitating								
3. Facilitation	.340	.328	1.000	.313	.283	.242	.262	.262
4. Sensations	.336	.402	.352	1.000	.388	.374	.384	.415
Branch 3: Understanding								
5. Changes	.225	.282	.255	.382	1.000	.575	.437	.417
6. Blends	.171	.260	.224	.375	.589	1.000	.425	.424
Branch 4: Managing								
7. Emotion manag.	.232	.300	.299	.395	.417	.416	1.000	.542
8. Emotional rel.	.191	.275	.269	.411	.395	.409	.575	1.000

Note. Correlations are based on the sample for which all data at the task level were complete (N = 1,985). General scoring appears in the lower left triangle; expert scoring appears in the upper right triangle. MSCEIT V2.0 = Mayer-Salovey-Caruso Emotional Intelligence Test, Version 2.0; manag. = management; rel. = relationships.

Confirmatory Factor Analyses. A factor analysis of the MSCEIT V2.0 can cross-validate earlier studies that support 1-, 2-, and 4- factor solutions of the EI domain (Ciarrochi, Chan, & Caputi, 2000; Mayer et al., 1999; Roberts et al., 2001). The 1-factor, "g" model, should load all eight MSCEIT tasks. The 2-factor model divides the scale into an "Experiential" area (Perception and Facilitating Thought Branches) and a "Strategic" area (Understanding and Managing Branches). The 4-factor model loads the two designated Branch tasks on each of the 4 branches (Mayer & Salovey, 1997; Mayer et al., 2001). These analyses are particularly interesting given that the MSCEIT V2.0 represents an entirely new collection of tasks and items.

We tested these models using AMOS (Arbuckle, 1999), and cross-checked them using LISREL (Joreskog & Sorbom, 2001) and STATISTICA (Statsoft, 2002). The confirmatory models shared in common that (a) error variances were uncorrelated, (b) latent variables were correlated, i.e., oblique, and (c) all other paths were set to zero. In the 4-factor solution only, the two within-area latent variable covariances (i.e., between Perceiving and Facilitating, and between Understanding and Managing) were additionally constrained to be equal so as to reduce a high covariance between the Perceiving and Facilitating branche scores.

There was a progressively better fit of models from the one- to the four-factor model, but all fit fairly well (four vs. two factors: x^2 (4) = 253, $p < .001$; two vs. one factors: x^2 (1) = 279, $p < .001$; see Table 3 for further details). The chi-square values are a function of sample size (N-1)F; and their size reflects the approximately 2,000 individuals involved, moreso than any absolute quality of fit. Fit indices independent of sample size include the normed fit index (NFI) which ranged from .99 to .98 across models, which is excellent (Bentler & Bonett, 1980), as well as the Tucker-Lewis index (TLI, Bentler & Bonett, 1980; Tucker & Lewis, 1973), which ranged from .98 to .96, and was also quite good, and Steiger's (1990) root mean square error of approximation (RMSEA), which ranged from .12 for the one-factor solution, which was a bit high, to an adequate .05 for the four-factor solution. A model fit using the four-factor solution with expert scoring was equivalent to that of general scoring (e.g., NFI = .97; TLI = .96; RMSEA = .04), and this correspondence between the expert and general consensus held for the one- and two-factor models as well.

MacCallum and Austin (2000) have noted that alternative models may be found that fit well, and this was the case with a 3-factor model described elsewhere that we tested on these data (Mayer et al., 1999). On the other hand, if one intentionally violates the 4-factor model, by shifting the second task on each branch to the next branch up (and placing Branch 4's second task back on Branch 1), the P^2 rises from 94 to 495, the fit indices become unacceptable (e.g., TLI drops from .96 to .78), and 4 of 6 correlations among branches are estimated at higher than 1.0. The four-branch model, in other words, does create a fit to the data that can be markedly superior to other models.

Table 3: MSCEIT V2.0 Parameter Estimates of the Observed Tasks on the Latent Variables, and Goodness-of-Fit Statistics for the One-, Two-, and Four- Factor Models

Variable[a]	Model tested		
	One-factor	Two-factor	Four-factor
Branch 1			
Perceiving	*I*	*I*	*I*
Faces	.40	.50	.55
Pictures	.50	.59	.68
Branch 2			
Facilitating			*II*
Facilitation	.46	.54	.53
Sensations	.64	.71	.72
Branch 3			
Understanding		*II*	*III*
Changes	.65	.68	.77
Blends	.64	.67	.76
Branch 4			
Managing			*IV*
Emotion manag.	.68	.70	.76
Emotional rel.	.66	.68	.74
Model fit	Goodness-of-fit index		
X^2	626.56	347.32	94.28
df	20	19	15
NFI	.988	.993	.977
TLI	.979	.988	.964
RMSEA	.124	.093	.052
N	1,985	1,985	1,985

Note. The factor models were specified such that error terms were uncorrelated. In the four-branch model, the two within-area covariances (i.e., between Perceiving and Facilitating, and between Understanding and Management) were constrained to be equal to one another. Boldfaced, italicized roman numerals indicate the factors specified in each model; beneath each roman numeral are the estimated factor loadings for each of the tasks associated with that specific factor. All other loadings were fixed at zero. MSCEIT V2.0 = Mayer-Salovey-Caruso Emotional Intelligent Test, Version 2.0; manag. = management; rel. = relationships; NFI = normed fit index; TLI = Tucker-Lewis index; RMSEA = root-mean-square error of approximation.
[a]Variables are ordered according to the four-branch model of emotional intelligence (Mayer & Salovey, 1997).

Discussion

In this study, emotions experts converged on correct test answers with greater reliability than did members of a general sample. The expert's convergence was better in areas where more emotions research has been conducted. If future research confirms these findings, then an expert criterion may become the criterion of choice for such tests. Critiques of the emotional intelligence concept have suggested, based on the use of one or two emotions experts, that expert and general consensus criteria might be quite different (e.g., correlate below r = .50, Roberts et al., 2001). Others have argued that, as more experts are employed, and their answers aggregated, their performance will resemble that of the consensus of a large, general, group (Mayer et al., 2001). The 21 experts in this study did exhibit superior agreement levels relative to the general sample. At the same time, the expert and general consensus criteria often agreed on the same answers as correct, $r = .91$. Participants' MSCEIT scores were also similar according to the two different criteria, $r = .98$.

Reliabilities for Branch, Area, and Total test scores were reasonably high for the MSCEIT, with reliabilities at the level of the individual tasks ranging lower. Two week test-retest reliabilities of $r(60) = .86$ are reported elsewhere (Brackett & Mayer, 2001). In addition, the findings from the factor analyses indicate that 1-, 2-, and 4-factor models provide viable representations of the emotional intelligence domain, as assessed by the MSCEIT V2.0.

No empirical findings by themselves can settle all the theoretical issues surrounding EI that were reflected in the September 2001 issue of <u>Emotion</u>. In addition, the applied use of emotional intelligence tests must proceed with great caution. That said, the findings here suggest that those who employ the MSCEIT can feel more confident about the quality of the measurement tool they use to assess EI. Ultimately, the value of the MSCEIT as a measure of emotional intelligence will be settled by studies of its validity and utility in predicting important outcomes over and above conventionally-measured emotion, intelligence, and related constructs. A number of such studies related to pro-social behavior, deviancy, and academic performance, have begun to appear (Mayer et al., 2002b). In the mean time, we hope that the present findings inform and, by doing so, clarify issues of scoring, of reliability, and of viable factorial representations.

References

Arbuckle, J. L. (1999). Amos 4.0. Chicago, IL: SmallWaters Corp.

Averill, J. R., & Nunley, E. P. (1992). *Voyages of the heart: Living an emotionally creative life.* New York: Free Press.

Bentler, P. M., & Bonett, D. G. (1980). Significance tests and goodness of fit in the analysis of covariance structures. *Psychological Bulletin, 88,* 588-606.

Brackett, M., & Mayer, J. D. (2001, October). *Comparing measures of emotional intelligence.* Paper presented at the Third Positive Psychology Summit, Washington, DC.

Buchanan, T., & Smith, J. L. (1999). Using the internet for psychological research: Personality testing on the World Wide Web. *British Journal of Psychology, 90,* 125-144.

Cattell, R. B., & Burdsal, C. A. (1975). The radial parcel double factoring design: A solution to the item-vs-parcel controversy. *Multivariate Behavioral Research, 10,* 165-179.

Ciarrochi, J. V., Chan, A. Y., & Caputi, P. (2000). A critical evaluation of the emotional intelligence concept. *Personality and Individual Differences, 28,* 539-561.

Ekman, P., & Friesen, W. V. (1975). *Unmasking the face: A guide to recognizing the emotions from facial cues.* Englewood Cliffs, NJ: Prentice Hall.

Izard, C. E. (2001). Emotional intelligence or adaptive emotions? *Emotion, 1,* 249-257.

Joreskog, K. G., & Sorbom, D. (2001). LISREL 8.51. Lincolnwood, IL: Scientific Software, Inc.

Kaufman, A. S., & Kaufman, J. C. (2001). Emotional intelligence as an aspect of general intelligence: What would David Wechsler say? *Emotion, 1,* 258-264.

Legree, P. I. (1995). Evidence for an oblique social intelligence factor established with a Likert-based testing procedure. *Intelligence, 21,* 247-266.

MacCallum, R. C., & Austin, J. T. (2000). Applications of structural equation modeling in psychological research. *Annual Review of Psychology, 51,* 201-226.

Mayer, J. D., Caruso, D. R., & Salovey, P. (1999). Emotional intelligence meets traditional standards for an intelligence. *Intelligence, 27,* 267-298.

Mayer, J. D., & Salovey, P. (1997). What is emotional intelligence? In P. Salovey & D. Sluyter (Eds.), *Emotional development and emotional intelligence: Educational implications* (pp. 3-31). New York: Basic Books.

Mayer, J. D., Salovey, P., & Caruso, D. R. (2002a). *Mayer-Salovey-Caruso Emotional Intelligence Test (MSCEIT) Item Booklet.* Toronto, Canada: MHS Publishers.

Mayer, J. D., Salovey, P., & Caruso, D. R. (2002b). *Mayer-Salovey-Caruso Emotional Intelligence Test (MSCEIT) User's Manual.* Toronto, Canada: MHS Publishers.

Mayer, J. D., Salovey, P., Caruso, D. R., & Sitaraneos, G. (2001). Emotional intelligence as a standard intelligence. *Emotion, 1,* 232-242.

Nunnally, J. C. (1978). *Psychometric theory.* New York: McGraw-Hill.

Ortony, A., Clore, G. L., & Collins, A. M. (1988). *The cognitive structure of emotions*. Cambridge: Cambridge University Press.

O'Sullivan, M., & Guilford, J. P. (1976). *Four factor tests of social intelligence: Manual of instructions and interpretations*. Orange, CA: Sheridan Psychological Services.

Roberts, R. D., Zeidner, M., & Matthews, G. (2001). Does emotional intelligence meet traditional standards for an intelligence? Some new data and conclusions. *Emotion, 1*, 196-231.

Rosenthal, R., Hall, J. A., DiMatteo, M. R., Rogers, P. L., & Archer, D. (1979). *The PONS Test*. Baltimore, MD: Johns Hopkins University Press.

Schaie, K. W. (2001). Emotional intelligence: Psychometric status and developmental characteristics: Comments on Roberts, Zeidner, and Matthews (2001). *Emotion, 1*, 243-248.

Scherer, K. R., Banse, R., & Wallbott, H. G. (2001). Emotion inferences from vocal expression correlate across languages and cultures. *Journal of Cross-Cultural Psychology., 32*, 76-92.

Statsoft. (2002). Statistica 6.0 Software. Tulsa, OK: Statsoft, Inc.

Steiger, J. H. (1990). Structural model evaluation and modification: An interval estimatin approach. *Multivariate Behavioral Research, 25*, 173-180.

Tucker, L. R., & Lewis, C. (1973). The reliability coefficient for maximum likelihood factor analysis. *Psychmetrika, 38*, 1-10.

Zeidner, M., Mathews, G., & Roberts, R. D. (2001). Slow down, you move too fast: Emotional intelligence remains an "elusive" intelligence. *Emotion, 1*, 265-275.

Convergent, Discriminant, and Incremental Validity of Competing Measures of Emotional Intelligence

Marc A. Brackett, University of New Hampshire
John D. Mayer, University of New Hampshire

This study investigated the convergent, discriminant and incremental validity of one ability test of emotional intelligence (EI): the Mayer-Salovey-Caruso-Emotional Intelligence Test (MSCEIT), and two self-report measures of EI: the Emotional Quotient Inventory (EQ-i), self-report EI test (SREIT). The MSCEIT showed minimal relations to the EQ-i and SREIT, whereas the latter two measures were moderately interrelated. Among EI measures, the MSCEIT was discriminable from well-studied personality and well-being measures, whereas the EQ-i and SREIT shared considerable variance with these measures. After personality and verbal intelligence were held constant, the MSCEIT was predictive of social deviance, the EQ-i was predictive of alcohol use, and the SREIT was inversely related to academic achievement. In general results showed that ability EI and self-report EI are weakly related and yield different measurements of the same person.

Research on emotional intelligence (EI) has expanded over the last decade and today there are a variety of tests to assess it. The three best known tests are the Mayer-Salovey-Caruso Emotional Intelligence Test (MSCEIT), the Emotional Quotient Inventory (EQ-i) (Bar-On, 1997a), and Schutte, et al.'s (1998) self-report EI test

(SREIT). There is a controversy, however, about what these tests actually measure, what they predict, and whether the tests are distinguishable from other abilities and personality attributes (Hedlund & Sternberg, 2000; McCrae, 2000; Mayer, Salovey, & Caruso, 2000).

Consider theories of EI. Mayer et al.'s (2000) original performance-based model of EI pertains to an individual's capacity to process and reason about emotions. These researchers distinguish their ability model from other "mixed" models of EI. They assert that the term EI has become "unmoored" from both emotion and intelligence because so-called mixed models combine mental abilities (e.g., ability to perceive emotion) with self-reported qualities such as optimism and well-being that are clearly distinct from their mental ability approach (Mayer et al., 2000; Salovey, Mayer, Caruso, & Lopes, 2001; Roberts, Zeidner, & Matthews, 2002).

Each approach to measuring EI can influence the validity of the construct. For example, in intelligence research, performance scales are standard because they are based on the capacity to solve mental tasks (Carroll, 1993). Self-report scales of intelligence on the other hand are based on people's endorsements of descriptive statements about themselves. If a person's self-concept is accurate then self-report data serve as an accurate measure. However, most people are inaccurate reporters of their own abilities. Correlations between ability and self-report measures of intelligence, for instance, are generally low ($r = .00$ to .35; Paulhus, Lysy, & Yik, 1998). Therefore, with respect to EI, it is likely that ability and self-report models will yield different representations of the same person.

In the present study one ability-based and two self-report tests of EI are employed. The MSCEIT is designed to measure EI as a mental ability. In this conception, EI is the capacity to reason in regard to emotions, and the capacity to use emotions to assist cognition (Mayer & Salovey, 1997). The EQ-i and SREIT are both mixed-model approaches to EI that are assessed with self-report inventories. The EQ-i measures an "array of non cognitive capabilities, competencies, and skills that influence one's ability to succeed in coping with environmental demands and pressures" (Bar-On, 1997b, p. 14). The SREIT is a brief self-report scale that is based on Schutte et al.'s (1998) understanding of Salovey and Mayer's (1990) original model of EI, which broadly defined EI as an ability. There also exist EI scales that are designed for organizational settings (e.g., Boyatzis, Goleman, & Rhee, 2000). These tests, which usually require informant reports, were not employed here.

To date, there are no studies comparing the MSCEIT, EQ-i, and SREIT. Do the three tests assess the same or different things? Are the tests distinguishable from verbal intelligence and measures of personality and well-being? Do the tests predict important behavioral criteria beyond what can be predicted by well-studied traits? After briefly describing the three EI tests, the present article addresses the questions just raised.

Convergent, Discriminant, and Incremental Validity of Competing Measures of Emotional Intelligence

Background

Research on ability EI started with academic psychologists in the early 1990's (Mayer, DiPaolo, & Salovey 1990; Salovey & Mayer, 1990). By mid-decade, the topic was popularized by Goleman (1995), who made new and extraordinary claims about the importance of EI, including that it is "as powerful and at times more powerful than IQ" (p. 34). Independent reviews of Goleman's (1995, 1998) popular writings have shown that his claims are unsubstantiated (Epstein, 1998; Hedlund & Sternberg, 2000; Mayer et al., 2000; Roberts et al., 2002). Presently, there are three full-scale tests of EI in the scholarly literature. The MSCEIT, EQ-i, and SREIT are three such tests for which preliminary empirical data are now available. Here, we describe these tests and their general characteristics and then discuss what each test appears to predict.

MSCEIT

Salovey & Mayer (1990) first defined EI as "the ability to monitor one's own and others' feelings and emotions, to discriminate among them and to use this information to guide one's thinking and actions" (p. 189). In that same year they also provided the first demonstration of how the construct may be measured (Mayer, et al., 1990). These researchers acknowledge that their initial conception of EI was partly a mixed model because it incorporated aspects of personality that might accompany emotional intelligence (Mayer et al., 2000, p. 402).

Mayer and Salovey (1993) gradually refined their definition of EI and argued that it was a real intelligence. They then offered a revised, more focused definition of EI as the ability to: a) perceive emotion, b) integrate emotion to facilitate thought, c) understand emotions, and d) regulate emotions to promote personal growth (Mayer & Salovey, 1997). The MSCEIT was designed to measure these four abilities.

The MSCEIT measures perception of emotion by having people rate how much of a particular emotion is being expressed in either a picture of a face expressing a basic emotion or in a picture of a design or landscape. Emotional facilitation of thought is measured by asking people to describe emotional sensations and their parallels to other sensory modalities and by having people assimilate predetermined mood into their thought processes concerning a fictional character. Understanding emotions is measured by asking people how emotions blend to form more complex emotions and how emotional reactions change over time. Finally, the MSCEIT measures emotion management by having test-takers choose effective ways to manage private emotions and the emotions of others in hypothetical situations.

The MSCEIT has a factor structure congruent with the four-part model of EI and it is both reliable and content valid. The authors assert that the MSCEIT meets several standard criteria for a new intelligence: it is operationalized as a set of abilities; it is objective in that answers on the test are either right or wrong as determined by consensus or expert scoring; its scores correlate with existing intelligences, while also

Convergent, Discriminant, and Incremental Validity of Competing Measures of Emotional Intelligence

showing unique variance; and scores increase with age (Mayer, Caruso, & Salovey, 1999; Mayer, et al., 2002; Mayer & Geher, 1996).

EQ-i

The EQ-i (Bar-On, 1997a) is a self-report test of EI that evolved out of the author's question, "Why do some people have better psychological well-being than others? And, why are some people able to succeed in life over others?" (Bar-On, 1997b, p. 1). In the EQ-i manual, Bar-On (1997b) broadly defines EI as addressing:

> ...the emotional, personal, social, and survival dimensions of intelligence, which are often more important for daily functioning than the more traditional cognitive aspects of intelligence. Emotional intelligence is concerned with understanding oneself and others, relating to people, and adapting to and coping with the immediate surroundings to be more successful in dealing with environmental demands...In a way, to measure emotional intelligence is to measure one's "common sense" and ability to get along in the world...(p. 1)

The EQ-i provides information on five composite factors that are comprised of 15 subscales, including: (a) intrapersonal EQ, composed of emotional self-awareness, assertiveness, self-regard, self-actualization,and independence, (b) interpersonal EQ, composed of empathy, relationship skills, and social responsibility, (c) adaptability, composed of problem solving, reality testing, and flexibility, (d) stress management, composed of stress tolerance, and impulse control, and (e) general mood, composed of happiness and optimism. Bar-On (2000), however, recently made a revision to his scale; he now views the general mood factor as a facilitator of EI rather than a part of it. Thus, total EQ-i scores are now computed by only summing the first four scales. The comparability of the two scoring methods has not been reported.

Bar-On (1997b) has written that exploratory and confirmatory factor analytic studies indicate that a 15-factor solution provides a good fit to the EQ-i. The subscales also have fairly high internal consistency. The reliability of the total EQ-i, however, has not been reported. Given the diverse factors that comprise the EQ-i, it is important to know if the scales represent a unidimensional or multidimensional construct.

SREIT

The SREIT is a brief self-report measure of EI that was developed by Schutte et al. (1998). These authors wrote a pool of 62 self-report items that were primarily based on their reading of Salovey & Mayer's (1990) early model of EI, which pertained to the ability to monitor and discriminate emotions and to use emotions to guide one's thinking and actions. For example, some items on the SREIT measure a person's self- perceived ability to monitor private feelings or the feelings of others.

Factor analysis of the initial 62 items resulted in the single-factor 33-item SREIT, which has good internal consistency and test-retest reliability. Petrides and Furnham

Convergent, Discriminant, and Incremental Validity of Competing Measures of Emotional Intelligence

(2000), however, have criticized the psychometric properties of the SREIT. These researchers claim that the scale does not appropriately map onto Salovey and Mayer's (1990) model of EI and that the scale is not unidimensional. They prefer the results of their exploratory factor analysis, which divided the SREIT into four provisional factors (optimism and mood regulation, appraisal of emotions, social skills, and utilization of emotions). Petrides and Furnham have not provided data on the reliability or validity of these subscales.

Comparative Performance of the MSCEIT, EQ-i, and SREIT

What do we know about these three EI tests? Remarkably, their intercorrelations have not been reported. However, we do know something about each test alone. For example, the MSCEIT, and its predecessor test, the Multi-factor Emotional Intelligence Scale (MEIS) have been correlated with verbal intelligence, the Big Five, and self-reported empathy (Bracket, 2001; Ciarrochi, Chan, & Caputi, 2000; Mayer et al., 1999; Salovey et al., 2001). These preliminary studies show that MSCEIT and MEIS only correlate moderately with these constructs ($rs < .40$).

The MSCEIT and MEIS have also been related to a number of life space criteria, which ask about the world outside and surrounding the individual such as daily activities and owned possessions (Brackett, 2001; also see Mayer, Carlsmith, & Chabot, 1998). Higher EI has been associated with higher levels of attending to health and appearance, positive interactions with friends and family, and owning objects that are reminders of their loved ones. Lower EI has been associated with higher reported use of drugs and alcohol, more deviant behavior, and owning large numbers of self-help books (Brackett , 2001; Formica, 1998; Mayer et al., 1999; Trinidad & Johnson, 2001). Self-reported parental warmth and secure attachment style also positively correlated with EI (Mayer et al., 1999). Finally, EI has been linked to informant reports of positive interpersonal relations. For example, school children with higher EI were rated as less aggressive by their peers and more prosocial by their teachers and leaders of an insurance company's customer claims team with higher EI were rated as more effective by their managers than those with lower EI (Rice, 1999; Rubin, 1999).

Most of the information on the validity of the EQ-i appears as data in the technical manual (Bar-On, 1997b). These reports and some recent published studies have shown that the EQ-i correlates strongly with a number of personality measures including Neuroticism on the Big Five, anxiety on the 16PF, depression with the BDI, and alexythymia (Dawda & Hart, 2000; Newsome, Day, and Catano, 2000; Parker, Taylor, & Bagby, 2001). The EQ-i also has discriminated between certain groups, such as successful and unsuccessful Air Force recruiters (Handley, 1997; cited in Bar-On, 1997b) and academically successful and unsuccessful students (Swart, 1996; cited in Bar-On, 1997b). The positive correlation with academic performance, however, has not been replicated (Newsome et al. 2000). Finally, the EQ-i appears unrelated to fluid intelligence (Bar-On, 1997b; Derksen, Kramer, & Katzko, 2002).

The SREIT correlates moderately to strongly with a number of personality constructs including alexithymia, optimism, impulse control, and openness to experience (Schutte et al., 1998). In Schutte et al.'s original study, the SREIT predicted end of the year college GPA and discriminated between groups expected to be higher and lower in EI. Specifically, women scored higher than men, and therapists scored higher than both psychotherapy patients and prisoners. In more recent studies, the scale significantly correlated with measures that assess interpersonal relations including: empathic perspective taking, social skills, marital satisfaction, and supervisor ratings of student counselors who worked at mental health agencies (Schutte, Malouff, Bobik, Coston, Greeson, Jedlicka, et al., 2001; Malouff & Schutte, 1998).

There is concern that EQ-i and SREIT, similar to earlier self-report EI tests, share large amounts of variance with existing personality scales (Davies, Stankov, & Roberts, 1998). For example, the EQ-i substantially overlaps with measures of anxiety ($r = -.70$) and the SCL-90 ($r = .85$), which is a general indicator of social and emotional functioning (Bar-On, 1997b, 2000). The SREIT correlates very highly with alexithymia ($r = -.65$), self-reported mood repair ($r = .68$), and a marital satisfaction scale ($r = .75$). These findings have led some researchers to believe that the EQ-i and SREIT may be best characterized as types of personality inventories and not as measures of EI (Hedlund & Sternberg, 2000; Mayer et al., 2000; McCrae, 2000). In fact, McCrae (2000) has hypothesized that these mixed conceptions of EI may simply measure the evaluatively positive poles of the Big Five (i.e., low scores for Neuroticism and high scores for Extraversion, Openness, Agreeableness, and Conscientiousness). Mayer and Cobb (2000, p. 177) also believe that mixed conceptions have "an all things bright and beautiful" quality to them, which makes them suspicious as descriptors of an emotionally intelligent person.

Introduction to the Present Study

Preliminary work on EI raises important questions concerning the convergent, discriminant, and incremental validity of the MSCEIT, EQ-i, and SREIT. This study addresses these questions by first comparing the three tests to one another and then to well-studied measures of personality, well-being, and verbal intelligence. We predict that ability (MSCEIT) and self-reported (EQ-i and SREIT) tests will yield different measurements of the same person because of their divergent definitions of EI and distinct measurement approaches. Because the MSCEIT is a well-defined ability model of EI in contrast to the EQ-i and SREIT, which are both mixed-conceptions of EI, we also predict that the MSCEIT will be mostly independent of existing personality constructs and that the EQ-i and SREIT will share considerable variance with these measures.

Each EI test author, researchers in the field, and popular writers on EI have predicted that EI is related to a number of behavioral criteria including academic performance and lower levels of violence and self-destructive behaviors (Bar-On, 1997b; Brackett, 2001; Formica, 1998; Goleman, 1995, 1998; Mayer et al., 1999; Mayer,

Convergent, Discriminant, and Incremental Validity of Competing Measures of Emotional Intelligence

Salovey, & Caruso, 2002b; Schutte et al., 1998). In this study two measures of academic performance (high school rank and college GPA) and four scales requiring individuals to report on cigarette smoking activity, alcohol use, drug use, and deviant behavior are used as the criteria. This will allow us to assess the comparative performance of each EI measure with respect to criteria they are purported to predict. We expect that all three EI measures will correlate with the criteria. However, once personality and well-being are controlled we predict that the EQ-i and SREIT will lose predictive value due to their shared variance with these existing measures.

Methods

Participants

Participants were 207 predominantly Caucasian-American (97%) college students (130 women and 77 men). The mean age for women was 18.93 ($SD = 1.51$) and for men was 19.51 ($SD = 1.17$). Each participant received 2 hours of course credit in undergraduate psychology courses for their involvement in the study. Due to incomplete questionnaires and the exclusion of extreme outliers on the measures, most of the data reported here are based on responses ranging from 188-202 participants. Analyses with high school rank and college GPA include 140 and 164 participants, respectively, due to the availability of data from the university registrar. Informed consent was obtained from each participant.

Measures of Emotional Intelligence

Mayer, Salovey, and Caruso Emotional Intelligence Test (MSCEIT). Emotional intelligence ability was measured with the MSCEIT Version 2.0 (Mayer et al., 2002a). The MSCEIT is a 141-item test that measures how well people perform tasks and solve emotional problems on eight tasks, which are divided into four classes or branches of abilities including (a) perceiving emotions, (b) facilitating thought, (c) understanding emotions, and (d) managing emotions. Correct answers are evaluated in terms of agreement with a general (or expert) consensus, which closely converge (Mayer, et al., 2002b). Analysis of the data by the test publisher provides five scores including one for each branch and one for total EI. As reported in the technical manual, split-half reliability coefficients for the four branches range from $r = .80$ to .91, and for the entire test $r = .91$.

Bar-On Emotional Intelligence Inventory (EQ-i). The EQ-i (Bar-On, 1997a) is a 133-item self-report measure of emotional intelligence. Respondents answer questions using a 5-point Likert-type scale (1 = very seldom or not true of me; 5 = very often true of me). Scores are provided by the test publisher and are calculated with reference to North American norms for the age group. Reported scores include total EQ-i and scores from the test's five composite scales: intrapersonal EQ, interpersonal EQ, adaptability, stress management, and general mood. Bar-On (2000) has recently changed his model and now considers the fifth factor, general mood, as a facilitator of EI and not part of it. Therefore, the total EQ-i score used here is based on the sum of the first four scales. Reliability coefficients for the 15 subscales that comprise the factor scores range from $a = .69$ to .86 across 10 studies (Bar-On, 1997b)[1].

Self-Report Emotional Intelligence Test (SREIT). The SREIT (Schutte et al., 1998) is a self-report test of EI that is based on Salovey and Mayer's (1990) original work on EI. Participants respond to 33 self-report items such as "I know why my emotions change," using a 5-point scale, on which 1 represents *strongly disagree* and a 5 represents *strongly agree*. The reliability of the scale in the present study was high (*a* = .93).

Measures of Personality and Well Being

Personality. Personality traits were assessed with the 240-item NEO-PI-R (Costa & McCrae, 1992), which measures five global dimensions of personality: Neuroticism, Extraversion, Openness to Experience, Agreeableness, and Conscientiousness. Each factor is a composite of 6 primary (facet) scales. Participants completed the scale using a 1 *strongly disagree* to 5 *strongly agree* response format. The reliability and validity of the measure has been established for college samples and is provided in the technical manual (Costa & McCrae, 1992b).

Psychological Well-Being. Ryff (1989) developed a theoretically based self-report inventory designed to measure six dimensions of psychological well-being (PWB). The six dimensions are: self-acceptance, environmental mastery, purpose in life, positive relations with others, personal growth, and autonomy. To accommodate computer scoring, each dimension was operationalized with a 1 *strongly disagree* to 5 *strongly agree* response format instead of the recommended six-item response format. The reliabilities of the six scales (*as* = .80 to .88) and composite PWB score (*a* = .94) were high.

Subjective Well-Being. Subjective well-being (SWB) was measured with the Satisfaction with Life Scale (SWLS) (Diener, 1984). This five-item scale assesses a person's general satisfaction with life. Participants responded using a 1 *strongly disagree* to 7 *strongly agree* response format. The scale has been widely used in college samples and the reliability and validity of the measure is established (Pavot & Diener, 1993).

Criterion Measures

External Life Space Criteria. Four life space scales, which provide data about people's daily activities, were employed as the criteria. These scales measured daily smoking behavior (e.g., packs of cigarettes owned, number of cigarettes smoked per day), illegal drug use (e.g., amount of marijuana owned, times used illegal drugs in the last month), alcohol consumption (e.g., bottles of beer and hard liquor owned, times in the last month fell asleep because of intoxication), and social deviance (e.g., number of physical fights, times vandalized something) (Brackett, 2001). Life space scales, similar to bio-data scales (Mael, 1991), differ from traditional self-report scales that inquire about a person's internal sentiments (e.g., "Do you enjoy smoking?") because they measure discrete, observable, and potentially verifiable behaviors (e.g., "How many cigarettes did you smoke yesterday?"). Reliabilities of the four scales, which had between 5 and 9 items, ranged from *a* = .62 to .91.

Convergent, Discriminant, and Incremental Validity of Competing Measures of Emotional Intelligence

Academic Ability. Participants signed an additional informed consent form that permitted the researchers to access their academic records. We obtained two indices for academic performance: high school rank and college GPA. Verbal SAT scores also were obtained as a proxy measure of verbal intelligence.

Procedure

Participants completed the self-administered materials in one testing session, which lasted about 1 1/2 to 2 hours. Participants first completed the informed consent forms. They then received a short demographics form, which was followed by the ability and self-report tests of EI, and then the personality, well-being, and life space scales. Upon completion, participants were given a debriefing statement.

Results

This section is divided into four parts. First, preliminary analyses were conducted within items on each scale. Second, EI measures were compared to one another, to verbal intelligence, and to well-studied measures of personality and well-being. Multivariate analyses were then used to further understand the interrelations among the EI and personality scales. Finally, the EI tests were related to academic performance and the external life space criteria.

Preliminary Analyses on each scale and its items. Before performing our central analyses, we first tried to replicate Petrides & Furnham's (2000) four-factor solution of the SREIT. Our factor analysis resulted in only one interpretable factor pertaining to the perception or appraisal of emotion. Therefore, we conducted all analyses with the 33-item SREIT as recommended by Schutte et al. (1998) given that no other meaningful factors were extractable.

Because we employed Bar-On's (2000) revised EQ-i scoring and the norms and most of the validity data are based on the original scoring of the EQ-i, we computed the correlation between the two scores. The correlation was almost perfect: $r(191) = .98$, $p < .001$. Thus, the elimination of the general mood factor from the original EQ-i composite score has relatively no effect on the total score.

We then assessed whether gender differences existed on any of the EI scales. Significant gender differences were only found on the MSCEIT, with women ($M = 105.13$, $SD = 11.09$) scoring higher than men ($M = 95.17$, $SD = 13.43$), $t(200) = -5.69$, $p < .001$. These gender differences are consistent with previous research (Brackett, 2001; Mayer et al., 1999). In contrast to Schutte et al.'s (1998) findings we did not obtain significant gender differences on the SREIT: men ($M = 3.71$, $SD = .51$) and women ($M = 3.75$, $SD = .39$). Parallel to Bar-On's (1997b) findings no gender differences existed on the EQ-i: men ($M = 93.26$, $SD = 11.10$) and women ($M = 92.37$, $SD = 11.53$).

Finally, we assessed the test-retest reliability of the MSCEIT by having 60 (18 men, 42 women) participants return 3 weeks after initial testing to re-take the MSCEIT.

The test-retest reliability was very high r (59) = .86, p < .001. The EQ-i and SREIT have already demonstrated adequate test-retest reliability (r = .73, .78, respectively) (Bar-On, 1997b; Schutte et al., 1998).

Relations Among Measures of EI, Personality, Well-Being, and Verbal SAT Scores

   Table 1 shows the zero-order correlations among the measures of EI, personality, well-being, and verbal SAT scores. As expected, the MSCEIT was most distinct among EI measures (rs = .21, .18, with the EQ-i and SREIT, respectively). The SREIT and EQ-i, however, were moderately interrelated (r = .43). The MSCEIT was also most distinct among EI measures with respect to personality and well-being. The MSCEIT only modestly correlated with openness, agreeableness, psychological well-being (PWB), and verbal SAT scores (rs = .25 to .32). These findings corroborate earlier findings (Brackett, 2001; Salovey et al., 2001). Similar to previous research, the EQ-i and SREIT had strong associations with the personality measures (Bar-On, 1997b; Dawda & Hart, 2000; Newsome et al., 2000; Schutte et al., 1998). The SREIT correlated with four of the Big Five factors and very highly with PWB (r = .69) and the EQ-i correlated significantly with each factor on the Big Five, and Neuroticism in particular (r = -.57).

   Next, we correlated the personality and well-being scales, which were all highly interrelated. For example, all of the Big Five factors correlated with PWB (rs = -.50 to .48). Only Neuroticism, Extraversion, and Conscientiousness correlated with SWB (rs = -.43 to .36). PWB and SWB also correlated with one another (r = .41). The interrelation among the personality and well-being scales is consistent with previous research (Emmons & Diener, 1985; McCrae & Costa, 1991; Schmutte & Ryff, 1997).

   To obtain a more detailed understanding of the relations between the MSCEIT and EQ-i, we correlated the subscales on the tests. As shown in Table 2, the highest correlation was between the MSCEIT regulation of emotion scale and the EQ-i interpersonal EQ scale (r = .40). We then went a step further and computed partial correlations among the EI tests, separately controlling for the Big Five and PWB because the EI measures shared considerable variance with the these measures, which may have inflated the coefficients in Tables 1 and 2. As shown in Table 3, when controlling for the Big Five or PWB, the MSCEIT became mostly independent of both self-report EI inventories. When both the Big Five and PWB were controlled, all of the relations between the MSCEIT and self-report measures became non-significant. The SREIT and EQ-i, however, remained correlated when the Big Five was controlled. When PWB was controlled the relations between the SREIT and the EQ-i became non-significant. Results indicate that the covariation between the EQ-i and SREIT is probably due to each scale's shared variance with PWB, whereas the covariation between the MSCEIT and EQ-i can be attributed, in part, to each scale's shared variance with the Big Five or PWB.

Discriminant Validity using Multivariate Statistics

To gain a more comprehensive perspective on the discriminant validity of the three EI tests, multiple regression analyses were performed using the Big Five and PWB scales as predictor variables and the three EI tests as the outcome measures. Figure 1 represents these results, which were all statistically significant ($p < .001$).

The MSCEIT was most distinct among EI measures ($Rs < .38$). With respect to the Big Five, only Agreeableness and Openness to Experience significantly contributed to the model; for PWB only the personal growth subscale significantly contributed to the model. In contrast, the EQ-i and SREIT both shared considerable variance with the Big Five and PWB. With respect to the Big Five, Extraversion, Openness to Experience, and Agreeableness were predictive of the SREIT ($R = .52$), and for PWB, five of the six scales significantly contributed to the model ($R = .70$). The EQ-i also shared substantial variance with four of the six PWB scales ($R = .58$) but shared most of its variance with the Big Five ($R = .75$). As predicted by McCrae (2000), all five factors significantly contributed to prediction of the EQ-i. These results provide further support that that the MSCEIT is mostly separable from personality and well-being, whereas the EQ-i and SREIT are not easily distinguished from these measures.

We then factor analyzed all of the personality, well-being, and EI tests, along with verbal SAT scores to gain a second perspective on the relations among the measures. The results (principal axis followed by oblique rotation) are presented in Table 4. The eigenvalues for the first five factors were 7.2, 2.7, 1.9, 1.8, 1.2, suggesting either a three or four-factor solution. We decided on the three-factor solution because the loadings were clear and interpretable ($\pm .35$), and the solution accounted for a reasonable amount of variance (44%). As can be seen, Factor 1 was composed of the five EQ-i scales, Neuroticism (reverse scored), Conscientiousness, and SWB. Factor 2 was composed of the four MSCEIT scales, along with verbal SAT scores and Agreeableness. Factor 3 was composed of the six PWB scales, the SREIT, Extraversion, and Openness to Experience. These results support our prior results and further demonstrate that among the EI measures the EQ-i is highly related to personality and the SREIT is highly related to well-being. The MSCEIT, although slightly correlated with Agreeableness and verbal SAT scores created its own factor. The MSCEIT factor was uncorrelated with factors 2 and 3, which were moderately correlated ($r = .50$) with one another.

Predictive and Incremental Validity

A limited number of behavioral life space criteria were employed based on their theoretical importance to EI. Table 5 shows the zero-order correlations among all measures with the life space criteria (drug use, alcohol use, cigarette smoking, social deviance) and scales of academic achievement (high school rank and college GPA). Both the MSCEIT and EQ-i correlated with some of the criteria. The SREIT was unrelated to any of the criteria. There were no significant gender differences in any of these correlations.

Table 1
Means, Standard Deviations, and Intercorrelations Among Measures of Emotional Intelligence, Personality and Well Being, and Verbal SAT scores.

	MSCEIT	SREIT	EQ-i	N	E	O	A	C	PWB	SWB	VSAT
Measures of Emotional IQ											
MSCEIT	1.00										
SREIT	**.18****	1.00									
EQ-i	**.21****	**.43*****	1.00								
Big Five											
Neuroticism	-.08	**-.19****	**-.57*****	1.00							
Extraversion	.11	**.32*****	**.37*****	**-.27*****	1.00						
Openness	**.25*****	**.43*****	**.16***	.00	**.23*****	1.00					
Agreeableness	**.28*****	.09	**.27*****	-.09	.05	**.19****	1.00				
Conscientiousness	.03	**.25*****	**.48*****	**-.29*****	**.30*****	-.03	**.18****	1.00			
Measures of Well-being											
Psychological Well-being	**.28*****	**.69*****	**.54*****	**-.50*****	**.48*****	**.33*****	**.21****	**.40*****	1.00		
Subjective Well-being	-.05	**.22*****	**.35*****	**-.43*****	**.34*****	.11	.11	**.36*****	**.41*****	1.00	
Verbal SAT	**.32*****	.05	-.03	-.04	**-.20****	**.26*****	.07	.08	.01	-.06	1.00
M	101.44	3.74	90.87	2.57	3.33	3.32	3.18	3.03	3.67	5.14	543.20
SD	12.91	.44	13.81	.56	.53	.53	.51	.58	.45	1.19	71.41

Note. N = 188 to 202. N = Neuroticism, E = Extraversion, O = Openness to Experience, A = Agreeableness, C = Conscientiousness. MSCEIT = Mayer-Salovey-Caruso-Emotional Intelligence Test, SREIT = self-report EI test, EQ-I = Emotional Quotient Inventory, PWB = psychological well-being, SWB = subjective well-being, VSAT = verbal Scholastic Aptitude Test (SAT) scores, IQ = intelligence quotient. Only significant correlations shown in boldface.
*p < .05; **p < .01; ***p < .001.

Convergent, Discriminant, and Incremental Validity of Competing Measures of Emotional Intelligence

Figure 1. Multiple R's for Big Five Traits versus Psychological Well-being Scales Regressed on Total Scores for the MSCEIT, EQ-i, and SREIT.

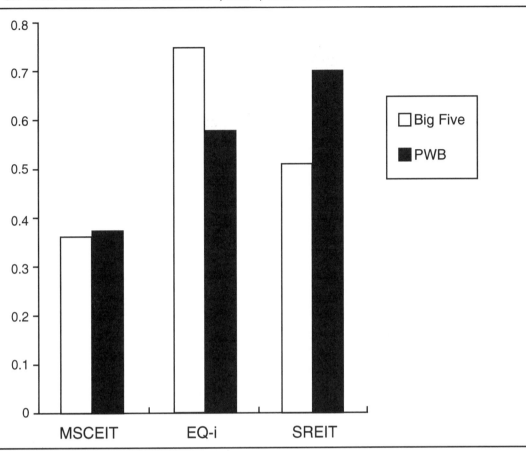

Note: MSCEIT = Mayer-Salovey-Caruso-Emotional Intelligence Test, SREIT = self-report EI test, EQ-I = Emotional Quotient Inventory, PWB = psychological well-being.

In order of strength of association (highest to lowest), the top three predictors of drug use were Conscientiousness, the EQ-i, and SWB. Alcohol use was predictable by the EQ-i and Agreeableness. Cigarette smoking was predictable by Conscientiousness and SWB. The top predictors of social deviance were Agreeableness, the MSCEIT, and the EQ-i. With respect to academic achievement, high school rank was predictable by verbal SAT scores, Agreeableness, and the MSCEIT. First semester college GPA was predictable by Conscientiousness, verbal SAT scores, PWB, and the MSCEIT.

Because our central concern was the incremental validity of the EI tests, we computed partial correlations between the EI tests and the criteria controlling for the Big Five and verbal SAT. The Big Five was held constant because it covaried with the EQ-i and the MSCEIT. Verbal SAT scores also were controlled because they covaried with the MSCEIT. As shown in Table 6, only three partial correlations were significant. Contrary to Schutte et al.'s (1998) finding, the SREIT was inversely related to academic achievement. The EQ-i remained negatively correlated with alcohol use and the MSCEIT remained negatively correlated with social deviance.

Table 2
Means, Standard Deviations, and Intercorrelations among Subscales of Measures of Emotional Intelligence.

	MSCEIT					SREIT	EQ-i					
	Total	P	I	U	R	Total	Total	Intra	Inter	AD	SM	GM
MSCEIT	1.00											
Perception (P)	.79***	1.00										
Integration (I)	.75***	.48***	1.00									
Understanding (U)	.68***	.35***	.37***	1.00								
Regulation (R)	.65***	.31***	.36***	.27***	1.00							
SREIT	.18**	.06	.15*	.12	.22**	1.00						
EQ-i	.21**	.07	.17*	.11	.28***	.43***	1.00					
Intrapersonal	.07	-.05	.11	.06	.13	.43***	.90***	1.00				
Interpersonal	.28***	.20**	.15*	.06	.40***	.37***	.68***	.49***	1.00			
Adaptability	.16*	.07	.14	.09	.18**	.33***	.81***	.64***	.40***	1.00		
Self Management	.15*	.02	.14	.14	.17*	.22**	.69***	.45***	.32***	.62***	1.00	
General Mood	.08	-.04	.11	.14	.19**	.36***	.83***	.75***	.53***	.57***	.50***	1.00
M	101.44	103.52	101.53	100.70	101.20	3.74	90.87	92.72	96.17	88.94	92.98	92.81
SD	12.91	15.04	12.95	12.68	12.53	.44	13.81	15.30	14.66	13.30	14.75	16.27

Note. N = 188 to 202. MSCEIT = Mayer-Salovey-Caruso-Emotional Intelligence Test, SREIT = self-report EI test, EQ-I = Emotional Quotient Inventory. Only significant correlations shown in boldface.
*p < .05; **p < .01; ***p < .001.

Convergent, Discriminant, and Incremental Validity of Competing Measures of Emotional Intelligence

Table 3
Partial Correlations among Measures of Emotional Intelligence Controlling for Big Five and Psychological Well-Being

| | Controlling for Big Five | | | | | | | Controlling for Psychological Well-being | | | | | | | |
| | SREIT | | | EQ-i | | | | SREIT | | | EQ-i | | | | |
	Total	Intra	Inter	Total	AD	SM	GM	Total	Intra	Inter	Total	Inter	AD	SM	GM
MSCEIT															
Perception	.05	.00	.12	.08	.12	.00	-.04	-.02	-.08	.12	.03	.12	.05	.00	-.07
Integration	.09	.06	.09	.12	.10	.09	.03	.02	.08	.10	.12	.10	.08	.09	.03
Understanding	.02	.08	.03	.06	.06	.09	-.07	.02	.03	.02	.07	.02	.05	.10	-.06
Regulation	.07	.00	**.18***	**.19***	.15	.14	.12	.00	.07	.07	**.20****	**.30*****	.10	.12	.14
SREIT	1.00	**.27****	**.27****	**.31*****	**.24****	.15	**.22****	1.00	.06	.19	.09	.19	.08	-.03	.02

(MSCEIT row: Controlling for Big Five — .08, .04, .14, .14, .13, .09, .00; Controlling for Psychological Well-being — -.01, .02, .14, .02, **.19***, .10, .10, .00)

Note. N = 191 to 202. Intra = intrapersonal, Inter = interpersonal, AD = adaptability, SM = self-management, GM = general mood. MSCEIT = Mayer-Salovey-Caruso-Emotional Intelligence Test, SREIT = self-report EI test, EQ-I = Emotional Quotient Inventory. Only significant correlations shown in boldface.
*p < .05; **p < .01; ***p < .001.

Discussion

Mayer and colleagues (Mayer & Salovey, 1997; Mayer et al., 2000; Salovey & Mayer, 1990) have consistently claimed that emotions pertain to signals about relationships and intelligence pertains to abstract reasoning. They argue that the correct definition of EI involves the ability to reason with emotions and of emotions to enhance reasoning. They further contend that broader definitions of EI are probably improper because when the term EI is used to include an array of attributes (Bar-On, 1997b; Goleman, 1995, 1998; Schutte et al., 1998) it becomes unclear what EI actually is and the construct begins to emulate existing measures.

If one adheres to Mayer and Salovey's (1997) mental ability model of EI, this study showed that MSCEIT is the measure of choice; it was discriminable from well-studied measures of personality and well-being and it showed some evidence that it predicts important life criteria. If, on the other hand, one defines EI in terms of a mixed array of "desirable" personality characteristics then the EQ-i and SREIT are both good choices. The drawback to these latter measures is that they are quite similar to already-existing measures of personality and well-being.

Convergent and Discriminant Validity

For the most part, ability and self-report EI tests were weakly related. The lack of convergence between the measures was probably due in part to the distinct ways the constructs are defined. Many items on the EQ-i and SREIT, for instance, pertain to personality attributes such as optimism and emotional stability, which are unrelated to the four abilities assessed by the MSCEIT. The low correlations between ability and self-report measures also may be due to their different measurement approaches (i.e., performance based versus self-report). It is well known that self-report and ability scales only modestly correlate because people are notoriously bad at assessing their own capacities (e.g., Paulhus et al., 1998).

As predicted, this study showed that MSCEIT was mostly distinguishable from well-being scales and the Big Five, whereas the EQ-i and SREIT were less separable from these constructs. Because EI ability is specifically defined as the ability to perceive, integrate, understand, and regulate emotions (Mayer & Salovey, 1997) it is unlikely to emulate existing personality measures. Indeed, the description of the four-branch model of EI is different from anything described by the Big Five. Although the Big Five explain large amounts of variance in personality, there are many traits and abilities such as masculinity/femininity or religiosity that are not covered by the Big Five (Paunonen & Jackson, 2000; Saucier & Goldberg, 1998). EI ability is one aspect of personality that is likely to fall outside the factor space of the Big five. There is no reason to believe that people higher in EI are more extraverted or open to experience than their less emotionally intelligent counterparts.

The EQ-i and SREIT, on the other hand were less separable from well-being constructs and the Big Five. This may be due to the similar semantic content between

Convergent, Discriminant, and Incremental Validity of Competing Measures of Emotional Intelligence

these self-report tests and the other existing self-report measures. Although Bar-On (2000, p. 364) stresses that the EQ-i was not developed to measure personality traits, in the present study, the EQ-i was highly correlated with the Big Five ($R = .75$). Indeed, our regression analyses showed that all five factors of the Big Five uniquely contributed to the prediction of the EQ-i at significant levels. This finding was in keeping with McCrae's (2000) prediction that the Big Five covers most of what is measured by mixed conceptions of EI, particularly when the Big Five is scored in an "ideal" way (i.e., low Neuroticism and high Extraversion, Agreeableness, Openness, and Conscientiousness). A comparable story could be told for the SREIT, which overlapped highly with Ryff's (1989) PWB scales ($R = .70$).

Table 4
Three Factor Solution of Measures of Personality, Well-being, Emotional Intelligence, and Verbal SAT's using Principal Axis Factoring with Oblique Rotation (Pattern Matrix).

Scale	I	II	III
EQ-i: Self Management	.800		
EQ-i: Adaptability	.753		
EQ-i: General Mood	.730		
Big Five: Neuroticism	-.719		
EQ-i: Intrapersonal	.667		
Subjective Well-being	.443		
Big Five: Conscientiousness	.439		
EQ-i: Interpersonal	.346		
MSCEIT: Perception		.601	
MSCEIT: Regulation		.570	
MSCEIT: Integration		.524	
MSCEIT: Understanding		.447	
Verbal SAT		.430	
Big Five: Agreeableness		.402	
PWB: Personal Growth			.740
SREIT			.723
PWB: Positive Relations			.695
PWB: Self-Acceptance			.693
PWB: Purpose in Life			.619
PWB: Environmental Mastery			.594
Big Five: Extraversion			.498
Big Five: Openness to Experience			.405
PWB: Autonomy			.348

Note: Only factor loadings above ±.35 are included. MSCEIT = Mayer-Salovey-Caruso-Emotional Intelligence Test, SREIT = self-report EI test, EQ-I = Emotional Quotient Inventory, PWB = psychological well-being, SAT = Scholastic Aptitude Test.

Table 5
Zero-Order Correlations among Measures of Personality, Well-being and Verbal SAT with External Criteria

Measures of Emotional IQ	DrugUse	AlcoholUse	Cigarette Smoking	Social Deviance	High School Rank	College GPA
MSCEIT	-.05	-.06	-.02	**-.27*****	**.21****	**.16***
EQ-i	**-.24*****	**-.20****	**-.21****	**-.21****	.04	.10
SREIT	-.04	-.05	.01	-.07	-.02	.06
Big Five						
Neuroticism	.09	.07	.03	.00	.07	-.03
Extraversion	**-.15***	.10	-.06	-.07	.05	**.15***
Openness	.04	-.03	.04	-.07	.15	.12
Agreeableness	-.11	**-.15***	-.06	**-.39*****	**.24*****	.06
Conscientiousness	**-.31*****	-.11	**-.19****	**-.20****	**.19***	**.33*****
Measures of Well-being						
Psychological Well-being	-.13	-.06	-.03	**-.16***	.06	**.19****
Subjective Well-being	**-.20****	.01	**-.17***	-.07	.01	**.16***
Verbal SAT	**.17***	-.09	-.03	-.08	**.39*****	**.27*****

Note: N = 188 to 202. For high school rank, N = 140, and for college grade point average (GPA), N = 164. MSCEIT = Mayer-Salovey-Caruso-Emotional Intelligence Test, SREIT = self-report EI test, EQ-I = Emotional Quotient Inventory. Only significant correlations shown in boldface.
*p < .05; **p < .01; ***p < .001.

Convergent, Discriminant, and Incremental Validity of Competing Measures of Emotional Intelligence

Incremental Validity

Most personality psychologists would agree that for a new construct to be welcomed into the field, it must explain variance that is not accounted for by well-established constructs. For that reason we were less interested in the zero-order correlations between the EI tests and criteria because of each tests' shared variance with existing measures that were themselves correlated with criteria. Furthermore, the self-report EI tests had so much in common with personality variables that the zero-order correlations may have just been a case of reinventing the wheel.

The MSCEIT and EQ-i showed some evidence of incremental validity, whereas the SREIT did not. With respect to the MSCEIT, after personality and verbal SAT scores were controlled, lower scores remained predictive of social deviance. This finding replicates a pattern of negative correlations between ability EI and deviant behavior (Formica, 1998; Brackett, & Mayer, 2002; Rubin, 1999). With respect to the EQ-i, lower scores were predictive of higher alcohol consumption. The SREIT did not correlate with any of the criteria in expected ways. Furthermore, this study challenged the importance of self-reported EI in the prediction of academic performance. In particular, the SREIT, contrary to previous findings (Schutte et al., 1998) had a negative partial correlation with academic performance.

It is plain that none of the correlations with the limited criteria employed here were high in absolute terms. Although predictions with other criteria may be higher, a realistic expectation is that the best new variables ought to increase predictive accuracy in important but modest ways. Of note, correlations in the .20 to .30 range with real-life criteria can have important implications (Abelson, 1985; Meyer, et al., 2001). Consider the case of a researcher who wishes to include as many individuals as possible that are at-risk for deviant behavior in a 6-month longitudinal study. Budgetary considerations allow for the selection of 100 participants out of an initial pool of 200. Pre-testing with the MSCEIT, and selection of individuals scoring below the average, would provide the researcher with an additional 10 participants (i.e., 60 versus 50 with no pre-testing) who are above-average in risk for behaving in a deviant fashion.[2] Thus, a test that correlates .20 with a criterion of interest can facilitate selection in consequential ways.

It is likely that more extensive criteria will yield additional interesting predictions, some stronger and some less strong than the above. The criterion and incremental validity of these tests needs to be developed over multiple studies with multiple criteria and diverse samples. The criteria employed here told us something about each measure of EI. The predictive validity findings here, however, are better interpreted in the context of more extensive studies, and more comprehensive reviews of evidence that are available for the MSCEIT (Brackett, & Mayer, 2002; Mayer, et al., 2002a) and the EQ-i and SREIT (e.g., Bar-On, 2000; Schutte et al., 2001).

Table 6

Partial Correlations between Measures of Emotional Intelligence and External Criteria Controlling for Big Five and verbal SAT scores.

	DrugUse	AlcoholUse	CigaretteSmoking	Social Deviance	High School Rank	College GPA
Measures of Emotional IQ						
MSCEIT	-.07	-.01	.02	**-.20****	.04	.05
EQ-i	-.12	**-.19***	-.08	-.06	-.12	-.08
SREIT	.05	-.05	.04	-.05	**-.16***	-.10

Note: N = 173 to 183, missing data for verbal SAT. For high school rank, N = 140 and for college grade point average (GPA), N = 164. MSCEIT = Mayer-Salovey-Caruso-Emotional Intelligence Test, SREIT = self-report EI test, EQ-I = Emotional Quotient Inventory. Only significant correlations shown in boldface.
* p < .05; ** p < .01

Convergent, Discriminant, and Incremental Validity of Competing Measures of Emotional Intelligence

Conclusions

There now exist two general models of EI: a mental ability model and a mixed model. In regard to mixed-models, most of the attributes measured by the EQ-i and SREIT substantially overlap with existing measures, which suggests that these scales have a breadth of coverage that is not all that different from well-studied personality and well-being scales. Mixed models are also somewhat misleading. Such models suggest that there is a new, integrated, single psychological entity called EI that combines diverse traits such as common sense, well-being, persistence, and good interpersonal skills. Furthermore, each of the Big Five scales individually predicts measures such as the EQ-i, which suggests that these mixed models are truly composed of distinct, somewhat uncorrelated, attributes. On the other hand, findings with the MSCEIT suggest that EI as a mental ability exists as a distinct, clearly defined construct that has evidence of incremental validity.

We assert that broad definitions of EI that do not refer exclusively to the terms "emotion" and "intelligence" are probably improper uses of the term. Although the traits that are theoretically covered by mixed models such as motivation, optimism, and self-esteem – and the traits that they empirically correlate with such as Extraversion, Agreeableness, and Openness — are important and predictive of real life criteria, they are better addressed directly and as distinct from EI. Keeping EI restricted to an ability model makes it possible to analyze the degree to which EI specifically contributes to a person's behavior.

References

Abelson, R. (1985). A variance explanation paradox: When a little is a lot. *Psyhological Bulletin, 97,* 129-133.

Bar-On, R. (1997a). *Bar-On Emotional Quotient Inventory (EQ-i): A test of emotional intelligence.* Toronto, Canada: Multi-Health Systems.

Bar-On, R. (1997b). *Bar-On Emotional Quotient Inventory (EQ-i): Technical manual.* Toronto, Canada: Multi-Health Systems.

Bar-On, R. (2000). Emotional and social intelligence: Insights from the emotional quotient inventory. In R. Bar-On, & J. D. A. Parker (Eds.). *The Handbook of Emotional Intelligence.* San Francisco: Jossey-Bass.

Boyatzsis, R. E., Goleman, D., & Rhee, K. S. (2000). Clustering competence in emotional intelligence. In R. Bar-On, & J. D. A. Parker (Eds.). *The Handbook of Emotional Intelligence.* San Francisco: Jossey-Bass.

Brackett, M. A. (2001). *Emotional intelligence and its expression in the life space.* Unpublished master's thesis, University of New Hampshire.

Brackett, M., & Mayer, J.D. (2002). *Emotional intelligence and its expression in the interactive life space.* Manuscript submitted for publication.

Carroll, J. B. (1993). *Human cognitive abilities: A survey of factor-analytic studies.* New York: Cambrige University Press.

Ciarrochi, J. V., Chan A. Y. C., & Caputi, P. (2000). A critical evaluation of the emotional intelligence construct. *Personality and Individual Differences, 28,* 539-561.

Costa, P. T., Jr., & McCrae, R. R. (1992). *NEO-PI-R Professional Manual – Revised NEO Personality Inventory (NEO-PIR) and NEO Five-Factor Inventory (NEO-FFI).* Odessa, FL: Psychological Assessment Resources.

Davies, M., Stankov, L., & Roberts, R. D. (1998). Emotional intelligence: In search of an elusive construct. *Journal of Personality and Social Psychology, 75,* 989-1015.

Dawda, D. & Hart, S. D. (2000). Assessing emotional intelligence: Reliability and validity of the Bar-On Emotional Quotient Inventory (EQ-i) in university students. *Personality and Individual Differences, 28,* 797-812.

Derksen, J., Kramer, I., & Katzko, M. (2002). Does a self –report measure for emotional intelligence assess something different than general intelligence? *Personality and Individual Differences, 32, 37-48.*

Diener, E. (1984). Subjective well-being. *Psychological Bulletin, 95,* 542-575.

Emmons, R. A., & Diener, E. (1985). Personality correlates of subjective well-being. *Personality and Social Psychology Bulletin, 11,* 89-97.

Epstein, S. (1998). *Constructive thinking: The key to emotional intelligence.* Westport, CT: Praeger Publishers/Greenwood Publishing Group.

Formica, S. (1998). *Describing the socio-emotional life space.* Unpublished senior's honor thesis, University of New Hampshire.

Goleman, D. (1995). *Emotional Intelligence.* New York: Bantam.

Goleman, D. (1998). *Working with Emotional Intelligence.* New York: Bantam.

Hedlund, J. & Sternberg, R. J. (2000). Too many intelligences? Integrating social, emotional, and practical intelligence. In R. Bar-On, & J. D. A. Parker (Eds.). *The Handbook of Emotional Intelligence.* San Francisco: Jossey-Bass.

Mael, F. A. (1991). A conceptual rationale for the domain and attributes of biodata items. *Personnel Psychology, 44,* 763-792.

Malouff, J., & Schutte, N. (1998, August). *Emotional intelligence scale scores predict counselor performance.* Paper presented at the Annual Convention of the American Psychological Society, Washington, D.C.

Mayer, J. D., & Cobb, C. D. (2000). Educational policy and emotional intelligence: Does it make sense? *Educational Psychology Review, 12,* 163-183.

Mayer, J. D., & Geher, G. (1996). Emotional intelligence and the identification of emotion. *Intelligence, 22,* 89-113.

Mayer, J. D., & Salovey, P. (1993). The intelligence of emotional intelligence. *Intelligence, 17,* 433-442.

Mayer, J. D., & Salovey, P. (1997). What is emotional intelligence? In P. Salovey and D. Sluyter (Eds.), *Emotional Development and Emotional Intelligence: Educational Implications.* New York: Basic Books.

Convergent, Discriminant, and Incremental Validity of Competing Measures of Emotional Intelligence

Mayer, J. D., Carlsmith, K. M., & Chabot, H. F. (1998). Describing the person's external environment: Conceptualizing and measuring the life space. *Journal of Research in Personality, 32,* 253-296.

Mayer, J. D., Caruso, D., & Salovey, P. (1999). Emotional intelligence meets traditional standards for an intelligence. *Intelligence, 27,* 267-298.

Mayer, J. D., Caruso, D., Salovey, P., & Sitarenios, G. (2002). Emotional intelligence as a standard intelligence. *Emotion, 1,* 232-242.

Mayer, J. D., DiPaolo, M., & Salovey, P. (1990). Perceiving affective content in ambiguous visual stimuli: A component of emotional intelligence. *Journal of Personality Assessment, 54,* 772-781.

Mayer, J. D., Salovey, P., & Caruso, D. R. (2000). Models of emotional intelligence. In R. J. Sternberg (Ed.), *Handbook of intelligence* (pp. 396-420). Cambridge, England: Cambridge University Press.

Mayer, J. D., Salovey, P., & Caruso, D. (2002a). *Mayer-Salovey-Caruso Emotional Intelligence Test (MSCEIT), Version 2.0.* Toronto, Canada: Multi-Health Systems.

Mayer, J. D., Salovey, P., & Caruso, D. (2002b). *MSCEIT technical manual.* Toronto, Canada: Multi-Health Systems.

McCrae, R. R. (2000). Emotional intelligence from the perspective of the five-factor model of personality. In R. Bar-On, & J. D. A. Parker (Eds.). *The Handbook of Emotional Intelligence.* San Francisco: Jossey-Bass.

McCrae, R. R. & Costa, P. T. (1991). Adding *Liebe und Arbeit:* The full five-factor model and well-being. *Personality and Social Psychology Bulletin, 17,* 227-232.

Meyer, G. J., Finn, S. E., Eyde, L. D., Kay, G. G., Moreland, L. K., Dies, R. R., et al. (2001). Psychological testing and psychological assessment: A review of evidence and issues. *American Psychologist, 56,* 128-165.

Newsome, S., Day, A. L., & Catano, V. M. (2000). Assessing the predictive validity of emotional intelligence. *Personality and Individual Differences, 29,* 1005-1016.

Parker, J. D. A., Taylor, G. J., & Bagby, R. M. (2001). The relationship between alexithymia and emotional intelligence. *Personality and individual differences, 30,* 107-115.

Paulhus, D. L., Lysy, D. C., & Yik, M. S. M. (1998). Self-report measures of intelligence: Are they useful as proxy IQ tests? *Journal of Personality, 66,* 525-553.

Paunonen, S. V., & Jackson, D. N. (2000). What is beyond the Big Five? Plenty! *Journal of Personality, 68,* 821-835.

Pavot, W. & Diener, E. (1993). Review of the satisfaction with life scale. *Psychological Assessment, 5,* 164-172.

Petrides, K. V. & Furnham, A. (2000). On the dimensional structure of emotional intelligence. *Personality and Individual Differences, 29,* 313-320.

Rice, C. L. (1999). *A quantitative study of emotional intelligence and its impact on team performance.* Unpublished master's thesis, Pepperdine University, CA.

Roberts, R. D., Zeidner, M., & Matthews, G. (2002). Does emotional intelligence meet traditional standards for an intelligence? Some new data and conclusions. *Emotion, 1,* 196-231.

Rosenthal, R., & Rubin, D. B. (1982). A simple, general purpose display of magnitude of experimental effect. *Journal of Educational Psychology, 74,* 166-169.

Rubin, M. M. (1999). *Emotional intelligence and its role in mitigating aggression: A correlational study of the relationship between emotional intelligence and aggression in urban adolescents.* Unpublished Dissertation, Immaculata College, Pennsylvania.

Ryff, C. D. (1989). Happiness is everything, or is it? Explorations on the meaning of psychological well-being. *Journal of Personality and Social Psychology, 57,* 1069-1081.

Salovey, P. & Mayer, J. D. (1990). Emotional intelligence. *Imagination, Cognition and Personality, 9,* 185-211.

Salovey, P., Mayer, J. D., Caruso, D., & Lopes, P. N. (2001). Measuring emotional intelligence as a set of mental abilities with the MSCEIT. In S. J. Lopez & C. R. Snyder (Eds.), *Handbook of Positive Psychology Assessment.* Washington DC: American Psychological Association.

Saucier, G., & Goldberg, L. R. (1998). What is beyond the Big Five? *Journal of Personality, 66,* 495-524.

Schmutte, P. S., & Ryff, C. D. (1997). Personality and well-being: Reexamining methods and meanings. *Journal of Personality and Social Psychology, 73,* 540-559.

Schutte, N. S., Malouff, J. M., Hall, L. E., Haggerty, D. J., Cooper, J. T., Golden, C. J., et al. (1998). Development and validation of a measure of emotional intelligence. *Personality and Individual Differences, 25,* 167-177.

Schutte, S., Malouff, J.M., Bobik, C., Coston, T. D., Greeson, C., Jedlicka, C., et al. (2001). Emotional intelligence and interpersonal relations. *Journal of Social Psychology, 141,* 523-536.

Trinidad, D. R., & Johnson, C. A. (2001). The association between emotional intelligence and early adolescent tobacco and alcohol use. *Personality and individual differences, 32,* 95-105.

Author Notes

The preparation of this article was facilitated by a grant from the National Science Foundation (Sigma Xi), a Research Enhancement Award from the University of New Hampshire, and a Summer Fellowship awarded from the University of New Hampshire to the first author. We thank our colleagues Zorana Ivcevic, Paulo Lopes, and Dr. Rebecca Warner from the University of New Hampshire for their comments on earlier versions of this article. The article also benefited a great deal from the helpful comments of three anonymous reviewers and Paula Niedenthal. Please address correspondence to Marc A. Brackett, Department of Psychology, Yale University, P.O. Box 208205, New Haven, CT 06520; e-mail: marc.brackett@yale.edu.

Footnote

[1] Bar-On (1997b) does not report reliabilities for the five composite factors. Because the EQ-i is computer scored by the test, publisher reliability for the measure in the present study was not available.

[2] Calculations for this example are based on Rosenthal and Rubin's (1982) Binomial Effect Size Display (BESD). This example, however, is just an approximation because the BESD assumes normality for both variables. For this example, the assumption was met for the predictor but not the criterion.

Part III

Application of EI: Everyday Behavior, Education, and the Workplace

This last section presents five articles (two empirical papers and three book chapters) that focus on the predictive validity and social significance of EI. The first two articles focus on the predictive (and incremental) validity of the MSCEIT (after statistically controlling for personality traits). In *Emotional intelligence and the prediction of everyday behaviour* by Brackett, Mayer, and Warner (2003), MSCEIT scores were associated with reported social deviance, drug use, and excessive alcohol consumption primarily for college-aged males. In *Emotional intelligence, personality, and the perceived quality of social relationships* by Lopes, Salovey, and Straus (2003), MSCEIT Branch 4 scores (the ability to manage emotions) were positively associated concurrent reports of positive social relationships and negatively associated with reports of conflict with friends.

The third and fourth articles describe how EI might be utilized in educational settings. In *Educational policy on emotional intelligence: does it make sense?* Mayer and Cobb (2000) provide an overview of potential links between EI, social and emotional learning, and character education. They warn that many policies are based on popularized models of EI that are not yet supported by reasonable scientific investigations of their efficacy. In *Toward a broader education: social, emotional, and practical skills,* Lopes and Salovey (in press) attempt to answer the question, "How should educators choose among different programs of social and emotional learning?" They also explore the theoretical and empirical underpinnings of social and emotional learning.

The last article in this section, *Emotional intelligence and emotional leadership* by Caruso, Mayer, and Salovey (2002) discusses how EI might be employed by various organizations for a number of purposes, such as: executive coaching and career development. The researchers differentiate between ability and mixed models and assert that EI as a mental ability offers insight into the competencies of effective leadership, which have not been previously examined. They also present a case study to illustrate the role of EI in leadership effectiveness.

Reprinted from *Personality & Individual Differences*, Vol. 35, by Lopes, P.N., Salovey, P., & Straus, R., (2003). Emotional Intelligence, personality, and the perceived quality of social relationships, with permission from Elsevier.

Emotional Intelligence and its Relation to Everyday Behaviour

Marc A. Brackett*, University of New Hampshire
John D. Mayer, University of New Hampshire
Rebecca M. Warner, University of New Hampshire

Acknowledgements

The authors gratefully acknowledge the contributions of Elizabeth Stine-Morrow and Zorana Ivcevic whose input throughout the project greatly improved it. This research was supported in part by a Research Enhancement Award, a Summer Fellowship from the University of New Hampshire, and a small grant from Sigma Xi, which were awarded to the first author. Parts of this research were presented at the Annual Conference for the Society of Personality and Social Psychology, Los Angeles, CA, February 2003. The Life Space scales can be obtained by writing to Marc A. Brackett. The MSCEIT is available from Multi-health Systems, Toronto, ON.

---
* Corresponding author. Department of Psychology, Yale University, PO Box 208205, New Haven, CT 06520, USA. Tel.: + 1-203-432-2322; fax: + 1-203-4321-7172. E-mail address: marc.brackett@yale.edu (M.A. Brackett).

Abstract

This study assessed the discriminant, criterion and incremental validity of an ability measure of emotional intelligence (EI). College students ($N =$ 330) took an ability test of EI, a measure of the Big Five personality traits, and provided information on Life Space scales that assessed an array of self-care behaviours, leisure pursuits, academic activities, and interpersonal relations. Women scored significantly higher in EI than men. EI, however, was more predictive of the Life Space criteria for men than for women. Lower EI in males, principally the inability to perceive emotions and to use emotion to facilitate thought, was associated with negative outcomes, including illegal drug and alcohol use, deviant behaviour, and poor relations with friends. The findings remained significant even after statistically controlling for scores on the Big Five and academic achievement. In this sample, EI was significantly associated with maladjustment and negative behaviours for college-aged males, but not for females. ©2003 Elsevier Ltd. All rights reserved.

Keywords: Emotional Intelligence; Emotions; Life Space; Maladjustment; Behaviour; MSCEIT; Personality; Big Five.

Evidence is accumulating that emotional intelligence (EI) is a distinct mental ability that can be reliably measured (Brackett & Mayer, 2003; Ciarrochi, Chan, Caputi, & Roberts, 2001; Mayer, Caruso, & Salovey, 1999; Mayer, Salovey, Caruso, & Sitarenios, 2003). However, there is as of yet little clarity as to what EI predicts. Some preliminary findings suggest that lower EI is related to involvement in self-destructive behaviours such as deviant behaviour and cigarette smoking (Brackett & Mayer, 2003; Rubin, 1999; Trinidad & Johnson, 2001), whereas higher EI is related to positive outcomes such as prosocial behaviour, parental warmth, and positive peer and family relations (Mayer, et al., 1999; Rice, 1999; Salovey, Mayer, Caruso, & Lopes, 2001). Beyond these preliminary studies, more research is necessary to assess the criterion validity of EI.

From a scientific perspective, ability traits such as EI should be understood in terms of their real world behavioural expressions (Funder, 2001). Surprisingly, few researchers have focused their attention on the criterion validity of personality variables with respect to behavioural criteria (Magnusson & Torestad, 1992). Paunonen and Ashton (2001), for instance, employed an assortment of self-report behavioural criteria in their research on the predictive validity of the Big Five personality traits (i.e., Neuroticism, Extraversion, Openness to Experience, Agreeableness, and Conscientiousness). They showed that these five super-traits were correlated with a number of behaviours. For example, Conscientiousness correlated with study habits and college GPA, and Extraversion correlated with frequent dating. However, many of the predictive validity coefficients in their research were low or non-significant. Two possible reasons for weak predictive validity include the use of single-item assessments of behaviours for which reliability cannot be assessed, and the use of fairly narrow behavioural criteria that are not organized according to any specific hypotheses (e.g., Epstein, 1979, 1983).

The goal of the present study is to assess the criterion validity of EI, and hence the social significance or external utility of EI by relating the Mayer-Salovey-Caruso

Emotional Intelligence and its Relation to Everyday Behaviour

Emotional Intelligence Test (MSCEIT, 2002a) to selected scales from the College Student Life Space Scale (CSLSS; Brackett, 2001). The CSLSS expands upon recent measures of self-reported Life Space data (e.g., Mayer, Carlsmith, & Chabot, 1998; Paunonen, 1998; Paunonen & Ashton, 2001) because each scale is comprised of multiple self-reported behaviours, which are internally consistent. For this study, 13 scales that assess hypothesized expressions of EI were selected, including measures of self-care behaviours, leisure pursuits, academic activities, and interpersonal relations. The present study will also examine the discriminant and incremental validity of EI; that is, the extent to which EI is independent of well-studied measures of personality and verbal intelligence, and the ability of EI to predict selected criteria beyond what can be predicted by these other constructs.

Background

Correlating EI with a few external criteria such as college grades or alcohol consumption, although worthwhile, provides an incomplete picture of the person. Thus, the present study takes a new ability measure of EI and relates it to a cluster of Life Space scales, which assess self-reported behaviours that have either been associated with EI in preliminary studies or have been hypothesized to be related to EI.

Unlike measures of internal personality, which ask people to endorse items such as "I like to attend parties" or "I enjoy smoking cigarettes", Life Space scales ask about the objective events and behaviours in the world surrounding the individual, such as "How many parties have you been to in the last month?" or "How many packs of cigarettes have you smoked in the last week?" (Mayer et al., 1998). In this section we discuss current conceptions and measures of EI and then do the same for the Life Space.

Emotional Intelligence

Emotional intelligence involves the capacity to carry out reasoning in regard to emotions, and the capacity of emotions to enhance reasoning. More specifically, EI is said to involve the ability to perceive and accurately express emotion, to use emotion to facilitate thought, to understand emotions, and to manage emotions for emotional growth (Mayer & Salovey, 1997). A number of related concepts exist, including emotional competence, emotional creativity, and empathic accuracy (Averill & Nunley, 1992; Lane, Quinlan, Schwartz, Walker, & Zeitlin, 1990; Saarni, 2001). There are also other approaches to EI. "Mixed" conceptions of EI (e.g., Bar-On, 1997; Goleman, 1995, 1998; Schutte, et al., 1998) are so-called because they mix in well-studied but mostly uncorrelated traits such as optimism, motivation, and well-being with aspects of ability EI (Mayer, Salovey, & Caruso, 2000). These mixed models are primarily based on a popularization of the concept (Goleman, 1995), and the measures that stem from them are related to the EI ability (Brackett & Mayer, 2003).

Earlier EI ability scales (e.g., Mayer, DiPaolo, & Salovey, 1990; Mayer et al., 1999) were criticized for possessing lower–than–desirable reliability (Davies, Stankov, & Roberts,

1998; Roberts, Zeidner, & Mathews, 2002). The Multi-factor Emotional Intelligence Test (MEIS; Mayer et al., 1999) has a full-scale reliability of $r = 0.96$, and subscores that also are quite reliable; earlier concerns about reliability were directed to individual tasks scores that are not typically studied (Mayer et al., 2003). Similarly, the most recent EI ability test, the Mayer-Salovey-Caruso Emotional Intelligence Scale (MSCEIT; 2002a), has a full-scale reliability of $r = 0.91$. The MSCEIT is content valid and possesses a factor structure congruent with the four-part model of EI (Mayer & Salovey, 1997; Mayer et al., 2003). The four EI abilities the MSCEIT measures are: (a) Perceiving Emotion, (b) Using Emotion to Facilitate Thought, (c) Understanding Emotion, and (d) Managing Emotion. The MSCEIT measures the ability to perceive emotion by showing people faces and designs and asking them to identify emotions in them. The Use of Emotion to Facilitate Thought is measured by assessing people's ability to describe emotional sensations and their parallels to other sensory modalities, and through an individual's ability to assimilate pre-determined mood into their thought processes. Understanding Emotions is measured by asking test-takers how emotions combine to form other emotions, and how emotional reactions change over time. Finally, Emotion Management is measured by having test-takers choose among more or less effective means of emotional management in private and interpersonal emotional situations.

The MSCEIT and its predecessor test, the MEIS appear to measure something that has not been measured before (Ciarrochi et al., 2001). Scores on both tests are related to but mostly independent of verbal intelligence, the Big Five, and empathy ($rs < 0.35$) (Brackett & Mayer, 2003; Mayer et al., 1999; Mayer et al., 2002a; Roberts et al., 2001; Salovey et al., 2001; Ciarrochi et al., 2001). Emotional intelligence also appears to predict important external criteria, as we will discuss shortly.

Emotional Intelligence in the Life Space
Conceptions of the Life Space
Mayer et al. (1998) designed an initial comprehensive measure of the Life Space. They borrowed the term "Life Space" from Lewin (1936, 1951), redefined it so that it pertained to the external environment, and divided it into four broad areas: (a) biological bases (e.g., height, weight, physical health), (b) situational elements (e.g., possessions such as clothing and pictures), (c) interactive situations (e.g., self-care behaviour, activities with friends), and (d) incorporative groups (e.g., sports team memberships). These four areas emerge as surrounding personality if one depicts personality in a two-dimensional space defined, first, by a vertical molecular-molar dimension (i.e., from the brain to the individual's psychology to groups of individuals) and, second, by a horizontal, internal-external dimension (e.g., from the individual brain and its psychology to the outside environment, situations, and groups) (Mayer, 1998; Mayer et al., 1998). Using such an approach Mayer et al. developed 26 Life Space scales, which were dispersed throughout these four domains. Many of the scales correlated with measures of internal personality.

Conceptually speaking, Life Space data fall into a different category than self-report data, in being a report of the external qualities of one's world (Mayer, 2003).

More specifically, Life Space data focus on external, observable, discrete aspects of a person's surrounding environment. The items require minimal interpretations on the part of the participant, and the answers are definite and potentially verifiable. For example, the life space question, "How many times in the last month have you said 'I love you' to your romantic partner?" is somewhat different from a parallel self-report of an internal sentiment such as, "How much do you love your partner?" (Buss & Craik, 1985; Mael, 1991; Mayer et al., 1998). Such question formats also minimize social desirability response bias (Shaffer, Saunders, & Owens, 1986).

Following Mayer et al. (1998), Formica (1998) related the MEIS with Life Space dimensions that assessed potential expressions of EI. Emotional intelligence correlated positively with a Relatedness scale (e.g., keeping a private journal of hopes and feelings, surrounding oneself with sentimental items such as photos of friends) and negatively with both a Rational Control scale (e.g., taking college courses in engineering, math, and computer science) and a Destructive Behaviour scale (e.g., drug and alcohol use, selling drugs, engaging in acts of mischief/destruction). Formica's research raised two important questions about EI: Can these relations between EI and real-world criteria be replicated? And, what else might EI correlate with? To address these questions, the present research correlated the MSCEIT with a more powerful measure of the Life Space.

Brackett (2001) extended both Mayer et al. (1998) and Formica's (1998) work by creating an omnibus measure of the Life Space, the College Student Life Space Scale (CSLSS). The CSLSS sampled a large set of items from each of the four domains previously described. Factor analysis of the CSLSS resulted in numerous meaningful and reliable scales. The 27 scales in the interactive domain provide a rich description of college students' daily lives, including: self care behaviours, leisure pursuits, academic activities, and interpersonal relations. The scales also correlated with the Big Five personality traits in expected ways. Intellect was related to an Introspective Lifestyle scale (e.g., time spent meditating, writing in diary); Extraversion correlated with a Promiscuous Lifestyle scale (e.g., number of sexual partners, age of first sexual intercourse); Agreeableness correlated (negatively) with a Deviant Behaviour scale (e.g., number of physical fights, times vandalized something); Conscientiousness was related to a Studious Lifestyle scale (e.g., time spent studying, hours spent in the library); and Neuroticism correlated with an Isolated Environment scale (e.g., lack of friends, spending entire weekends alone).

In the present study, we examined relations between the MSCEIT and 13 scales from the CSLSS in order to replicate and expand upon the range of behaviours that have been hypothesized as expressions of EI. For example, preliminary validity evidence indicates that high EI is related to self-reported parental warmth, secure attachment, and informant reports of both children's pro-social behaviour in school and manager effectiveness (Mayer et al., 1999; Rice, 1999). Therefore, we predict that EI will be positively correlated with better-quality relationships with peers and family members. Lower EI, however, has been related to higher levels of smoking, alcohol

Emotional Intelligence and its Relation to Everyday Behaviour

consumption, and social deviance (Brackett & Mayer, 2003; Formica, 1998; Rubin, 1999; Trinidad & Johnson, 2001). Therefore, we predict that EI will be negatively correlated with these adverse life conditions.

Introduction to the Present Study

In the present research we investigate relations between the MSCEIT and self-reported behaviours that are potential expressions of EI. First, preliminary analyses will be conducted on the MSCEIT and Life Space scales. Then, the MSCEIT will be compared to the Big Five and to verbal intelligence. In our main analyses, relations between the MSCEIT and the Life Space will be examined.

Methods

Participants

Analyses are based on participants ($N = 330$; 241 females, 89 males) who were part of a larger study that examined the relation between the Big Five personality traits and the Life Space. The participants were between 17 and 20 years old, 96% were Caucasian. All were recruited from introductory psychology courses and received course credit for their involvement in the study. Each participant signed an informed consent upon arrival to the study and received a debriefing sheet upon completion.

Measures

College Student Life Space Scale (CSLSS; Brackett, 2001): Interactive Domain
The 13 scales from the CSLSS improve upon earlier developed Life Space scales (Formica, 1998; Mayer et al., 1998) and other self-report measures of everyday behaviour (Paunonen, 1998; Paunonen & Ashton, 2001). The scales are organized according to three broad content areas: healthy versus unhealthy behaviour (e.g., attending to one's physical appearance, alcohol consumption), general leisure and academic activities (e.g., having a studious lifestyle, engaging in deviant behaviour), and interpersonal relations (e.g., positive or negative relations with mother or best friend). The items measure discrete, observable and potentially verifiable behaviours in a person's life. For example, the question, "How many hours did you study yesterday?" is followed by response options "0," "1," "2-3," and so on. Each of the 13 scales had between 3 and 14 items ($M = 8.7$) and reliabilities ranging from alpha = .62 to .88 ($M = .81$).

The construction of the Life Space scales is described elsewhere (Brackett, 2001). Here, only a few of the scales from each content area (i.e., self-care, daily activities, interpersonal relations) will be discussed. In the self-care area, there is an Illegal Drug User scale (e.g., smokes marijuana, spends money on illegal drugs) and a Care of Physical Appearance scale (e.g., wears makeup or uses skin care products, spends time grooming and choosing clothes). In the daily activities area there is a Deviant Behaviour scale (e.g., physical fights, gambling behaviour). Finally, in the interpersonal relations area, there are scales such as Positive Relations with Father (e.g., displays affection, laughs, seeks advice), and Negative Relations with Friends (e.g., screams, fights, and uses illegal drugs). In Table 2 of the Results Section, the most representative items from each scale are presented.

Emotional Intelligence and its Relation to Everyday Behaviour

Mayer-Salovey-Caruso Emotional Intelligence Test (MSCEIT, 2002a)

Emotional Intelligence was measured with the MSCEIT Version 2.0 (Mayer et al., 2002a). The test contains 141 items that are answered in approximately 35 minutes. The test consists of eight tasks, which are divided into four classes or branches of abilities including (a) perceiving emotion, (b) using emotion to facilitate thought, (c) understanding emotion, and (d) managing emotions. Analysis of the data provides three scores reported here: a total EI score, and two area scores: Experiencing EI (comprised of perceiving emotion and facilitating thought) and a Strategic EI (comprised of understanding and regulating of emotion). Correct answers on the test are evaluated in terms of agreement with a general or expert consensus, which closely converge (Mayer et al., 2003). The split-half reliability of the scale in this sample was high ($r = .90$). The mean MSCEIT score for females was 96.62 ($SD = 10.34$) and for males it was 89.33 ($SD = 11.61$). More detailed information on the construct validity of the MSCEIT is available in the User's Manual (Mayer et al., 2002b).

Big Five Personality Traits

Personality was assessed using the 50-item personality scale from the International Personality Item Pool (Goldberg, in press). The scale assesses the five personality factors (Neuroticism, Extraversion, Intellect (or Openness), Agreeableness, and Conscientiousness) of the Big Five. The internal consistency of each scale was high: Neuroticism ($a = 0.85$; $M = 3.02$, $SD = 0.72$), Extraversion ($a = 0.84$; $M = 3.43$, $SD = 0.70$), Intellect ($a = 0.80$; $M = 3.49$, $SD = 0.58$), Agreeableness ($a = 0.82$; $M = 4.16$, $SD = 0.58$), and Conscientiousness ($a = 0.80$; $M = 3.58$, $SD = 0.62$).

Academic Ability

We obtained permission from the participants to acquire their verbal SAT scores ($M = 533.33$, $SD = 71.78$) and college grade-point averages ($M = 2.89$, $SD = 0.58$) from the university registrar.

Procedure

All participants took the CSLSS, the Big Five, and the MSCEIT in two testing sessions, each lasting two hours.

Results

We first conducted preliminary analyses on the MSCEIT and the Life Space scales. The MSCEIT was then compared to the Big Five measure of personality and to verbal SAT scores to assess its discriminant validity. Following these analyses, we focused on the predictive and incremental validity of the MSCEIT (relative to the Big Five and verbal intelligence).

Preliminary Analyses on the MSCEIT and Life Space

We obtained both consensus and expert scores for the MSCEIT from the test publisher. Consensus scores reflect the proportion of people in the normative sample (over 5,000 people from various countries) who endorsed each MSCEIT test item.

Expert norms were obtained from a sample of 21 members of the International Society Research on Emotions (ISRE) who provided their expert judgment on each of the test's items. The correlation between the two scoring methods was nearly perfect ($r = 0.98$), which is consistent with the information in the technical manual (Mayer et al., 2002b; see also Mayer et al., 2003). We conducted all subsequent analyses using consensus scores. Rechecking them with expert scoring led to no meaningful differences. Next, we correlated the two area scores (Experiencing EI and Strategic EI). There was a moderate relationship between the two ($r = .46$), which indicated that the abilities associated with the two EI areas are related to one another but still distinguishable warranting separate analyses with the criteria.

Because gender differences in EI were found in earlier studies (Mayer et al., 2000), we assessed the extent to which these differences existed in the present study. Consistent with previous research, overall female EI ($M = 96.62$, $SD = 10.34$) was significantly higher than overall male EI ($M = 89.33$, $SD = 11.61$), $t(328) = -5.48$, $P < 0.001$. This effect, however, was small, $h^2 = 0.08$. Similar gender differences were also found for the Experiencing EI and Strategic EI subscores on the MSCEIT.

We then assessed whether gender differences existed on the 13 Life Space scales. Independent sample t tests showed significant differences between males and females on 10 of the 13 scales ($P < 0.05$). For example, the mean score on the Care of Physical Appearance Scale was higher for females than for males, but for the Deviant Behaviour scale the reverse was true.

Because significant gender differences were found on both the MSCEIT and the Life Space scales we conducted analyses separately for males and females, in addition to the analyses on the full sample. We thought there might be gender differences in the correlations between EI and the Life Space in addition to the mean gender differences on both scales.

Discriminant Validity of the MSCEIT

In order to evaluate whether MSCEIT scores were redundant with Big Five scales and academic achievement, correlations between all scales were examined. Table 1 shows the zero-order correlations among the MSCEIT, Big Five, and measures of academic achievement. MSCEIT scores were modestly correlated with just two Big Five dimensions: Agreeableness and Intellect ($rs < 0.24$). MSCEIT total scores also correlated with verbal SAT scores ($r = 0.35$, for the full sample) and to a much lesser extent with college GPA. No significant gender differences were found in any of these correlations. These findings mirror previous research, which showed that MSCEIT scores are mostly independent from personality and verbal intelligence (Brackett & Mayer, 2003; Salovey et al., 2001). The MSCEIT, therefore, has discriminant validity; it taps information about individual differences not contained in the Big Five or measures of academic achievement.

Table 1
Correlations Among Measures of Emotional Intelligence, Personality, and Academic Performance

| | Emotional Intelligence | | | | | | | | |
| | Experiencing EI | | | Strategic EI | | | Total EI | | |
	A	M	F	A	M	F	A	M	F
Extraversion	0.04	0.04	0.06	-0.01	-0.05	-0.03	0.03	0.00	-0.02
Agreeableness	**0.21*****	**0.21***	**0.15***	**0.17****	0.05	**0.14***	**0.24*****	0.16	**0.19****
Conscientiousness	0.07	-0.04	0.08	0.02	-0.03	-0.02	0.05	-0.04	0.04
Neuroticism	0.02	0.02	0.06	0.01	0.02	0.04	0.02	0.02	0.06
Intellect	**0.13***	**0.28****	0.11	**0.14****	0.13	**0.20****	**0.17****	**0.24***	**0.19****
Verbal SAT	**0.23*****	0.20	**0.27*****	**0.39*****	**0.27***	**0.47*****	**0.35*****	**0.29***	**0.42*****
College GPA	0.07	0.13	-0.02	**0.18****	-0.02	**0.22****	**0.14***	0.01	0.10

Sample size for all subjects = 302 $\leq N \leq$ 332, for males = 74 $\leq N \leq$ 89, and for females = 209 $\leq N \leq$ 242. A = all subjects, M = males, F = females. All significant correlations are shown in boldface.
* $p < 0.05$.
** $p < 0.01$.
*** $p < 0.001$, two tailed.

Emotional Intelligence and its Relation to Everyday Behaviour

Table 2
Zero-Order Correlations Between Emotional Intelligence and Life Space Scales

Life Space Scale	a	Sample Items	Emotional Intelligence								
			Experiencing EI			Strategic EI			Total EI		
			A	M	F	A	M	F	A	M	F
Self care behaviours											
Illegal Drug User	0.87	Times smoked marijuana in last month, money spent on drugs in last month	-0.09	**-0.34***	0.11	-0.10	**-0.23***	0.02	**-0.11***	**-0.32***	0.09
Care of Physical Appearance	0.78	Time spent grooming yesterday, time spent choosing clothes yesterday	0.07	-0.14	-0.04	**0.13***	-0.05	0.00	**0.12***	-0.11	0.02
Smoking Behaviour	0.84	Cigarettes smoked yesterday, packs of cigarettes smoked last week	0.05	-0.04	0.09	0.08	0.09	0.08	0.08	0.03	0.11
Alcohol User	0.81	Most amount of alcohol consumed in one day, days drank in last two weeks	**-0.13***	**-0.32***	0.01	-0.10	-0.16	-0.02	**-0.13***	**-0.28***	0.02
General Leisure and Academic Activities											
Studious Lifestyle	0.62	Time spent studying alone last week, amount of time studied last weekend	-0.04	-0.01	-0.11	-0.01	-0.02	-0.08	-0.03	-0.02	-0.10
Deviant Behaviour	0.71	Number of physical fights in last year, times vandalized something in last year	**-0.27***	**-0.45***	0.01	**-0.18***	**-0.21***	0.05	**-0.27***	**-0.40***	-0.03
Promiscuous Lifestyle	0.79	Number of different sexual partners, age had first sexual intercourse(r)	-0.02	-0.21	0.04	0.03	-0.05	0.05	0.01	-0.16	0.11

(continued on next page)

Emotional Intelligence and its Relation to Everyday Behaviour

Table 2 (continued)

Life Space Scale	a	Sample Items	Emotional Intelligence								
			Experiencing EI			Strategic EI			Total EI		
			A	M	F	A	M	F	A	M	F
Interpersonal relations											
Best Friend (positive relations)	0.85	Times had 30 minute or longer conversations, times sought advice from friend	0.08	0.06	0.02	0.06	-0.03	0.03	0.07	0.00	0.02
Best and New Friend (negative relations)	0.83	Times been screamed at by in last month, times used illegal drugs with friend	**-0.15***	**-0.28***	0.03	**-0.15***	-0.10	-0.09	**-0.18***	**-0.23***	-0.03
New Friend (positive relations)	0.82	Times ate dinner with last week, times had long conversation with friend	**0.13***	-0.02	0.06	**0.16***	0.05	0.06	**0.17***	0.00	0.08
Father (positive relations)	0.88	Times ate dinner with last summer, times displayed affection with father	-0.04	-0.21	-0.02	-0.02	-0.11	-0.02	-0.03	-0.20	-0.02
Mother (positive relations)	0.85	Times called last month, times said, "I love you" to mother in last month	0.04	-0.13	-0.02	0.01	-0.06	-0.10	0.04	-0.12	-0.06
Family (negative relations)	0.83	Times screamed at parents last year, times had fight and didn't speak to parents	-0.02	-0.13	0.01	-0.07	-0.10	-0.08	-0.04	-0.14	-0.04

Sample size for males = $74 \leq N \leq 89$, for females = $209 \leq N \leq 242$, for entire sample $302 \leq N \leq 332$. A = all subjects, M = males, F = females, r = reverse scored. All significant correlations are shown in boldface.
*$p < 0.05$, two tailed.

Emotional Intelligence and its Relation to Everyday Behaviour

Criterion Validity of the MSCEIT

To assess whether EI predicted the Life Space criteria, we first examined zero-order correlations between MSCEIT scores and the Life Space scales. Table 2 shows the correlations between these scales for the full sample, and separately for males and females. Six of the 13 life space scales significantly correlated with EI. A careful examination of the correlations shows a pattern of expected negative relations between EI and the Life Space scales, but for the male subgroup only. For males, lower EI (particularly Experiencing EI, which combines the ability to perceive emotions and the ability to use emotions to facilitate thought) was related a number of scales measuring adverse aspects of life such as Illegal Drug Use, Alcohol Consumption, Deviant Behaviour, and Negative Relations with Friends (rs = -0.28 to -0.45). Of note, the absolute value of the correlation for males was statistically significantly higher than that for females when directly tested against each other with a z-test ($P < 0.05$). Only two small positive relations between EI and the Life Space were found for the full sample, Care of Physical Appearance, and Positive Relations with Friends scales (rs = 0.12, 0.17, respectively).

In contrast to our expectations, EI was not related to many positive aspects of the Life Space. Specifically, the MSCEIT did not correlate with scales that measured positive relations with parents or best friends. Furthermore, in our sample of college students lower EI was not predictive of smoking behaviour as it was in Trinidad and Johnson's (2001) sample of adolescent males and females.

Many of the findings pointed to the importance of conducting analyses separately for each gender. First, most of the correlations suggested an interaction between gender and EI as predictors of life space criteria. In other words, the size of the correlation between EI and life space scales was different for men versus women. For example, the correlation between the Illegal Drug User scale and EI for males was -0.34, whereas for females it was 0.09. The difference in this correlation for males and females was statistically significant, which suggests that the relations between these variables were different for each gender. Second, some of the correlations between EI and the criteria (e.g., Care of Physical Appearance) were not significant within the male only or female only subgroups, but were significant for the full sample. As shown in Figure 1, the correlation between EI and the Care of Physical Appearance scale probably occurred because women scored higher than men on both measures. In that sense, the correlation for the full sample reflects group differences on both measures rather than individual differences.

Incremental Validity of the MSCEIT

Although EI was only modestly correlated with the Big Five and verbal SAT scores, we thought it was important to report the incremental validity of the MSCEIT. That is we examined partial correlations between the MSCEIT and the Life Space controlling for selected Big Five variables and SAT scores. This would ensure that the correlations in Table 2 were not due to other variables that covary with EI. Table 3 shows the partial correlations for the six scales that were significantly related to EI after

Figure 1
Illustration of how between gender differences in means on Emotional Intelligence and Life Space criteria can lead to a spurious correlation in the overall sample.

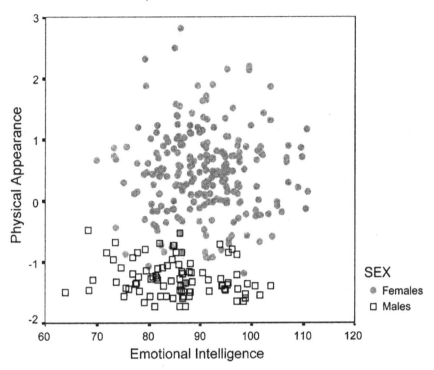

Table 3
Partial correlations between Emotional Intelligences and Life Space Scales

| | Life Space Scale | Emotional Intelligence | | | | | |
| | | Experiencing EI | | Strategic EI | | Total EI | |
		M	F	M	F	M	F
Remained significant	Illegal Drug User	**-0.37*****	0.12	-0.21	0.02	**-0.34****	0.09
	Alcohol User	**-0.29****	0.02	-0.13	0.01	**-0.26***	0.02
	Deviant Behaviour	**-0.35*****	-0.04	-0.08	0.00	**-0.27***	-0.03
	Best/New Friend Relations (-)	**-0.28****	0.06	-0.08	-0.05	-0.22	0.02
Became non-significant	New Friend Positive Relations	-0.11	0.01	-0.03	0.02	-0.12	0.01
	Care of Physical Appearance	-0.10	-0.02	0.01	0.07	-0.05	0.02

Sample size for males = 74 ≤ N ≤ 89, for females = 209 ≤ N ≤ 242. M = males, F = females. All significant correlations are shown in boldface.
*P < 0.05.
**P < 0.01.
***P < 0.001, two tailed.

Emotional Intelligence and its Relation to Everyday Behaviour

Agreeableness, Intellect, and verbal SAT scores were statistically controlled. Four of the negative correlations between EI and the Life Space remained significant for the male subgroup and the two scales for which there were small positive correlations with EI became non-significant. The MSCEIT, therefore, has incremental validity; it is predictive of behavioural criteria over and above the predictions that can be made from the Big Five and verbal intelligence.

In sum, the present research suggests that EI predicts important behavioural criteria, particularly for the male college students in our sample. The results support and expand upon earlier studies (Brackett & Mayer, 2003; Formica, 1998; Rubin, 1999; Trinidad & Johnson, 2001) and indicate that a male's lower EI may be predictive of poor adjustment and negative life outcomes such as illegal drug use, excessive alcohol consumption, deviant behaviour, and poor relations with friends. With respect to females, few distinguishing qualities in the Life Space were found for EI in this study.

Discussion

Psychologists and educators are interested in EI because they want to know its implications for people's lives. What is its relation to academic success and to leisure pursuits? How does it affect interpersonal relations? Do people with high EI behave differently than people with low EI? One way to answer these questions is in the context of a person's external Life Space. A number of studies in the past have related EI to a few aspects of daily life such as children's pro-social behaviour and smoking habits (e.g., Rubin, 1999; Trinidad & Johnson, 2001). However, examining just a few variables in a person's life provides a limited view of how EI may be expressed.

This article presented a research program that jointly studied EI and multiple assessments of positive and negative aspects of a person's everyday behaviour. Many of the Life Space scales, chiefly for males, conveyed information about EI is expressed in people's lives. For example, males with lower EI reported having poor quality peer relations, suggesting that individuals with low EI may have trouble establishing meaningful social interactions. Furthermore, males with lower EI demonstrated significantly more involvement than females in potentially harmful behaviours such as using illegal drugs, drinking alcohol excessively, and engaging in deviant behaviour. Thus, the present study supports an emerging pattern of correlations between lower EI and larger amounts of alcohol consumption, illegal drug use, and involvement in deviant behaviour (Brackett & Mayer, 2003; Formica, 1998; Trinidad & Johnson, 2001). Moreover, these findings remained significant after the Big Five and verbal SAT scores were statistically controlled. Finally, this study pointed to the importance of examining relations between EI and external criteria separately for males and females. There were more correlations large enough to be judged statistically significant for males than for females in spite of the fact that the size of the male sample was substantially smaller than the female sample.

Future Directions

The present study raised many interesting questions. Why were women higher in EI than men? Why was lower EI more predictive of negative aspects of a male's life than of positive aspects? Why wasn't EI predictive of aspects of the Life Space for females?

With respect to the first question, there is a large body of research that shows women are better able to read unstated social information, including feelings from facial expressions and other nonverbal clues (e.g., Hall, 1978, 1984; Rosenthal, Hall, DiMatteo, Rogers, & Archer, 1979). Perhaps women develop higher EI because of early child-parent interactions. Brody (1985), for example, reviewed research showing that mothers not only speak more to daughters about feelings but actually display a wider range of feelings to them as well. In contrast, with their sons, mothers tend to hold back and to respond less expressively. Brody reports that when communicating with their daughters (as compared with their sons) mothers also use more vivid facial expressions, which may help girls to develop better skills at recognizing each other's emotions. Furthermore, recent research has shown that areas of the brain devoted to emotional processing may be larger in women than men, which may also be related to the observed gender differences in EI (Gur, Gunning-Dixon, Bilker, & Gur, 2002).

It is not clear why EI was related to more negative aspects of a male's life than of positive or negative aspects of a female's life. However, studies on a related construct, alexithymia (i.e., self-reported difficulty in identifying and expressing emotions), yield similar findings. Researchers have shown that males with high scores on alexithymia measures report increased alcohol consumption and drug use, and psychoactive substance dependence (Helmers & Mente, 1999; Kauhanen, Julkunen, & Salonen, 1992; Taylor, Parker, & Bagby, 1990).

It is also possible that there is a threshold effect; there may be some minimum level of EI that is necessary for good judgment in social situations, and the proportion of males who fall below this threshold may be higher than the proportion of females. Perhaps above this threshold, further increases in EI do not correlate highly with behaviour. Furthermore, the lack of predictive validity for females on some scales such as the social deviance scale may also be related to the lower frequency and range of violent acts for females than for males (White, 2001). For example, the variance of the social deviance scale was more restricted for females than for males. The social deviance scale used in this study only contained overt physical aggressive behaviours; perhaps stronger associations for females may have emerged if more covert or verbal aggressive tactics like ostracism, gossip, and indirect vendettas had been included (White, 2001).

Finally, a person with low EI may have less emotional knowledge than others. It is very likely that emotional knowledge can be improved through education (note that such training is different from raising or lowering an intelligence). If these relations are causal, perhaps training children and adults in EI, and males in particular, can lead to their more adaptive behavior. For example, it appears that infusing emotional literacy programs into existing school curricula can help increase emotional knowledge and work against the initiation and progression of harmful behaviours such as excessive alcohol consumption, illegal drug use and deviant behaviour (Bruene-Butler, Hampson, Elias, Clabby, Schuyler, 1997; Elias, Gara, Schuyler, Branden-Muller, Sayette, 1991). Only well-designed longitudinal studies will help us see if EI develops naturally through maturation, or the extent to which EI can be changed.

Limitations

In the present study, we did not expect EI to explain large amounts of variance, but to increase predictive accuracy in important but modest ways. The correlations between EI and the criteria were not high ($rs < 0.45$) in absolute terms. It is likely that more extensive criteria will yield additional interesting predictions, some stronger and some less strong than the above. For example, it is possible that the negative association between smoking behaviour and EI found by Trinidad & Johnson (2001) would have been replicated had we used standardized scales of smoking behaviour.

Another concern is whether the group differences in EI and the predictive validity of EI for males and females will replicate in larger and more diverse samples. It is possible that the effects found in this study are unique to college students in the New England area of the United States and will not generalize to individuals in ethnically diverse areas.

Finally, given the gender differences in EI and in its relation to the Life Space criteria, future research should examine the possible gender differences in the factor structure of the MSCEIT and whether other variables such as gender role orientation will account for the observed group differences in EI between men and women. Clearly, this study could not address all of these issues. The validity of the MSCEIT will need to be developed over multiple studies with numerous samples and a variety of theoretically related criteria.

Conclusion

This study examined relations between EI and everyday life conditions. Emotional intelligence was measured as an ability by the MSCEIT; life conditions were measured by a scale of Life Space, the CSLSS. We thought it was important to conduct such a study, as we believed the results would yield a better picture of EI as it is lived in the real world. Because males and females had significantly different scores on the MSCEIT and many of the Life Space scales, we examined the correlations separately for each gender. Emotional intelligence was related to many aspects of the Life Space for our sample of male college students. Our findings suggest that EI may protect males from engaging in potentially harmful behaviours such as drug use and social deviance. There were fewer relations obtained in this sample for women. More research is needed to understand how EI is expressed in people's lives.

References

Averill, J. R., & Nunley, E. P. (1992). *Voyages of the heart: Living an emotionally creative life.* New York: Free Press.

Bar-On, R. (1997). *Bar-On Emotional Quotient Inventory.* Toronto, ON: Multi-Health Systems.

Brackett, M. A. (2001). *Personality and its expression in the life space.* Unpublished master's thesis, University of New Hampshire.

Brackett, M. A. & Mayer, J. D. (2003). Convergent, discriminant, and incremental validity of competing measures of emotional intelligence, *Personality and Social Psychology Bulletin, 29,* 1147-1158.

Brody, L. R. (1985). Gender differences in emotional development: A review of theories and research. *Journal of Personality, 53,* 102-149.

Bruene-Butler, I., Hampson, J., Elias, M. J., Clabby, J., & Schuyler, T. (1997). The improving social awareness-social problem-solving project. In G. Albee & T. Gullotta (Eds.) *Primary prevention works* (pp. 239-267). Newbury Park, CA: Sage.

Buss, D. M. & Craik, K. H. (1985). Why not measure that trait? Alternative criteria for identifying important disposition. *Journal of Personality & Social Psychology, 48,* 934-946.

Ciarrochi, J., Chan, A.Y.C., Caputi, P, & Roberts, R. (2001). Measuring emotional intelligence. In C. Ciarrochi, J. P. Forgas, & J. D. Mayer (Eds.). *Emotional intelligence in everyday life: A scientific inquiry* (pp. 25-45). Philadelphia, PA: Psychology Press.

Davies, M., Stankov, L., & Roberts, R. D. (1998). Emotional intelligence: In search of an elusive construct. *Journal of Personality and Social Psychology, 75,* 989-1015.

Elias, M. J., Gara, M. A., Schuyler, T. F., Branden-Muller, L. R., & Sayette, M. A. (1991). The promotion of social competence: longitudinal study of a preventive school-based program. *American Journal of Orthopsychiatry, 61,* 409-417.

Epstein, S. (1979). The stability of behaviour: I. On predicting most of the people much of the time. *Journal of Personality and Social Psychology, 37,* 1092-1126.

Epstein, S. (1983). Aggregation and beyond: some basic issues on the prediction of behaviour. *Journal of Personality, 51,* 360-392.

Formica, S. (1998). *Describing the socio-emotional life space.* Unpublished senior honor's thesis, University of New Hampshire.

Funder, D. C. (2001). Personality. *Annual Review of Psychology, 52,* 197-221.

Goldberg, L. R. (in press). The comparative validity of adult personality inventories: Applications of a consumer-testing framework. In S. R. Briggs, J. M. Cheek, & E. M. Donahue (Eds.), *Handbook of Adult Personality Inventories.*

Goleman, D. (1995). *Emotional Intelligence.* New York: Bantam.

Goleman, D. (1998). *Working with Emotional Intelligence.* New York: Bantam.

Gur, R., Gunning-Dixon, F., Bilker, W. B., & Gur, R. E. (2002). Sex differences in temporo-limbic and frontal brain volumes of healthy adults. *Cerebral Cortex, 12,* 998-1003.

Hall, J. A. (1978). Gender effects in decoding nonverbal cues. *Psychological Bulletin, 85,* 845-857.

Hall, J. A. (1984). *Nonverbal sex differences: communication accuracy and expressive style.* Baltimore, MD: The Johns Hopkins University Press.

Helmers, K. f., & Mente, A. (1999). Alexithymia and health behaviours in healthy male volunteers. *Journal of Psychosomatic Research, 47,* 635-645.

Kauhanen, J., Julkunen, J. & Salonen, J. (1992). Coping with inner feelings and stress: heavy alcohol use in the context of alexithymia. *Behavioural Medicine, 18,* 121-126.

Lane, R. D., Quinlan, D. M., Schwartz, G. E., Walker, P. A., & Zeitlin, S. B. (1990). The Levels of Emotional Awareness Scale: A cognitive-developmental measure of emotion. *Journal of Personality Assessment, 55,* 124-134.

Lewin, K. (1936). *A Dynamic Theory of Personality.* New York: McGraw-Hill.

Lewin, K. (1951). *Field theory in social science.* New York: Harper Torch Books.

Mael, F. A. (1991). A conceptual rationale for the domain and attributes of biodata items. *Personnel Psychology, 44,* 763-792.

Magnusson, D., & Torestad, B. (1992). The individual as an interactive agent in the environment. In W. B. Walsh, K. F. Craik, & R. H. Price (Eds.). *Person-Environment Psychology: models and perspectives.* Hillsdale, NJ: Lawrence Erlbaum Associates.

Mayer, J. D. (2003). A classification system for the data of personality psychology. *Review of General Psychology* (in press).

Mayer, J. D. (1998). A systems framework for the field of personality. *Psychological Inquiry, 9,* 118-144.

Mayer, J. D., Carlsmith, K. M., & Chabot, H. F. (1998). Describing the person's external environment: conceptualizing and measuring the life space. *Journal of Research in Personality, 32,* 253-296.

Mayer, J. D., Caruso, D. R., & Salovey, P. (1999). Emotional intelligence meets traditional standards for an intelligence. *Intelligence, 27,* 267-298.

Mayer, J. D., DiPaolo, M., & Salovey, P. (1990). Perceiving affective content in ambiguous visual stimuli: a component of emotional intelligence. *Journal of Personality Assessment, 54,* 772-781.

Mayer, J. D., & Salovey, P. (1997). What is emotional intelligence? In P. Salovey and D. Sluyter (Eds.), *Emotional Development and Emotional Intelligence: educational Implications.* New York: Basic Books.

Mayer, J. D., Salovey, P., & Caruso, D. R. (2000). Models of emotional intelligence. In R. J. Sternberg (Ed.), *Handbook of intelligence* (pp. 396-420). Cambridge, England: Cambridge University Press.

Mayer, J. D., Salovey, P., & Caruso, D. (2002a). *Mayer-Salovey-Caruso Emotional Intelligence Test (MSCEIT), Version 2.0.* Toronto, Canada: Multi-Health Systems.

Mayer, J. D., Salovey, P., & Caruso, D. (2002b). *MSCEIT technical manual.* Toronto, Canada: Multi-Health Systems.

Mayer, J. D., Salovey, P., Caruso, D. R., & Sitarenios, G. (2003). Measuring emotional intelligence with the MSCEIT 2.0. *Emotion, 3.*

Paunonen, S. V. (1998). Hierarchical organization of personality and prediction of behaviour. *Journal of Personality and Social Psychology, 74,* 538-556.

Paunonen, S. V., & Ashton, M. C. (2001). Big Five factors and facets and the prediction of behaviour. *Journal of Personality & Social Psychology, 81,* 524-539.

Rice, C. L. (1999). *A quantitative study of emotional intelligence and its impact on team performance.* Unpublished master's thesis, Pepperdine University, Malibu, CA.

Roberts, R. D., Zeidner, M., & Matthews, G. (2001). Does emotional intelligence meet traditional standards for an intelligence? Some new data and conclusions. *Emotion, 1,* 196-231.

Rosenthal, R., Hall, J. A., DiMatteo, M. R., Rogers, P. L., & Archer, D. (1979*). Sensitivity to nonverbal communication: the PONS test.* Baltimore, MD: The Johns Hopkins University Press.

Rubin, M. M. (1999). *Emotional intelligence and its role in mitigating aggression: a correlational study of the relationship between emotional intelligence and aggression in urban adolescents.* Unpublished Dissertation, Immaculata College, Immaculata, Pennsylvania.

Saarni, C. (2001). Emotional competence: A developmental perspective. In R. Bar-On & J. D. A. Parker (Eds.), *The Handbook of Emotional Intelligence* (pp. 68-91). San Francisco: Jossey-Bass.

Salovey, P., Mayer, J. D., Caruso, D., & Lopes, P. N. (2001). Measuring emotional intelligence as a set of mental abilities with the MSCEIT. In S. J. Lopez & C. R. Snyder (Eds.), *Handbook of Positive Psychology Assessment.* Washington DC: American Psychological Association.

Schutte, N. S., Malouff, J. M., Hall, L. E., Haggerty, D. J., Cooper, J. T., Golden, C. J., & Dornheim, L. L. (1998). Development and validation of a measure of emotional intelligence. *Personality and Individual Differences, 25,* 167-177.

Shaffer, G. S., Saunders, V., & Owens, W. A. (1986). Additional evidence for the accuracy of biographical data: long-term retest and observer ratings. *Personnel Psychology, 39,* 791-809.

Taylor, G. J., Parker, J. D. A., & Bagby, R. M. (1990). A preliminary investigation of alexithymia in men with psychoactive substance dependence. *American Journal of Psychiatry, 147,* 1228-1230.

Trinidad, D. R., & Johnson, C. A. (2001). The association between emotional intelligence and early adolescent tobacco and alcohol use. *Personality and Individual Differences, 32,* 95-105.

White, J. W. (2001). Aggression and gender. In J. Worell (Ed.). *Encyclopedia of women and gender* (pp. 81-93). New York: Academic Press.

Reprinted from *Personality & Individual Differences*, Vol. 35, pp 641-658, by Lopes, P.N., Salovey, P., & Straus, R. (2003). Emotional intelligence, personality, and the perceived quality of social relationships, with permission from Elsevier.

Emotional Intelligence, Personality, and the Perceived Quality of Social Relationships

Paulo N. Lopes, Yale University
Peter Salovey, Yale University
Rebecca Straus, Yale University

Abstract

This study explored links between emotional intelligence, measured as a set of abilities, and personality traits, as well as the contribution of both to the perceived quality of one's interpersonal relationships. In a sample of 103 college students, we found that both emotional intelligence and personality traits were associated with concurrent self-reports of satisfaction with social relationships. Individuals scoring highly on the managing emotions subscale of the Mayer, Salovey, and Caruso Emotional Intelligence Test (MSCEIT), were more likely to report positive relations with others, as well as perceived parental support, and less likely to report negative interactions with close friends. These associations remained statistically significant even controlling for significant Big Five personality traits and verbal intelligence. Global satisfaction with one's relationships was associated with extraversion, neuroticism (negatively), and the ability to manage one's emotions, as assessed by the MSCEIT. ©2003 Elsevier Ltd. All rights reserved.
Keywords: Emotional intelligence; Emotions; Personality: Intelligence; Social competence; Social relationships.

In spite of a large body of research, it has proved difficult to integrate existing knowledge about social and emotional competence into a cohesive theoretical framework. Social skills seem to be weakly intercorrelated and somewhat context- or domain-specific. As a result, numerous studies have failed to uncover a coherent and interrelated set of abilities that could be labeled social intelligence (for reviews see Cantor & Kihlstrom, 1987; Kihlstrom & Cantor, 2000; Sternberg et al., 2000).

The theory of emotional intelligence proposed by Salovey and Mayer (1990; Mayer & Salovey, 1997) provides a new framework to investigate social and emotional adaptation. It focuses on emotional skills that can be developed through learning and experience, and posits four central abilities: perceiving, using, understanding, and managing emotions. In order to facilitate research in this area, the authors have developed ability tests to assess these skills. The first test was called the MEIS (*Multifactor Emotional Intelligence Test*; Mayer, Caruso, & Salovey, 1998). This instrument was subsequently improved upon, leading to a shorter, more reliable, and better-normed test, called the MSCEIT (*Mayer, Salovey, and Caruso Emotional Intelligence Test*; Mayer, Salovey, & Caruso, 2001).

Mayer, Caruso, and Salovey (1999; Mayer, Salovey, Caruso, & Sitarenios, 2001) have argued that the emotional skills mapped by their model can be viewed as an intelligence, because: (a) they represent an intercorrelated set of competencies that can be statistically interpreted as a single factor with four subfactors mapping onto the four branches of the theoretical model; (b) they are distinct from, but meaningfully related to, abilities such as verbal intelligence; and (c) they develop with age. Studies with the MEIS provided preliminary evidence that emotional intelligence, measured as a set of abilities, shows convergent, discriminant, and predictive validity (for reviews see Mayer, Salovey & Caruso, 2000; Salovey, Mayer, Caruso, & Lopes, in press).

A large body of evidence, drawn from different lines of research, suggests that emotional skills are important for social and emotional adaptation (Salovey, Mayer, & Caruso, 2002). Damásio's (1994) studies of brain-damaged patients suggest that the ability to integrate emotional information with rational decision-making and other cognitive processes is essential for people to manage their lives. Studies with children, using a variety of assessment tools, have linked the abilities to read emotions in faces, understand emotional vocabulary, and regulate affect, on the one hand, to social competence and adaptation, as rated by peers, parents and teachers, on the other (for reviews see Eisenberg, Fabes, Guthrie, & Reiser, 2000; Feldman, Philippot & Custrini, 1991; Halberstadt, Denham & Dunsmore, 2001; Saarni, 1999). School-based interventions that emphasize emotional competencies, such as PATHS (Promoting Alternative Thinking Strategies), suggest that training emotional skills contributes to social adaptation (Greenberg, Kusche, Cook, & Quamma, 1995; Kusché & Greenberg, 2001).

The concept of emotional intelligence has inspired numerous school-based programs of social and emotional learning, as well as management training programs.

Emotional Intelligence, Personality, and the Perceived Quality of Social Relationships

However, there has been much debate about how emotional intelligence should be defined and assessed, and what it may predict. Does emotional intelligence contribute to social and emotional adaptation over and above personality traits and traditional intelligence? To what extent are emotional skills domain- or context-specific? These questions have implications both for our understanding of social and emotional adaptation, and for the design of school- or work-based social and emotional training programs.

Whereas Salovey and Mayer proposed a theory narrowly focused on emotional skills, others have written about emotional intelligence as a general capacity for social and emotional adaptation, or as an umbrella term to designate a wide array of competencies (e.g., Bar-On, 2000; Boyatzis, Goleman, & Rhee, 2000; Goleman, 1995, 1998). These broader views encompass social and emotional skills and traits, overlapping with personality and motivation. Mayer, Salovey, and Caruso (2000a) have argued that researchers need to retain a narrow definition of emotional intelligence, focused on skills rather than traits. This is important to ensure discriminant validity in relation to personality and other constructs. In fact, recent studies have suggested that broad, self-report measures purportedly assessing emotional intelligence lack adequate discriminant validity (Davies, Stankov & Roberts, 1998; Dawda & Hart, 2000; Roberts, Zeidner, & Matthews, 2001). This problem appears not to characterize ability-based measures of emotional intelligence.

Ciarrochi, Chan, and Caputi (2000) found that emotional intelligence, as assessed by the MEIS, correlates with empathy, and shares little overlap with extraversion and neuroticism. Other studies using the MEIS provided preliminary evidence of its predictive validity. For example, schoolchildren scoring higher on the MEIS were rated by their peers as less aggressive, and by their teachers as more prosocial, than students scoring lower on emotional intelligence (Rubin, 1999). Adolescents scoring higher on the MEIS were less likely to have smoked cigarettes recently, and were less likely to have used alcohol in the recent past (Trinidad & Johnson, 2002). Nonetheless, further research is needed to establish the construct validity of emotional intelligence.

There have been few studies using the more professionally-produced and most recently developed test of emotional intelligence, the MSCEIT. This test includes eight tasks to assess four branches of emotional intelligence: perceiving, using, understanding, and managing emotions. The tasks include, for example, reading facial expressions of emotions, identifying feelings likely to facilitate different activities, understanding emotional dynamics, and evaluating the effectiveness of different responses to interpersonal problems.

The MSCEIT can be scored using consensus or expert norms. These were drawn from a normative sample of several thousand individuals in different countries, and a sample of 21 emotion researchers. Split-half reliabilities for the branch scores, computed from the normative sample, range from 0.79 to 0.91. There is a high degree of convergence between consensus and expert scores, as evidenced by correlations greater than 0.90 (Mayer, Salovey, & Caruso, 2001; Mayer, Salovey, Caruso, & Sitarenios, in press).

The present study was designed to explore the construct validity of emotional intelligence by analyzing the relationships between emotional intelligence, verbal intelligence, personality, and the perceived quality of interpersonal relationships. In particular, we also evaluated whether emotional intelligence predicted concurrent self-reports about the quality of one's social relationships, controlling for the Big Five and verbal intelligence. This is a stringent test of the incremental validity of emotional intelligence, because: (a) there is conceptual overlap between some of the Big Five personality traits (e.g., social extraversion and agreeableness) and our outcome variables, which tapped into the perceived quality of social interaction; (b) there is also common method variance between the measures of personality and satisfaction with social relationships that we used, both of which relied on self-report; (c) an ability test of emotional intelligence such as the MSCEIT does not encompass all the skills that contribute to emotionally intelligent behavior; (d) there may be conceptual overlap between emotional regulation skills (one of the branches of the MSCEIT) and the Big Five.

While personality theory emphasizes temperamentally-driven dispositions, Mayer and Salovey's (1997) theory of emotional intelligence focuses on skills that can be acquired through learning and experience. However, traits and skills are most likely intertwined. Personality traits may be, in part, genetically based and fairly stable over time. However, adult personality is not rigidly determined from birth, and there is room for change. For example, a sizeable portion of children who seem temperamentally inhibited early on grow up not to be shy (Kagan, 1998). Individual learning and experience, in interaction with the environment, mold the development of personality (Caspi, 2000; Kagan, 1998; McCrae et al., 2000; Watson, 2000). The Big Five reflect emotional dispositions that may be influenced by emotional regulation skills: extraversion and neuroticism are associated with the propensity to experience positive and negative emotions, respectively, (e.g. Diener & Lucas, 1999; Larsen & Ketelaar, 1989, 1991; Rusting & Larsen, 1997; Watson, 2000), while agreeableness and conscientiousness may reflect emotional regulation in interpersonal and work settings (Larsen, 2000). Empirically, however, the overlap between emotional intelligence and personality is likely to be minimized when we assess emotional intelligence through an ability test, and personality through self-report, as in the present study. Personality measures tend to reflect typical performance, while ability tests may reflect optimal performance. Using different methods of assessment minimizes common method variance as well.

Ability tests of emotional intelligence cannot encompass all the skills that contribute to people's capacity for emotional regulation. The predictive power of such tests may therefore be somewhat restricted. Emotional regulation includes both reactive and proactive coping (Frijda, 1999), and the latter can draw upon all sorts of skills, including analytical, creative, and practical competencies. The MSCEIT clearly does not evaluate all the skills that contribute to emotional regulation. Moreover, it assesses knowledge of appropriate strategies for managing emotions, rather than actual skill in implementing them. This may restrict the predictive power of the MSCEIT, as well as minimize the overlap between the MSCEIT and the Big Five.

1. Hypotheses

In line with the idea that we need to take into account both emotional intelligence and personality traits in order to understand better the perceived quality of one's social relationships, we hypothesized that:

H1. Emotional intelligence, as assessed by the MSCEIT, shows limited overlap with personality traits and verbal intelligence.

H2. Both emotional intelligence and personality traits predict concurrent self-reports of satisfaction with social relationships. Emotional intelligence remains a significant predictor when the Big Five and verbal intelligence are controlled for statistically.

2. Method

2.1. Participants

One hundred and three students (37 men, 66 women) enrolled at Yale University participated in this study, either for pay or in partial fulfillment of credit requirements for an introductory psychology course. The sample was 47% white/Caucasian, 22% Asian, 19% black/African-American, 11% Hispanic, and 2% other. The mean age was 19.2 years. Participants were recruited to include only native English speakers and individuals who had spent at least four years in English-language countries or schools.

2.2. Procedure

Participants completed the MSCEIT emotional intelligence test, a measure of verbal intelligence, personality scales, and self-report measures of satisfaction with interpersonal relationships, all in the same session. The emotional intelligence test was administered first, on paper, and then participants completed the remaining measures via computer. We were unable to collect responses to three measures (Positive Relations with Others, Private and Public Self-Consciousness, and Social Skills) for the first 12 participants.

2.3. Emotional Intelligence: The MSCEIT

We used the MSCEIT emotional intelligence test, version 2.0 (Mayer, Salovey, & Caruso, 2001). This test assesses four branches of emotional intelligence: perceiving, using, understanding, and regulating emotions. Each branch consists of two tasks. For the Perceiving Emotions to Facilitate Thought branch of the MSCEIT, respondents are asked to identify the emotions in photographs of faces (Faces task), as well as in designs and landscapes (Pictures task). For the Using Emotions branch, respondents are asked to describe emotions using non-emotional vocabulary (Sensations), and to indicate the feelings that might facilitate or interfere with the successful performance of various cognitive and behavioral tasks (Facilitation). Understanding Emotions is assessed with questions concerning the manner in which emotions evolve and transition over time (Changes), and how some feelings are produced by blends of emotions (Blends). The ability to Manage Emotions is assessed through a series of scenarios asking the test-taker to identify the most adaptive ways to regulate one's own feelings (Emotion Management), and the feelings of others in social situations (Social Management).

Answer sheets for the MSCEIT were scored by the test publishers, Multi-Health Systems (MHS), using consensus-scoring norms. Participants' scores reflect the degree of fit between their responses and those of the normative sample, consisting of more than 5,000 individuals who have taken the MSCEIT before. Scores based on consensus norms correlate highly ($r > 0.90$) with those based on expert ratings (Mayer, Salovey, Caruso, & Sitarenios, 2001; Mayer et al., in press). Scores on the MSCEIT are standardized in relation to the normative sample, with a mean of 100 and a standard deviation of 15. Split-half reliabilities reported for the normative sample range from 0.79 to 0.91 for the four branches (Mayer et al., in press). In this sample, split-half reliabilities ranged from 0.60 to 0.89, for the four branches, and 0.88 for the whole test.

2.4. Verbal Intelligence

We estimated verbal intelligence using an abridged version of the vocabulary subtest of the Wechsler Adult Intelligence Scale - Third Edition, Revised (WAIS III; Wechsler, 1997), which asks participants to define words. We omitted the first 10 items because they were too easy for our sample. The WAIS was administered as a written test, rather than as an interview. We also collected self-reported Scholastic Aptitude Test (SAT) scores.

2.5. Personality and Related Scales

We assessed the Big Five personality factors using the NEO Five Factor Inventory (NEO-FFI; Costa & McCrae, 1992). Cronbach alphas in this sample were 0.86 for neuroticism, 0.83 for extraversion, 0.76 for openness, 0.70 for agreeableness, and 0.87 for conscientiousness.

We used the Fenigstein, Scheier, and Buss (1975) Self-consciousness Scale, yielding scores for Private Self-consciousness, designed to assess self-reflection (á = 0.74); Public Self-consciousness, measuring concern about others' evaluation of the self (á = 0.86); and Social Anxiety, tapping into anxiety or discomfort in the presence of others (á =0.72).

For self-esteem we used an abridged version of the Rosenberg (1965) scale, with four items (á = 0.82). We adapted the wording to avoid restriction of range by preceding each question with the phrase "Compared to other Yale students..."

Emotional Intelligence, Personality, and the Perceived Quality of Social Relationships

2.6. Self-Perceived Emotional Intelligence

The Trait Meta-Mood Scale (TMMS; Salovey, Mayer, Goldman, Turvey, & Palfai, 1995) was designed to assess how people reflect upon their moods, but can also be used as a proxy for self-perceived emotional intelligence. It evaluates the extent to which people report attending to and valuing their feelings (Attention), feeling clear rather than confused about their emotions (Clarity), and use positive thinking to repair negative moods (Repair). Salovey et al. (1995) reported adequate internal consistency, as well as convergent and discriminative validity for this scale. We used an abridged scale with 15 items, and obtained Cronbach alphas of 0.71 for Attention, 0.71 for Clarity, and 0.74 for Repair.

2.7. Self-Perceived Social Skills

Because we found no short, well-established measure of social skills, we created an exploratory scale, adapting 28 items from various inventories (á = 0.83). Questions included: "Would others say that you are good at handling people?", "Would your friends say that you are good at figuring people out?", and "Do you find it difficult to work in teams?".

2.8. Mood

We asked participants to rate the extent to which they presently felt happy, sad, anxious, and angry/irritated, on five-point Likert scales, and computed a state mood composite score (á = 0.50).

2.9. Social Desirability

Participants also completed the Crowne and Marlowe (1960) Social Desirability Scale during a follow-up study that took place a few weeks after the present study (á = 0.73).

2.10. Quality of Interpersonal Relationships

We used two self-report measures to assess self-perceived quality of interpersonal relationships. The Positive Relations with Others subscale of Ryff's (1989) Scales of Psychological Well-Being assesses satisfaction with the quality of one's engagement in, and support obtained from, the social domain of life, broadly construed. We used a 14-item version recommended by Ryff (á = 0.83).

The Network of Relationships Inventory (NRI; Furman & Buhrmester, 1985; see also Furman, 1996) asks participants to report about the quality of their relationships with other individuals along 10 dimensions, yielding three factor scores: social support, negative interaction, and power imbalance. The social support factor taps into companionship, instrumental aid, intimacy, nurturance, affection, admiration, and alliance. The negative interaction factor taps into conflict and antagonism. In this study, we asked participants to report about the parent or parental figure they felt closest to, as well as about their closest, non-romantic friend. We computed separate factor scores for parent and close friend. Cronbach alphas ranged from 0.89 to 0.94.

3. Results

The scales included in this study generally revealed adequate reliabilities, as summarized in Table 1, which also reports means and standard deviations for all measures. The main exception was the four-item mood scale (á = 0.50). The reliabilities for the Understanding and Managing Emotions branches of the MSCEIT (split-half r = 0.67 and 0.60, respectively) were lower than expected, and lower than those reported by Mayer, Salovey, Caruso, and Sitarenios (2001), and Mayer, et al. (in press) for the normative sample (split-half r = 0.80 and 0.83, respectively). This could be due to the characteristics of our sample and the conditions under which they completed the MSCEIT. All analyses reported in this article are based on scores computed by the test publisher, which include 124 of the 141 MSCEIT items. A set of 123 items with positive item-total correlations in this sample yielded improved split-half reliabilities (0.89, 0.75, 0.71, and 0.65, for the four branches, respectively). [1]

Statistical analyses based on scores adjusted through exclusion of the items with negative item-total correlations yielded results that were very similar to those reported here.

We eliminated two subjects from all analyses. One was an outlier who scored 48.6 on the MSCEIT, more than four standard deviations below the mean for our sample. The other reported not being a native English speaker, and having spent less than four years in English-language countries or schools, the criteria we used for selecting participants for this study.

Although we used a sizeable battery of questionnaires, participant fatigue was apparently not a problem. Inspection of the data revealed no anomalies, and the scales administered toward the end of the first session still yielded adequate internal consistencies, as well as sound inter-item correlations for reverse-scored items.

3.1. Correlations Among the MSCEIT, Personality, and Other Measures

Correlations between scores on the test of emotional intelligence and other measures are presented in Table 2. The MSCEIT showed limited overlap with the Big Five personality traits and with verbal intelligence, thus confirming our first hypothesis. Scores on the MSCEIT correlated with some of the Big Five personality factors, but the highest correlation was 0.33. The Managing Emotions branch of the MSCEIT correlated positively with Agreeableness and Conscientiousness, and negatively with Openness to Experience.

Verbal intelligence, assessed by the WAIS-III vocabulary subscale, correlated modestly (0.39) with the Understanding Emotions branch of the MSCEIT, which relies on knowledge of emotional vocabulary. It did not correlate significantly with the other branches of emotional intelligence. Note that the range of verbal intelligence was somewhat restricted in this sample of Yale University students.

Table 1
Descriptive Statistics on Included Measures

Scale	Mean	SD	Reliability [a]
MSCEIT – Total score	103.6	10.6	$r = 0.88$
MSCEIT – Perceiving emotions	102.0	13.3	$r = 0.89$
MSCEIT – Using emotions	100.7	11.8	$r = 0.74$
MSCEIT – Understanding emotions	109.3	10.3	$r = 0.67$
MSCEIT – Managing emotions	101.7	9.5	$r = 0.60$
WAIS-III – Vocabulary [b]	66.7	17.4	$r = 0.69$
SAT – Verbal – Self-reported	725.3	56.9	
SAT – Math – Self-reported	720.8	65.9	
NEO-FFI – Neuroticism	3.05	0.72	á = 0.86
NEO-FFI – Extraversion	3.49	0.58	á = 0.83
NEO-FFI – Openness	3.69	0.54	á = 0.76
NEO-FFI – Agreeableness	3.64	0.46	á = 0.70
NEO-FFI – Conscientiousness	3.45	0.62	á = 0.87
Private Self-consciousness	3.75	0.62	á = 0.74
Public Self-consciousness	3.79	0.78	á = 0.86
Social Anxiety	3.22	0.81	á = 0.72
Self-esteem	3.44	0.82	á = 0.82
TMMS – Attention	3.96	0.71	á = 0.71
TMMS – Clarity	3.15	0.82	á = 0.71
TMMS – Repair	3.36	0.99	á = 0.74
Self-perceived social skills	3.38	0.54	á = 0.83
Social Desirability [b]	41.0	14.4	á = 0.73
State Mood Composite	3.51	0.63	á = 0.50
Positive relations with others	3.84	0.61	á = 0.83
NRI – Social Support – Parent	3.43	0.73	á = 0.93
NRI – Social Support – Close friend	3.50	0.65	á = 0.92
NRI – Negative Interaction – Parent	2.25	0.96	á = 0.94
NRI – Negative Interaction – Close friend	1.58	0.61	á = 0.89

$90 \leq N \leq 101$ due to missing data.
[a] We report split-half reliabilities for MSCEIT scales (due to item heterogeneity, as each branch of the test is comprised of two different tasks) and for the WAIS-III Vocabulary Scale. We report Cronbach alpha standardized item coefficients for all other measures.
[b] WAIS-III Vocabulary and Social Desirability scores are on a scale from 0 to 100.

Table 2
Correlations Between the MSCEIT and Other Measures[a]

	MSCEIT: Perceiving emotions	MSCEIT: Using emotions	MSCEIT: Understanding emotions	MSCEIT: Managing emotions	MSCEIT: Total score
Verbal Intelligence (WAIS-III Vocabulary)	0.06	-0.03	**0.39**	0.05	0.17
Verbal SAT (Self-reported)	-0.10	**-0.22**	**0.36**	-0.10	-0.04
Math SAT (Self-reported)	-0.09	-0.06	0.19	-0.13	-0.03
NEO-FFI – Neuroticism	-0.07	-0.03	-0.09	-0.15	-0.12
NEO-FFI – Extraversion	-0.04	-0.01	0.10	0.06	0.03
NEO-FFI – Agreeableness	0.19	**0.24**	0.15	**0.33**	**0.32**
NEO-FFI – Conscientiousness	0.11	0.12	**0.22**	**0.24**	**0.23**
NEO-FFI – Openness	-0.13	**-0.28**	-0.01	**-0.22**	**-0.22**
Self-esteem	0.01	-0.07	-0.05	0.08	-0.01
Private Self-Consciousness	0.00	-0.11	-0.16	-0.12	-0.12
Public Self-Consciousness	0.02	0.08	0.04	0.05	0.06
Social Anxiety	0.02	-0.02	-0.07	0.02	-0.01
TMMS – Attention	0.05	-0.10	0.04	0.05	0.01
TMMS – Clarity	0.08	-0.13	0.09	0.04	0.04
TMMS – Mood Repair	0.00	0.00	**0.21**	**0.27**	0.15
Self-perceived Social Skills	-0.05	-0.08	0.08	**0.24**	0.05
Social Desirability	0.09	0.01	0.08	0.15	0.11
State Mood Composite	-0.01	-0.09	0.03	0.12	0.01
Positive Relations with Others	-0.01	-0.06	0.20	**0.27**	0.11
NRI – Social Support / Parent	-0.14	-0.07	0.09	**0.22**	0.01
NRI – Social Support / Close Friend	-0.09	-0.05	0.02	0.10	-0.03
NRI – Negative Interaction / Parent	-0.05	-0.08	-0.03	-0.10	-0.09
NRI – Negative Interaction / Close friend	**-0.25**	**-0.33**	**-0.36**	**-0.36**	**-0.45**

Significant correlations are marked in bold ($P < 0.05$, two-tailed). $90 \leq N \leq 101$ due to missing data.

[a]Measures included (in alphabetical order): MOOD: a state mood composite (happy, sad, anxious, and angry/irritated); MSCEIT (emotional intelligence ability test): MSCEIT Version 2.0 (Mayer, Salovey & Caruso, 2001); NRI: Network of Relationship Inventory (Furman, 1996; Furman & Buhrmester, 1985); NEO-FFI: NEO Five-Factor Inventory (Costa & McCrae, 1992); Private self-consciousness, Public self-consciousness, and Social anxiety: (Fenigstein et al., 1975); Positive relations with others: Scales of Psychological Well-Being (Ryff, 1989, 14-item version); SAT: Scholastic Aptitude Test, self-reported; Self-perceived social skills: Exploratory scale; Self-esteem: (Rosenberg, 1965), abridged; Social desirability: (Crowne & Marlowe, 1960); TMMS attention, clarity and repair: Trait Meta-Mood Scale (Salovey et al., 1995), abridged; Verbal intelligence: Wechsler Adult Intelligence Scale – Third edition (Wechsler, 1997) vocabulary subscale.

The MSCEIT was unrelated to public and private self-consciousness, self-esteem, social desirability, and mood, as expected. MSCEIT scores did not correlate significantly with the Attention and Clarity factors of the Trait Meta-Mood Scale (TMMS), which can be seen as a proxy for self-perceived emotional intelligence. The Mood Repair scale of the TMMS, which taps into the use of optimistic thinking to regulate negative moods, correlated 0.21 and 0.27 with the MSCEIT branches of Understanding and Managing Emotions, respectively.

3.2. Self-reported Satisfaction with Relationships in Life

Two self-report measures tapping into the quality of interpersonal relationships provide some evidence for the convergent and incremental validity of the MSCEIT: the Positive Relations with Others subscale of Ryff's (1989) scales of psychological well-being, and the Network of Relationship Inventory (NRI; Furman & Buhrmester, 1985).

Table 3 shows the correlations between these measures, on the one hand, and the MSCEIT, verbal intelligence, and the Big Five, on the other. The Managing Emotions branch of the MSCEIT correlated with the Positive Relations with Others scale, and with the Social Support factor of the NRI in relation to a close parent or parent figure. This last scale measures the companionship, intimacy, aid and affection in the relationship. All four branches of the MSCEIT were inversely correlated with the Negative Interaction Factor of the Network of Relationship Inventory, in relation to a close friend. This scale assesses conflict and antagonism in the relationship.

To assess the incremental validity of emotional intelligence, we used multiple regression to analyze the variables that concurrently predicted self-reported satisfaction with interpersonal relationships. The predictors entered were: the Big Five personality traits, verbal intelligence, and the four MSCEIT branch scores. We followed a forward stepping strategy, entering the Big Five and verbal intelligence first, and the MSCEIT branch scores last. At each step, we retained only those variables that proved statistically significant, to avoid overstretching the carrying capacity of the data with too many predictors. We followed this strategy systematically for the five outcome variables referred above: Ryff's (1989) scale of Positive Relations with Others; and the NRI Social Support and Negative Interaction factors, for parent and friend. The final models are reported in Table 4.

Emotional intelligence revealed significant zero-order correlations with three out of these five outcome variables (positive relations with others, social support with parent, and negative interaction with friend). These associations remained statistically significant when we controlled for significant Big Five and verbal intelligence variables in multiple regression as described above. This suggests that emotional intelligence has incremental validity in relation to personality and verbal intelligence, supporting our second hypothesis.

Table 3
Correlations Between Scales of Self-Perceived Satisfaction with Social Relationships and Other Measures[a]

	Positive Relations with Others	NRI Social Support/ Parent	NRI Social Support/ Friend	NRI Negative Interaction/ Parent	NRI Negative Interaction/ Friend
MSCEIT – Perceiving Emotions	-0.01	-0.14	-0.09	-0.05	**-0.25**
MSCEIT – Using Emotions	-0.06	-0.07	-0.05	-0.08	**-0.33**
MSCEIT – Understanding Emotions	0.20	0.09	0.02	-0.03	**-0.36**
MSCEIT – Managing Emotions	**0.27**	**0.22**	0.10	-0.10	**-0.36**
MSCEIT – Total Score	0.11	0.01	-0.03	-0.09	**-0.45**
NEO-FFI – Neuroticism	**-0.53**	-0.02	**-0.28**	**0.30**	0.07
NEO-FFI – Extraversion	**0.51**	0.08	**0.42**	-0.10	0.04
NEO-FFI – Agreeableness	0.20	0.03	0.14	**-0.32**	-0.16
NEO-FFI – Conscientiousness	**0.37**	0.16	**0.27**	**-0.26**	**-0.22**
NEO-FFI – Openness	0.02	-0.18	-0.05	0.16	0.09
Verbal Intelligence (WAIS-III Vocabulary)	0.00	-0.18	-0.15	0.11	-0.18

Significant correlations are marked in bold (P < 0.05, two-tailed). $90 \leq N \leq 101$ due to missing data.
[a]Measures included (in alphabetical order): MSCEIT Version 2.0 (Mayer, Salovey & Caruso, 2001); NRI: Network of Relationship Inventory (Furman, 1996; Furman & Buhrmester, 1985); NEO-FFI: NEO Five-Factor Inventory (Costa & McCrae, 1992); VERBAL INTELLIGENCE: Wechsler Adult Intelligence Scale – Third edition (Wechsler, 1997) vocabulary subscale.

Table 4
Predicting Self-Perceived Satisfaction With Social Relationships, Using Multiple Regression

	Beta	P-value	R^2 change
(a) Predicting "Positive Relations With Others" (Ryff, 1989)[a]			
Neuroticism	-0.33	0.001	0.28
Extraversion	0.35	<0.001	0.09
MSCEIT—Managing Emotions	0.22	0.01	0.05
(b) Predicting "Social Support With Friend" (NRI: Furman & Buhrmester, 1985)[b]			
MSCEIT—Managing Emotions	0.22	0.03	0.05
(c) Predicting "Social Support With Friend" (NRI: Furman & Buhrmester, 1985)[c]			
Extraversion	0.39	<.01	0.18
Conscientiousness	0.21	0.02	0.04
(d) Predicting "Negative Interaction With Parent" (NRI: Furman & Buhrmester, 1985)[d]			
Agreeableness	-0.30	0.001	0.10
Conscientiousness	-0.24	0.01	0.06
(e) Predicting "Negative Interaction With Friend" (NRI: Furman & Buhrmester, 1985)[e]			
Conscientiousness	-0.10	0.30	0.05
MSCEIT—Understanding Emotions	-0.23	0.02	0.10
MSCEIT—Using Emotions	-0.21	0.02	0.06
MSCEIT—Managing Emotions	-0.20	0.04	0.03

[a]Model F (3, 86) = 20.24, $P < 0.001$; adjusted $R^2 = 0.39$
[b]Model F (1, 99) = 4.86, $P = 0.03$; adjusted $R^2 = 0.04$
[c]Model F (2, 98) = 13.82, $P < 0.001$; adjusted $R^2 = 0.20$
[d]Model F (2, 98) = 9.30, $P < 0.001$; adjusted $R^2 = 0.14$
[e]Model F (4, 96) = 7.75, $P < 0.001$; adjusted $R^2 = 0.21$

Using scores from Ryff's (1989) Positive Relations with Others scale as the dependent variable, the final model, reported in Table 4(a), included as significant predictors neuroticism, extraversion, and the managing emotions branch of the MSCEIT ($F(3, 86) = 20.24$, $P < 0.001$, adjusted $R^2 = 0.39$). In this model, the variance explained by the MSCEIT managing emotions branch was small but statistically significant. No other variables explained significant additional variance.

Using the social support with parent score from the NRI as the dependent variable, the final model, reported in Table 4(b), included only the managing emotions branch of the MSCEIT, as a positive predictor. None of the Big Five nor verbal intelligence entered the model.

For the two outcome variables that did not reveal significant zero-order correlations with emotional intelligence ("social support with friend" and "negative interaction with parent"), the only significant predictors retained in the final models were personality variables. These models are reported in Tables 4(c) and 4(d).

Using the negative interaction with friend score from the NRI as a dependent variable in multiple regression, the final model, reported in Table 4(e), included the understanding, using, and managing emotions branches of emotional intelligence ($F(4, 96) = 7.75$, $p < 0.001$; adjusted $R^2 = 0.21$). Conscientiousness entered the model in step one but did not remain statistically significant when emotional intelligence was included.

We replicated these findings following a more conservative strategy: entering all of the Big Five and verbal intelligence simultaneously as a first block of variables, and forward-stepping MSCEIT branch scores last. The results were generally similar to those reported above, though some predictors no longer remained statistically significant. Emotional intelligence still accounted for significant variance in two out of five outcome measures (Positive Relations with Others, and Negative Interaction with Friend), after apportioning the maximum possible variance to personality traits and verbal intelligence. In predicting Social Support with Parent, the managing emotions branch of the MSCEIT became marginally significant ($P < 0.10$).

4. Discussion

We found preliminary evidence for the convergent, discriminant, and incremental validity of emotional intelligence, in relation to verbal intelligence and personality measures. Both of the hypotheses were supported. There was a general pattern of low correlations between scores on an emotional intelligence test, on the one hand, and personality traits and verbal intelligence, on the other. Emotional intelligence showed significant (though modest) correlations with several indicators of quality of social interaction. These findings provide some evidence of both convergent and discriminant validity for the MSCEIT, supporting the first hypothesis.

Multiple regression analyses provided preliminary support for the incremental validity of the MSCEIT in relation to personality and verbal intelligence. The managing emotions branch of the MSCEIT retained a significant association with three out of five outcome variables tapping into the self-perceived quality of interpersonal relationships, even when we controlled for significant Big Five and verbal intelligence measures. The fact that both the MSCEIT and the Big Five concurrently predicted self-reported satisfaction with relationships in life suggests that we need to take into account both emotional skills and personality dispositions in order to understand social and emotional adaptation. This finding supports the second hypothesis.

Our findings should be viewed as tentative, and interpreted with caution, as there are several limitations to this study.[2] Until these results are replicated with other samples, we do not know if they generalize. Reliance on self-report measures of satisfaction with social relationships is another limitation. Note, however, that we used an ability measure of emotional intelligence to "predict" self-reported satisfaction with social relationships - we did not use a self-report measure to predict self-reported outcomes. Moreover, we used a rather stringent test of incremental validity (controlling for personality), as discussed above.

Lower than expected reliabilities for some branches of the MSCEIT may have attenuated correlations with other measures. On the other hand, this increases our confidence that correlations reported as statistically significant were not due to chance. There was substantial variability in the amount of time participants took to complete the MSCEIT, and we do not know to what extent this may have influenced emotional intelligence scores.

It is also possible that the measure of verbal intelligence that we used was not as valid as we might wish. For logistical reasons we asked participants to provide written rather than oral responses to the WAIS Vocabulary Scale, which entails describing the meaning of words. Participants wishing to finish the study faster might have typed shorter replies, which are more likely to be incomplete or unsatisfactory, and thereby received scores that do not accurately reflect their true verbal intelligence.

The general pattern of low correlations found in the present study between emotional intelligence, measured as a set of abilities, and the Big Five personality traits, has been replicated in other recent studies – even though the exact associations vary (Brackett & Mayer, 2001; Ciarrochi et al., 2000; Lopes, Schütz, Sellin, Nezlek, & Salovey, in preparation). Together, these findings suggest that, when emotional intelligence is assessed as a set of skills, discriminant validity in relation to personality and verbal intelligence is substantial. Several researchers have questioned the construct validity of emotional intelligence because self-report scales of emotional intelligence share substantial overlap with personality measures (Davies et al., 1998; Dawda & Hart, 2000). This criticism does not seem to apply to an ability measure of emotional intelligence such as the MSCEIT.

The results we obtained with the Trait Meta-Mood Scale (TMMS), which can be seen as a proxy for self-perceived emotional intelligence, also suggest that self-report and ability measures of emotional intelligence yield different findings. We found low correlations between the MSCEIT and the TMMS. Correlations between the TMMS and the Big Five were higher than those between the MSCEIT and the Big Five.[3]

The Using and Managing Emotions branches of the MSCEIT were positively (though modestly) associated with the Big Five trait of agreeableness, which taps into altruism, interpersonal trust, and compliance, among other facets. Managing Emotions also correlated with several indicators of relationship quality. These results strengthen previous findings based on the MEIS, suggesting that emotional intelligence is associated with prosocial tendencies (e.g. Rubin, 1999) and relationship quality (Ciarrochi et al., 2000). Scores on the Understanding and Managing Emotions branches were also positively (though modestly) associated with conscientiousness, possibly reflecting self-control. The conscientiousness factor of the Big Five taps into self-discipline, dutifulness, and deliberation.

We did not expect to find non-significant correlations between the managing emotions branch of the MSCEIT, on the one hand, and neuroticism, extraversion, and social anxiety, on the other. In a subsequent study with a German sample (Lopes et al., in preparation), we did find small but significant correlations (in the 0.2 range) with neuroticism (negative) and extraversion (positive), as well as with agreeableness and conscientiousness (both positive). We expected to find somewhat higher correlations because neuroticism and social anxiety reflect self-perceived difficulties with emotional regulation, and extraversion reflects positive emotionality. Neuroticism, sometimes also labeled emotional instability, assesses a disposition to experience negative emotional states, such as anxiety, depression, anger and hostility, feelings of vulnerability, and self-consciousness. Extraversion is associated with positive emotionality, energy, and interpersonal warmth or gregariousness (Costa & McCrae, 1992).

Larsen (2000) draws a distinction between temperamental differences in susceptibility to affective stimuli, or emotional reactivity (which he associates more with neuroticism and extraversion), and individual differences in response modulation (which he associates more with agreeableness, conscientiousness, and openness). We would expect the development of emotional regulation skills to improve emotional balance, contributing to lower neuroticism and higher extraversion, agreeableness, and conscientiousness. However, it is likely that people also develop social and emotional skills to compensate for their temperamental dispositions, as Kagan (1998) has suggested.

Someone who is prone to negative emotions may need to work harder to develop emotional control, thereby acquiring a more sophisticated repertoire and understanding of emotional regulation strategies. This person might then obtain a high score on a test of emotional intelligence, while still reporting a disposition to experience negative emotions, or neuroticism. Similarly, someone who is dispositionally prone to

Emotional Intelligence, Personality, and the Perceived Quality of Social Relationships

experience more positive emotions may feel less need to pay attention to emotional regulation strategies. Such compensation mechanisms would weaken the link between the emotional skills assessed by the MSCEIT and personality traits, thus helping to explain the low correlations we found here.

We did not expect to find negative (although small) correlations between two branches of the MSCEIT and openness to experience. We think that openness to feelings, which is one facet of openness to experience, is important for emotional intelligence (see also McCrae, 2000). Previous findings with the MEIS indicate that emotional intelligence is positively associated with openness to feelings (r = 0.24), but unrelated to openness to aesthetics (Ciarrochi et al., 2000). The Big Five scale used in the present study (the NEO-FFI) does not assess openness to feelings. In the Lopes et al. (in preparation) study conducted in Germany, we did find a positive correlation between the managing emotions branch of the MSCEIT and openness to experience, assessed with a different instrument.

It is possible that the negative correlation between the MSCEIT and openness to experience in this study was due to chance or, perhaps, an artifact of conformity bias. The MSCEIT is designed to assess emotional skills, but the method of consensus scoring used in this study may also reflect conformity with, or attunement to, social norms. If people who score high on openness to experience provide somewhat unusual responses to the emotional stimuli used in the MSCEIT, they may receive lower scores on this test, because responses are scored according to how well they match the normative sample.

In interpreting findings from the MSCEIT, it is unclear to what extent we are truly assessing skill, rather than conformity or adjustment to social norms. Roberts et al. (2001) have criticized ability tests of emotional intelligence for this reason. However, there are several reasons to pursue the development of such measures, in spite of this criticism. The first is that there is a high degree of agreement between expert and consensus scoring (Mayer, Salovey, Caruso, and Sitarenios, 2001; in press), which enhances our confidence in this scoring method. The second is that social and emotional skills, used to interact and communicate with others, necessarily reflect attunement to social norms and expectations, so that it may be difficult to distinguish skill and adjustment. The third is that complex, real-life problems often allow more than one correct solution, and therefore need to be assessed using expert or consensus norms if we want to avoid relying on self-report. One faces a similar challenge in evaluating practical intelligence or creativity (Sternberg, 1999; Sternberg et al., 2000).

Finally, we should note that scores on the MSCEIT were unrelated to social desirability and mood. This supports the idea that a skills-based measure of emotional intelligence is not influenced by some of the biases that may undermine the credibility of self-report measures, especially for assessment purposes.

Emotional intelligence, assessed as a set of abilities, shares limited overlap with verbal intelligence and personality measures. The MSCEIT, designed to assess emotional skills, and the Big Five, intended to measure social and emotional dispositions, seem to tap into different aspects of psychological functioning. Different methods of assessment (ability testing and self-report) seem to minimize overlap. Both the MSCEIT and personality traits concurrently "predicted" self-reported satisfaction with relationships in life. These findings suggest that we need to take into account both emotional skills and dispositions to better understand social and emotional functioning. The fact that the MSCEIT explained unique variance in self-reported satisfaction with interpersonal relationships supports the incremental validity of this ability-based measure of emotional intelligence.

Future research should seek to establish the predictive validity of emotional intelligence, using outcomes measures that do not rely on self-report. If future studies confirm that the MSCEIT has adequate psychometric properties, convergent and discriminant validity, the crucial issue is to determine whether ability-based measures of emotional intelligence can predict other important outcomes.

References

Bar-On, R. (2000). Emotional and social intelligence: insights from the Emotional Quotient Inventory. In R. Bar-On & J. D. A. Parker (Eds.), *The handbook of emotional intelligence* (pp. 363-388). San Francisco: Jossey-Bass.

Boyatzis, R. E., Goleman, D., & Rhee, K. S. (2000). Clustering competence in emotional intelligence: insights from the Emotional Competence Inventory. In R. Bar-On & J. D. A. Parker (Eds.), *The handbook of emotional intelligence* (pp. 343-362). San Francisco: Jossey-Bass.

Brackett, M. A., & Mayer, J. D. (2001, October). *Comparing measures of emotional intelligence.* Poster presented at the Third Positive Psychology Summit, Washington, DC.

Cantor, N., & Kihlstrom, J. F. (1987). *Personality and social intelligence.* New Jersey: Prentice-Hall.

Caspi, A. (2000). The child is father to the man: Personality continuities from childhood to adulthood. *Journal of Personality and Social Psychology, 78*, 158-172.

Ciarrochi, J. V., Chan, A. Y. C., & Caputi, P. (2000). A critical evaluation of the emotional intelligence construct. *Personality and Individual Differences, 28*, 539-561.

Costa, P. T., Jr., & McCrae, R. R. (1992). *NEO-PI-R professional manual - revised NEO Personality Inventory (NEO-PIR) and NEO Five-Factor Inventory (NEO-FFI).* Odessa, FL: Psychological Assessment Resources.

Crowne, D. P., & Marlowe, D. (1960). A new scale of social desirability independent of psychopathology. *Journal of Consulting Psychology, 24*, 349-354.

Damásio, A. R. (1994). *Descartes' error: Emotion, reason, and the human brain.* New York: Putnam.

Davies, M., Stankov, L., & Roberts, R. D. (1998). Emotional intelligence: In search of an elusive construct. *Journal of Personality and Social Psychology, 75,* 989-1015.

Dawda, D., & Hart, S. D. (2000). Assessing emotional intelligence: Reliability and validity of the Bar-On Emotional Quotient Inventory (EQ-i) in university students. *Personality and Individual Differences, 28,* 797-812.

Diener, E., & Lucas, R. E. (1999). Personality and subjective well-being. In D. Kahneman, E. Diener, & N. Schwarz (Eds.), *Well-being: The foundations of hedonic psychology* (pp. 213-229). New York: Russell Sage.

Eisenberg, N., Fabes, R. A., Guthrie, I. K., & Reiser, M. (2000). Dispositional emotionality and regulation: their role in predicting quality of social functioning. *Journal of Personality and Social Psychology, 78,* 136-157.

Feldman, R. S., Philippot, P., & Custrini, R. J. (1991). Social competence and nonverbal behavior. In R. S. Feldman & B. Rime (Eds.), *Fundamentals of nonverbal behavior* (pp. 329-350). New York: Cambridge University Press.

Fenigstein, A., Scheier, M. F., & Buss, A. H. (1975). Public and private self-consciousness: assessment and theory. *Journal of Consulting and Clinical Psychology, 43,* 522-527.

Frijda, N. H. (1999). Emotions and hedonic experience. In D. Kahneman, E. Diener, & N. Schwarz (Eds.), *Well-being: the foundations of hedonic psychology* (pp. 190-210). New York: Russell Sage.

Furman, W. (1996). The measurement of children and adolescents' perceptions of friendships: conceptual and methodological issues. In W. M. Bukowski, A. F. Newcomb, & W. W. Hartup (Eds.), *The company they keep: Friendships in childhood and adolescence. Cambridge studies in social and emotional development* (pp. 41-65). New York, NY: Cambridge University Press.

Furman, W., & Buhrmester, D. (1985). Children's perceptions of the personal relationships in their social networks. *Developmental Psychology, 21,* 1016-1024.

Goleman, D. (1995). *Emotional intelligence.* New York: Bantam.

Goleman, D. (1998). *Working with emotional intelligence.* New York: Bantam.

Greenberg, M. T., Kusche, C. A., Cook, E. T., & Quamma, J. P. (1995). Promoting emotional competence in school-aged children: The effects of the PATHS curriculum. *Development and Psychopathology, 7,* 117-136.

Halberstadt, A. G., Denham, S. A., & Dunsmore, J. C. (2001). Affective social competence. *Social Development, 10,* 79-119.

Kagan, J. (1998). *Galen's prophecy.* Boulder, CO: Westview Press.

Kihlstrom, J. F., & Cantor, N. (2000). Social intelligence. In R. J. Sternberg (Ed.), *Handbook of intelligence* (2nd ed., pp. 359-379). New York: Cambridge University Press.

Kusché, C. A., & Greenberg, M. T. (2001). PATHS in your classroom: Promoting emotional literacy and alleviating emotional distress. In J. Cohen (Ed.), *Social-emotional learning and the elementary school child: A guide for educators* (pp. 140-161). New York: Teachers College Press.

Larsen, R. J. (2000). Toward a science of mood regulation. *Psychological Inquiry, 11,* 129-141.

Larsen, R. J., & Ketelaar, T. (1989). Extraversion, neuroticism and susceptibility to positive and negative mood induction procedures. *Personality and Individual Differences, 10,* 1221-1228.

Larsen, R. J., & Ketelaar, T. (1991). Personality and susceptibility to positive and negative emotional states. *Journal of Personality and Social Psychology, 61,* 132-140.

Lopes, P. N., Schütz, A., Sellin, I., Nezlek, J., & Salovey, P. (in preparation). Unpublished data, Yale University.

Mayer, J. D., Caruso, D. R., & Salovey, P. (1998). *Multifactor Emotional Intelligence Test (MEIS).* (Available from John D. Mayer, Department of Psychology, University of New Hampshire, Conant Hall, Durham, NH 03824 USA.)

Mayer, J. D., Caruso, D. R., & Salovey, P. (1999). Emotional intelligence meets traditional standards for an intelligence. *Intelligence, 27,* 267-298.

Mayer, J. D., & Salovey, P. (1997). What is emotional intelligence? In P. Salovey & D. Sluyter (Eds.), *Emotional development and emotional intelligence: Implications for educators* (pp. 3-31). New York: Basic Books.

Mayer, J. D., Salovey, P., & Caruso, D. (2000a). Models of emotional intelligence. In R. J. Sternberg (Ed.), *Handbook of human intelligence* (2nd ed., pp. 396-420). New York: Cambridge University Press.

Mayer, J. D., Salovey, P., & Caruso, D. (2000b). Selecting a measure of emotional intelligence: The case for ability scales. In R. Bar-On & J. D. A. Parker (Eds.), *The handbook of emotional intelligence* (pp. 320-342). San Francisco: Jossey-Bass.

Mayer, J. D., Salovey, P., & Caruso, D. (2001a). *The Mayer-Salovey-Caruso Emotional Intelligence Test (MSCEIT).* Toronto: Multi-Health Systems, Inc.

Mayer, J. D., Salovey, P., Caruso, D. R., & Sitarenios, G. (2001). Emotional intelligence as a standard Intelligence. *Emotion, 1,* 232-242.

Mayer, J. D., Salovey, P., Caruso, D. R., & Sitarenios, G. (in press). Measuring emotional intelligence with the MSCEIT V2.0. *Emotion.* (in press).

McCrae, R. R. (2000). Emotional intelligence from the perspective of the Five-Factor Model of Personality. In R. Bar-On & J. D. A. Parker (Eds.), *The handbook of emotional intelligence* (pp. 263-276). San Francisco: Jossey-Bass.

McCrae, R. R., Costa, P. T., Ostendorf, F., Angleitner, A., Hrebícková, M., Avia, M. D., Sanz, J., & Sánchez-Bernardos, M. L. (2000). Nature over nurture: temperament, personality, and life span development. *Journal of Personality and Social Psychology, 78,* 173-186.

Emotional Intelligence, Personality, and the Perceived Quality of Social Relationships

Roberts, R. D., Zeidner, M., & Matthews, G. (2001). Does emotional intelligence meet traditional standards for an intelligence? Some new data and conclusions. *Emotion, 1,* 196-231.

Rosenberg, M. (1965). *Society and the adolescent self-image.* Princeton, NJ: Princeton University Press.

Rubin, M. M. (1999). *Emotional intelligence and its role in mitigating aggression: A correlational study of the relationship between emotional intelligence and aggression in urban adolescents.* Unpublished manuscript, Immaculata College, Immaculata, PA.

Rusting, C. L., & Larsen, R. (1997). Extraversion, neuroticism, and susceptibility to positive and negative affect: A test of two theoretical models. *Personality and Individual Differences, 22,* 607-612.

Ryff, C. D. (1989). Happiness is everything, or is it? Explorations on the meaning of psychological well-being. *Journal of Personality and Social Psychology, 57,* 1069-1081.

Saarni, C. (1999). Developing emotional competence. New York: Guilford.

Salovey, P., & Mayer, J. D. (1990). Emotional intelligence. *Imagination, Cognition, and Personality, 9,* 185-211.

Salovey, P., Mayer, J. D., Caruso, D. (2002). The positive psychology of emotional intelligence. In C. R. Synder & S. J. Lopez (Eds.), *Handbook of positive psychology* (pp. 159-171). Oxford: Oxford University Press.

Salovey, P., Mayer, J. D., Caruso, D., & Lopes, P. N. Measuring emotional intelligence as a set of abilities with the MSCEIT. In S. J. Lopez & C. R. Snyder (Eds.), *Handbook of positive psychology assessment.* Washington, DC: American Psychological Association.

Salovey, P., Mayer, J. D., Goldman, S. L., Turvey, C., & Palfai, T. P. (1995). Emotional attention, clarity, and repair: Exploring emotional intelligence using the Trait Meta-Mood Scale. In J. W. Pennebaker (Ed.), *Emotion, disclosure, and health* (pp. 125-154). Washington, DC: American Psychological Association.

Sternberg, R. J. (1999). The theory of successful intelligence. *Review of General Psychology, 3,* 292-316.

Sternberg, R. J., Forsythe, G. B., Hedlund, J., Horvath, J. A., Wagner, R. K., Williams, W. M., Snook, S. A., & Grigorenko, E. L. (2000). *Practical intelligence in everyday life.* New York: Cambridge University Press.

Trinidad, D. R., & Johnson, C. A. (2002). The association between emotional intelligence and early adolescent tobacco and alcohol use. *Personality and Individual Differences, 32,* 95-105.

Watson, D. (2000). *Mood and temperament.* New York: Guilford.

Wechsler, D. (1997). *WAIS-III: Wechsler Adult Intelligence Scale* (3rd ed.). San Antonio, TX: The Psychological Corporation.

Emotional Intelligence, Personality, and the Perceived Quality of Social Relationships

Acknowledgements

We thank the following individuals for their suggestions and comments during the preparation and running of this study, data analysis, and writing: Sigal Barsade, David Caruso, Geoffrey Cohen, J. Richard Hackman, Alan Kazdin, Chinyelu Lee, Helena Lopes, John Mayer, John Nezlek, Jerome Singer, Gill Sitarenios, Robert Sternberg, Victor Vroom, and Edward Zigler.

We also acknowledge support from the National Cancer Institute (R01-CA68427), the National Institute of Mental Health (P01-MH/DA56826), and the Donaghue Women's Health Investigator Program at Yale to Peter Salovey.

Footnotes

[1] We report split-half reliabilities for MSCEIT branch scores due to item heterogeneity, as each branch of the test is comprised of two distinct tasks. Based on the 124 items used by the test publisher for computing MSCEIT scores, Cronbach alpha for the four branches of the MSCEIT and for the total score were 0.85, 0.64, 0.67, 0.45, and 0.85, respectively. The set of 123 items with positive item-total correlations in this sample yielded improved Cronbach alphas of 0.86, 0.69, 0.69, and 0.58 for branches 1 to 4, respectively, and 0.87 for the total score.

[2] We should also note that, in a follow-up study with the same participants, emotional intelligence did not significantly predict how people were evaluated by others following a half-hour group negotiation exercise. This could be due to the nature and constraints of the situation, or to the difficulty of predicting specific instances of behavior from general traits and skills.

[3] Due to limitations of space, we do not report correlations between the TMMS and measures other than the MSCEIT.

Reprinted with permission of Kluwer Academic/Plenum Publishers.
Mayer, John D., & Cobb, Casey D. (2000). Educational Policy on Emotional Intelligence: Does It Make Sense? *Educational Psychology Review*, Vol. 12, No. 2, pp. 163-183.

Educational Policy on Emotional Intelligence: Does It Make Sense?

John D. Mayer, University of New Hampshire
Casey D. Cobb, University of New Hampshire

Abstract

Educational policy on emotional intelligence appears to be based more on mass-media science journalism than on actual educational and psychological research. The first section of this article provides an overview of the research areas of emotional intelligence, social and emotional learning, and character education; it further examines how these areas became linked in the popular press. The second section examines the scientific evidence for whether emotional intelligence underpins social and emotional learning, how emotional intelligence relates to success, and whether it is central to character. We conclude that educational policy in this area has outpaced the science on which it is ostensibly based; recommendations for the future are made.

Emotional intelligence was formally defined, and aspects of it first measured, in two journal articles in 1990 (Mayer, DiPaolo, & Salovey, 1990; Salovey & Mayer, 1990). Just five years later, the concept was popularized in a best-selling book entitled, Emotional Intelligence (Goleman, 1995), and featured on the cover of TIME (Gibbs, 1995). The popular book made three points which caught the imagination of the public

— and of educators. First, the book saw rudeness, irresponsibility, and violence as a serious problem plaguing the nation's schools and the nation. Second, the book claimed that scientists had discovered a link between high emotional intelligence and prosocial behavior. Third, the book claimed that emotional intelligence was "as powerful, and at times more powerful, than IQ" in predicting success in life (Goleman, 1995, p. 34).

Such claims rapidly entered the educational policy arena. Writing in <u>Educational Leadership</u>, Scherer (1997, p. 5) echoed Goleman by stating "emotional intelligence, more than IQ, ...is the most reliable predictor of success in life and in school." Research in emotional intelligence was viewed as providing a foundation for those working in socio-emotional learning, and the two became closely identified (Elias, et al., 1997, p. 1). By 1997, at least 22 formal programs of socio-emotional learning had been tested in one or more schools or school systems, with some programs emphasizing emotional intelligence throughout the school's entire curriculum (Elias et al., 1997, Appendix C). In Rhode Island, Goleman noted, "they are attempting to make the whole state emotionally intelligent" (Klein, 1997, p. 2), and, in fact, the Rhode Island state government created a plan calling for an integration of emotional learning in its social, health, and education programs (Rhode Island Emotional Competency Partnership, 1998).

An initial question raised by all this is whether schools should be designing policy centered on raising emotional intelligence. It may be that emotional intelligence will be of value to the curriculum, but the history of curricular innovation suggests that caution is in order. For example, beginning in 1986, a State of California task force spent three years and three-quarters of a million dollars on a study of whether to add self-esteem programs to school curricula (Joachim, 1996; Leo, 1990). Amazingly, the task force recommended adopting such programs despite the absence of research evidence that self esteem would improve learning — or improve any other important school problem such as violence or drug use. Based on the task force's recommendation, self-esteem programs flooded the California public schools, only to be viewed as a waste of school resources and a dismal failure several years later. Had the task force placed sufficient weight on its scientific findings, it might have averted this outcome.

This article examines the scientific findings concerning emotional intelligence. It explores the degree to which educational policies are logically connected to the science pertaining to the intelligence. The first section of this article provides some brief background on the areas of emotional intelligence and of socio-emotional learning, how the two areas became linked, and what happened afterward. We pay particular attention to the development of the Mayer and Salovey ability model of emotional intelligence in the science domain (e.g., Mayer & Salovey, 1997), although we review other approaches as well. In addition we focus on a concern that education policy on emotional intelligence was driven by science journalists as much as by educators and psychologists. The second section examines the scientific bases for educational policy on emotional intelligence. The last section evaluates where scientists and educators might wish to head from here.

How Emotional Intelligence Became a Topic of Educational Policy

<u>The Beginnings of Emotional Intelligence Research</u>
The term "emotional intelligence" was employed on an occasional basis in the academic literature from the mid 1960's forward, without much attention paid to defining it, or to creating an area around it (e.g., Greenspan, 1979, pp. 254-270; Leuner, 1966; Payne, 1986/1983). For example, one tradition considered emotional intelligence to be a Piagetian stage of development (Greenspan, 1979), but couched the concept in a jointly Freudian and Piagetian theoretical model — that did little to define or clarify it for most readers.

In an unpublished dissertation, Wayne Payne came close to a first definition of the concept when he wrote that emotional intelligence was a basic intelligence in which:

> ... the facts, meanings, truths, relationships, etc., are those that exist in the realm of emotion. Thus, feelings are facts...The meanings are <u>felt</u> meanings; the truths are emotional truths; the relationships are interpersonal relationships. And the problems we solve are emotional problems, that is, problems in the way we feel" (Payne, 1986, p. 165).

Payne's definition left open such questions as what a "felt meaning" means, and what kind of truth "emotional truth" is.

The work of Mayer and Salovey more clearly developed the idea of emotional intelligence as an intelligence (e.g., Mayer & Salovey, 1997; 1993; Salovey & Mayer, 1990). In 1990, Salovey & Mayer first formally defined emotional intelligence, and demonstrated that aspects of it could be measured (Mayer, DiPaolo & Salovey, 1990; Salovey & Mayer, 1990). Those authors currently define emotional intelligence as *the capacity to process emotional information accurately and efficiently, including the capacity to perceive, assimilate, understand, and manage emotion* (Mayer, Salovey, & Caruso, in press).[1]

Mayer and Salovey's approach viewed emotional meanings as signals about relationships. For example, angry emotional expressions are viewed as having evolved across species and as signaling a cross-species message of warning. In human beings, such feelings convey important meanings about relationships — the relationships one has with other people, groups, and even objects, as well as the relationships one has with oneself (e.g., guilt signals regret over one's own actions).

In this theory, emotional intelligence involves four broad classes of abilities: the perception, the integration, the understanding, and the management of emotion (see Table 1, Column 1). The first ability, perceiving emotions, involves attending to and recognizing feelings. For example, a mother may perceive her son's ill-at-ease posture and accurately perceive that he has done something wrong. The second ability, integrating emotion in thought, involves using personal emotions in thought and

Educational Policy on Emotional Intelligence: Does It Make Sense?

communication. For example, she may then tell her son about a time when she had difficulty telling her mother about something she had done wrong, and her own mother's response, in order to encourage him to tell her about the problem. The third ability, understanding emotions, involves reasoning with feelings. This might occur if her son then admits to getting a speeding ticket. She may want to understand the relations among her fear for her son's safety, her anger over possibly-rising automobile insurance premiums, and her son's shame over his own behavior. The last group of skills concern management. How will she deal with her own and her son's feelings and behavior, to come up with a response that includes a good balance between empathy and discipline? The best feeling management will depend in part upon her successful perception of emotion, use of it, and understanding of the feelings involved in the situation to that point, as well as an understanding of how her actions will determine longer term emotional relations with her son (Mayer & Salovey, 1997).

In addition to providing a more formal definition of emotional intelligence, Mayer and Salovey's 1990 articles described an emotionally intelligent character — a well adjusted, genuine and warm, persistent, and optimistic person (Mayer, DiPaolo, & Salovey, 1990, pp. 773, 781; Salovey & Mayer, 1990, pp. 199-200).

A Brief Overview of Character Education and Socio-emotional Learning

Educators since the time of the Ancient Greeks have been interested in the character of their students. Some educators desired well adjusted, genuine, warm and persistent students; others sought disciplined, respectful, good citizens, and still others sought some other constellation of characteristics (Nucci, 1989, p. xiv). There was a recognizable character education movement in the United States in the late 1920's (Artman & Jacobs, 1928). Character education refers to the attempt to form a person's character, particularly as it involves heightening a sense of belonging to and responsibility for others (Benninga & Wynne, 1998). As such, its curricula promote a set of values, such as fairness and honesty, that lead to proper or virtuous behavior (See Table 1, Column 2). The character education movement made its mark even beyond the public schools, for example, in the scouting traditions. The Girl Scouts were established in this country in 1912, and the Girl Scout law states: I will do my best to be honest and fair, friendly and helpful, considerate and caring, courageous and strong, and responsible for what I say and do, and to respect myself and others, respect authority, use resources wisely, make the world a better place, and be a sister to every Girl Scout. (Girl Scouts USA, 1999). The Boy Scouts, similarly, aspire to be "trustworthy, loyal, helpful, friendly, courteous, kind, obedient, cheerful, thrifty, brave, clean, and reverent" (Boy Scouts of America, 1999).

A more recent movement, called the socio-emotional learning movement, appears closely related to character education. Socio-emotional theorists have identified long lists of values associated with their curricula (see Table 1, Column 3). For example Elias et al. (1997, p. 33) identify 27 values that fall into five broad areas.[2] These five areas are *self-development* (e.g., confidence, creativity, excellence, purposefulness, and self-discipline), *caring* (e.g., helpfulness, and love), *respect* (e.g., courtesy, honor,

Educational Policy on Emotional Intelligence: Does It Make Sense?

Table 1
A Comparison of the Concepts of Emotional Intelligence, Socio-emotional Learning, and Character Education

	Emotional Intelligence	Character Education	Socio-emotional Learning	Popular Emotional Intelligence
Definition	Emotional intelligence is the ability to process emotional information, particularly as it involves the perception, assimilation, understanding, and management of emotion (after Mayer & Salovey, 1997).	The long-term process of helping young people develop good character, i.e., knowing, caring about, and acting upon core ethical values such as fairness, honesty, compassion, responsibility, and respect for self and others. (The Character Education Partnership, 1998).	"Socioemotional learning is the process through which children and adults develop the skills, attitudes, and values necessary to acquire social and emotional competence (Elias et al., 1997, p. 2).	Emotional intelligence, popularly conceived, involves "abilities such as being able to motivate oneself and persist in the face of frustrations; to control impulse and delay gratification; to regulate one's moods and keep distress from swamping the ability to think; to empathize, and to hope" (Goleman, 1995, p. 34)
Further Specification	Four main areas of abilities: (a) Perception and expression of emotion (b) Integrating emotions in thought (c) Understanding emotions (d) Managing emotions	Values emphasized include: (a) fairness (b) honesty, (c) compassion, (d) responsibility (e) respect for self and others (The Character Education Partnership, 1998).	Skills in four domains of learning: (a) Life skills and social competencies (b) Health-promotion and problem-prevention skills(c) Coping skills and social support for transitions and crises(d) Positive contributory service (Elias et al., pp. 21-22).	Five main areas: (a) Knowing one's emotions (b) Managing emotions (c) Motivating oneself (d) Recognizing emotions in others (e) Handling relationships

and tolerance), *responsibility* (e.g., honesty, justice, loyalty, and service), and *spiritual values* (e.g., peacefulness, reflectiveness, reverence, and thankfulness). The list bears a strong resemblance to those adhered to by the Girl Scouts and Boy Scouts.

Socio-emotional learning is said to require skills for navigating the social world, such as the ability to communicate effectively, to plan, and to exert emotional self-control (Elias, 1997). Advocates of socio-emotional learning want to teach these ideas both in and outside the regular curriculum. For example, students might be told to put a "gotcha" sticker on another student exhibiting caring or respect, so as to reward those students for their behavior (Elias et al., 1997, p. 34).

The socio-emotional learning movement also draws some of its heritage from that of the affective education movement, which stemmed from the work of humanistic psychologists such as Abraham Maslow and Carl Rogers in the 1950's (Miller, 1976, p. 83). Affective education promoted experiential approaches for building a student's internal personal skills, self knowledge, and feeling-recognition, with a focus on promoting self-esteem and a positive self-image (e.g., Wood, 1996, p. 126). The affective education movement was itself rather broadly defined, and often considered synonymous with "humanistic education," and "psychological education" (Miller, 1976, p. 5).

Both the character education and socio-emotional learning movements share in common the idea that much of human personality can be modified for the better through learning.[3] Character educators engage in "developing civic virtue and moral character in our youth for a more compassionate and responsible society" (The Character Education Partnership, 1998). Socio-emotional educators engage in educating for a safe, secure, caring society.

There is much to admire in the socio-emotional learning and character education traditions. Their values of self-development, caring, respect, responsibility, and spirituality appear to cross many perspectives and ideologies. They represent values that are considered of importance in many societies and religions, precisely because they promote the advancement of a society. These particular values seem well-tailored to socialization within democratic, diverse societies. It is almost as if one generation of socializers was creating the next.

Linking Emotional Intelligence and Education Policy

How did emotional intelligence, which in the early 1990's was a fairly modest academic area, become a subject of educational policy? In the period leading up to 1995, the Fetzer Institute provided financial support to Daniel Goleman, a New York Times science journalist, to tie his interests in emotions and the brain to educational work in emotional literacy (Goleman, 1995, p. 341). In addition, the Institute arranged for a series of meetings between researchers in emotional intelligence and related areas, on the one hand, and educators and curriculum developers, on the other (Salovey & Sluyter, 1997, p. xii). The Fetzer Institute also assisted with the development of organizations such as the Collaborative for the Advancement of Social and Emotional Learning (CASEL).

Educational Policy on Emotional Intelligence: Does It Make Sense?

It was Goleman who provided the link between emotional intelligence and education. In the academic literature, emotional intelligence was increasingly viewed as a focused set of mental abilities. To link emotional intelligence to character it was useful to equate the two as much as possible. Goleman thus expanded and emphasized the view of emotional intelligence as a list of personality characteristics including optimism, adjustment, and motivation (see Table 1, Column 4). Goleman stated, "There is an old-fashioned word for the body of skills that emotional intelligence represents: *character*"(Goleman, 1995, p. 285). This character, Goleman asserted, will enhance our schools. Attending to students' emotional competencies will result in a "'caring community,' a place where students feel respected, cared about, and bonded to classmates..." (Goleman, 1995, p. 280).

Goleman's popularization of the concept of emotional intelligence depended in part on broadening it from a specific psychological entity – a mental capacity for processing emotion – to a broader collection of scientific ideas. Earlier, Salovey and Mayer had described character outcomes of emotional intelligence as including optimism and motivation. Goleman equated these character outcomes with the intelligence itself. Emotional intelligence became a catch phrase for anything that involved motivation, emotion, or good character. Virtually any link between personality and good school outcomes could be attributed to this broad conception of emotional intelligence. The problem was that the collection of character attributes labeled as emotional intelligence was no longer one definable entity, and indeed, could consist of entities that were entirely independent of one another, and that could even come into conflict at times (e.g., persistence versus sensitivity).

Using the Link between Emotional Intelligence and Education

Educators interested in policy found the link between emotional intelligence and socio-emotional learning enticing. First, there appeared to be a quick, public acceptance of the idea that emotional intelligence was required to learn and to behave well. One leader in curriculum development referred to emotional intelligence as "the integrative concept" underlying socio-emotional learning (Elias et al., 1997, pp. 27, 29).

Second, policy experts quickly accepted the idea that emotional intelligence predicted success. The senior editor of Educational Leadership stated that "emotional well-being is the strongest predictor of achievement in school and on the job"; and that "...recent studies have shown that emotional intelligence predicts about 80 percent of a person's success in life." (Pool, 1997, p. 12)

Third, these individuals concluded that emotional intelligence was readily observable and assessable in students. For example good citizenship was evidence of high emotional intelligence (Pool, 1997, p. 12), whereas "dramatic displays of low emotional IQ..." could be discerned from temper tantrums and " The inability to regain your composure quickly..." (Stufft, 1997, p. 42).

Educational Policy on Emotional Intelligence: Does It Make Sense?

Finally, throughout the policy literature are references to "fostering" (Novick, 1998, p. 200) or "enhancing" emotional intelligence (Duhon-Haynes, Duhon-Sells, Sells, & Duhon-Ross, 1996, p. 2). Stufft (1996, p. 43) noted that "Fortunately, emotional temperament is not set in concrete. Unlike one's intellectual IQ, which is difficult to change, one's emotional IQ is somewhat easier to modify". And Pasi (1997) added, "the good news about emotional intelligence is that it is virtually all learned, according to Daniel Goleman..." (p. 40).

The previous quotes indicate that certain educators and policy analysts became truly involved with the promise of emotional intelligence. Those quotes further suggest that policy makers were informed by journalistic accounts of the science rather than by the science itself. In essence, the science and policy were connected through science journalism rather than involving direct readings of the emotional intelligence literature (cf. Franknel, 1995; Jerome, 1981).

What is the Scientific Justification for Including Emotional Intelligence in the Curriculum?

Policy experts appeared to accept emotional intelligence as central to emotional learning, highly predictive of success, essential to character, and readily taught. But does emotional intelligence really underpin emotional learning? Is it the best predictor of success in life, readily taught, or otherwise important for education? This section of our article tries to find some answers to these questions.

Does Emotional Intelligence Underpin Socio-emotional Learning?

Theoretically speaking, emotional intelligence, defined as the capacity to perceive, integrate, understand, and manage emotions, is a good candidate for a capacity underlying emotional learning. (Another possible candidate would be social intelligence, which, in comparison to emotional intelligence, concerns both the emotional and non-emotional understanding of group dynamics, social status, political relationships, interpersonal activities and impact, and leadership).

For the statement "emotional intelligence underlies emotional learning" to prove correct, however, emotional intelligence must be demonstrated to be a useful model of an actual intelligence. Otherwise, the statement is no more sensible than saying "algebraic intelligence" underlies algebra, or even, that "pythagorean intelligence" underlies understanding the Pythagorean formula, $A^2 = B^2 + C^2$. Thus far, there are no specific algebraic intelligences or Pythagorean intelligences. Rather, we speak of more general "verbal-propositional" intelligences, or "spatial intelligences," or other intelligences for which there exist coherent, distinct areas of abilities. Those more general intelligences are inferred from groups of mental skills that rise and fall together (Carroll, 1993).

This is not the place for an extensive elaboration of the criteria for identifying a part of personality. One central criterion that is worth mentioning here, however, is that a personality part must be unitary in some sense: it must be a unitary mechanism like memory, or describe a unitary area of knowledge like self-concept, or be unitary in function like intelligence (Mayer, 1998).

For a concept such as emotional intelligence to gain credibility, it must be clearly defined, and then measurement instruments based on the definition must be developed and evaluated. Mayer and Salovey's (1997) ability definition of emotional intelligence has the longest history (the first version originating in 1990) and the most support in the psychological literature, and for that reason we will focus on it here. It should be mentioned that a variety of other concepts are more-or-less closely related to it, including intrapersonal intelligence (Gardner, 1993), pragmatic intelligence (Sternberg & Caruso, 1985), and emotional creativity (Averill & Nunley, 1992).

Mayer and Salovey think of intelligence as a hierarchy of mental abilities, with general intelligence at the top of the hierarchy, and dividing next into verbal (or crystallized) and spatial/performance (or fluid) intelligences, and then more specific intelligences thereafter (e.g., Carroll, 1993; Horn & Noll, 1994), such as, perhaps, abilities at memorization, vocabulary skills, and object rotation. Each of these intelligences represents a partially distinct part of general intelligence.

The most direct measures of emotional intelligence are in the form of ability tests. That is, they ask people to solve emotional problems. The recent introduction of the Multifactor Emotional Intelligence Scale (MEIS), which has 12 ability tasks related to emotional intelligence, has gone some way toward demonstrating the validity of the Mayer and Salovey model. A representative item from the MEIS is as follows:

Contempt most closely combines which two emotions?
  1. anger and fear
  2. fear and surprise
  3. disgust and anger
  4. surprise and disgust

The best answer to the above question is "3" because contempt involves angry dismissal, along with disgust at poor performance or poor behavior. Other MEIS items, such as perceiving emotion in faces, designs, and music, are less verbal. Factor analysis indicates that the MEIS has one overall general factor of emotional intelligence, and three subfactors. The three subfactors correspond to (I) The accurate perception of emotion (e.g., in faces and music), (II) the understanding of emotional meaning (e.g., how emotions combine and progress over time), and, (III) the regulation of emotion (e.g., identifying good alternatives for the social management of emotion). A weaker, fourth factor (IV), integrating emotion in thought, may also be present.

Scores based on each factor and the full test are highly reliable (full test alpha reliability is $r = .96$). In a sample of 503 people, overall emotional intelligence correlated significantly, and modestly, with verbal intelligence ($r = .36$) indicating that it is a member of the family of intelligences that is distinct from verbal comprehension. It also correlated with self-reported empathy ($r = .33$). Results from the MEIS argue strongly for the existence of an emotional intelligence (see Mayer, Caruso, & Salovey, 1999, for more details).

Empirical research on such measures has just begun, and is by no means widely accepted as of now. In a recent study of early-developed measures of the field, Davies, Stankov, and Roberts (1998) dismissed self-report scales of emotional intelligence, but even worried over "objective" ability measures, including precursors to the MEIS. They concluded that: "...as presently postulated, little remains of emotional intelligence that is unique and psychometrically sound. Thus, questionnaire measures are too closely related to "established" personality traits [to be considered anything new], whereas objective measures of emotional intelligence suffer from poor reliability" (p. 1013).

The Davies et al. study preceded publication of the highly reliable MEIS. Nonetheless the quote illustrates the skepticism with which emotional intelligence has been met by some.

If the existence of emotional intelligence as a part of personality becomes widely accepted within the scientific community, then such statements as the one opening this section – that emotional intelligence underlies socio-emotional learning – will be reasonable. If evidence against the intelligence mounts, then this connection will no longer obtain.

How Does Emotional Intelligence Relate to Success?

Academic reviewers of the field agree that there is little published at present that indicates what this ability version of emotional intelligence predicts. Some have suggested that predictive validity has escaped the attention of the workers in the field (Davies et al., 1998, p. 1013), but it is more accurate to say that validation has just begun. Ability scales such as the MEIS have existed only for the last few years and have not been widely distributed. Nonetheless, there is considerable evidence that high performance on tasks resembling those on the "emotion perception" scales of the MEIS are correlated with reduced involvement in violent and drug-related behavior (Mayer, Caruso, Salovey, Formica, & Woolery, 1999).

Is it possible that emotional intelligence, defined in the broader popularized fashion (e.g., including motivation, social skills, and so on), predicts a great deal? Goleman (1995) argues that if we look at sets of different variables – persistence, warmth, optimism, and so forth – we can predict important life outcomes. Looking at such a broad collection of variables, however, seems no different from everyday personality research. From this perspective, Goleman is probably correct that multiple variables predict important outcomes. Emotional intelligence used in this fashion, however, refers to nothing new.

The second way to interpret the claim that this broadly defined emotional intelligence predicts success is to take seriously the idea that its specific traits are of a special class that are highly important. Although this may be the case, there is little evidence to support it at present. The idea that different traits, such as motivation, empathy, and so on, contribute to a unitary function that contributes dramatically to success is as-of-yet undemonstrated. Epstein (1998, p. 19) has remarked, "Nothing like this has yet been attempted, and...all we have is unsupported speculation about the existence of an undefined concept referred to as emotional intelligence" (see also, Davies et al., p. 1012; Mayer, Salovey, & Caruso, in press).

There is not much to suggest that the individual traits in the broader, 1995 Goleman list predict success highly on their own. For example, to the degree that Goleman's concept of "handling relationships" relates to traits of altruism, or to warmth, or to good feelings, it makes no unusual contribution to success. A study of nearly 24,000 workers found that the Big Five personality trait, Agreeableness, which includes (self-reported) altruism and modesty was irrelevant to job success (Barrick & Mount, 1991). Similarly, extroversion, which includes warmth and good feelings, did not predict success among teachers, lawyers, or accountants, although it did among salespeople. In the few places where traits such as positive feelings did predict success, such as for salespeople, it typically did so at the 2-3% variance level, a far cry from outperforming intelligence (which predicts in the 10-25% range).

Some recent studies in the area do indicate positive outcomes can be found with self-report scales that might measure Goleman's 1995 concept, but those studies' outcomes are no larger in terms of the percentage "success" they predict than many other modest but interesting effects found in personality research (see Mayer, Salovey, & Caruso, in press, for a review). Because self-report scales correlate with positive affect – happy, joyful feelings – it may be that happiness, as opposed to the emotional intelligence, contributes to the success. Happiness is sometimes found to contribute to school achievement (Wessman & Ricks, 1966) and on-the-job performance (e.g., Staw & Barsade, 1993).

The claim that emotional intelligence outpredicts IQ originates in a section of Goleman's 1995 book, in which he implies that emotional intelligence might predict up to 80% of the success in life. We have critiqued that section of his book elsewhere and will not repeat our critique here.[4] Goleman's argument shifted, however, in his 1998 book. He now implies that emotional intelligence predicts 67% of success at work. In his own words: I compared which competencies listed [from job descriptions in numerous organizations] as essential for a given job, role, or field, could be classed as purely cognitive...and which were emotional competencies. When I applied this method...I found that *67 percent* – two out of three – of abilities deemed essential for effective performance were emotional competencies. Compared to IQ and expertise, emotional competence mattered *twice* as much (Goleman, 1988, p.31). Given Goleman's broad definition of emotional intelligence — by 1998 he focuses on 25 socio-emotional skills — the 67% outcome is unsurprising.

Educational Policy on Emotional Intelligence: Does It Make Sense?

What personnel managers (or anyone else) desire on-the-whole, however, is unlikely to characterize a single job applicant. In a list of 25 characteristics, some attributes are likely to conflict. For example, some applicants with a high need-to-achieve may be lower in cooperation than average. Moreover, what personnel managers desire may not necessarily determine an employee's success. Although traits such as "people skills," "initiative" and "persuasiveness," appear in 67% of job descriptions, it doesn't mean such attributes predict success — only that such attributes successfully make it into job advertisements. It overlooks the underlying communication of such lists, which may be simply: "when you come to work here, we'll expect you to work hard and get along." Only rigorous scientific investigation can determine whether a trait really leads to success on the job.

Is Emotional Intelligence Central to Character?

Emotional intelligence was originally associated with specific character attributes in the ability literature, but those character attributes were then de-emphasized (Mayer & Salovey, 1993; 1997; Mayer & Geher, 1996; Mayer, Caruso, & Salovey, 1999). Intelligence is plastic – it can be used for many different purposes. For example, optimism depends in part on biological/brain underpinnings, on life experiences, and on specific learned styles (e.g., Seligman, Reivich, Jaycox, & Gillham, 1995). Although emotional intelligence may contribute to optimism, much more is at work in determining whether a person is optimistic. Ability scales of emotional intelligence do appear fairly independent of many personality traits – one exception is with self-reported empathy, with which it shares a correlation of about $r = .35$ (Mayer & Geher, 1996; Mayer, Salovey, & Caruso, 1999).

Intelligence, emotional intelligence included, is not synonymous with good feeling. Good classroom behavior includes intellectual dissension, argument, and skeptical critiques as well as supportive, feel-good commentaries. Arguments void of negative emotion can be sterile and otherworldly. Emotionally intense materials — either positive or negative — are better recalled than neutral ones (Rapaport, 1950, p. 94). In addition, mood variation — including precipitous declines into negative feelings such as sadness, anger, and fear — fosters multiple perspective taking, and, perhaps, creativity and genius (Jamison, 1995; Mayer & Hanson, 1995; Richards et al., 1988).

When a policy maker such as Pool (1997) states that "the good citizen...[is]...the person with a high emotional intelligence" (p. 12), he is, at that very abstract level, equating emotional intelligence with goodness. Who among us, after all, is against good citizenship (defined our own way)? Researchers have joined in the search for an all-good character. The Emotional Quotient Inventory (Bar-On, 1997) measures optimism, assertiveness, self-actualization, self-esteem, and positive mood, among others. There is an "all things bright and beautiful" quality to these descriptions that both makes them hard to criticize in the abstract, but also makes them rather suspicious as a description of the emotionally intelligent character. This positive emphasis doesn't entirely come to grips with the necessity to cope with, and even fight against, the dangerous or impoverished side of life, let alone the boring, conventional side (Phillips, 1995).

Educational Policy on Emotional Intelligence: Does It Make Sense?

Emotional intelligence emphasizes the selection among values appropriate to the circumstances, recognizing the impossibility of expressing all good things all the time.

Finally, good character is probably possible without emotional intelligence. A person who follows social standards of politeness and good behavior will be perceived as having a good character, independent of their measured level of emotional intelligence.

Is Emotional Intelligence Readily Taught?

With a few exceptions, it does not make sense to us to speak of teaching an intelligence. An intelligence refers to a capacity to learn. Most policy experts seem to be discussing teaching emotional knowledge. We have little quarrel with the possibility of teaching in that area. Human beings are wonderful learners, and can be taught many things, understanding emotions is no doubt one of them (Elias, 1997). Thus, although we don't think it makes sense to talk about the ready acquisition of emotional intelligence, a slight change in language – to socio-emotional learning – is entirely acceptable to us. How much socio-emotional learning improves school performance or positively impacts behavior remains to be seen, however, as outcome studies are sparse to date (Zins, Travis, & Freppon, 1997, p. 262).

Is Emotional Intelligence Important in Education?

One area in which there is agreement among the scientific, popular, and policy versions of emotional intelligence is that emotional intelligence broadens what it means to be smart. It means that among some people who are labeled "bleeding hearts," "romantics," or "overly sensitive," there is some important information processing going on. Keeping that in mind may help educators better grasp the whole learner – that the information we convey as educators is both cognitive and emotional.

Discussion and Conclusion

It is easy to see why the popular version of emotional intelligence is appealing to policy makers. Popularizers of the concept have promised that raising students' emotional and social competencies will improve their academic and lifelong pursuits, their interpersonal relationships, and the climate of schools and organizations. "...[E]xperience and research," wrote Elias et al. (1997, p. 1), "show that promoting social and emotional development in children is 'the missing piece' in efforts to reach the array of goals associated with improving schooling in the United States."

Educational policy on emotional intelligence, however, turns out to be based on a very young scientific enterprise. The ability conception of emotional intelligence has some solid studies supporting it, although it has also been criticized in places. The broader, popular models of emotional intelligence, which combine abilities and dispositions or traits, have not been operationalized adequately as of yet. There is no established literature on what the popular version of emotional intelligence might predict. Although some important predictions from the mental ability model are likely, they can be expected to be in the modest but important range of most other personality prediction. There is no reason to believe that emotional intelligence will outperform intelligence as a predictor of school performance — but neither do most variables. Personality variables predicting at lower levels are still of societal significance. Emotional intelligence may predict reductions in bad behavior, which will be a matter of some importance. It is also of considerable value to broaden out understanding of what it means to be intelligent, should the evidence for emotional intelligence become widely accepted, as we expect.

It certainly seems likely that aspects of socio-emotional skills can be taught, and that many of these teachable skills have found their way into curricula for socio-emotional learning (Greenberg, Kusche, Cook, & Quamma, 1995). Still, no one knows what such education might bring about at this time. For example, the first scholarly volume in the area , Emotional Development and Emotional Intelligence, contained only one chapter on research evaluation of socio-emotional learning, which concluded, regarding programs to reduce school violence, "little evaluation information is available about the various approaches" (Zins, Travis, & Freppon, 1997, p. 262). Nor was any research on the outcomes of other programs cited. Goleman's (1995) chapter reviewing "Schooling the emotions," which also examined such programs, also failed to cite any relevant outcome studies of socio-emotional learning, although the chapter reports some anecdotal evidence for their success. One promising, potentially related area of research is in violence prevention (Catalano, Arthur, Hawkins, Berglund, & Olson, 1998).

In the short-term, therefore, it is worth acknowledging that we are only beginning to learn about emotional intelligence, and we don't know the degree to which it would predict success either for individuals or for schools. This does not mean that emotional intelligence is unimportant; nor does it mean that socio-emotional curricula aren't good or should be abandoned. All it means is that socio-emotional programs are implemented, at present, with reasonable hopes that they will have beneficial effects, independent of scientific findings concerning that fascinating newly-defined part of personality—emotional intelligence. The developers of socio-emotional learning programs, to their credit, have shown interest in program evaluation (Elias et al., 1997, Chapter 7). Such serious interest, if taken up by policy makers, can help prevent policy failures of the sort we outlined at the outset of this article regarding the California self-esteem movement. Findings about how socio-emotional learning programs improve schools are directly relevant to their use, and worth examining as they are reported.

If emotional intelligence becomes better established, as we expect it will, it could be integrated into policy in several ways. It might lead to an understanding of how socio-emotional programs work. Emotional intelligence also may be integrated into existing curricula. For example, we believe that emotional intelligence may well be fostered by courses in the liberal arts and the creative arts. These areas are often economically squeezed in today's curriculum because it is hard to explain exactly what they are teaching. One important thing they may foster is emotional reasoning. A student who is discussing what a character in a story feels, or what emotions a piece of music or art conveys, is actively using and perhaps fostering emotional perception and understanding. Understanding emotions on a case by case basis, as in literature, may be an important way people become experts in an area (Dreyfus & Dreyfus, 1986). Such links, if borne out by research, may re-legitimize areas of education which are presently suffering some loss of status and support.

In the long term, we believe the rush by policymakers to embrace emotional intelligence is part of a broader syndrome, that consists of successive waves of interest, directed at educating one or another single parts of the mind, that have occurred during the past 50 years. These waves of interest often represent shifts in cultural direction or zeitgeist. For example, in the early 1960s, a rising confidence in science and engineering focused attention on the person as machine — and reinforcing the organism to behave in a particular way. The result? An emphasis on teaching machines in education. The later 1960s and 1970s saw an emphasis on the experiential part of personality by such humanistic psychologists as Abraham Maslow and Carl Rogers; this coincided with the affective education movement (Wood, 1996). In the 1980s, the cognitive part of personality was reflected in both the cognitive revolution in psychology, and, in education, in a renewed emphasis on basic academic skills, along with an increased emphasis on testing. In the late 1980s, growing international competition gave rise to a renewed focus on intelligence within psychology, and to an increased emphasis on educational accountability, including the idea of state- or nation-wide testing. Perhaps as a reaction to the intense academic competition, a sub-theme of that decade was also a focus on raising children's self-esteem in school; concomitantly, self-esteem received renewed attention in psychology (Joachim, 1996; Leo, 1990). In the early 1990s in psychology, emotional parts of personality became a focus of attention, crystalizing in the concept of emotional intelligence, and in educational programs in socio-emotional learning.

What is consistent in this pattern is that both psychologically and educationally speaking, personality is often reduced to a focus on a single area, or even a single part – e.g., learning capacity, intelligence, learning disability, self-esteem, or emotional intelligence. Part of the reason for this is that models for the total personality have been woefully inadequate over the last several decades (see Mayer, 1998a, for a review). Personality psychology is undergoing an integration that has not been seen since the 1930s (Craik, 1998). The field now has possesses organizational frameworks to examine all the parts of personality together (e.g., Buss & Finn, 1978; Mayer, 1998a; 1998b; McAdams, 1996). It may be possible to use some of the new integrations of personality to take a new, more sophisticated approach to educating students about themselves as people. This new approach would not be dependent upon a single — often amorphous — part of personality. Rather, it would take a look at the articulated whole of personality and address education to this more balanced picture.

Educational policy related to emotional intelligence is of considerable interest. The policies are well-meaning and often executed through promising curricula devoted to socio-emotional learning. An examination of the emotional intelligence concept in educational policy indicates some weaknesses in how that policy was formulated, however, and some serious lapses in how it is tied to science. Most centrally, the policies are based on popularizations of a very young science which is, at present, still developing support for its central hypothesis that emotional intelligence exists. Various popularizations of the scientific field have included highly enthusiastic claims for emotional intelligence which, thus far, at least, appear unsubstantiated by reasonable scientific standards. Once that disconnect between policy and science is accounted for, the policies may still stand, but their justifications will require reworking. One policy goal worth considering for the future is an educational curriculum based on new integrations in personality psychology.

References

Artman, J. M., & Jacobs, J. A. (1928). The significance of present trends is the character education movement. Religious Education, 23, 240-253.

Averill, J. R. & Nunley, E. P. (1992). Voyages of the heart: Living an emotionally creative life. New York: Free Press.

Barrick, M. R. & Mount, M. K. (1991). The Big Five personality dimensions and job performance: A meta-analysis. Personnel Psychology, 44, 1-26.

Bar-On, R. (1997). Bar-On Emotional Quotient Inventory: A measure of emotional intelligence. Toronto, ON: Multi-Health Systems, Inc.

Benedict, M. (1990) Rating your story's EQ: Ethics quotient. Quill and Scroll, 64, 4-5.

Benninga, J. S., & Wynne, E. A. (1998). Keeping in character: A time-tested solution. Phi Delta Kappan, 79(6), 439-445.

Boy Scouts of America (1999). [Online]. Scout Law. Available: www.bsa.scouting.org/factsheets/02-503a.html.

Buss, A. H., & Finn, S. E. (1987). Classification of personality traits. Journal of Personality and Social Psychology, 52, 432-444.

Carroll, J. B. (1993). Human cognitive abilities: A survey of factor-analytic studies. New York: Cambridge University Press.

Catalano, R. F., Arthur, M. W., Hawkins, D. J., Berglund, L., & Olson, J. J. (1998).

Comprehensive community- and school-based interventions to prevent antisocial behavior. In R. Loeber & D. P. Farrington (Eds.). Serious and violent juvenile offenders: Risk factors and successful interventions (pp. 248-283). Thousand Oaks, CA: Sage.

Character Education Partnership (see "The Character Education Partnership.")

Craik, K. H. (1998). Personality systems concepts and their implications. Psychological Inquiry, 9, 145-148.

Davies, M., Stankov, L., & Roberts, R.D. (1998). Emotional Intelligence: In search of an elusive construct. Journal of Personality and Social Psychology, 75, 989-1015.

Dockrell, W. B. (1959). The relationship between socio-economic status, intelligence and attainment in some Scottish primary schools. Indian Psychological Bulletin, 4, 1-6.

Drench, M. (1994). Your effectiveness quotient! Total health, 16, 36-37.

Dreyfus, H. L., & Dreyfus, S. E. (1986). Why skills cannot be represented by rules. In N. Sharkey (Ed.) Advances in cognitive science. Chichester, England: Horwood.

Duhon-Haynes, G., Duhon-Sells, R., Sells, H., & Duhon-Ross, A. (1996). Peace education: Enhancing caring skills and emotional intelligence in children (Report No. CG027266). Lousiana: Counseling and Personnel Services. (ERIC Document Reproduction Service No. ED 399 489)

Elias, M. J., (December 3rd, 1997). The missing piece. Education Week, 17, 36ff.

Elias, M. J., Zins, J. E., Weissberg, R. P., Frey, K. S., Greenberg, M. T., Haynes, N. M., Kessler, R., Schwab-Stone, M.E., & Shriver, T.P. (1997). Promoting social and emotional learning: Guidelines for educators. Alexandria, VA: Association for Supervision and Curriculum Development.

Entrepreneur (1993). What's your EQ? Entrepreneur, 21, 15.

Epstein, S. (1998). Constructive thinking: The key to emotional intelligence. Praeger, Westport, CT.

Feinberg, H. (1941). IQ correlated with EQ. Journal of Educational Psychology, 32, 617-632.

Franknel, D. A. (April 29, 1995). Fatal attraction between scientists and journalists? Lancet, 345, 1105-1106.

Gardner, H. (1993). Frames of mind: The theory of multiple intelligences. (10th Anniversary Edition). New York: Basic Books.

Gibbs, N. (1995, October 2). The EQ factor. Time, pp. 60-68.

Girl Scouts USA (1999). The Law. Available: www.gsusa.org/ organization/ program.html.

Glanzer, P. L. (1998). The character to seek justice: Showing fairness to diverse visions of character education. Phi Delta Kappan, 79(6), 434-438; 448.

Goleman, D. (1995). Emotional intelligence. New York: Bantam.

Goleman, D. (1998). Working with emotional intelligence. New York: Bantam.

Greenberg, M. T., Kusche, C. A., Cook, E. T., Quamma, J. P. (1995). Promoting emotional competence in school-aged children: The effects of the PATHS curriculum. Development and Psychology, 7, 117-136.

Greenspan, S. I. (1979). Intelligence and adaptation. New York: International Universities Press.

Horn, J. & Noll, J. (1994). A system for understanding cognitive capacities: A theory and the evidence on which it is based. In D. K. Detterman (Ed.). Current topics in human intelligence, Vol 4: Theories, tests, and issues. New York: Guilford Press.

Jamison, K. R. (1995). Manic-depressive illness and creativity. Scientific American, 272, 62-00.

Jerome, F. (1981). Prime time science and newstand technology: Is it all just hoopla? Professional Engineer, 51, 12-14.

Joachim, K. (1996). The politics of self esteem. American Educational Research Journal, 33, 3-22.

Klein, R. (1997). Emotional appeal. Times Educational Supplement, 4-5.

Leibman, B. (1995). What's your EQ (eating quotient)? Nutrition Action Health Letter, 22, 9-10.

Leo, J. (April 2nd 1990). The trouble with self-esteem. U.S. News & World Report, 108, 16.

Leuner, B. (1966). Emotional intelligence and emancipation. Praxis der Kinderpsychologie und Kinderpsychiatrie, 15, 196-203. [German]

Mayer, J. D. (1998a). A systems framework for the field of personality. Psychological Inquiry, 9, 118-144.

Mayer, J. D. (1998b). The Systems Framework: Reception, Improvement, and Implementation. Psychological Inquiry, 9, 169-179.

Mayer, J. D., Caruso, D. R., & Salovey, P. (1999). Emotional intelligence meets standards for a traditional intelligence. Manuscript submitted for publication.

Mayer, J. D., Caruso, D. R., Salovey, P. Formica, S., & Woolery, A. (1999). Validity studies of the Multifactor Emotional Intelligence Scales [Unpublished raw data].

Mayer, J. D., DiPaolo, M. T., & Salovey, P. (1990). Perceiving affective content in ambiguous visual stimuli: A component of emotional intelligence. Journal of Personality Assessment, 54, 772-781.

Mayer, J. D. & Geher, G. (1996). Emotional intelligence and the identification of emotion. Intelligence, 22, 89-113.

Mayer, J. D., & Hanson, E. (1995). Mood-congruent judgment over time. Personality and Social Psychology Bulletin, 21, 237-244.

Mayer, J. D., & Salovey, P. (1993). The intelligence of emotional intelligence. Intelligence, 17(4), 433-442.

Mayer, J. D. & Salovey, P. (1997). What is emotional intelligence? In P. Salovey & D. Sluyter (Eds). Emotional Development and Emotional Intelligence: Implications for Educators (pp. 3-31). New York: Basic Books.

Mayer, J. D., Salovey, P., & Caruso, D. R. (in press). Competing models of emotional intelligence. In R. J. Sternberg (Ed.). Handbook of Human Intelligence (2nd ed.).

McAdams, D. P. (1996). Personality, modernity, and the storied self: A contemporary framework for studying persons. Psychological Inquiry, 7, 295-321.

Miller, J. P. (1976). Humanizing the classroom. New York: Praeger Publishers.

Mischel, W. (1968). Personality and assessment. New York: Wiley.

Nucci, L. P. (1989). Moral development and character education: A dialogue. Berkeley, CA: McCutchan Publishing.

Educational Policy on Emotional Intelligence: Does It Make Sense?

Pasi, R. J. (1997). Success in high school—and beyond. Educational Leadership, 54, 43-46.

Payne, W. L. (1986). A study of emotion: Developing emotional intelligence; self-integration; relating to fear, pain, and desire. Doctoral Dissertation at the Union Graduate School. Cincinnati, OH. [Original dissertation work submitted and accepted, May, 1983].

Pool, C. R. (1997). Up with emotional health. Educational Leadership, 54, 12-14.

Phillips, L. (1995). How do you feel, stupid? Nation, 261, p. 585.

Rapaport, D. (1950). Emotions and memory. New York: International Universities Press.

Richards, R., Kinney, D. K., Lunde, I., Benet, M., & Merzel, A. P. C. (1988). Creativity in manicdepressives, cyclothymes, their normal relatives, and control subjects. Journal of Abnormal Psychology, 97, 281-288.

Rhode Island Emotional Competency Partnership (1998). Update on Emotional Competency. Rhode Island State Government

Salovey, P. & Mayer, J. D. (1990). Emotional intelligence. Imagination, Cognition, and Personality, 9, 185-211.

Salovey, P. & Sluyter, D. J. (1997). A note from the editors. In P. Salovey & D. J. Sluyter, (Eds.). Emotional development and emotional intelligence (pp. xi-xii). New York: Basic Books.

Scarr, S. (1989). Protecting general intelligence: Constructs and consequences for intervention. In R. L. Linn (Ed.). Intelligence: Measurement, theory, and public policy. Ubrana, IL: University of Illinois Press.

Scherer, M. (1997). Perspectives: Heart start. Educational Leadership, 54, 5.

Seligman, M. E. P., Reivich, K., Jaycox, L., & Gillham, J. (1995). The optimistic child. Boston, MA: Houghton Mifflin.

Shapiro, L. E. (1997) How to raise a child with a high E.Q: A parents' guide to Emotional Intelligence. New York: HarperCollins Publishers.

Staw, B. M., & Barsade, S. G. (1993). Affect and managerial performance: A test of the sadder-but-wiser versus happier-and-smarter hypothesis. Administrative Science Quarterly, 38, 304-331.

Sternberg, R. J. & Caruso, D. R. (1985). Practical modes of knowing. In E. Eisner (Ed.) Learning and teaching the ways of knowing: 84th Yearbook of the National Society for the Study of Education (Part II, pp. 133-158). Chicago: University of Chicago Press.

Stufft, W. D. (1996). Assessing your emotional IQ. Teaching music, 4, 42-43.

The Character Education Partnership (No date). [Online]. Available: http://www.character.org/ [1998, January 15].

Tyron, G. S., & Tyron, W. W. (1986). Factors associated with clinical practicum trainees' engagements of clients in counseling. Professional Psychology: Research & Practice, 17, 586-589.

Weisinger, H. (1997). Emotional intelligence at work. New York: Jossey-Bass.

Wessman, A. E., & Ricks, D. F. (1966). Mood and personality. New York: Holt, Rinehart, & Winston, Inc.

Wood, S. J. (1996). Implementing a successful affective curriculum. Intervention in School & Clinic, 32, 126-129.

Wynne, E. A., & Walberg, H. J. (1986). The complementary goals of character development and academic excellence. Educational Leadership, 43, 15-18.

Zins, J. E., Travis, L. F., & Freppon, P. A. (1997). Linking research and educational programming to promote social and emotional learning. In P. Salovey & D. J. Sluyter, (Eds.). Emotional development and emotional intelligence (pp. 257-274). New York: Basic Books.

Footnotes

[1]EQ. Like emotional intelligence, the term "EQ," was employed on an occasional basis over many years. One early use of EQ was, in fact, to denote education quotient, (e.g., Feinberg, 1941). Its current incarnation as "emotional quotient" was the consequence of the earlier-mentioned TIME magazine story that featured EQ in block letters on the magazine's cover. EQ is a rather confusing abbreviation, from our standpoint. IQ, as intelligence quotient, refers to a person's degree of intelligence. Similarly, in the 1930's EQ, as education quotient, referred to a person's degree of education. A high emotion quotient should therefore index how moody or emotionally reactive a person is. In fact, however, EQ was successfully recognized by TIME readers as referring to the degree of emotional intelligence a person possessed. That is, EQ is a condensed E-IQ, or Emotional IQ. Through the years, EQ has stood not only for Educational Quotient and Emotional Quotient, but for the English Quotient (Dockrell, 1959), Engagement Quotient (Tryon & Tryon, 1986), Ethics Quotient (Benedict, 1990), Entrepreneurial Quotient (Entrepreneur, 1993), Effectiveness Quotient (Drench, 1994), and even Eating Quotient! (Liebman, 1995).

[2] The original Elias et al. (1997) list was alphabetized. The five-area grouping in the text represents our own classificaton of those values.

[3] Today, most educators make a political distinction between character education and socio-emotional learning. Character education is associated with conservative, right-wing values, and socio-emotional learning is associated with left-wing values. It is important to note, however, that this is a historical accident, and that either approach could serve either ideology. Among character educators, teaching such virtues as "patriotism, hard work, and citizenship" may serve a conservative agenda whereas teaching "skepticism and tolerance" may serve a more liberal agenda (Glanzer, 1998, p. 436). Take away this difference and, perhaps, the movements are not very dissimilar. Perhaps socio-emotional learning emphasizes teaching interpersonal skills whereas

character education emphasizes a more general educational approach toward thinking and reasoning about morals. These are complementary approaches.

[4] Briefly, the logic of the 1995 claim began with the widely-accepted idea that intelligence predicts about 20% of the individual differences variability in achievement in school. Goleman implied that the remaining 80% therefore had to be predicted by something else...and that something else was emotional intelligence. A century of personality research, however, makes it reasonably certain that intelligence is the single largest predictor of variance in all of personality psychology (e.g., Mischel, 1968). That is, there has never been found a single other variable that predicts as well. When other variables — achievement motivation, extroversion, good mood, and the like — are added in to predictions of school performance, for example, they typically account for 2% or 3% or sometimes 5% of the variance. Why is this? Predicting a person's future success is not much different than making long range forecasts of earthquakes, hurricanes, the stock market, or geopolitics. It is limited by complexity. The unexplained 80% of success appears to be in large part the consequence of complex, chaotic interactions among hundreds of variables playing out over time.

Toward a Broader Education:
Social, Emotional, and Practical Skills

Paulo N. Lopes, Yale University
Peter Salovey, Yale University

Author Notes

We thank the following individuals for their comments on earlier drafts of this chapter: Kathryn Estes, Cory Head, Linda Jarvin, Chinyelu Lee, Helena Lopes, David Pizarro, Robert Sternberg, Roger Weissberg, Andreas Xenachis, and Joseph Zins.

We also acknowledge support from the National Cancer Institute (R01-CA68427), the National Institute of Mental Health (P01-MH/DA56826), the National Institute of Drug Abuse (P50-DA13334), and the Donaghue Women's Health Investigator Program at Yale to Peter Salovey. Paulo N. Lopes was supported by a fellowship from the Portuguese Science and Technology Foundation.

How should educators choose among different programs of social and emotional learning? What skills should one really focus on? Every intervention program is inspired by different goals and assumptions. Every theory has its strengths and limitations. Studies often yield mixed findings. How are educators to make sense of it all?

In this chapter, we explore some of the theoretical and empirical underpinnings of social and emotional learning (SEL). Obviously, one chapter cannot do justice to all of the theory and research addressing children's social and emotional development. We focus on theories of intelligence — social, emotional, and practical intelligence — even though much of the research in these areas has been conducted with adults.

Overall, there is good evidence that well-designed SEL programs can promote children's social and emotional adjustment. The number of SEL programs that have been rigorously evaluated, using adequate comparison groups and following children over time, is still limited. When we synthesize the evidence for some of the best SEL programs, however, the overall picture is quite encouraging. Programs such as Promoting Alternative Thinking Strategies, the Seattle Social Development Project, and Resolving Conflicts Creatively have undergone rigorous evaluations, and the results are promising (e.g., Hawkins, Catalano, Kosterman, Abbott, & Hill, 1999; Kusché & Greenberg, 2001; Weissberg & Greenberg, 1998).

Still, important questions remain to be addressed. Exactly how do these programs benefit children? How long do the benefits last? To what extent can social and emotional skills be generalized across settings and situations? The quality of curricula and teaching materials is important. But does choosing one quality program over another make much of a difference? How much should we emphasize formal instruction as compared with learning from experience? What approaches work best for different groups of students? How can we improve these programs to prepare children better for the challenges they are likely to face throughout life?

These are difficult questions, and we cannot wait for research to clarify them all. Given reasonable evidence that SEL programs are effective, we should seek to implement social and emotional learning on a wider scale. But exactly how should we go about this? Researchers associated with the Collaborative for Academic, Social, and Emotional Learning (CASEL) have outlined useful guidelines for effective SEL practice (Zins, Elias, Greenberg, & Weissberg, 2000; see also Payton et al., 2000). SEL programs should be comprehensive, multiyear programs, integrated into the school curriculum and extracurricular activities. They should be theoretically based, as well as developmentally and culturally appropriate. They should promote a caring, supportive, and challenging classroom and school climate; teach a broad range of skills; be undertaken by well-trained staff with adequate, ongoing support; promote school, family, and community partnerships; and be systematically monitored and evaluated.

Difficulties arise, however, when researchers try to identify a set of key skills to focus on. Payton and colleagues(2000) list key social and emotional competencies

Toward a Broader Education: Social, Emotional, & Practical Skills

under four headings: awareness of self and others; positive attitudes and values; responsible decision making; and social interaction skills. In drawing up any such list of key skills for a domain as broad as social and emotional learning, we face several challenges:

1. Overall, the list is likely to represent a very broad range of skills, and it may be difficult to address all these skills through formal classroom instruction.
2. The skills listed (e.g., managing feelings) may encompass, or depend on, a wide array of other skills, which are not part of the list.
3. The skills to be taught may be partly domain- or context-specific, failing to transfer across situations.
4. There may be more common ground between educational programs stressing different key skills than usually is acknowledged, as these programs may operate through similar mechanisms (e.g., enhancing intrinsic motivation).
5. For all these reasons, the theoretical and empirical rationale for emphasizing one set of skills over another is often less than compelling.

It may be argued that lists of key skills are intended merely to give readers some idea about the breadth of SEL programs, rather than to present a theoretically and empirically based hierarchy of skills. But then the question remains: Given limited time and resources, what skills should educators focus on?

This question is likely to have no clear-cut answer. If schools are to prepare children for the challenges they will face in the future, then the skills emphasized depend to some extent at least on what we think these challenges will be. Such assessments are necessarily subjective because they depend on our goals and values — namely, how we would like to shape our children's development and influence the course of events in the world. Empirical studies may tell us what contributes to adaptation in the present, but they cannot always tell us how to prepare for the future. In other words, theory and research can guide decision making, but decisions about education also must be based on consensual goals and values and an appreciation of the challenges that children are likely to face over the course of their lives.

We argue that, in the absence of a clear rationale for focusing on one set of skills over another, our best bet may be to teach a broad a set of competencies and capitalize on informal learning, that is, learning through experience, modeling, and observation. These ideas already figure among the guidelines outlined by CASEL, and we think they should be taken further.

Proponents of social and emotional learning often seek to teach to the whole child and promote students' balanced development. This involves going beyond the type

Toward a Broader Education: Social, Emotional, & Practical Skills

of memory-based learning and logical-abstract thinking that has been emphasized in Western schools. We think the range of competencies addressed in schools should be broadened to encompass not only social and emotional skills, but also creative and practical abilities. We now know about different education or intervention programs that seem to be effective in promoting different goals, such as developing social and emotional skills, enhancing creativity and practical thinking, training optimism, or stimulating intrinsic motivation for school. Ultimately, education would be better if we managed effectively to integrate important ideas and practices from these very different lines of research and intervention work.

We also need to capitalize on informal learning because we may not be able to teach through explicit instruction many of the skills that will help children to become healthy and productive adults. The number of skills involved is very large, and we may not have time to teach them effectively in the classroom. Moreover, many abilities, such as managing feelings, thinking creatively, or developing intrinsic motivation, cannot be learned through explicit instruction alone. They have to be developed through personal experience and practice. We can help children to develop such skills by constructing stimulating learning environments, creating opportunities for them to practice, providing constructive feedback, and having teachers model those skills and behaviors. To do this, we need good schools, good teachers, and quality teacher training.

SEL and Academic Achievement

Social, emotional, and practical skills are likely to be important for academic achievement, both directly and indirectly. For example, emotional regulation skills may facilitate control of attention and the development of intrinsic motivation for challenging pursuits, thus contributing to sustained intellectual engagement and studying. Children also need to control emotional outbursts and impulsive reactions in order to sit still through class and interact with teachers and peers. Children's social and emotional adaptation and their bonding to prosocial peers and adults may further contribute to their motivation for learning.

As far as we know, there is little empirical evidence linking the school-based promotion of social and emotional skills to qualities such as attention control, which are hard to assess. However, there is evidence that children's social and emotional adaptation is associated with bonding to school, and with academic outcomes such as school dropout (Hawkins et al., 1999).

In this chapter we often discuss the benefits of SEL programs in terms of social and emotional adaptation, rather than academic achievement. We do this because there is a large body of theory and research on social and emotional adaptation, but little empirical data on the relationship between social and emotional skills and academic outcomes. We also think that social and emotional adaptation to school is likely to contribute to academic achievement. Moreover, we believe that social and emotional adaptation should be viewed as an essential goal of education.

Toward a Broader Education: Social, Emotional, & Practical Skills

Generally speaking, the extent to which social and emotional learning contributes to academic achievement is likely to depend on several factors: (1) how we define and assess academic achievement; (2) whether social and emotional learning is weaved into traditional subject matters so as to make school learning more interesting and enjoyable; and (3) the degree to which SEL programs enhance children's social and emotional adaptation to school, and bonding to prosocial peers and adults.

If developing social, emotional, practical, and creative competencies is important so that children can lead healthy and productive lives, this should be viewed as an essential goal of education. We need to revise the way that we define and assess achievement in school. We need to incorporate such skills into evaluations of academic achievement. Accountability is crucial, and decision makers will likely be wary of efforts to broaden the range of competencies addressed in schools unless these competencies can be evaluated and children's progress in these areas can be tracked over time. One of the reasons that rote learning and analytical skills have been overemphasized in Western schools is that such knowledge and skills can be assessed easily and objectively. In our discussion of emotional and practical intelligence, we describe recent efforts to develop ability measures of emotional and practical skills.

Preparing Children for the Challenges Ahead

Three or four generations ago, most children would spend only a few years in school. Classroom instruction focused on basic skills such as reading, writing, and arithmetic and a few other traditional subjects. Parents might have been able to teach their children basic discipline, but often could not teach them to read and write. Although educators also had to enforce discipline in the classroom, they could not pay much attention to social and emotional competencies.

Times have changed. Young people are now more exposed to problems of depression, social isolation, and drug abuse. They need to build social and emotional resources to cope with these risks. Children also spend many more years in school. This requires that they develop concentration, impulse control, and emotional regulation.

Work settings now require teamwork, participative leadership, informal networks, and quality customer service. People's capacity to establish good relationships with others weighs heavily in hiring and promotion decisions. All this demands the development of elaborate social and emotional skills.

In a society undergoing rapid change, young people no longer learn a trade for life. They must constantly learn new skills, and adapt to changing technology and market demands. The freedom they enjoy to make career and lifestyle decisions also requires that they plan ahead and actively manage their lives. All this puts a premium on initiative, motivation, adaptability, and self-management.

As the world has changed, so have schools. Young people spend more years in school, develop higher proficiency in basic disciplines, and study a greater range of subjects. Critical thinking is replacing rote learning. Yet educational reform continues to lag behind the changes required by modern society. As Sternberg (1985, 1999) has argued, schooling still focuses excessively on analytical skills, encompassing logical, abstract, and critical thinking. We are neglecting the sort of practical and creative abilities that allow people to deal with real-life problems and unforeseen challenges.

Analytical intelligence (i.e., IQ) seems to account for about 10% to 15% of job performance ratings and other real-world outcomes (Herrnstein & Murray, 1994). What accounts for the rest? Children who outshine others in school are not necessarily the most successful in life. The relationship between educational achievement and life satisfaction is very weak indeed (Diener & Lucas, 1999). How can we make education more useful for what really matters?

On What Skills Should We Focus?

Most people probably agree that schools are not teaching some of the skills that are important for life. Yet they may also question whether these skills should be taught in schools at all, and whether we should be diverting time and effort away from traditional subject matters in order to do so.

It is possible to infuse social and emotional learning into existing curricula, so as to avoid overburdening teachers and students with more demands on their time. Some trade-offs are inevitable, however. Paying more attention to one set of skills is likely to detract from investment in others. So many skills are important for life that, given limited school time and resources, we cannot address them all through explicit instruction. How should we decide on what skills to focus?

There are at least three ways to approach this question. The first is that specific intervention goals may entail an emphasis on particular skills. For example, many SEL programs consider the prevention of violent and antisocial behavior a top priority, and therefore emphasize conflict resolution skills. However, prevention goals are not equally salient for all communities. If there are no acute problems and the general goal is to promote social and emotional adaptation, then the rationale for a particular focus is less clear.

The second approach is to emphasize skills that are likely to generalize across settings and situations. Self-management skills, for example, involving planning and deliberation, self-monitoring and self-reflection, are applicable to practically all domains of life. Some learning skills, including strategies for acquiring knowledge and learning from feedback, also are likely to generalize.

The third approach is to capitalize on implicit or informal learning. We may not be able to teach all relevant skills through formal instruction, but we can help children to learn through experience and practice, modeling and observation. We can use teamwork, collaborative learning, and small group discussions to provide opportunities for children to learn to interact with others in a supportive environment. A healthy school atmosphere can help children to nurture positive relationships with others. We can take advantage of everyday problems and disputes as they arise in the classroom to help children develop perspective taking and conflict resolution skills. We can infuse social and emotional learning into the teaching of traditional subject matters.

Some of the best SEL programs use all three approaches. Still, it would be useful to have more guidance on how to promote positive youth development. While some SEL programs aim to prevent specific problems, many have much broader goals — namely, to help children lead more fulfilling lives. Whether or not it is stated as such, their ultimate goal is to help children to become healthy, well-adjusted, and happy individuals.

But what is the best way to educate children so that they will be happy and well adjusted? We may know a lot about parental and educational practices associated with positive and negative outcomes for children. In general, however, we know how to treat psychological problems much better than we understand how to promote psychological health. There are so many factors that can influence adjustment over the life course, that it becomes difficult to identify optimal strategies.

Moreover, what do we mean by happiness and adjustment? Happiness can mean different things to different people. We can think of a well-adjusted individual as one who experiences joy and excitement, peace and contentment, self-acceptance, satisfaction with life, fulfillment, meaningful engagement, or enjoyment of daily pursuits. There may be many ways to lead a good life. There may be many ways to be successful in any field. And there may be many ways to promote positive youth development.

Developing skill in any domain requires training and practice, and investing more in one set of abilities may detract from investment in others. We cannot excel at everything. Emphasizing one set of skills over another entails advantages and disadvantages, and these may be more or less salient in different environments and at different points in the life course. Every approach has its strengths and weaknesses. There may be no single best solution.

This suggests that different programs may be effective and beneficial for children, even if they target somewhat different goals and rely on different curricula. There is evidence that some SEL programs effectively promote children's social and emotional adjustment, but we have no strong reasons for claiming that one of these approaches is better than another. Can theory and research on social, emotional, and practical skills provide further guidance?

Social Skills

We all seem to think that some people are especially adept at interacting with others. We might say that these people have good social skills. But what does it take to establish and sustain good relationships with others? If we can identify a coherent and interrelated set of skills associated with positive social outcomes, perhaps we should incorporate these skills into SEL programs.

Think of all the skills and traits that may be useful for dealing with others: emotional understanding, perspective taking, communication skills, cheerfulness, sense of humor, emotional regulation, respect for social norms, empathy, agreeableness, assertiveness, negotiation skills, ability to engage in interesting conversation, plain intelligence, charm. We could go on. But do these skills and traits really go together?

Think of someone who has good social skills. Perhaps you will think of someone who might thrive at parties, receptions, and large gatherings. Maybe you will think of somebody who is generally cheerful and extroverted. But this person may not be equally adept at handling romantic relationships and intimate friendships, children and old people, subordinates and peers, teamwork and conflict.

For researchers, the attempt to define and measure social intelligence has been a frustrating endeavor. There have been more than a dozen studies of social intelligence, undertaken mostly with young adults. Although the evidence is mixed, it suggests that diverse social skills are weakly correlated (for reviews see Cantor & Kihlstrom, 1987; Hall & Bernieri, 2001; Kihlstrom & Cantor, 2000; Sternberg et al., 2000). Developing ability in one area may not ensure competence in another. Teaching some of these skills does not ensure that children will learn all the others. Because people draw upon many different skills for social interaction, and we cannot teach all of these competencies through formal instruction, we have to rely on informal learning.

Social skills training is used effectively in clinical and other settings for treating or preventing problem behaviors. However, various evaluation studies suggest that social skills training in the classroom may not always translate well into natural settings or have a strong impact on children's peer relations (La Greca, 1993). One set of skills that seems to generalize across domains and situations is linked to the theory of social information processing, which looks at how people interpret and respond to social events. They have to analyze what happened, consider possible responses, choose and plan a course of action, then monitor and evaluate the effectiveness of their reply. Deficits in these skills are associated with aggressive behavior and poor social adjustment (Crick & Dodge, 1994).

In particular, children prone to aggression often reveal deficits and biases in the way that they detect and interpret cues of aggression. They tend to attribute hostile intentions to others, even when there was no hostile intent. They tend to have limited response repertoires and generate few alternative strategies for dealing with interpersonal problems. They also tend to evaluate the outcomes of their actions from a biased perspective, so that they continue to believe that fighting is the only way to deal with similar situations, for example.

Many SEL programs now teach children that when faced with interpersonal problems, they should stop and think; identify the problem and their feelings about it; plan the best course of action by generating alternative solutions and evaluating the possible consequences of different strategies; and go ahead and try the best plan (Zins et al., 2000). Several studies suggest that this type of training helps to reduce problem behaviors, as rated by children and teachers (e.g., Caplan et al., 1992).

Practical and Creative Skills

Sternberg (1985) has argued that we should think of intelligence as something broader than IQ. His theory of successful intelligence (Sternberg, 1985, 1999b) posits three broad domains of ability in addition to memory: analytical, creative, and practical intelligence. Analytical intelligence, involving logical-abstract reasoning and critical thinking, is the one that our educational system tends to favor. Creative intelligence helps us find original solutions for new problems as we adapt to new situations. Practical intelligence helps us solve everyday, real-life problems effectively and is based on the know-how and common sense that we acquire through experience.

Sternberg defines intelligence as one's ability to achieve success in life, given one's personal standards, and within one's sociocultural context. He views intelligence as a form of developing expertise (Sternberg, 1999a). According to him, what IQ tests really measure is achievement at the type of logical-abstract thinking skills that children learn in Western schools. The fact that IQ scores have risen significantly over the past decades suggests that intelligence can be developed. Cross-cultural studies further suggest that in communities where different skills are emphasized, IQ has less value (Sternberg, 1999b).

In Sternberg's overarching framework, practical intelligence encompasses social and emotional competencies. Among the lessons outlined by Sternberg and Grigorenko (2000) for promoting practical skills in schools are several units that one also might find in SEL programs: motivation, controlling impulses, persevering, managing self-pity, handling personal difficulties, and developing self-confidence. However, Sternberg's work tends to emphasize cognitive processes and pays less attention to emotions.

Sternberg's approach to practical intelligence focuses on the concept of tacit knowledge. This is the know-how that we acquire through experience, usually without thinking about it, so that we have trouble putting it into words. The problems we train children to solve at school are very different from the problems they often will face later in life. Academic problems usually are clearly spelled out, involve a limited number of variables, and allow only one solution. Students can solve these problems using abstract rules and principles in sequential order. And the problems allow only one correct solution. In contrast, practical problems often are poorly defined and can be tackled in many different ways. They often require creative reformulation. And they draw upon tacit knowledge that may be largely domain-specific (Sternberg et al., 2000).

Sternberg and his team have shown that taking into account analytical, creative, and practical skills permits understanding and predicting people's performance better than IQ alone (Sternberg, 1999b). Practical skills can be assessed through tests of tacit knowledge, which ask people to rate the effectiveness of different strategies for dealing with given school or workplace scenarios, for example. This type of tacit knowledge is associated with supervisors' ratings of job performance, over and above traditional measures of IQ (Grigorenko, Guillermo, Jarvin, & Sternberg, 2001; Sternberg et al., 2000).

Sternberg's team is now applying these ideas to education. They have adapted existing curricula and teaching materials for students at different grade levels, to address analytical, creative, and practical skills in a balanced way. They found that teaching children in this way improves their academic achievement on reading and other skills, as compared with focusing solely on memory or critical thinking (Grigorenko, Jarvin, & Sternberg, 2002; Sternberg, Grigorenko & Jarvin, 2001).

Instead of asking educators to teach a whole new curriculum, Sternberg's team is infusing creative and practical skills into existing curricula and teaching materials. This makes it easier for educators and policy makers to buy into their program. It also makes it easier to link their program to academic achievement. Moreover, they are trying to broaden the definition and assessment of academic achievement. They are developing tests of creative and practical ability to ensure that children's progress in these areas can be evaluated on a continuing basis.

Sternberg's team has done a lot to show that the range of competencies taught in school should be broadened. Many of their ideas about creative and practical skills also could be usefully applied to social and emotional learning. However, their work pays little attention to emotions and does not specify what subskills to focus on for different abilities. Moreover, we still do not know to what extent these abilities generalize across domains, cultures, and situations.

Emotional Skills

For a long time, emotions were seen as processes that disrupted rational thought and decision making. Only recently have investigators started to emphasize the adaptive value of emotions. For example, people whose capacity to process emotional information has been impaired due to brain injury have difficulty making everyday decisions and managing their lives (Damásio, 1994). Emotions tell us what we like and what to do. Feelings guide our everyday behavior and allow us to make choices without considering all the pros and cons of every option.

Moreover, some people seem to handle feelings and emotions better than others. People who are otherwise very intelligent sometimes make disastrous decisions because they fail to take into account their own and other people's feelings. Bright politicians can lose elections because their emotional reactions come across as inappropriate.

Salovey and Mayer (1990) posited a theory of emotional intelligence encompassing four basic abilities: perceiving and understanding emotions, using emotions in thought, and managing emotions (see also Mayer & Salovey, 1997). Inspired by this functional view of emotions, they focused on skills that allow people to process and interpret emotional information. Evidence suggests that these skills represent a coherent and interrelated set of information-processing abilities, distinct from other types of intelligence, and that they develop with age (Mayer, Caruso, & Salovey, 1999).

Mayer, Salovey, and Caruso (2001) developed a test to assess emotional abilities without relying on self-report: the Mayer, Salovey and Caruso Emotional Intelligence Test (MSCEIT). This test involves various tasks, including decoding facial expressions of emotion, understanding blends of emotions and emotional dynamics, integrating emotional information with other thinking processes, and managing emotions for purposes of self-regulation and social interaction. Answers on the MSCEIT can be scored against those of a sample of experts from an international society of emotion researchers, or a normative sample of several thousand people. The two scoring methods yield similar results, and the test has been shown to be reliable (Mayer, Salovey, Caruso, & Sitarenios, 2001; Salovey, Mayer, Caruso, & Lopes, in press). Although this test was designed for adults, a version for elementary and middle school children is in the works.

A number of studies suggest that emotional intelligence, assessed in this way, is associated with a range of positive outcomes. Among school children, it was associated with lower peer ratings of aggressiveness and higher teacher ratings of prosocial behavior (Rubin, 1999). Among teenagers, it was linked to less tobacco and alcohol consumption (Trinidad & Johnson, 2002). Among college students, it was related to higher self-reported empathy, relationship quality, and psychological well-being (Brackett & Mayer, in press; Ciarrochi, Chan, & Caputi, 2000). College students' scores on the MSCEIT were associated with the self-reported quality of relationships with both friends and parents, the self-perceived quality of daily social interactions, and peer nominations for positive social and emotional characteristics, even when basic personality traits and academic intelligence were statistically controlled (Lopes, Salovey, & Straus, in press; Lopes, Nezlek, Schütz, Sellin, & Salovey, 2003; Lopes, Salovey, & Beers, 2002). Among leaders of an insurance company's customer claims teams, emotional intelligence was linked to higher manager ratings of effectiveness and higher team performance (Rice, 1999).

Emotional abilities are also likely to be important for academic achievement (see Salovey & Sluyter, 1997). For example, perceiving emotions may be important for

Toward a Broader Education: Social, Emotional, & Practical Skills

artistic expression and writing, as well as for interpreting literature and works of art. Using emotions to facilitate thinking may help students to decide what activities to focus on, depending on how they feel. It may be easier to write a creative essay if one is feeling cheerful, because positive moods enhance divergent thinking and imagination. Negative moods may facilitate careful attention to detail and be more suitable for doing geometry proofs, for example. Understanding emotional vocabulary and emotional dynamics helps children to develop a good command of language and analyze the characters and plot of a novel. The ability to manage emotions may help students to handle anxiety-arousing situations, such as taking tests or starting creative projects. However, we do not yet have strong evidence linking emotional intelligence and academic achievement.

Solid evidence that emotional skills are associated with social adaptation comes from research with children, involving a variety of different assessment tools. In a large number of studies, children's abilities to read emotions in faces, understand emotional vocabulary, and regulate their emotions have been associated with their social competence and adaptation, as rated by peers, parents, and teachers (for reviews see Eisenberg, Fabes, Guthrie, & Reiser, 2000; Feldman, Philippot, & Custrini, 1991; Halberstadt, Denham, & Dunsmore, 2001; Saarni, 1999).

People's capacity for emotional regulation may be linked to genetically driven temperamental dispositions, which tend to be fairly stable. Over time, however, children can learn to cope with, and compensate for, their temperamental dispositions. In fact, about one-third of the infants who seem temperamentally predisposed to become inhibited and shy grow up to be relatively uninhibited (Kagan, 1998). Furthermore, evaluations of intervention programs that emphasize emotional competencies indicate that training in emotional skills contributes to social adaptation (Greenberg, Kusché & Riggs, this volume).

Emotional intelligence gained popularity through Goleman's (1995) best-selling book. The idea captured educators' attention and contributed to the growing interest in social and emotional learning programs. In Goleman's writings, however, the concept was vastly expanded to include personality traits, social skills, and motivational and other factors. Other authors also have used the term to designate very broad conceptions of social and emotional adaptation.

To determine whether emotional intelligence is truly important, we need to distinguish it from other dimensions of psychological functioning to show that we are not rehashing old ideas with a new name (Brackett & Mayer, 2003). We therefore distinguish emotional intelligence, designating a set of skills for processing emotional information, as outlined above, from broader conceptions of social and emotional competence and adaptation (Mayer, Salovey, & Caruso, 2000). The skills subsumed by this definition of emotional intelligence are only a subset of the skills and qualities that SEL programs seek to address. Available evidence suggests that they are important, but further research is needed to determine to what extent they should be emphasized in programs of social and emotional learning.

In drawing implications from this type of research, we also need to keep in mind that although basic emotional skills may be important everywhere, the way that they are applied or expressed should vary according to culture and context. Particular coping strategies may be more appropriate in some contexts than others. Some people may control anger or anxiety quite well in some situations, but not in others.

Teaching Social and Emotional Skills

Teachers can enrich classroom instruction regardless of whether their schools adopt new curricula or endorse a given program of educational reform. Schoolwide changes may have far greater impact. Using appropriate teaching materials greatly facilitates teachers' work. Support from school administrators, parents, and colleagues makes it easier to implement changes. Nonetheless, teachers can start to address a broader range of competencies in their classrooms, even if changing educational practice on a broader scale takes a long time (e.g., Elias et al., 1997).

For example, teachers can use everyday situations that arise in the classroom, or in the schoolyard, as opportunities to promote a richer understanding of social and emotional issues. Conflicts and arguments may be particularly fruitful for modeling or practicing negotiation skills, perspective taking, and emotional regulation. Teachers can use literature or history classes, essays and art projects, or even sports, to discuss human nature, people's feelings, and emotional reactions. They can promote teamwork, group projects, and small discussion groups to help children learn to interact with others through experience. They can encourage children to express and discuss their emotions, listen to others, and respect other people's points of view. They can train children to breathe deeply, look at a problem from different angles, and think things through before taking action on a stressful situation.

This may be challenging. Teachers who are overwhelmed, with too many students or discipline problems, may be reluctant to take on new challenges. Some educators may feel less comfortable with social and emotional learning than others. Children's emotional reactions and coping habits may be deeply engraved and hard to change. It takes a lot of training and practice for children to develop new habits and skills. We should not expect quick changes.

Managing our emotions, and relating to others, are among the greatest challenges that we face in life. Helping children to face these challenges may not be easy, but it is essential that we try. There are no simple formulas to be applied to all children and circumstances. More than drilling a limited set of skills over and over again, we should strive to expand children's repertoire of skills and enhance their capacity to respond flexibly to the demands of the moment. Ideally, we would help our youth to relate to others by promoting a deeper appreciation of the complexity of human nature.

Conclusion

To prepare children for the challenges they are likely to face in a fast-changing society, we should broaden the range of competencies addressed in schools. There is evidence that SEL programs can promote children's social and emotional adaptation and bonding to school. There is also evidence that promoting a balanced mix of analytical, creative, and practical abilities may enhance children's interest in learning and school achievement. Integrating these two approaches may be a good way to help children become well-adjusted and productive adults.

There may be many ways of promoting positive youth development. We do not know exactly what components of different programs are most effective and for what purposes, groups, and contexts. We should avoid focusing public debate too much on issues of program content, as this may inadvertently undermine the higher goal of investing in quality education. In the end, investing in good schools, good teachers, and quality teacher training is likely to be more important than choosing between one quality program and another.

Future research will clarify the importance of specific social, emotional, and practical skills for adaptation over the life course. However, educators should not wait for research to clarify all questions and doubts. By adopting better curricula, or changing the way they teach, teachers can help improve children's lives. Given all the factors that impinge upon children's development, and the vast array of competencies that contribute to social and emotional adaptation, we should not expect to see dramatic changes from educational reform or intervention programs. In the long run, however, small changes can have tremendous impact.

References

Brackett, M. A., & Mayer, J. D. (in press). Convergent, discriminant, and incremental validity of competing measures of emotional intelligence. *Personality and Social Psychology Bulletin.*

Cantor, N., & Kihlstrom, J. F. (1987). *Personality and social intelligence.* Englewood Cliffs, NJ: Prentice-Hall.

Caplan, M., Weissberg, R. P., Grober, J. H., Sivo, P. J., Grady, K., & Jacoby, C. (1992). Social competence promotion with inner-city and suburban young adolescents: Effects on social adjustment and alcohol use. *Journal of Consulting and Clinical Psychology, 60,* 56-63.

Ciarrochi, J. V., Chan, A. Y. C., & Caputi, P. (2000). A critical evaluation of the emotional intelligence construct. *Personality and Individual Differences, 28,* 539-561.

Crick, N. R., & Dodge, K. A. (1994). A review and reformulation of social information-processing mechanisms in children's social adjustment. *Psychological Bulletin, 115,* 74-101.

Toward a Broader Education: Social, Emotional, & Practical Skills

Damásio, A. R. (1994). *Descartes' error: Emotion, reason, and the human brain.* New York: Putnam.

Davies, M., Stankov, L., & Roberts, R. D. (1998). Emotional intelligence: In search of an elusive construct. *Journal of Personality and Social Psychology, 75,* 989-1015.

Denham, S. A. (1998). *Emotional development in young children.* New York: Guilford Press.

Diener, E., & Lucas, R. E. (1999). Personality and subjective well-being. In D. Kahneman, E. Diener, & N. Schwarz (Eds.), *Well-being: The foundations of hedonic psychology* (pp. 213-229). New York: Russell Sage.

Eisenberg, N., Fabes, R. A., Guthrie, I. K., & Reiser, M. (2000). Dispositional emotionality and regulation: Their role in predicting quality of social functioning. *Journal of Personality and Social Psychology, 78,* 136-157.

Elias, M. J., Zins, J. E., Weissberg, R. P., Frey, K. S., Greenberg, M. T., Haynes, N. M., Kessler, R., Schwab-Stone, M. E., & Shriver, T. P. (1997). *Promoting social and emotional learning: Guidelines for educators.* Alexandria, VA: Association for Supervision and Curriculum Development.

Feldman, R. S., Philippot, P., & Custrini, R. J. (1991). Social competence and nonverbal behavior. In R. S. Feldman & B. Rime (Eds.), *Fundamentals of nonverbal behavior* (pp. 329-350). New York: Cambridge University Press.

Gardner, H. (1983/1993). *Frames of mind: The theory of multiple intelligences. 10th Anniversary Edition,* (original work published 1983). New York: Basic Books.

Goleman, D. (1995). Emotional intelligence. New York: Bantam Books.

Grigorenko, E. L., Guillermo, G., Jarvin, L., & Sternberg, R. J. (2001). *Toward a validation of aspects of the theory of successful intelligence.* Unpublished manuscript, Yale University.

Grigorenko, E. L., Jarvin, L., & Sternberg, R. J. (2002). School-based tests of the triarchic theory of intelligence: Three settings, three samples, three syllabi. *Contemporary Educational Psychology, 27,* 167-208.

Halberstadt, A. G., Denham, S. A., & Dunsmore, J. C. (2001). Affective social competence. *Social Development, 10,* 79-119.

Hall, J. A., & Bernieri, F. J. (2001). *Interpersonal sensitivity: Theory and measurement.* Mahwah, NJ: Erlbaum.

Hawkins, J. D., Catalano, R. F., Kosterman, R., Abbott, R., & Hill, K. G. (1999). Preventing adolescent health-risk behaviors by strengthening protection during childhood. *Archives of Pediatric & Adolescent Medicine, 153,* 226-334.

Herrnstein, R. J., & Murray, C. (1994). *The bell curve.* New York: Free Press.

Kagan, J. (1998). *Galen's prophecy.* Boulder, CO: Westview Press.

Kihlstrom, J. F., & Cantor, N. (2000). Social intelligence. In R. J. Sternberg (Ed.), Handbook of intelligence (2nd ed., pp. 359-379). New York: Cambridge University Press.

Kusché, C. A., & Greenberg, M. T. (2001). PATHS in your classroom: Promoting emotional literacy and alleviating emotional distress. In J. Cohen (Ed.), *Social emotional learning and the elementary school child: A guide for educators* (pp. 140-161). New York: Teachers College Press.

La Greca, A. M. (1993). Social skills training with children: Where do we go from here? *Journal of Clinical Child Psychology,* 22, 288-298.

Lopes, P. N., Nezlek, J., Schütz, A., Sellin, I., & Salovey, P. (2003). *Emotional intelligence and daily social interaction.* Manuscript submitted for publication.

Lopes, P. N., Salovey, P., & Beers, M. (2002). *Emotional and social networks.* Unpublished data, Yale University.

Lopes, P. N., Salovey, P., & Straus, R. (in press). Emotional intelligence, personality, and the perceived quality of social relationships. *Personality and Individual Differences.*

Mayer, J. D., Caruso, D. R., & Salovey, P. (1999). Emotional intelligence meets traditional standards for an intelligence. *Intelligence,* 27, 267-298.

Mayer, J. D., & Salovey, P. (1997). What is emotional intelligence? In P. Salovey & D. J. Sluyter (Eds.), *Emotional development and emotional intelligence: Implications for educators* (pp. 3-31). New York: Basic Books.

Mayer, J. D., Salovey, P., & Caruso, D. (2000). Models of emotional intelligence. In R. J. Sternberg (Ed.), *Handbook of human intelligence, 2ne Edition* (pp. 396-420). New York: Cambridge University Press.

Mayer, J. D., Salovey, P., & Caruso, D. (2001). *The Mayer, Salovey, and Caruso Emotional Intelligence Test (MSCEIT).* Toronto, ON: Multi-Health Systems, Inc.

Mayer, J. D., Salovey, P., Caruso, D., & Sitarenios, G. (2001). Emotional Intelligence as a standard intelligence. *Emotion,* 1, 232-242.

Payton, J. W., Graczyk, P. A., Wardlaw, D. M., Bloodworth, M.R., Tompsett, C. J., & Weissberg, R. P. (2000). Social and emotional learning: A framework for promoting mental health and reducing risk behavior in children and youth. *Journal of School Health,* 70, 179-185.

Rice, C. L. (1999). *A quantitative study of emotional intelligence and its impact on team performance.* Unpublished master's thesis, Pepperdine University, Malibu, CA.

Rubin, M. M. (1999). *Emotional intelligence and its role in mitigating aggression: A correlational study of the relationship between emotional intelligence and aggression in urban adolescents.* Unpublished dissertation, Immaculata College, Immaculata, PA.

Saarni, C. (1999). *Developing emotional competence.* New York: Guilford.

Salovey, P., & Mayer, J. D. (1990). Emotional intelligence. *Imagination, Cognition, and Personality,* 9, 185-211.

Salovey, P., Mayer, J. D., Caruso, D., & Lopes, P. N. (in press). Measuring emotional intelligence as a set of abilities with the MSCEIT. In S. J. Lopez & C. R. Snyder (Eds.), *Handbook of positive psychology assessment.* Washington, DC: American Psychological Association.

Salovey, P., & Sluyter, D. J. (Eds.) (1997). *Emotional development and emotional intelligence: Educational implications.* New York: Basic Books.

Sternberg, R. J. (1985). *The triarchic mind: A new theory of human intelligence.* New York: Penguin.

Sternberg, R. J. (1999a). Intelligence as developing expertise. *Contemporary Educational Psychology,* 24, 359-275.

Sternberg, R. J. (1999b). The theory of successful intelligence. *Review of General Psychology,* 3, 292-316.

Sternberg, R. J., Forsythe, G. B., Hedlund, J., Horvath, J. A., Wagner, R. K., Williams, W. M., Snook, S. A., & Grigorenko, E. L. (2000). *Practical intelligence in everyday life.* New York: Cambridge University Press.

Sternberg, R. J., & Grigorenko, E. L. (2000). *Teaching for successful intelligence: To increase student learning and achievement.* Arlington Heights, IL: SkyLight Professional Development.

Sternberg, R. J., Grigorenko, E. L., & Jarvin, L. (2001). Improving reading instruction: The triarchic model. *Educational Leadership,* 58, 48-52.

Sternberg, R. J., Torff, B., & Grigorenko, E. L. (1998). Teaching triarchically improves school achievement. *Journal of Educational Psychology,* 90, 374-384.

Trinidad, D. R., & Johnson, C. A. (2002). The association between emotional intelligence and early adolescent tobacco and alcohol use. *Personality and Individual Differences,* 32, 95-105.

Weissberg, R. P., & Greenberg, M. T. (1998). School and community competence-enhancement and prevention programs. In W. Damen (Series Ed.) & I. E. Sigel & K. A. Renninger (Vol. Eds.), *Handbook of child psychology: Vol. 4. Child psychology in practice* (5th edition; pp. 877-954). New York: Wiley.

Zins, J. E., Elias, M. J., Greenberg, M. T., & Weissberg, R. P. (2000). Promoting social and emotional competence in children. In K. M. Minke & G. C. Bear (Eds.), *Preventing school problems -- promoting school success: Strategies and programs that work* (pp. 71-99). Washington, DC: National Association of School Psychologists.

Reprinted with permission of Lawrence Erlbaum, Associates.
Caruso, D.R., Mayer, J.D., Salovey, P. (2003). *Emotional intelligence and emotional leadership.* In R.E. Riggio and S.E. Murphy (eds.), Multiple intelligences and leadership (pp. 55-73). Mahway, NJ: Erlbaum.

Emotional Intelligence and Emotional Leadership

David R. Caruso, Work-Life Strategies
Peter Salovey, Yale University
John D. Mayer, State University of New York

Author Notes

We would like to thank Alan Harris, President of Harris-McCully Associates, Inc. where David Caruso is Vice President of Assessment. In that role, he has been given the opportunity of working with many emotionally intelligent and unintelligent senior executives. We are grateful to Neal Ashkanasy, Sigal Barsade and Cheryl Rice for providing us with their work on emotional intelligence and leadership.

Introducing Models of Emotional Intelligence

Phil Watkins[1] was the President of a division of a large paper brokerage firm. A paper broker buys paper from a paper mill, and then sells it to a manufacturer or printer. It's a risky business, with paper-thin margins, as it were, but it can also be a profitable one. The paper business is also one of the last vestiges of old-fashioned salesmanship, the kind where expense accounts sometimes include customer entertainment at "gentleman's clubs," complete with a huge bar tab. Watkins had been in the business for almost 20 years and was thinking about getting out. He felt that he didn't fit in. "I'm not a sales guy, I'm not a financial guy, I just fell into this business when I was a kid," he once said.

Watkins did not seem to fit the mold. For one thing, he believed that his company could do good business by being tough, but ethical in their dealings with customers and suppliers. In terms of personal interactions, Watkins sometimes was blindsided by others and their behavior. As a result, he was often taken advantage of by co-workers. He bent over backwards to rescue employees, one of whom was siphoning business to his personal account, and another who complained that he needed his bonus just to meet his house payments, but who at the same time, wasn't even making his minimum sales commission. The CEO was just as bad, and Watkins had to manage his own business, as well as take care of the CEO and clean up after him. The business in general was profitable, so Watkins was not in danger of losing his job.

Is Watkins an effective leader? By most objective financial yardsticks, the answer is certainly "yes". By some subjective ratings of effectiveness, the answer would be mixed. Colleagues and employees enjoyed working with him, but Watkins had several serious, unresolved management issues. In addition, Watkins was not happy in his role. He had the potential to be an effective leader, but he had not gotten there, and perhaps, never would. In this chapter we attempt to discover the reasons for Watkins' successes and difficulties by addressing the role of emotional intelligence in leadership effectiveness.

There are two broad approaches to emotional intelligence: an ability approach (that views emotional intelligence as a set of cognitive abilities) and a mixed approach (that combines abilities and a broad range of personality traits). We examine each of these models, and apply the models to our analysis of Watkins. (For further discussion of competing models of emotional intelligence, see Mayer, Salovey, & Caruso, 2000.)

Ability Model of Emotional Intelligence

Is Watkins emotionally intelligent if we examine his leadership skills using an ability model? According to Mayer and Salovey's (1997) four-branch model of emotional intelligence, emotional intelligence is the ability to perceive emotions, to access and generate emotions to assist thought, to understand emotions and emotional knowledge, and to regulate emotions reflectively to promote emotional and intellectual growth. This revised model was based upon the first sustained academic development of the concept (Mayer, DiPaolo, & Salovey, 1990; Salovey & Mayer, 1990). (Table 1 presents an analysis of Watkins on the four branches from Mayer and Salovey's ability model [1997], and on all 25 competencies drawn from a mixed model of emotional intelligence [Goleman, 1998a]).

The first branch of the ability model is *Identifying Emotions.* This branch includes a number of skills, such as the ability to identify feelings, to express emotions accurately, and to differentiate between real and phony emotional expressions. Is Watkins good at Identifying Emotions?[2] Watkins is capable of accurately identifying and expressing emotion, as he often makes insightful observations about his staff. He knows how others are feeling, and he can read the emotions of his staff, customers and suppliers with great accuracy. He does this, in part, by carefully attending to emotions. His recognition of his own emotions was sometimes inaccurate, as he would often claim to be feeling calm toward an employee when it was obvious to everyone else that he was angry with that person. Watkins appears to be skilled in some areas of Identifying Emotions.

The second branch of the ability model is *Using Emotions*. Using Emotions includes the ability to use emotions to redirect attention to important events, to generate emotions that facilitate decision making, to use mood swings as a means to consider multiple points of view, and to use different emotions to encourage different approaches to problem solving (for instance, to use a happy mood to assist in generating creative, new ideas). We know that Watkins motivates others and is fairly innovative. He harnesses certain moods and uses them to come up with new ideas. Watkins was known to be able to generate great excitement during sales conferences, and grab the attention of his senior staff at weekly staff meetings. Watkins' ability to Use Emotions is high.

The third branch is *Understanding Emotions*. This is the ability to understand complex emotions and emotional "chains", how emotions transition from one stage to another, the ability to recognize the causes of emotions, and the ability to understand relationships among emotions. Watkins' ability to Understand Emotions is not as high as is his ability to Identify or Use Emotions. Watkins appears to be somewhat blind to the true nature of some of his employees. This, if anything, was Watkins' fatal flaw: He often misunderstood what others' feelings would lead to. He did not seem to understand that the salesman who missed his quota would get angry with Watkins for setting his quota too high in the first place. This was not a problem of accurate assessment of emotions. Rather, it was a problem of being naïve and too trusting, perhaps. Watkins did not dig deep enough into his people, and he was often unable to determine how they would react. The less scrupulous employees played off of Watkins' naiveté about people and took advantage of him and the company.

The fourth branch of the ability model is *Managing Emotions*. Managing Emotions includes the ability to stay aware of one's emotions, even those that are unpleasant, the ability to determine whether an emotion is clear or typical, and the ability to solve emotion-laden problems without necessarily suppressing negative emotions. Watkins manages emotions fairly effectively: He does not react blindly but integrates his emotions into his actions. Watkins assists his people in a constructive way when they are upset about a deal gone bad. Usually, when things go wrong, Watkins doesn't "think about it tomorrow," like Scarlett O'Hara, instead, he deals with the situation immediately for maximal effectiveness. But Watkins sometimes avoids confrontations that involve anger. This style causes him to live with pent-up frustration, and key people in his organization never get the feedback they need to do their jobs well.

What does the ability approach to emotional intelligence tell us about Watkins' leadership? We see that Watkins is an effective leader because he is able to harness his emotions to build a team, motivate his staff, and integrate his emotions into his

Table 1:
Evaluation of Phil Watkins on Ability and Mixed Models of Emotional Intelligence

Ability Model Of Emotional Intelligence

Ability	Level	Analysis
Perceiving Identify emotions in thoughts Identify emotions in other people Express emotions accurately Discriminate between accurate and inaccurate feelings	High	He attended to emotions, but especially those of his staff. Sometimes, he misread his own emotions.
Using Prioritize thinking by directing attention Generate emotions to assist judgment Mood swings change perspective Emotional states encourage problem solving	High	Very able to generate and use emotions to think creatively and make decisions.
Understanding Label and recognize relations among emotions Interpret meanings emotion convey Understand complex feelings Recognize emotional transitions	Average	Although he could understand of the basics of emotions, he often misunderstood people's motives
Managing Stay open to feelings Engage/detach from an emotion Reflectively monitor emotions	High/ Average	He was a master at managing emotions. Never defensive or closed off, he could put aside the blinding passions and make informed decisions, expect when angry.

...continued on next page...

Emotional Intelligence and Emotional Leadership

Mixed Model of Emotional Intelligence

Competency	Level	Analysis
Self-Awareness		
Emotional awareness	High	He had a rich, inner life, although some of his
Accurate self-assessment	Average	self-perceptions were inaccurate, and was
Self-confidence	Low	confident in only a few areas.
Self-Regulation		
Self control	Average	He was a man of his word, and promoted
Trustworthiness	Very High	innovation in the workplace. However, he
Conscientiousness	High	was not especially adaptable, being set
Adaptability	Average	in some of his ways.
Innovation	High	
Motivation		
Achievement	Low	He worked hard when he was at the office
Commitment	Low	but he was not ambitious, and in fact, was
Initiative	High	looking for an exit strategy. He did enjoy
Optimism	High	generating enthusiasm and new ideas.
Empathy		
Understanding others	Low	He misread people while at the same time
Developing others	High	believing in his people's potential.
Service orientation	High	He cared about customer's needs, was
Diversity	Average	happy working in a white-male environment
Political awareness	Low	but was politically naïve.
Social Skills		
Influence	High	He was unaware of just how good he was.
Communication	High	He avoided direct conflict, but managed
Conflict management	Average	situations effectively.
Leadership	High	Watkins wanted things to change in the
Change catalyst	High	organization and was motivated to
Building bonds	High	build a sense of team.
Collaboration/cooperation	High	
Team capabilities	High	

planning and decision making. Frustration and anger were also managing him, and this caused him to be less effective, and much less happy, in his role. Watkins' career dissatisfaction may stem from his lack of understanding the motives of his staff, and the unpleasant performance surprises this entails. Viewing Watkins in this way, we can conclude that he has a few obstacles to becoming a highly effective leader, but the seeds of excellence are also apparent in his emotional intelligence profile. The ability model is deep and focused on emotion. Although it was not intended as a theory of leadership, it has much to offer leadership theory. Its value lies in the new insights it offers into the competencies of leadership which have not previously been examined.

Mixed Model of Emotional Intelligence

Mixed models of emotional intelligence are based upon the ability model (see, for instance, Goleman, 1995) but add other psychological attributes. Goleman's initial approach to emotional intelligence included five components: knowing one's emotions; managing emotions; motivating yourself; recognizing emotions in other people; and, handling relationships (largely derived from Salovey and Mayer, 1990). There are other mixed models of emotional intelligence as well, most notably, that of Bar-On (Bar-On, 1997). Bar-On's model includes five broad categories: intrapersonal skills, interpersonal skills, adaptability, stress management, and general mood.

Goleman's ideas on emotional intelligence (1998a) were expanded to include 25 competencies grouped into the same, five basic categories (although the labels changed): Self-Awareness (emotional awareness, accurate self-assessment, self-confidence); Self-Regulation (self control, trustworthiness, conscientiousness, adaptability, innovation); Motivation (achievement, commitment, initiative, optimism); Empathy (understanding others, developing others, service orientation, diversity, political awareness); and Social Skills (influence, communication, conflict management, leadership, change catalyst, building bonds, collaboration/ cooperation, team capabilities). In a way, he has combined in the same model both emotional abilities and the product of those abilities.

According to Goleman (1998a), to be emotionally intelligent, Watkins would have to have many of these 25 competencies, presumably all at a high, or high enough, level. We'll examine a few of these. Watkins has a rich, inner life and is emotionally self-aware (the matching competency is Emotional Awareness). However, his self-perceptions were sometimes inaccurate (Accurate Self-assessment), and he was confident in just a few areas of his work life (either Accurate Self-assessment or Self-confidence). Watkins was a trusting and trustworthy leader, and colleagues could always count on him (Trustworthiness). While he was president of the division, he was not particularly ambitious (Achievement). He worked hard (Conscientiousness), but lacked the motivation to go to the next level, and retirement beckoned (Commitment). Part of Watkins' effectiveness was due to his high level of optimism (Optimism), something that he was not aware of, but that his staff perceived. He misread people and their motives much of the time (Understanding Others), but he believed in his people and tried to get them to do their best (Developing Others). He wanted to serve his customers and meet their needs (Service Orientation). Politically, Watkins was very naïve, and didn't seem to know how things really worked (Political Awareness). Watkins was a communicator (Influence, or Communication), and was invested in change (Change Agent, or Innovation). He spent a lot of time and energy in forming friendly relationships with his staff (Building Bonds), and was reasonably good at managing many types of emotional situations (Self-Control, or Understanding Others).

What does this mixed approach to emotional intelligence tell us about Watkins? We see Watkins as a complex individual, and understand some of the reasons for his effectiveness. But the bottom line is unclear, because the list is so long. This is a wonderful list of things for a leader to aspire to, but where should one even begin? This analysis would likely predict that Watkins would fail in his role as a leader, or that he would not be a star performer. We will revisit Watkins at the conclusion of this chapter, and discover whether he made it or not.

Evaluating Models of Emotional Intelligence

Let us consider the case study and the two approaches to emotional intelligence in greater detail.

The Strengths of the Ability Model

The ability model of emotional intelligence is focused on how emotions can facilitate thinking and adaptive behavior. It has to do with how people think, decide, plan and create. Second, the ability model of emotional intelligence is skill based. Emotional Intelligence is considered a special class of mental attributes, either cognitive capacities parallel but separate from traits, (e.g., McCrae & Costa, 1996), or as a distinct class of traits referred to as ability or cognitive traits (e.g., Cattell & Warburton, 1967, p. 10; Mayer, 1995, pp. 859-864). The model does not focus on personality traits, or dispositions, per se, except as a product of having these underlying skills. Similarly, emotional intelligence conceived of as an ability can be measured using objective, ability-based measures. Third, the ability model has been empirically validated. The four branches of emotional intelligence have been shown to be separable, but also related to a single construct (Mayer, Caruso, & Salovey, 1999). Most importantly, the ability model of emotional intelligence has utility in that it offers new insights to our understanding and prediction of effective leadership.

The Limitations of the Ability Model

The ability model, as presented in its academic context, is not a complete theory of workplace management (and does not claim to be). It is a model of a type of intelligence, and therefore, it is intended to co-exist with, supplement, and clarify existing models of leadership – not replace them. Second, although data do support the model itself, and there are examples of what it predicts, the ability model of emotional intelligence is too new to have extensive empirical data in support of its predictive validity. Third, because of the depth of the model (and because it does not include products of emotional intelligence as part of the model), it is not likely to achieve the level of prediction that popular models of emotional intelligence boast, although we believe it will make significant contributions to our understanding of leadership.

The Strengths of the Mixed Model

There are several strengths of the mixed model and several reasons for its popularity. First, the mixed model includes a multitude of traits, and it is grand in its scope. Many traits have face validity as well: Few would argue that leadership, encouraging diversity, or team capabilities, for instance, are not important skills in the workplace. Second, the list of traits in the mixed model resonates with leaders, as well as human resource (HR) professionals. The model covers most of the present-day thinking on effectiveness, including traits such as service orientation, diversity, political awareness, and being a change catalyst. It is an amalgamation of many of the standard competency models put together by HR professionals every day. Third, the model claims to have tremendous predictive validity, accounting for up to 80% of the variance in life outcomes (Goleman, 1995).

The Limitations of the Mixed Model

It appears that the traits included in mixed models are essentially captured by the five-factor model of personality (Digman, 1990) as well as much of the existing trait research on leadership (see, for instance, Hogan, Curphy, & Hogan, 1994). For instance, Yukl's (1981) 14 leadership behaviors are remarkably similar to mixed models of emotional intelligence: planning and organizing, clarifying, informing, monitoring, consulting, recognizing, networking, rewarding, mentoring, delegating, team building and conflict resolution, problem solving, supporting, and motivating.

Another difficulty is that Goleman's revised (1998 a) approach appears to be unclear in its grouping of competencies. For instance, the Empathy category includes Service Orientation, Diversity and Political Awareness. In addition, the emotional competencies include not just traits or skills, but outcomes. Building bonds, Commitment, or Political Awareness, for instance, appear to be more the product of emotional intelligence, as opposed to a skill or a trait. Similarly, it is difficult to determine how some traits differ from one another, such as Influence and Communication.

Some researchers (i.e., Davies, Stankov, & Roberts, 1998) believe that emotional intelligence defined as a mixed model does not exist as a construct separable from other aspects of personality. These authors collected data on a diverse set of instruments purporting to measure emotional intelligence. They based their approach on both an early scientific definition of emotional intelligence (Salovey & Mayer, 1990) and Goleman's (1995) approach, as well as a mixture of early self-report and ability measures. They concluded that "little remains of emotional intelligence", as the measures were either unreliable or failed to load on non-personality trait factors. That is, measures of emotional intelligence drawn from the mixed model were better described using standard personality measures and traits. The one exception to this conclusion was for the early ability scales that came to make up one of our current scales (emotional perception).

How Should Emotional Intelligence Be Defined?

A mixed model approach to emotional intelligence offers little that is new to leadership theorists and practitioners. As noted above, existing theories of leadership and personality models already describe the traits included in the mixed approach. An ability model of emotional intelligence offers something new: a means to understand how leaders manage their own emotions, and that of others, to get results. We next examine the relationship of emotional intelligence to leadership functions.

Emotional Intelligence and Theories of Leadership

What Leaders Do

If we wish to examine leadership - emotional intelligence relationships, then we must first understand what it is that leaders do. We generally blur the distinction between management and leadership, although there are critical differences (e.g., Hersey & Blanchard, 1988; Kotter, 1990). Management is focused on specific functions or activities: planning, motivating staff, decision making, facilitating creative thinking, and social effectiveness (Yukl, Wall, & Lepsinger, 1990). Leadership is the influencing of others in order to achieve a goal. Emotional intelligence can facilitate these functions, but the successful leader will require more than just emotional intelligence in order to carry these out. We next examine ways in which emotional intelligence can assist these leadership functions.

Why Leaders Need to Be Able to Identify Emotions

The ability to identify emotions allows leaders to be aware of their own feelings and emotions. This ability also allows the leader to accurately identify the emotions of the group and of individual followers, to express emotions accurately, and to differentiate between honest and phony emotional expressions.

Greater self-awareness does indeed influence managerial performance. High-performing managers' self-ratings were more congruent with their direct reports' ratings than were average-performing managers (Church, 1997). Manager self-awareness (MSA) was viewed in this study as leading to greater management performance, and self-monitoring was positively related to MSA.

Why Leaders Need to be Able to Use Emotions

Using Emotions allows leaders to understand and motivate others by making emotions available, engage in multiple perspective taking that can help planning, and to engage in activities facilitated by emotions (e.g., detail work when feeling neutral or down, or creative brainstorming activities when feeling happy). Leaders high on Using Emotions may be able to encourage open-minded decision making, planning, and idea generation by considering multiple points of view. Leaders can generate enthusiasm for a project and energize, direct, and motivate the group, and themselves.

That leadership comprises, in part, the utilization of emotions, then emotional intelligence may indeed be an important component of effective leadership. In fact,

Emotional Intelligence and Emotional Leadership

leadership has been defined along these lines: "Leadership, which embraces the emotional side of directing organizations, pumps life and meaning into management structures, bringing them to full life" (Barach & Eckhardt, 1996, p. 4). Certain forms of effective leadership may also involve the spreading of emotions among the group, a phenomenon known as emotional contagion (Barsade & Gibson, 1998). *Emotional contagion* can enhance group cooperation and reduce group conflict (Barsade, 1999). In addition, positive affect, and teams with homogenous positive affect, has a beneficial influence on team relationships (Barsade, et al., 1999).

Similarly, effective leadership directly involves the use of emotion, often through symbolic management. In symbolic management, the manager uses symbols – stories, rituals, myths, fables – to rouse and motivate staff to guide them toward achievement of a shared vision. Symbolic management depends on an emotional or intuitive, "buy-in" from the followers: "Symbolic management is effective because it draws on the qualities of the heart and of the head - and, at times, it entirely bypasses the latter for the former" (Ashforth & Humphreys, 1995, p. 111).

Why Leaders Need to be Able to Understand Emotions

Understanding Emotions includes the ability to recognize relationships between emotions, determine the meaning that emotions convey, understand complex feelings, and to recognize how emotions change from one state to another. Understanding Emotions is the ability that provides a leader with the information on what makes people tick. This is the ability that also provides the leader with an understanding of other people's points of view. When trait-based, and other, leadership models talk about the human aspect of leadership, they often refer to social skills, people skills, or human relationship skills without clearly defining them. They talk about managing people, communication, influence and other skills, but often, these terms are not operationalized to a sufficient enough extent to measure them and study them closely.

There are, of course, exceptions, but we believe that the skills of emotional intelligence might provide some insight into these heretofore slippery skills of leadership. For example, Hersey and Blanchard (1988) list the three skills of a manager as consisting of technical, human and conceptual. They define human skills as the "ability and judgment in working with and through people, including an understanding of motivation and an application of effective leadership" (p. 7). They cite an American Management Association study that claimed that the ability to "get along with people" was "more vital than intelligence, decisiveness, knowledge, or job skills" (p. 8).

Communication has been studied as a factor in successful leadership. Research on leader-member exchange has suggested that the relationship between a leader and his or her subordinates is predictive of important outcomes (Gerstner & Day, 1997). Emotional intelligence may enhance our understanding of such exchanges.

Why Leaders Need to be Able to Manage Emotions

Managing Emotions allows leaders to handle the stress of two quarters of disappointing sales, or not to fear a new competitive product introduction so that the disappointment or fear either paralyzes them or causes them to make poor decisions. An emotionally intelligent response to problem solving is viewed as being emotion-focused, wherein you use the emotions created by the situation to diagnose and solve the underlying problem (Mayer & Salovey, 1993). For instance, Weiss and Cropanzano (1996) indicate that a more effective coping strategy deals directly with the emotions while a less effective coping strategy deals with the emotion itself, rather than its causes, through techniques such as denial.[3] These authors add that problem-focused coping is usually the more productive alternative, but that there are times when a denial strategy may be a better way to get a specific task accomplished, at least in the short run, a position with which we agree.

One of the goals of effective leadership is to create and enhance individual and group relationships. Relationship-formation has been studied by Kahn (1993) who views work relationships as emotional attachments. These attachments bind workers to each other, with these attachments created in a caregiving-care receiving environment. Kahn discusses eight dimensions of caregiving that form anchoring relationships at work, such as empathy, support, compassion, and consistency. Emotions, and emotional skills, play an integral role in the everyday life of leaders.

George (1995) suggests that managerial mood, specifically positive mood, increases employee work performance. It is likely that emotional intelligence, specifically the ability to regulate one's own and other emotions, is one of the skills that allow leaders to maintain such beneficial moods. Similarly, charisma, the regulation of the emotions of team members by its leader (Friedman, Riggio & Casella, 1988; Wasielewski, 1985), appears to require the ability to enhance pleasant emotions and de-emphasize unpleasant emotions in others. Charismatic leadership, a form of transformational leadership (Bass, 1985, 1997; Bass, Avolio, & Goodheim, 1987), may also have its roots in Managing Emotions (Ashkanasy & Tse, 1998).

Emotional Intelligence and Leadership Traits

In order to understand better how this global ability – emotional intelligence – plays a role in effective leadership, we will also examine how it relates to other traits believed to be important to leadership. Trait models of leadership examine specific personality attributes thought to underlie leadership (e.g., Bass, 1985, 1997; Fiedler, 1967; Hogan, Curphy, & Hogan, 1994; Sternberg, 1997; Stogdill, 1974). Hundreds of traits have been examined, such as intelligence, extroversion, dominance, masculinity, adjustment (Lord et al., 1986); drive, motivation, honesty, self-confidence, cognitive ability, knowledge of the business (Kirkpatrick & Locke, 1991); self-confidence, sociability, ambition, perseverance, and height (Porter, Lawler, & Hackman, 1975).

In a comprehensive review of leadership traits (Bass, 1981), three groups of traits were listed as being contributors to leadership effectiveness: intelligence (such as judgment, knowledge, decisiveness); personality (adaptability, alertness, creativity, personal integrity, self-confidence, emotional control, independence), and abilities (cooperativeness, popularity, sociability, social participation, tact). In fact, this comprehensive trait model appears to have a great deal of overlap with Goleman's (1998a) mixed approach.

More recently, Hogan (Hogan, Curphy, & Hogan, 1994) reviewed the extensive literature on leadership traits and concluded that the data could best be understood using the Big Five approach to personality. According to their analysis, leaders are high in surgency (dominance and sociability), emotional stability, and conscientiousness, as well as intellectance (or Openness). Hogan recommends selecting personality predictors based on job analyses and that the personality traits should be chosen from a select group of traits. He further believes that leaders should be screened for "dark side" traits using criteria from the DSM (Axis II personality disorders such as Narcissistic or Borderline Personality Disorder) and observer ratings. Hogan notes that personality traits "often lead to correlations in the .20 to .40 range; observer's ratings lead to correlations in the .30 to .60 range." (p. 501) for leadership potential.

Emotional intelligence, from an ability perspective, offers a distinctive and unique approach to an understanding of leadership, and supplements such a list of traits. Emotional intelligence may be a new trait to consider, along with these other central traits that predict leadership excellence. Emotional intelligence may also provide a means to better operationalize these traits.

Applying Emotional Intelligence To Leaders: How Ability Models of Emotional Intelligence Can Assist Leadership Practitioners and Researchers

We believe that an ability-based model of emotional intelligence provides HR professionals with the conceptual approach and the specific tools they need to enhance organization effectiveness. Although leaders and senior executives are often loathe to discuss soft skills, and reject ambiguous claims and terms regarding people skills or personality traits, they may be more likely to embrace an ability-based approach to leadership. In this section, we discuss ways in which emotional intelligence theory can help HR professionals and leadership researchers to develop, test, and utilize skill-based models of leadership.

Measurement

Ability-based models of emotional intelligence require performance measures to assess emotional intelligence. That is, if emotional intelligence is conceptualized as a set of skills or abilities, then it is imperative to measure emotional intelligence using ability-based, or performance, measures rather than self-report measures. The data indicate that emotional intelligence – conceived of as an *ability* – can be reliably measured, and has divergent and convergent validity (see, for instance, Mayer, DiPaolo, & Salovey, 1990; Mayer & Geher, 1996; Mayer, Caruso, & Salovey, 1999).

The Multifactor Emotional Intelligence Scale (MEIS) is an ability-based test (Mayer, Salovey, & Caruso, 1997).[4] Initial research with these scales suggests that they are internally consistent, have adequate content validity and construct validity. The scales have interesting relationships with important real-life criteria, such as how one was parented and life style behaviors (Mayer, Caruso, & Salovey, 1999).

Ability measures of emotional intelligence directly measure emotional skills. For instance, on one subtest of the MEIS that measures Identifying Emotions, the test taker views a face and then reports the amount of specific emotional content in it using a five-point scale. A subtest that measures Managing Emotions presents the test taker with an emotional problem, such as how to cheer up a sad person, and asks the test taker to rate the effectiveness of various alternatives (such as "eating a big meal" or "taking a walk alone").

Using the MEIS in Team Leadership Research

Rice (1999) suggests that emotional intelligence plays a role in effective team leadership and team performance, but that it does not play a role in all aspects of such performance. These results, although preliminary, provide a useful model for leadership researchers interested in emotional intelligence.

Rice administered a short form of the MEIS to 164 people (159 of whom were women), in 26 teams, led by 11 team leaders. The teams were part of a processing facility at a large insurance company. The two department managers of these teams rated the team leaders and each team on six variables: customer service, accuracy of claims processing, productivity, commitment to continuous improvement, team leader overall performance, and team overall performance. Department managers then ranked the 11 leaders and 26 teams in terms of their overall effectiveness. An emotional intelligence score was computed for each of the 11 leaders, and an average team emotional intelligence score was also computed.[5]

Although team emotional intelligence did not significantly correlate with the department manager's rankings, there was a significant relationship between customer service and team emotional intelligence ($r = .46$). There was also a significant relationship between the emotional intelligence of the team and the manager-ranked effectiveness of the team leader ($r = .34$). Lastly, the team leader's emotional intelligence correlated .54 with the manager's ranking of the team leader's effectiveness.

This study, the first of its kind using an ability approach to emotional intelligence, indicates that emotional intelligence plays a role in team performance, but that the role is a complex one.

Competency Models

We believe that competency models of leadership, and specific careers, should address the role of emotional intelligence. However, emotional intelligence is not always an important component of leadership, nor is it always a key factor for many different careers.

Emotional Intelligence and Emotional Leadership

Competency models of leadership, when addressing the role of emotional intelligence, must explicitly (a) analyze the nature of the leadership position; (b) state the model of emotional intelligence being employed; (c) list the specific emotional skills included in the competency model; and, (d) demonstrate that the emotional skills are relevant to a critical aspect of the leadership position. It will no longer suffice to say that a leadership position requires a high level of emotional intelligence: one must specify the competencies or skills.

Selection

Should emotional intelligence be used to select leaders? In some ways, it already is, through the use of behavioral interviewing, and by judging leadership candidates as to whether they are competent to lead teams and organizations. However, we feel that ability-based measures of emotional intelligence may add to the selection process in a unique way, with a unique contribution to decision making. Assessment of emotional intelligence will need to be tied tightly to the competency model or job analysis for a specific position, which in turn, will explicitly list the specific emotional intelligence skills.

Senior executives are often loathe to submit to psychological assessment, and many are uncomfortable discussing their inner emotional lives. They feel that their privacy is being invaded, and that the questions have little to do with the job itself[6]. We don't expect that senior executives will embrace emotional intelligence testing as part of pre-employment screening, but we have found that they have a greater acceptance of emotional intelligence tests than they do other measures (e.g., personality inventories). For instance, a sub-scale of the MEIS and MSCEIT requires the examinee to indicate the presence or absence of a set of emotions in photos of people. Certainly, most senior executives will realize that the ability to "read" people is an important management skill, and will be more likely to accept the use of such an assessment tool.

Gender

The role of gender in leadership selection and development should include a discussion of emotional intelligence. Our data indicate that women score somewhat higher on measures of emotional intelligence than do men (Mayer, Caruso, & Salovey, 1999; Mayer & Geher, 1996). Extensive reviews of the data on leadership and gender indicate that women leaders are devalued in comparison to their male counterparts, but especially when women employ a stereotypical male leadership style, namely an autocratic as opposed to democratic, style (Eagly, Makhijani, & Klonsky, 1992). If emotional intelligence plays a role in effective leadership, and if women, as a group, are higher in emotional intelligence than are men, then we need to realize that women possess a critical leadership skill. Emotional intelligence, conceived of as an ability, also allows us to get away from "soft" or stereotypically feminine ways of describing leaders who are good with people and reason well with and about emotions. We do not need to steer clear of discussions of emotional skills in the workplace for fear that such discussions will center on "touchy-feely" skills. Emotionally intelligent female leaders can be viewed as being more intelligent than they are "emotional", and we need to consider the skills of emotional intelligence as objective, hard skills.

Training and Development

Can emotional intelligence be taught? Mixed models of emotional intelligence posit that these are emotional competencies, and as such, can be learned, although little support is offered. In fact, if we look at the literature on emotional stability, while techniques to reduce anxiety and depression certainly exist, one has to wonder whether this, and other traits, can be learned or trained easily.

We prefer to speak of teaching emotional knowledge and skills, and we believe that people can acquire emotional knowledge and emotional skills. For instance, it is relatively straightforward to teach an executive how to recognize emotional signals in others, especially non-verbal emotional signals. Executive coaching programs are designed to enhance managers' emotional and social skills. Anecdotal evidence from executive coaching programs indicates that emotional knowledge can be taught, and that doing so sometimes can have dramatic impact on a leader and an organization. These results also suggest that emotional intelligence is important in leadership effectiveness. For the most part, effective coaching programs will combine formal instruction in emotions, as well as hands-on instruction through the use of role playing and similar methods.

Keeping Things in Perspective

Emotional intelligence, like a winning smile, helps. The lack of emotional intelligence does not always spell doom and disaster. Recently, one of the authors was involved in an executive coaching case in which a department head was asked to work on her interpersonal skills. She would frequently engage in very inappropriate behavior (she dealt with very tough personalities, and could curse fluently in four languages), to the point where turn-over in her area, production and distribution, was much higher than in any other department in the company. Exit interviews uniformly blamed her leadership style as the reason the employee was quitting. Coaching included detailed career assessment (including the MEIS), which indicated that the production manager lacked even the basic skills of emotional intelligence. Her awareness of her own, and others', emotions was almost nil. She was moody and unable to generate enthusiasm or interest in her employees. She did not understand why employees would get upset with her. She seemed unable to manage her emotions, often selecting the most ineffectual of responses to handle emotional situations.

Yet, her employer will not fire her, nor will she be demoted. The reason is simple: she gets things done, and she accomplishes a mission-critical task for her company. Although she burns through lower-level employees, she, and her boss, view these employees as expendable resources. Certainly, if she could bolster her emotional skills, she would be a more effective leader, the company would save money and production would run more efficiently. But she, and they, are willing to make this trade-off.

If she does not have emotional intelligence, she does possess a quality that is critical to her success: She knows the ropes. Her tacit knowledge is exceedingly high, and this knowledge is her power, providing her with the means to do her job, and achieve her goals. Indeed, Wagner and Sternberg (1985) examined the importance of practical intelligence in management effectiveness, and found that knowledge about how to manage your career and yourself in practical contexts is an important correlate of job performance.

Many other skills are required to be an effective leader. For instance, the management skills of the next generation of leaders have been hypothesized to include five components (Allred, Snow, & Miles, 1996). These components are a knowledge-based technical specialty (such as accounting or chemistry); cross-functional and international experience; collaborative leadership (leading a project team or being a team member); self-management skills (such as career planning and continuous learning); and, personal traits (which include flexibility, integrity, and trustworthiness). Emotional intelligence plays a role in some of these areas, of course, but not in all areas. Therefore, we urge leadership researchers and practitioners to include other skills in their model, including intellectual ability, practical intelligence, tacit knowledge, and functional skills[8].

Conclusions

We opened this chapter with the story of the reluctant leader, Phil Watkins. There is more to this story. Watkins participated in an in-depth, one-on-one, executive coaching program. As part of the program, he took the MEIS, the ability test of emotional intelligence. His results were intriguing: He scored above the 90th percentile on most of the subtests. However, he was low on a few subtests. One was Perspectives, a measure of the ability to understand emotions to reason about people. Watkins sometimes was blindsided by others and their behavior, and as a result, he sometimes was taken advantage of by coworkers. He was also lower on one subtest of Managing Emotions. Watkins' anger and frustration often greatly interfered with his decision making. His coaching focused on learning to understand other people better, and to form accurate judgments about his coworkers, even though he was their colleague, and in some cases, their friend. Watkins was also assisted in not repressing his negative emotions, but instead, utilizing them to approach his staff and provide them with negative, but constructive feedback. Much of the coaching involved working through the mechanics of staff interactions, and getting Watkins to develop and practice new emotion-management behaviors. Watkins was able to develop his ability in these areas and to grow more comfortable with his role. Within one year, Watkins ousted the CEO, who was believed to be engaging in a host of unethical business practices. Profits were off significantly as well when Watkins took the reigns. Although he bent over backwards to rescue a few key employees, he grew to realize that they would not change, and would, in one case, continue to siphon off business. Watkins made several personnel changes, revised sales compensation, and instituted stricter financial controls. By the following year, the company posted greatly improved financial results – gross revenue was lower, but profit margins and the bottom line were vastly improved. Just as striking, in a company-wide climate survey, employees rated the company much higher than average, and were generally very satisfied with their work. A multirater assessment of Watkins resulted in well above-average ratings on 20 of the 21 individual leadership scales (only the Thrifty scale was below average, meaning that Watkins was somewhat extravagant). He was seen as caring, credible, persuasive and enterprising. Just as important, Watkins' own feelings about his work had a dramatic turn-around: He grew to love his job. In Watkins' case, emotional intelligence did make a difference, and diagnosis and coaching tied to an ability model had significant, positive results.

We believe that emotional intelligence is an important theoretical concept that can contribute positively to the literature on leadership. We have stated a clear preference for an ability model, but mixed models are very appealing. Such models have excited the imagination of the public at large and human resources professionals in particular. These models have given new respectability to the discussion of emotions in the workplace, and in that way, they have proven to be of immense value.

Such enthusiasm is important, because leaders of today are still being chosen for their functional expertise.[9] If leaders do lack emotional intelligence, they may be unmoved by calls for greater understanding of emotions in the workplace. We suggest that HR practitioners and leadership researchers focus on the ability model because it offers a unique and valuable perspective on leadership. The ability approach will also avoid the problem of the CEO realizing that they are footing the bill – and sometimes a large bill – for selection and training that still talks about "people skills". However, the mere mention that emotions can be intelligent may grab the attention of bottom-line oriented, technically-focused leaders.

Lastly, we believe that organizations, teams and individuals all stand to benefit from choosing leaders who are high in emotional intelligence, and by developing the skills of less emotionally intelligent leaders.

References

Allred, B.B., Snow, C.C., & Miles, R.E. (1996). Characteristics of managerial careers in the 21st century. Academy of Management Review, 10, 17-27.

Ashkanasy, N.M., & Tse, B. (1998). Transformational leadership as management of emotion: A conceptual review. Presented at First Conference on Emotions and Organizational Life. San Diego, CA.

Ashforth, B.E., & Humphreys, R.H. (1995). Emotion in the workplace: A reappraisal. Human Relations, 48, 97 – 125.

Barach, J.A., &Eckhardt, D.R. (1996). Leadership and the job of the executive. Westport, CT: Quorum Books.

Bar-On, R. (1997). Bar-On Emotional Quotient Inventory: A measure of emotional intelligence. Toronto, ON: Multi-Health Systems, Inc.

Barsade, S.G. (1999). The ripple effect: Emotional contagion in groups. Manuscript submitted for publication.

Barsade, S.G., & Gibson, D.E. (1998). Group emotion: A view from top and bottom. Research on managing groups and teams (Vol. 1), 81-102. Westport, CT: JAI Press.

Barsade, S.G., Ward, A.J., Turner, J.D.F., & Sonnenfeld, J.A. (1999). To your heart's content: The influence of affective diversity in top management teams. Manuscript submitted for publication.

Bass, B.M. (1981) Stogdill's handbook of leadership (2nd Rev.). New York: Free Press.

Bass, B.M. (1985). Leadership and performance beyond expectations. New York: Free Press.

Bass, B.M. (1997). Does the transactional-transformational leadership paradigm transcend organizational and national boundaries? American Psychologist, 52, 130 – 139.

Bass, B.M., Avolio, B.J., & Goodheim, L. (1987). Biography and the assessment of transformational leadership at the world class level. Journal of Management, 13, 7 – 20.

Cattell, R. B., & Warburton, F. W. (1967). Objective personality and motivation tests. Urbana: University of Illinois Press.

Church, A.H. (1997). Managerial self-awareness in high-performing individuals in organizations. Journal of Applied Psychology, 82, 281-292.

Costa, P. T., & McCrae, R. R. (1992). The NEOPI-R Professional Manual. Odessa,FU: Psychological Assessment Resources.

Davies, M., Stankov, L., & Roberts, R.D. (1998). Emotional intelligence: In search of an elusive construct. Journal of Personality and Social Psychology, 75, 989-1015.

Digman, J.M. (1990). Personality structure: Emergence of the five-factor model. In Annual Review of Psychology (Vol. 41, pp. 417–440). Palo Alto, CA: Annual Reviews.

Eagly, A.H., Makhijani, M.G., & Klonsky, B.G. (1992). Gender and the evaluation of leaders: A meta-analysis. Psychological Bulletin, 111, 3-22.

Fiedler, F.E. (1967). A theory of leadership effectiveness. New York: McGraw-Hill.

Friedman, H.S., Riggio, R.E., & Casella, D.F. (1988). Nonverbal skill, personal charisma, and initial attraction. Personality and Social Psychology Bulletin, 14, 203-211.

George, J.M. (1995). Leader positive mood and group performance: The case of customer service. Journal of Applied Social Psychology, 25, 778-794.

Gerstner, C.R., & Day, D.V. (1997). Meta-analytic review of leader-member exchange theory: Correlates and construct issues. Journal of Applied Psychology, 82, 827-844.

Goleman, D. (1995). Emotional intelligence. New York: Bantam.

Goleman, D. (1998-a). Working with emotional intelligence. New York: Bantam.

Goleman, D. (1998-b). What makes a good leader? Harvard Business Review, November-December, 93-102.

Hersey, P., & Blanchard, K.H. (1988). Management of organizational behavior. Englewood Cliffs, NJ: Prentice-Hall.

Hogan, R., Curphy, G.J., & Hogan, J. (1994). What we know about leadership. American Psychologist, 49, 493-504.

Kahn, W.A. (1993). Caring for the caregivers: Patterns of organizational care giving. Administrative Science Quarterly, 38, 539-563.

Kirkpatrick, S.A., & Locke, E.A. (1991). Leadership: Traits do matter. The Executive, 5, 48-60.

Kotter, J.P. (1990). A force for change: How leadership differs from management. New York: Free Press.

Lord, R.G., DeVader, C.L., & Alliger, G.M. (1986). A meta-analysis of the relation between personality traits and leadership perceptions: An application of validity generalization procedures. Journal of Applied Psychology, 71, 402-410.

Martell, K, & Carroll, S. (1994). Stress the functional skills when hiring top managers. HR Magazine, July, 85-87.

Mayer, J. D. (1995). A framework for the classification of personality components. Journal of Personality, 63, 819-879.

Mayer, J. D., Caruso, D. R., & Salovey, P. (1999). Emotional intelligence meets traditional standards for an intelligence. Intelligence. 27, 267-298.

Mayer, J.D., DiPaolo, M.T., & Salovey, P. (1990). Perceiving affective content in ambiguous visual stimuli: A component of emotional intelligence. Journal of Personality Assessment, 54, 772-781.

Mayer, J.D., & Geher, G. (1996). Emotional intelligence and the identification of emotion. Intelligence, 22, 89-113.

Mayer, J.D., & Salovey, P. (1993). The intelligence of emotional intelligence. Intelligence, 17, 433-442.

Mayer, J.D. & Salovey, P. (1997). What is emotional intelligence? In P. Salovey & D. Sluyter (Eds). Emotional development and emotional intelligence: Implications for educators (pp. 3-31). New York: Basic Books.

Mayer, J. D., Salovey, P., & Caruso, D. R. (1997). The Multifactor Emotional Intelligence Scale (MEIS). Simsbury, CT: www.EmotionalIQ.com.

Mayer, J. D., Salovey, P., & Caruso, D. R. (2000). Models of emotional intelligence. In R. J. Sternberg (Ed.). The handbook of intelligence (pp. 396-420). New York: Cambridge University Press.

McCrae, R. R., & Costa, P. T. (1996). Toward a new generation of personality theories: Theoretical contexts for the five-factor model. In J. S. Wiggins (Ed.). The Five-Factor Model of Personality. New York: Guilford.

Porter, L.W., Lawler, E.E., & Hackman, J.R. (1975). Behavior in organizations. New York: McGraw-Hill.

Rice, C.L. (1999). A quantitative study of emotional intelligence and its impact on team performance. Unpublished master's thesis, Pepperdine University.

Rosse, J.G., Miller, J.L., & Stecher, M.D. (1994). A field study of job applicants' reactions to personality and cognitive ability testing. Journal of Applied Psychology, 79, 987-992.

Salovey, P., & Mayer, J.D. (1990). Emotional intelligence. Imagination, Cognition, and Personality, 9, 185-211.

Sternberg, R.J. (1997). Successful intelligence. New York: Plume

Stogdill, R.M. (1974). Handbook of leadership. New York: Free Press.

Wagner, R. K. & Sternberg, R. J. (1985). Practical intelligence in real-world pursuits: The role of tacit knowledge. Journal of Personality and Social Psychology, 49, 436-458.

Wasielewski, P.L. (1985). The emotional basis of charisma. Symbolic Interaction, 8, 207-222.

Weiss, H.A., & Cropanzano, R. (1996). Affective events theory: A theoretical discussion of the structure, causes, and consequences of affective experiences at work. In B.M. Staw & L.L. Cummings (Eds.), Research in organizational behavior (Vol. 18), 1-74.

Yukl, G.A. (1981). Leadership in organizations. Englewood Cliffs, NJ: Prentice-Hall.

Yukl, GA, Wall, S., & Lepsinger, R (1990). Preliminary report on the validation of the management practices survey. In KE Clark and MB Clark (Eds.), Measures of leadership (pp 223-238). West Orange NJ: Leadership Library of America.

Footnotes

[1] Names and details of the cases have been altered to protect the identity of clients.

[2] While emotional intelligence ability testing is the best way to determine whether a person is emotionally intelligent, we will utilize Watkins' case study to illustrate important principles about these models.

[3] We do not use their terms here since they use them in a different way than we do.

[4] The best way to measure the traits in a mixed model is through the standard personality inventories (e.g. NEO Personality Inventory, Costa & McCrae, 1992).

[5] Team leader correlations are based upon a sample of 11 leaders, and team correlations are based on a sample of 26 teams.

[6] Although they studied entry-level job applicants, Rosse, Miller, & Stecher (1994) found that personality tests were viewed as overly intrusive in the selection process, while personality tests in combination with ability measures had no such negative impact on applicants' perceptions.

[7] Emotional stability is sometimes referred to as neuroticism, and consists of traits such as anxiety and depression. It is one of the traits previously noted to be important in leadership effectiveness.

[8] Proponents of the mixed approach also indicate that "IQ" and technical skills still are important in leadership effectiveness (Goleman, 1998-b).

[9] In a survey of Fortune 500 general managers (Martell & Carroll, 1994), functional skills (e.g., technical expertise) were rated as more important than management skills for marketing, R&D and production top management. The article noted that "a manager must be highly proficient in his or her functional area to be an effective leader" (p. 86).

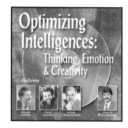

Editors' Bios

Peter Salovey. Dr. Salovey's research has focused on the psychological significance and function of human moods and emotions, and the application of social psychological principles to motivate people to adopt behaviors that protect their health. His recent work concerns the ways in which emotions facilitate adaptive cognitive and behavioral functioning. With John D. Mayer, he developed a broad framework, coined "emotional intelligence," to describe how people understand, manage and use their emotions. His recent work on health behavior has included field experiments evaluating how educational and public health messages can best be tailored to promote prevention and early detection behaviors relevant to cancer and HIV/AIDS. Dr. Salovey has published about 200 articles and chapters, and he has authored, coauthored, or edited 11 books including *The wisdom in feeling: Psychological processes in emotional intelligence*. In his leisure time, he plays stand-up bass with The Professors of Bluegrass.

Marc Brackett. Dr. Brackett's first line of research focuses on emotional intelligence and its associations with the quality of interpersonal relationships and adaptive versus maladaptive behavioral outcomes (e.g., physical and mental health, drug use, and social deviance). Over a series of studies Dr. Brackett has also developed a theoretical model and measurement tool of the Life Space, which organizes a person's external environment into four broad domains (biological underpinnings, situational elements, interactions, and group memberships). The Life Space scales he has developed provide extensive external criteria to test associations between internal personality characteristics and people's personal surroundings and behavior. Dr. Brackett is co-Author of *Voices of the Children: Unleashing Emotional Literacy,* a field-tested curriculum that provides middle school teachers the tools to incorporate lessons pertaining to children's feelings into existing programming. Dr. Brackett regularly teaches introductory and personality psychology. He also holds a 5th degree black belt in Hapkido, a Korean martial art.

John D. (Jack) Mayer. Dr. Mayer's scholarly work has encompassed both empirical research and theory development. His research has focused on broad issues such as how feelings influence thought, how intelligence influences life attainments, and, more generally, how a person's traits are expressed in their surrounding lives. Regarding the mutual influences of feelings and thought, he developed, with his colleague Peter Salovey, the scientific theory of emotional intelligence, and a series of ability tests for its measure, culminating in the Mayer-Salovey-Caruso Emotional Intelligence Test (MSCEIT). He also developed a framework for the description of an individual's overall psychological functioning.

Professor Mayer has published nearly 100 theoretical and empirical scientific publications, including peer-reviewed articles, book chapters, edited books, and psychological tests. Dr. Mayer is coeditor, with J. Ciarrochi and J. P. Forgas of *Emotional Intelligence in Everyday Life: A Scientific Inquiry.* He regularly teaches courses in personality psychology, tests and measures, and related areas. He enjoys relaxing with his family, cooking, walking, and reading.